OUT OF THE FOG

Also published by Scott Marshall

Love, Explained

(available on Amazon and at Barnes & Noble)

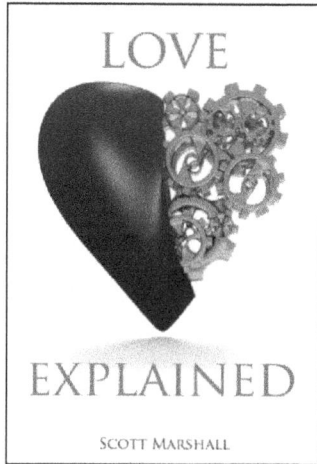

Animals Love Just Like Us

(available at Barnes & Noble)

OUT OF THE FOG

A Hungarian Baptist's Personal Memoir of Immigration,
Conversion, and Success in America

by Edwin Lucas Kautz

Edited by Scott Marshall

Published by Scott Marshall

Written between 1949 and 1966 by Edwin Lucas Kautz
Manuscript scanned by Todd Marshall
OCR edited by Robert Allen Kautz
Designed, edited, and typeset by Scott Marshall © 2019

V 1.2

First U.S. Edition 2019

ISBN: 978-0-9994506-4-2 (hardcover)

Library of Congress Control Number:1-8033492311

Typeset on Chromebooks with Google Docs.
Set in Libre Baskerville 9pt.

OUT OF THE FOG

A Hungarian Baptist's Personal Memoir of
Immigration, Conversion, and Success in America

Table of Contents

Anna Lukas (1894 – 1988), Edwin L. Kautz (1891 – 1972)

Preface

The urge to communicate is present in all of us. So is the need to understand ourselves. Both of these are responsible for my stumbling into the teaching profession and the ministry. Yet, although I started to write this story at least ten times, I became discouraged by what appeared to be its insignificance in the vast frame of the world-shaking events of our time. But the compulsion returned with the feeling that perhaps no human life and effort is insignificant. Certainly, that is one of the most important teachings of the Man this world cannot forget, Jesus of Nazareth.

In addition, every person needs to come to terms with himself. With the perspective of the years, the training of a social scientist in objectivity, the calming of passions and ambitions, it is my hope that some illumination and meaning may emerge from experiences pleasant and otherwise.

There is a kind of compulsion to share what one has experienced and found in the struggle of life, especially when a major part of a man's life has been spent in teaching. If in addition, a person loves to teach, as I do, then the attitudes and habits of such a life will greatly reinforce the human desire to communicate.

There is a lyrical quality in autobiography, such as poets know, and the writer needs to share himself with others. He can only hope that the readers will not deal too harshly with his efforts.

Coupled with all this is a sense of indebtedness to parents who had vision and heroism to match it, to teachers who were beacons of light pointing the way, to America our great foster parent who adopted us and provided opportunities for the poor underprivileged masses fleeing to her shores, to friends and loved ones, to ministers and churches and to the Eternal Goodness "Watching o'er His own." Frankly, I despair of giving due recognition to all. I can only hint at their contributions and the deep sense of obligation they engendered.

Then there is the never-ceasing need to understand oneself. This may be, and often is, quite mortifying, and one needs to be aware of and on guard against those conscious and subconscious face-saving devices that obscure the truth. But I faced this vividly some years ago, when, after a praiseworthy deed that filled me with a warm glow, I analyzed my motives for the same. To my astonishment and humiliation, I discovered that the motives behind the lovely deed were a mix of good, evil, and amoral impulses. I trust that the experience cured me of whatever spiritual snobberies persisted in me and helped me achieve the ultimate in objectivity: "I am a sinner." Along with this there continues a need for a sense of personal worth, dignity, and recognition. So, if one can find a divine spark in oneself now and then, that is also necessary in order to balance the feelings of insignificance and unworthiness.

In writing this story, I discovered what doubtless many other writers discovered in writing theirs — that there are areas in my memory where fact and fancy coalesce and intertwine to such an extent that it becomes impossible to separate them — but I made a genuine effort to do so. And it is too long and tedious a process to have an analyst unwind the tangled skein of the past.

What puzzled me more is whether I can resurrect the emotions that originally surrounded and suffused the experiences herein described. If I succeed, the story might evoke the interest of even those who enjoy only vast spectacles. For there is plenty of drama here of a humbler sort and not without significance, but to organize the apparently unrelated details so that something meaningful may appear, and to give a setting to experiences that will make them real to others — that is labor, indeed.

There are a great many people in America with immigrant parents or grandparents. Some of these, perhaps many, never appreciated them. It may be that they appeared odd, strange, and inexplicable, and it is not impossible that the bridge of understanding between the generations was never built. In my classes in sociology, the members of the newer American generation not infrequently remained after class to thank me for the greater understanding and empathy they had achieved in studying the immigrant family — often their own. If this book helps a few others to arrive at a similar appreciation of their immigrant ancestry, and so incidentally develop greater sympathy, perhaps even in empathy for strangers and for living, I shall have my reward.

This is also a story for my grandchildren. Like all privileged folk growing up in affluent suburban communities, they are menaced by a lack of understanding and fellow-feeling that would come from shared experience. This story is an attempt to inspire empathy for all less-privileged people by describing the struggles of our immigrant ancestors.

I dread to think that my own grandchildren may grow up to swell the ranks of the ignorant, unfeeling, indifferent, and privileged and so hasten a social explosion that may destroy them and many others. Because America has meant so much to me, and because, I am convinced, she means so much to the world, I pray that they may grow up to meet the challenge of these terrifying days with the wisdom and concern worthy of the citizens of the greatest and, I believe, noblest nation in the world. May they march with the choice sons of every people who carry in their hearts a vision of global loyalty to that common brotherhood of which our Heavenly Father is the ground and the assurance.

A noted clergyman of our country illuminates such peril with a story from his own ministry. It happened during the terrible days of the Great Depression. He had spent days in Chicago watching the long lines in front of employment offices, the free soup kitchens, the men selling apples on street corners, and listening to stories of helpless, bleak misery, and watching the endless tramp of unemployed millions. The following Sunday he preached a fiery sermon on the shame of it all in the richest country in the world, challenging his people to think and to do something about it and to apply the Gospel to our social problems. There were not many thanks from his affluent parishioners as they filed out after the service. The climax came in the words of a lovely, sweet old lady, with plenty of this world's goods, who patted his hand with real concern and said, "Don't worry pastor. It is not as bad as you think."

All in all, this is a simple human story, simply told, about the forces of life as they close in on people or permit them to escape. Now and then the reader may be moved to laughter, harsh and sardonic, or gentle and kind at the sight of our common human frailties, or happy over a bit of poetic justice.

This is not an earthshaking story. Little people, of whom there are so many, flit across the stage of life, pushed hither and yon by forces beyond their control or understanding. Now and then there is a flash of heroism, but mostly it is the common struggle of multitudes. They share the virtues and follies, victories and defeats, and the joys and sorrows of the common people. Sometimes a divine spark lights up the long, dull days with sudden meaning before the same old grey settles back on the scene.

Music may be heard here, "the still sad music of humanity," the fragile music of dreams and visions; achievements rising above the roar of the breakers along the shore of the wild, mystic sea of life out of which all living things emerge and which threatens to destroy this fragile loveliness. It may even happen that to some there will come insights of something divine, a beauty not of this world and haunting human life.

So be it to each reader according to his needs and capacity. May this tiny sliver of life's mirror reflect some new perspective, reveal a bit of truth or beauty that will make our struggle more meaningful and significant. Perhaps there may even come to some of us that inner cleansing, the catharsis that the ancient Greek dramatists so often achieved, and that all of us need.

1 - Early Memories of Hungary

Whose fault was it that the new baby was spoiled? Three children were born to the parents in rapid succession, and all three were dead when I was born — not an isolated experience in the good old days. The last one was almost two when the dreaded disease diphtheria slowly choked him to death, for this was 1890 when a child contracting diphtheria was equivalent to a death sentence. So my desperate parents, determined to save little me, their fourth child, gave me every attention, and in consequence spoiled me thoroughly. I insisted on sleeping during the day and on playing at night. With the curious sociability of babies, I also insisted vociferously that someone play with me and amuse me. As a result, a violent emotional storm shattered the peace of the little family every few days.

"I'll smash you against the wall if you don't stop screaming," cried my maddened mother.

"Na-Na!"

Grandma soothed her. "I'll take the child. I know you must get up early to go to that stinking cigar factory. Come, my baby, let mamma sleep."

To tell the truth, I was a puny child, and remained rather delicate into adulthood. Yet there was something tough in me too, as mother discovered, when, for the third time, she had me in the doctor's office after vaccinations for smallpox. They didn't take, even after the third attempt, and the doctor threw me back into my mother's lap with a disgusted snort and the consoling remark, "Take him, Mrs. Kautz, not even the devil wants him!"

Not much of dramatic importance happened after that, at least nothing I can recall — until that dreadful sixth year when I had to enter school. School in those days back in the Old Country, Hungary, was a sobering experience. There were rumors among the children, passed on with hushed voices when adults were out of hearing, of canings, kneeling for hours, and, once, of a principal giving a child such a beating with a meter stick that he died. I had never thrived well on fear.

One day I brought home my little reader. Grandfather Meszaros, probably intrigued by my puckered brows and fearful looks, asked me to read. I stuttered and stumbled through the first few words and finally buried my head in the book, sobbing bitterly.

"Now, now," said grandpa, with a curious mixture of sternness and tender inflection, "Will my grandson, whose grandpa was a veteran in the Italian War, behave like a coward? Why I was in the battle of Salerno ..." and there followed one of his gory tales in which he inevitably was a hero and his side won the battle. "Now, let me see that book. Why, you're not scared of a tiny book like this and those funny little marks in it, are you, my grandson?"

My tears dried up in amazement as I watched Grandpa take out an eraser and meticulously rub out the four blue fives — marks of failure — and with the same kind of blue pencil write ones in their places — marks of excellence. What would the teacher say? Would this mean my first caning in school? That disgraceful sight when a teacher pulled a helpless, crying child over her knee or the desk and laid it on with a stinging cane? And could I tell on my grandpa? Well, anyhow, a comforting notion, my teacher had never been a soldier and never fought on the battlefield like my grandpa — so why be afraid? Then, grandfather took me in hand and went over the lessons, and even helped me learn the following two.

Class recitations did not go well the next day. About halfway through the reading period the teacher suddenly stopped in her pacing up and down the aisles. Her eyes fixed an astonished, bewildered and stern gaze upon my reader. In a hard, determined voice she commanded me to read. I was so scared I almost forgot the lesson, but then my grandpa's strong patriarchal face, whiskers and all, rose like a hero in my consciousness and I read his first lesson almost perfectly.

"The next!" demanded the incredulous teacher.

I read the second lesson perfectly.

"The third! ... The fourth! ... Maybe you would want to try the new lesson for today?" she inquired, evidently hoping to put another hated five on the clean page. Victory! I read it perfectly! And she, with amazement registered in her every move, marked a one on each page.

Grandpa's heroic tales became even more credible after that. Had he not foiled my greatest enemy, the harsh first-grade teacher? Sometimes grandpa's tales became pretty gruesome and rather horribly vindictive. Once, he told Brother Steve and me how, after a sanguinary battle, he and his buddies went over the battlefield and bashed in the teeth of the dead and wounded Italians. As a grandfather myself, I recall this story with a deep revulsion that must have its roots in the abyss of childhood memories. Nor did it help me to discover, years later, that grandpa was a minion of the hated Habsburgs who used him, a fervent fighter for Hungarian freedom, to drown in blood the same urge for freedom in Italy that Grandfather admired so in his own nation, Hungary.

I was grateful to grandpa for the many little tokens of his affection and interest. I recall with a thrill the second or third Christmas in the village school. Somehow grandpa wangled a place on the program me. For weeks he drilled me in the poem I was to recite. The great day came. The assembly room of the school was filled with the village notables. The judge, sheriff, priest, school principal, teachers, and the Baron and Baroness alongside an enormous Christmas tree that reached the lofty ceiling and was covered with tiny candles flaming merrily. I was on a table, to be clearly visible to all. Grandpa gazed deeply into my eyes and stepped back. I recited my poem, just as Grandpa had taught me. A veritable thunder of clapping followed Grandpa and me to our seats, and after the program all the lovely ladies, as well as some not so lovely, covered him with kisses and loaded my arms with presents. I was too little to notice that Grandpa's eyes were filled with tears, and did not hear him say to my mother; "Now I am ready to die; I see that my grandson will amount to something." Years later, in America, my mother often repeated these words.

One day I saw Grandpapa engage two gendarmes in animated conversation. Odd, I thought, since grandpapa was not very fond of gendarmes, although I was never told why. They patrolled the village two-by-two in spotless dark green uniforms, rifle hanging by a strap from the shoulder and sword by the side, bluish-green feathers fastened on the side of their *csákó* ("shako" tall, cylindrical military caps) flying in the breeze. They were a brave sight, but grandfather never talked to them. That morning, however, he guided them down the street in eager conversation. When they had gone, he sat down under the mulberry tree, wiped the perspiration from his face and said: "God in heaven, but those damned gendarmes gave me a bad time."

"Why, grand-papa?"

"They looked too carefully at our garden."

"But why should that trouble you?"

"Because I have planted some tobacco, you numbskull. Not much, just enough for my own pipe for a few months. But that is illegal. Tobacco is a government monopoly and those who break the law may find themselves in the village jail, or worse, have to pay a fine." Thereafter, grandfather was at the garden gate each morning bidding his new friends a smiling good morning and cultivating their blind goodwill. And why should they examine the pretty garden of this courteous gentleman with rude, inquisitive eyes? They did not.

In a few years, all too short, grandpa died. He was only sixty but his campaigns, or his love for strong drink, brought on the inevitable early end. But who cares? He was a tough old soldier to the end. His wife and daughters, feeling that his end was near, pleaded with him to make his confession and receive the last rites, but he sternly and curtly turned them down. Finally, in spite of him, they sent for a priest. To their horror, he rose in his deathbed, pointed to the door, and with a blue streak of profanity drove the astonished and frightened cleric from the room. The shocked priest made the sign of the cross and departed in a hurry. The incident did not hurt the religious feelings of his grandchildren, who were now more than ever convinced of his heroism!

Perhaps it was fortunate that he passed away. He could not be reconciled to Ludwig, his son-in-law, who was a hated Austrian, one of those whose nation had crushed the Hungarians when they made their classic fight for liberty under the leadership of Louis Kossuth in 1848-49. Ludwig was around 24 when he migrated to Budapest from Vienna, because he had heard that the economic opportunities for upholsterers and comforter makers were far better there. He had been in Budapest for about a year when he met a dashing Hungarian beauty at a dancing school. He could hardly say even a few words in her "barbaric tongue" (his words) and she spoke even less German, but love has a language all its own and this story had its beginning right there.

It was a love match. All through the years, I saw them embrace and kiss each other fondly, at times passionately. But Grandpa never quite forgave his daughter for marrying an Austrian, and certainly was never reconciled to his son-in-law to whom he always referred to as *az a Budos nemet* (that stinking Dutchman).

So early did race-prejudice enter my life. Only much, much later did I recognize how illogical it was. My father had never fought against the Hungarians on the side of the oppressing Habsburgs, but Grandpa had actually done just that against the Italians when they were fighting for independence. But by some strange indoctrination that seemed proper to Grandpa, he was unable to perceive the contradiction. Why, he could even stand for hours on the sidewalk of the Korut in Budapest, the capitol building, to see the King drive by and then shout "Long live Francis Joseph the First, King of the Hungarians." I wonder if it ever occurred to him that his King was also the emperor of the hated Austrians, who invited the czar of Russia to help him crush the Hungarian revolt of 1849. At elections Grandpa always voted for the "of '48," the party of Kossuth, now led by the son, and he rejoiced in the filibusters of that party in Parliament and in the small concessions wrung from the Party of '67 — the party of compromise. And it helped Ludwig not one whit in Grandpa's eyes that he copied exactly the mustache and beard of Francis Joseph.

Until electric street lights were introduced, Christmas was a particularly magical festival in the village of Erzsebetfalva. How well I remember the tolling of church bells on Christmas eve calling the faithful to midnight mass, and the fantastic procession as the families, wrapped in their warmest garments and lantern in hand, stepped out into the dark, cold night. It seemed like a ray of light with hundreds of tiny trickles uniting into a mighty stream. Their quick steps squeaked in the snow, long streamers of vapor issued from their nostrils as they progressed through the streets, dimly lit by the flickering lights they carried, creating solemnly dancing shadows as they moved toward the church and disappeared to reappear again after the service in a blaze of lamps separating, retreating, and disappearing again. Only the brilliant sparkle of God's own diamonds in the black velvet sky remained, reflected by His tiny diamonds in the snow.

Sometime before Christmas came the slaughtering season. The children stood at the window and watched the scene in the yard. About a dozen of father's friends had been invited to help in butchering the hogs, burning off the hair with straw, and the making of blood and liver sausages. It was great fun for them, and they could gorge themselves on good country food. One by one the porkers were brought out, thrown on their side, stabbed in the throat and held until the blood stopped flowing into the pans. Now and then one of the men would fill a cup and down the hot blood. We were disgusted and sobbed bitterly. Had we not fed those pigs for a year, made pets of them? Now our father and his friends had murdered them. I've forgotten how long it took before I could eat of that meat.

The children remembered all too vividly that miraculous day when father brought home a dozen squealing, hairless little pigs in his overcoat pockets. They watched him cut up a sponge into little pieces, throw these into a shallow pan of milk and guide their cunning little snouts to those artificial teats. How quickly they caught on and sucked noisily. The pan was empty in no time. They grew, too, but only two of them grew into big, fat porkers. And now, horrible world, they were dead. Murdered before their eyes!

The summer had its own joys. We fished and frogged in the creek, about a block from our house. We made our own fish hooks by bending pins, and dug our own worms or caught our own insects for bait. The frogs seemed especially excited by tiny bits of red rags, at which they jumped eagerly. We were never very successful, but to true sportsmen that did not matter very much.

For some reason, we were not allowed to bathe in the creek. The water only reached our middles. But children of the gypsies labored under no such disability, and shocked but envious village children watched them bathe and frolic without a stitch of clothing, boys and girls together, with now and then the wistful notion: "How nice it is to be a gypsy!" But we did not envy them in winter for they had to negotiate the snow with bare feet. The stream was open to the village only in unfenced fields. Elsewhere the owners drove their fences right into the brook. This made us particularly angry in winter when we had only short stretches here and there for skating. The kids did not appreciate the restrictions imposed by adult notions about private property.

Every house in the village had its garden fenced in by a tall fence. As the children walked along the unpaved sidewalks, they gazed with longing at the treasures in the gardens: golden apricots, purple plums, red cherries, apples, mulberries, gooseberries, etc. Sometimes they stopped, licking their lips and asking the man in the garden, "*Bacsi* (uncle), please may I have some of this or that?" Sometimes Bacsi did, and as often refused.

One of the favorite stories of mother centered around such an experience. In her village, there was a large estate with a very large cherry orchard. She had never tasted the largest, sweetest cherries. As a girl of twelve in the company of her more adventurous playmates, she was in the habit of climbing over the fence and up the tree with the choicest fruit, stuffing herself to bursting.

One day, her watchfulness was dulled by the challenge of an unusually tempting branch, and suddenly the threatening voice of the *"csosz"* (watchman) brought her back to reality:

"Come down at once!" He commanded, but the pert little miss quickly recovered her poise.

"Ah," she considered, he is an old man, he can never climb this tree, and if he does, I'll climb higher where he would be afraid to follow. "I will not!" she cried.

"Come down at once, you unprofitable one! I know who you are. The Meszaros girl!"

"Come and get me," goaded the little witch.

"Well, I can wait," growled the *csosz*, and seating himself at the base of the tree, he lit his pipe and waited, glancing surreptitiously up at the branches now and then. She watched him like a hawk.

Enervated by the heat, and comfortably leaning against the trunk, secure in the knowledge that his prey was safe, the *csosz* became very sleepy. At first, he fought against the overwhelming drowsiness, then slowly his head sank to his chest and his pipe glided from his mouth to the ground. Like a squirrel, the waiting girl crawled noiselessly to the lowest branch and out as far as she could without breaking it. Hanging on with her hands she dropped lightly to the ground and quietly ran to the fence. When she was safely on the other side she cried, "Here I am, uncle watchman, catch me," and ran home.

On a memorable morning, after a breakfast of rolls and coffee but mostly milk, my brother Steve and I and a friend from the city, Kalman (ages eight, ten, and eleven) stepped out on the unpaved street. We turned right and walked in the shade of the tall acacias. These were everywhere, clothed in green and white or green and pink. We watched the white and pink blossoms fall and form a lovely carpet along the street. The air was heavy with their sweet scent and graceful swallows in their formal suits of black with lemon breast, and vividly colored butterflies flitted over meadow and garden. The sun shone in a deep blue sky and played hide and seek with the snow-white clouds.

Three barefoot boys, full of the wonder and joy of life and eagerly looking forward to the adventures of a new day, hurried down the street. Suddenly, we stopped in shocked amazement at a lifeless swallow on the ground. We picked him up, examined him in turn, and discovered a slight flutter of life. Anxiously, we ran home determined to nurse him back to health so that he might join his mates again on their swift dashes. We gathered some of the crumbs from the breakfast table, a little dish of water, and sneaked out into the garden. We were not going to let any snooping adults pry into our secret. Oh so slowly and pitifully the little bird recovered while we discussed what possible unfortunate accident had disabled him. Was he a young bird just learning to fly? Had he been mauled by a wicked old cat? But there was no bruise on his sleek body.

Soon he could stand on his feet. We lifted him to the top of a stake to which a tomato bush was tied. He flew just a little way then dropped to the ground. So we put him back into the soft little bed we had made of dry grass and feathers, then fed him and gave him a drink. After a while, we lifted him to a higher stake and urged him to fly. Suddenly he rose on an ambitious arc and headed over the meadow toward the creek. But about halfway over the meadow, he dropped like a stone. Us three boys dashed through the gate and into the meadow. We found him dead. Nothing helped this time.

Again, we were face-to-face with the stark, dreadful fact of death. Not only the death of pigs that men must have for food, not only that of brave old grandpa, but even the death of the lovely, graceful swallow who made his nest under the eaves of our house. And we had tried to save its life in vain. Perhaps this added concern made the experience with implacable death the more poignant.

What now? Our dead friend must have a burial. One of us secured a beautiful candy box treasured by Grandma. We lined it carefully with dry grass, chicken feathers gathered from the barnyard, and a strip of muslin from mother's store of rags. Then, imitating as faithfully as we were able, the priest, ministrant, cantor and mourners, we laid the little bird to rest in a deep grave so that no tomcat could dig him up, and raised a mound and a cross as we recited an Our Father, a Hail Mary, and the Creed in unison, weeping copiously through it all.

About this time, I became intoxicated by the fairy tales I was learning to read. I was particularly intrigued by the stories of those mysterious little inhabitants of fairyland, dwarfs, who performed all sorts of wonderful labors in the bowels of the earth and sometimes surprised people with unexpected deeds of helpfulness. Also, we heard the big folks discuss a new saint of extraordinary powers, whose statue had just been consecrated in the church, Roman Catholic of course, The only church they knew in the village. St. Anthony could grant any request of believers if they carried out the devotions outlined in his little prayer book for nine consecutive Tuesdays and deposited a contribution for the poor of the parish in the box at the foot of his statue.

Grown into manhood, I no longer remember where we secured the few *kreutzers* (pennies) for the contributions, but under the inspiration of our elders' marvelous stories concerning the miracles of the saint and the fascination of the fantastic little men of fairyland we determined to try an experiment in faith. With the absolute trust of childhood, we began the prescribed devotions. To make it even more efficacious we appropriated a little framed picture of the Virgin Mother, and with the free imagination of devout children, converted it into the sacrament, abstracting a few strands of angel's hair to make the rays of *szentségtartó* (monstrance, an angel's hair in yard-long strips of golden stuff spread over Christmas trees).

Grandma had sent us to the sexton to buy frankincense to place on her aching teeth. We added another to grandma's few kreutzers and withheld two or three grains of the incense for our own secret worship. Sneaking a lump of live coal from the kitchen fire, grinding up the incense between stones, reciting the responses of the mass, as much as we remembered, we placed the incense on the coal and offered the fragrance to their homemade sacrament. We burned our fingers severely in the process and received a thorough scolding from grandma, but we concluded this would make our offering and adoration more acceptable.

Our absolute faith revealed itself in other ways, too. We set about preparing a place for the little men St. Anthony was to send us. In the vacant but fenced-in lot next door, we planted branches and in their shade provided primitive benches and tables. It looked a lot like a public square with a ramp leading up to it. A little distance away we put up a small tent with a dais, for the dwarf king, should he decide to come also, and we waited for the miracle. Every morning, as early as possible before breakfast, whenever we could elude the watchfulness of the big people, we secretly made our way to the dwarf town we had built, wondering if the little people had arrived. Several times a day we made our way quietly, cautiously, to the secret place and watched and waited.

Then one day it happened! One of us saw a tiny oxcart slowly making its way up the ramp. Two of the little people, an inch or two tall sat in front. We all saw them. Whispering excitedly, we drew near but suddenly the dwarfs disappeared. From that time on, we saw them repeatedly. Sometimes they appeared in the room where we slept, usually under the bed.

The climax occurred in the tent. One day, Steve crawled up to it slowly, cautiously lifted the flap at one end, and in the next moment, rushed towards the house while shrieking, "I'm going to tell grandma! I'm going to tell grandma!"

"Stupid!" I hissed into his ear, dragging him to the ground. "I'll fill your mouth full of sand. Do you want to make St. Anthony angry? What are you scared of?"

"But I saw him, I saw him!" Steve fearfully confided.

In turn, Kalman and I too lifted the flap of the tent and there on the dais of sand lay a tall dwarf, with a peaked cap smoking a pipe with a long stem, smiling benevolently. We gazed at each other and marveled at the great miracle. The land of make-believe was true and St. Anthony's power vindicated. So what if, as we looked again, the little man had disappeared? Only a depression in the sand marked the place where he had lain. All three of us saw the empty little depression where his body had rested. For some reason, however, we were frightened and decided to ask St. Anthony to take back the dwarfs. This he did almost at once, although Kalman and I saw them now and then in various places for another two or three years even after we moved to Budapest.

Oh, lovely childhood, arising out of the unconscious and the dimness of the undifferentiated, confusing impact of the world, miraculous roseate dawn of life, full of golden marvels, strange sights and sounds, yet so palpable, physical and sensuous. All too soon the miracles and visions recede in the harsh light of the factual world, and the big people, who had lost the wonder of it long ago, slowly teach the children to trace the inexorable chain of cause and effect. Once the greatest teachers of all said "Let the children come unto me for of such is the kingdom of heaven."

Fortunately, us three little friends were untroubled by such philosophical reflections. It was enough for the day and the wonder thereof. Nor did the big people learn about this miracle until many years later in the far, undreamed-of land of America, when Steve and I became parents themselves.

One night as adults, we sat in Steve's apartment with our wives, children asleep, talking about childhood memories. I recited the above experience while the women looked on with incredulous smiles. When Steve vouched for the story the women sat in silence. Then the talk went on about other matters. None of them had studied psychology and so could not analyze and kill the remnants of wonder still in the hearts of these grown-up boys.

Mother's sister had married Uncle Gregor. He was a good man. I still remember with gratitude his gift of silkworms. They were tiny, thin creatures almost thread-like. Uncle Gregor assured me that if I fed them fresh mulberry leaves each day through the summer, they would grow big and produce silk. Real silk? Yes, indeed. So I cared for them devotedly, and they grew and grew. One day I noted that the biggest, fattest one was rather sluggish. When I told Uncle Gregor, he said, "Watch it very carefully now, something wonderful will happen."

One morning his sluggish worm could not be found. However, among the leaves, I found a small egg-shaped cream-colored silky thing.

"Ah," said Uncle Gregor, "he made his coffin. He is inside. Watch more closely than ever, for now, you'll see a miracle."

After several days, I opened the box rather impatiently and carelessly. The miracle was taking too long. A white moth or butterfly swept out of the box and was soon lost to sight. When Uncle Gregor heard of it in the evening, he said, "Bring me that yellow cocoon." Then he pointed to a hole at one end. "That's where he escaped. Your ugly, sluggish worm turned into a lovely butterfly. No longer does he need to climb laboriously and eat green leaves, but flies freely from flower to flower and feeds on honey. Now, if you want silk, you must put these cocoons into the oven for a while and then you can unwind it."

How could I ever have dreamed that this would be the best illustration of the resurrection in far-off America, on the other side of the world, where I'd become a minister. It was always especially meaningful to young people and children, and comforted many broken-hearted families, especially one that had lost a baby.

Uncle Gregor came from Gratz, in the Tyrol, and was a trusted machinist at the Gellert Mills in Budapest — probably the largest flour mill in Hungary. The engine room, with its spotless walls and stone floors, gleaming machinery, polished brass oiling cups, enormous flywheel, and terrific clatter made an indelible impression on me. My uncle was the boss in that amazing hall and must have been a very smart man! He was very religious, too. Every Sunday he took me with him to mass. Very devoutly he followed the service. On the way home, we stopped in at Roth's, their grocer, for a bottle of beer or a spot of *siluorium* (plum brandy). After a generous dinner, Uncle Gregor would continue his drinking until comfortably confused, then take to bed with his pipe and go to sleep. Once or twice he almost set the bed on fire when his pipe slipped into the bed with him instead of onto the floor. After that, they always watched him carefully.

Kalman, our city friend from Budapest, was a puny chap. My parents had offered to take him for the summer, certain that the country air and plenty of good fresh food would make him strong. I remember the day when Kalman and his sister Ilonka arrived. Particularly Ilonka. Not that she was pretty but rather the magic of the pink, pleated dress that moved with fairy-like grace whenever *she* moved. Folds opening and closing on the ten-year-old like a fairy's accordion. Even now I see her, daintily stepping off the train — a princess. She was the first girl I noticed. They came on the *vicinalis* (local train) with short coaches and a high square box of a locomotive with a few inches of a smokestack. It was nicknamed "the coffee grinder." The coaches were second and third class, the former with upholstered, leather-covered seats. The latter had wooden seats. Only the aristocracy and the rich could afford to travel second class. All of our relatives and friends traveled third class. No matter — the train was a benevolent monster that carried people to high adventure, particularly in Budapest all of ten kilometers away.

I was fascinated by my new friend Kalman and could not bear having him out of my sight. If we sat together, my arms inevitably went around his shoulder or gently stroked his back. On awakening in the morning, I fairly covered him with kisses, inhaling his clean, warm, intoxicating body smell. Yet, it may be registered truthfully that there never was the slightest suggestion of the overtly sexual, and I would have recoiled in disgust had there been. Freud was too young to trouble the minds of the big people with his horribly fascinating theories. This childish infatuation passed like others through the years to come without leaving ugly suspicions in my mind or in those of my parents.

Right next to the house there was a large, wide-spreading mulberry tree. It must have been grafted, for unlike several other trees in our yard that bore tiny berries, this tree produced large, purple-black berries as large as the upper half of a man's thumb and sweet as honey. It was an annual treat for daddy's friends in the city to come pick the tree clean and gorge themselves with its heavenly fruit. Usually we spread some sheets on the ground, then these nimble young men climbed the tree, stood on the roof or the branches and ate and ate, shaking the tree lustily now and then for the women and children below.

On Saturdays, every family heated a big kettle of water, set up the *teknő* (wooden trough) in the kitchen, and the entire family took its weekly bath. The children came first, starting with the youngest and ending with the eldest and then the adults. From time to time hot water was added until all had been washed and scrubbed clean.

Occasionally, father treated his family to a bath at the village bathhouse, a private institution and rather expensive for a working man's family. It had a large stone or marble tub in each room with steps leading into it. Here, from gleaming brass faucets, one could draw all the hot and cold water desired. Mother wore a gown, dad wore an apron, and the children splashed about in nude happiness.

Life was pleasant to this growing boy. There were no paved streets, only a few electric lights, and plenty of space between the houses and wide spreading meadows at the boundaries of the village. The nameless little creek that flowed through the gardens and orchards made merry music.

The teachers, in general, must have been kind because I have very few unhappy memories, and they must have been without any unusual or cruel traits for I cannot remember any of them. Still, I do remember the cantor who had the double function of playing the organ at the Roman Catholic Church, lustily singing the responses, leading a kind of impromptu choir, and teaching the fourth grade at the elementary school. He was a well built, muscular man in his thirties, with a generous, impeccably twirled and pointed mustache and rosy cheeks. He was leisurely in his movements and incessantly sucking on peppermint drops, for which he would send us to the nearest grocery store. He was fairly strict and rather quick with the use of a cane. The penalty for talking was a strike on one's palm, for drinking ink, two strokes, and so on until one got a thorough beating on the posterior as the class looked on with fright and horror, and one's enemies looked on with sadistic satisfaction. It only made matters worse if a boy's courage failed and he tried to snatch his hand away as the cane descended. It might catch him on a finger, or the cantor would have a second and more energetic try at the culprit. He might even add an extra blow to punish him for such impudence. I still remember vividly how the blow stung and how he nursed his hand throughout the period after a single blow of the cane.

One of the chaplains of the village church who taught religion two or three times a week had a particularly painful way of caning. I can still see him pulling a youngster over a bench and apply the stick with light but stinging blows, the thin cane bending and snapping as it came down on the soft body.

Fortunately, I liked religion, always received a '1', the mark of excellence, and occasionally performed the lesser duties of second altar boy. I observed that the old rector never fully bent his knee before the altar. My folks explained that he was crippled with rheumatism. I noticed also that some of the fathers mixed wine and water at the mass in about equal parts, while others used very little water. Some of the observant faithful made humorous remarks about him "liking his wine rather well."

I was particularly fond of one of the younger priests, whom I greeted on the street one day with a resounding "Blessed be Jesus Christ."

This was the customary greeting for priests, to which they responded with, "Forever. Amen."

The young priest stopped me, asked my name and where I lived and remarked that one who greeted a father so wholeheartedly deserved a reward, and pulled from his pocket a beautiful picture of a young and handsome Christ with a flaming heart almost covering the entire breast, and blessed me.

The family had a beautiful garden, and no wonder — the contents of the outdoor latrines were carefully spread over it. Many years later in far-off America, I discovered in my sociological studies that the Chinese had practiced the same method and kept their farms fertile through centuries. I recall that the big people were particularly proud of their enormous, brilliant red and sweet tomatoes. Father ate them raw by the dozen, but the others preferred them cooked.

I might not have been so happy had I known how hard my father and mother worked. Years later I learned that my mother, after working all day in the cigar factory, got off the evening train, unfolded a sack, and went through the open fields gathering weeds for the pigs and lugging it home on her back. My father, a short, slender man, did not come home for days at a time but stayed in the shop, often working twenty hours a day, throwing himself on a mattress for a few hours rest when his eyes simply refused to stay open.

Now and then on a Sunday, my father took me for a stroll. Usually, we would stop at the inn for a spritzer (a deciliter of wine with a generous mixture of *vichy*, varied according to taste, lightening the alcohol content, and giving the wine a sparkle). Sometimes father ordered a couple of *virshli* with rolls, an Old Country version of a hot dog served with freshly grated and warmed horseradish. It was very strong and always brought tears to my eyes. It certainly increased one's thirst and the desire for wine. On one such excursion, father did not watch closely enough and I drank more than usual. When we started walking home, I staggered. Laughing, father let me hold on to the horn-top of his cane while he held the lower part and so dragged me home. Often father told this to his friends in my presence and they laughed long and loud, even winking to each other, until I was quite ashamed to be the object of their fun. Did father realize that he was employing good psychology on me, or was this only an expression of his Viennese *gemutlichkeit* (geniality)? I never learned. I know, however, that I never saw father even tipsy.

It was a lazy, warm summer afternoon. As we walked about the garden, we picked up some purple berries, sweet as honey. There above us, next to the house, was the tall mulberry tree spreading its branches richly laden with luscious purple fruit, eagerly visited by the wasps of the neighborhood. This was just what us three lazy boys unconsciously longed for. In quick succession, we climbed the tree and stepped off onto the roof where one needed even less effort to pick the sweet berries. All went well until Steve discovered a wasp's nest. In his boredom, he began to throw dry little branches at it. Out buzzed a horde of angry insects and we withdrew to a safe distance. Suddenly Kalman started to slide down the trunk.

"Where are you going?"

"Oh, I had enough."

Steve followed him with the same question and same reply.

Then one of the angry wasps settled on me with a fiery sting. Down I scuttled and plunged my arm into a barrel of rainwater under the tree. Then the other two shamefacedly confessed that they'd had enough of the berries for the same reason.

Here in this quiet little village, I had one of the most delicious surprises of my life. A little wagon went on rounds selling a delicacy. I went to inquire. It was something called "frozen" that I had never tasted before. I ran back home and told about this novel something and begged grandma for the few pennies that it cost. But poor people did not spend pennies freely in my native land. However, my pleading wore down her penurious resistance, and soon I had some of this new amazing something in my hand. I tasted it. It was something cold, frozen, with a heavenly flavor, literally. I recall it with a longing to this day. Never, never again did ice cream taste so delicious!

But living in the country had its disadvantages, too. Our rabbits burrowed their way out of their pen by making tunnels under the fence. My grandparents were mystified by their periodic disappearance until one day grandma, walking across our broad yard, almost broke her foot as it fell through and into one of the tunnels. After that, we frequently had rabbit stew or roast for dinner.

Nor can I ever forget the time we had a hailstorm. These were not infrequent but this one was memorable because the hailstones were the size of hen's eggs. Grandpa, with his fierce beard flying in the wind and heavy cover on his head, and grandma with the heaviest shawl she could find, rushed into the yard and all the pens and drove the animals under cover. They brought in some of the ice stones. That is how I remember. I still do not understand how we escaped the smashing of all our windows.

One vivid memory dates back to volunteer maneuvers by thousands of participants on the Island of Csepel just below Budapest. The Boer War was on in South Africa. The participants were in British and Boer uniforms. Everybody's sympathies were with the tiny Boer Republic defying the might of one of the greatest world powers. We watched every edition of the newspapers with feverish anxiety for the Boers, cheering their every victory and praying for their ultimate success. Doubtless, the tragic history of our own nation Hungary, oppressed for centuries by Tartar, Turk, German, and Slav hordes, decimated by almost continuous warfare — all but destroyed, rising again and again out of what had seemed to be the death of our nation, was the rich soil of our sympathy. Little did we dream that one day the Boers would do to the natives of Africa all that the British did to them, and much, much worse.

Nor could we forget the role played by Russian power in our War of Independence under the leadership of Louis Kossuth in 1848-49, how the raw troops recruited by the golden tongue of Kossuth drove every army of Francis Joseph out of the country, and how in desperation he turned to the Czar who sent a large army of 200,000 fresh, well-disciplined troops, and together they crushed our little nation.

During my boyhood, there was much talk about the terrible Russian

Bear. By that time the interests of the Austro-Hungarian monarchy and of the Russian empire were in conflict. All of the Slavic peoples of the polyglot monarchy; Czechs, Slovaks, Poles, Ukrainians, Serbs, and Croats; looked to Russia as their big brother who would aid them in their struggles for independence. Many if not all of the Orthodox churches of Hungary were centers of pan-slav intrigue and agitation against the Monarchy. One cannot help but wonder if any of them, the elderly at least, now under the heavy hand of the Soviets, ever think of former times in the monarchy when the comparison must bring nostalgic longings for the "good old days," at least on the part of those old enough to remember the past. Nor is it to the credit to Hungary's leaders and statesmen of the monarchy that, in their blind chauvinism, they failed to see the challenge of a new day and the opportunity to reconstitute the empire into a multilingual nation like Switzerland, and save that political and economic unit so necessary to the peace and prosperity of that very mixed and confused area. Once again the blindness of the privileged, composed of the aristocrats, the hierarchy of the Roman Catholic Church, and the chauvinist leaders of the various nationalities, won its millennial victory and the common people paid the price in misery, blood, and new tyrannies. Well, the fierce Russian Bear, bloodier than ever, knocked their heads together and forced them to live together in the hegemony of the Soviet empire, exploiting them as they had never dreamed possible. Of such stuff does history make its stern judgments. So the inchoate, distant fear of the Russian Bear has turned into an immediate day-by-day terror that turns every thought of freedom into despair.

From the vast distance of those pre-jet days came the faint rumbles of the Spanish-American War, more like ancient history than a contemporary event. The Hungarians were on the side of Cuba, the Philippines, and the United States, and glad to learn about the defeat of another empire, an autocratic dynasty and the freeing of their colonies.

The Turkish Empire was crumbling. Hungarian patriots watched its destruction with mixed feelings. They had no sympathy for the corrupt, decadent autocracy of the Sultans, but they remembered gratefully that Louis Kossuth was given refuge by the Porte, after the Hungarian Revolution of 1849 collapsed. When it could no longer guarantee his safety from the Habsburg vultures, Kossuth escaped on board an American battleship. In the Crimean War, the Russian autocrat crushed the Porte. But the spoils were snatched from the jaws of the Bear by the other European empires. Bosnia-Herzegovina was Austria's share, and another block of indigestible people was added to the crazy-quilt pattern of the monarchy. Wars, and rumors of wars: The Balkans were in a ferment with military maneuvers everywhere. Soldiers filled the streets of the towns. Universal military service extracted three years from the youth of Hungary — three years of brutal discipline.

2 - Life in Budapest

After several years in the country, my parents discovered that life was too hard and too expensive when they both had to work in the city. They spent too much time away from the children.

Our parents, especially mother, had ambitions for their children. The schools of *Erzsébetfalva* (present day Pesterzsébet) were limited in scope. I was almost ready for *polgari* (a kind of junior high school) but I would have to live in Budapest to attend it. Accordingly, they began to plan moving back to the city that they had left for the fresh air, sunshine, homegrown vegetables, and fruits of the country, and the freedom to roam in safety for their children.

In addition, my parents found commuting increasingly burdensome. After working nine or ten hours in shop and factory and spending another hour reaching home, the chores waiting for them at home with chickens, rabbits, pigs, and the garden life became rather monotonous. Not even the joys of rural life, especially for the children, were able to balance in favor of the country. There were times when my poor father stayed in his cellar workshop on *Nagy Diófa utca* (Great Waldorf Street) in order to increase his earnings — for now there were five of us — working eighteen to twenty hours of the twenty-four, throwing himself on the mattress when he was exhausted and back to his task after a few hours of sleep. The cellar was so damp that beads of moisture gathered on the walls. I often saw him wipe it off with some rags. He began to develop rheumatism that stayed with him the rest of his life inflicting the agony of endless pain and sleepless nights until tempted by thoughts of suicide. Sometimes we did not see him for days. Mother worried about him, although he seldom complained. They finally decided to move into one of the cheaper apartment houses in a workingman's district close to mother's cigar factory where she was a forelady, and not too far from father's shop and a tiny park within a minute's walk.

My parents had to find living quarters for their ten-year-old (myself). One of mother's forelady friends in the factory offered to take me in until they moved to the city. She and her husband lived alone. They had no children and were able to afford a beautifully-furnished apartment. Although depressed and sad at leaving home to live alone with two strange adults, I was quite impressed by the loveliness of my temporary home. My aesthetic sense found deep satisfaction in the beauty surrounding me.

But in those days no apartments had indoor toilets or bathrooms, so we used night pots. Those pots of my new foster parents were left uncovered at night and my nostrils suffered agonies with the smell. I recall being awakened at night by the awful stench and burying my face in the pillow to escape it. My consolation was to join mother in a coffee break at noon and be treated to delicious coffee with whipped cream called *Habos kávé* (foamy coffee). Fortunately, this lasted only for two or three weeks and I was very glad to rejoin my family in our new apartment.

We did not have many small rooms, like Americans, but only one very large room with an alcove and a kitchen. Father and mother slept in the alcove. Grand Mama and we children slept in large double beds in the other larger section. Our furniture consisted of a divan (father's masterpiece with a very high ornate and upholstered back), a table, a few chairs, a cupboard for our good dishes, a high wardrobe for our suits and clothes, and Grand Mama's trunk into which nobody but she was allowed even a glimpse. As I think of our American housing arrangements, it would seem that our new home in Budapest was terribly cluttered up, but as I recall the situation it appears that we could have danced in the middle and, oh yes, we even had a stove in the room.

Life in *polgari* school was cold and difficult. I had no friends and the standard was considerably higher than that of the village school I had attended. Here we had separate teachers we called professors for each subject. Each class had a homeroom to which the professors came, and each class had a class-head — one of our professors. The name of mine was Professor Merey Zoltan. I remember him as a very pleasant, good-looking man, and quite young. We all liked him. He was tall, straight and forever bending his head to one side or the other as if it were too heavy to hold up straight with all the knowledge he carried in it. He taught beginner's mathematics and geometry — very elementary but quite difficult for me. All through life I have had extraordinary difficulties with math.

My favorite was Professor Bongerfi, who taught grammar, composition, and literature — subjects that I have always liked. He was short, stocky, and hot-tempered — his eyes shooting fiery darts at us through his glasses whenever we displeased him. He was a typical *Magyar* (Hungarian). Always before teaching he would spend five minutes reading in a book he had been writing, making corrections with a blue pencil.

One morning, as the previous period came to an end, I recalled with a shock that in all probability I would be called on to recite, and I had not studied the lesson for Professor Bongerfi. I already felt his fiery eyes on me, heard his scathing words, saw him write "5" in his big *naplo* (logbook), and was humiliated by shame. I grabbed my textbook and feverishly concentrated on the lesson for the day. I heard nothing and saw nothing of the animated talk and movements of my fellow students. Suddenly there was silence, then we stood, respectfully, as the professor entered the room until he took his seat at the desk on the platform.

As he worked in his book I worked in mine until he put his aside, took the *naplo*, and began to read the names of about six pupils who were to recite that day. These few seconds were a century to the tortured me. My name was first. The professor looked at me benignly. Evidently, he was pleased with something, that only increased my trepidation, and said, "Well, Kautz, what have you learned for today?" I recited my lesson with emphasis and speed — eager to make a good impression and afraid of forgetting something. When I finished, he looked at me with a pleased smile, then turned to the class and said, in a warm, pleasant tone, "You see, boys? Here is a pupil after my own heart. He has even studied the lesson for tomorrow and recited it perfectly. There's a student for you!"

I almost fainted, but went back to my seat, head up, proud, and quite satisfied with the unintended yet nonetheless mean trick I had perpetrated on my good professor. Not until years later in far-off America did I dare to tell this story to anyone.

I was not so fortunate with my German professor, whose name escapes me. Perhaps it is still buried under feelings of shame and guilt, because I did so poorly in his class. It must have been the accursed masculine, feminine, and neuter words and endings. Sometimes as unreasonable and fantastic as, later on, English spelling and words would be, with identical sound but different meanings. Nothing like this had ever bothered my Hungarian ear, and getting accustomed to such an impossible language was quite a trial. Oh, I passed, but barely. I was so conscience-stricken that I entertained thoughts of suicide.

Why? First, because my poor parents had the notion that they had a gifted son. Second, because from my infancy I had learned German as well as Hungarian, for to my poor Viennese papa, Hungarian was the most difficult and the most terrible language. Therefore German should not have been too difficult for me. Third, all of us in school took our education more seriously than children in America. Finally, one of the important reasons we moved to the capitol was to give me this educational opportunity. I can still see the disappointment on the faces of my parents. What happened? I really don't know. Selective memory still draws a curtain over it.

Then there was bleary-eyed Professor Hickl. The boys called him Jonah, the name of the hippopotamus in the city's zoo. It must have been because of his fat body and quite striking, fat neck, that almost formed another shorter torso as it rested on his upper body. We learned very little from him because he was forever gazing out of the window at every passing skirt. I still remember standing at the head of a group of us, reciting the lesson. A comely female or two passed by the window, and Professor Hickl paid no attention to me. When I was through, I waited patiently until he turned to me and said: "Now, my son, recite the lesson for the day." Was I disgusted!

There was a fourth professor, whose name also refuses to rise to the surface of my mind, perhaps because I did so poorly in his course. He taught gymnastics, soccer, and sports in general. He was a very tall, very spare man and always carried a light coat on his arm and had gleaming pince-nez glasses on his big nose. I was not the athletic type. I was among the poorest in the class. Yet he gave me a fair mark, and for this, I remember him with gratitude.

One of the nicest memories of my boyhood is a trip with him to Visegrad, where we climbed over the ruins of the ancient fort built by King Matthias the Just, whose court was one of the important centers of the Renaissance. Entranced, we listened to stories and true anecdotes of his reign.

Classes lasted from eight to one o'clock, then home for lunch and out again to carry papa's lunch to his cellar workshop. I'm afraid I dawdled on the way sometimes. The Maria Theresa Barracks that I had to pass always fascinated me. In the big open courtyard surrounded by a high iron picket fence, soldiers drilled to the sounds of harsh commands, oaths, and curses as the non-commissioned officers whipped them into orderly, obedient, disciplined units. One day they were drilling some new recruits — frightened peasant youths they must have been because they often did the opposite of the roared command. I watched with horror as the non-coms slapped them across their faces and beat upon their legs with a rifle when they turned the wrong way. They made me hate and fear the military.

Yet the officers attracted me too in their handsome uniforms, often carrying their swords on one arm and twirling their beautiful large mustaches with the other hand, or returning the smart salutes of their inferiors in the indolent way of officers everywhere. The ring of star-shaped spurs attached to well-fitting, highly-polished boots, and the clatter of their swords on the pavement dragging after them created a martial atmosphere that drew me toward the life I hated. Much more so, the military bands that marched frequently along the main thoroughfares of the city playing stirring marches always compelled a group of us boys to march after them in rhythm.

At least once a year, the armed forces would station in the city. With colors flying, bands playing and oak leaves on the csákó (military hat) of every soldier who was led by their elegant mounted officers, they converged on *Vérmező*, the Field of Bloody, for a review by the king, or for an outdoor mass, or perhaps the consecration of weapons by the Cardinal-Primate of Hungary. Only much later, as a youth in America in rebellion against the church and, by implication, against all forms of religion, did I reflect upon this terrible, out-of-date perversion of Christianity, the religion of divine love, used to bless weapons of mass murder of our brothers.

On patriotic holidays we crowded into the streets and public places to view the parade of the soldiers: swords and bayonets gleaming, flags flapping, and the earth reverberating under the heavy stamping of thousands. Nearly always, however, these occasions were spoiled for Hungarians by the playing of the Habsburg anthem *Gott erhalte unser Kaiser* (God save our Emperor) when ours was an Apostolic King, not an emperor! Only many years later in America was I able to appreciate this glorious music of Hayden, set to church hymns, that slowly eradicated my first, unhappy impressions.

But I was on my way to my hungry father. How patient he was! I do not remember a single scolding for my late arrivals. One day I loitered too long and when I realized how late it was getting I started to run. I tripped and spilled the contents of the little can I was carrying. Fortunately, it was filled only with noodles instead of thick soup, stew or paprika. So I hastily scraped them back into the can leaving only the dirtiest to decorate the sidewalk.

My poor papa started to eat. Usually, this was a very tasty dish for the noodles were rolled in finely ground and fried bread crumbs, salted and sweetened to taste. The stuff crackled between his teeth. "*Krucinezer!*" he exploded with his favorite toned-down curse. "These noodles are gritty. What happened to them?"

Laughter and tears struggled for expression in me, but respect and fear enabled me to keep an innocent face as I replied, "I don't know, papa!" So the meal passed without further incidents. Was I glad to be out and on my way home!

There was a big cafe on the way where I stopped regularly to watch the drivers of the carriages, just like those still operating in New York's Central Park, play billiards and sip their coffee, usually black, from large glasses, while their horses waited patiently outside until passengers came. One day I noticed an unusual commotion on *Rákos utca* (Rákos Street). Police, called "guardians of order" in Budapest, were hastily clearing the street for a splendid equipage, with outriders and footmen in expensive livery on the driver's seat and in the back. I recognized the occupant. What loyal Hungarian could not? My king, Francis Joseph I. He came to see the ruins of a famous department store that had burnt the day before and to visit the injured in the *Rokus Korhaz*, a hospital. He jumped from his carriage like a youth and with quick steps disappeared into the building while the street rang with shouts of "Long live the King, Francis Joseph the First." It was very thrilling for a twelve-year-old boy.

Many, many years later, on my first return visit to Europe, myself now a grandfather, stood before the sarcophagus of the king in the crypt of the Habsburgs, under the Church of the Capuchins in Vienna. While the guide, a monk, knelt and said a prayer for the salvation of the royal soul, the man, and the boy inside him, pondered the meaning of history. "How the mighty have fallen!"

There was the coffin of Queen Elizabeth, too, the wife of Francis Joseph, who died prematurely by the dagger of an assassin. She was on one of her continuous trips, trying to flee from the mournful memories of the tragic death of Rudolph, the crown-prince, her only son. It was his misfortune to fall in love with the Countess Chotek whom he refused to give up, even if he had to surrender his right to the succession. Finally, he was shot to death by assassins at his chateau along with the countess. The assassins escaped and were never discovered. It was long suspected that they were known at court, perhaps even inspired by the inner circle.

Here lay Rudolph united with his family in death. I remembered these tragedies well for they were often told with horror by the adults. Nor can I forget the adulation that surrounded the Queen because she had made peace between the alienated nation and its ruler. Especially on the occasion of Kossuth's death, leader of the rebellion against the Habsburgs in 1848-49. He never returned from his self-appointed exile in Turin, Italy, although the king wanted him back, and the government had granted him a pardon. Elizabeth laid a gorgeous wreath on his coffin when he was laid out in Budapest, as a token of reconciliation. The heart of the nation went out to her in profound affection and sympathy when she lost Rudolf.

This increased as gossip broadcast the King's devotion to Frau Schratt, a Viennese actress, at whose home he had often sought consolation and recreation instead of with his lovely queen. Fifty years later I still recall the shocking headlines, black-bordered pictures of the queen and of the assassin. The senseless attack on a woman who was lovely and good, and the idol of the Hungarian nation shook us all and made us hate the anarchists as never before.

Often on the way home from Papa's workshop, I stopped in front of a picture store. The scene I studied most often was the capture of Peking and the rescue of the European consulates' staff during the Boxer rebellion. Little did the boy dream that the dread vision of Napoleon, that of an awakened giant, China, would come true in his lifetime and cause sleepless nights in the chancelleries of the world, including that of the other great giant — Soviet Russia. He wondered at the outlandish features, eyes, dress and fierce looks of the "yellow men."

Wars and rumors of wars. Faint but discernible rumbles of great earthquakes along the geological faults of the empire system in an apparently solid, stable world. But the privileged races, nations, and classes were too busy scrapping with each other for immediate advantages of pelf, power, and profit to do anything about it. And if black clouds appeared on their horizon, it was considered only a passing storm that like many others would soon pass.

Then the Russo-Japanese War broke out. There could be but one outcome, of course — the defeat of the little island empire that had barely stepped over the threshold from a feudal regime into modern nationhood. The gigantic Bear would flatten the rash pigmy with one blow of its terrible paw, but the wise ones in power rubbed their eyes in unbelief as they watched the imperial might of the Czar go down in ignominious defeat — its great navy sunk, bottled-up, and dispersed. But the little people were glad. Little nations, oppressed races and even the great White nations, the underprivileged who were not drunk with chauvinism like the simple villager, the father of my wife, predicted the victory of the "little yellow men."

Hungarians, remembering the Czar's troops on their soil in 1849, were rather jubilant, and so were other European nations who feared the peril of the Russian flood of pan-slavism and autocracy. But my poor, blind, misled little nation, fired by the heroic traditions of the past and the military virtues necessitated by its tragic history, still dreamed of glory — for did not the high command of the Imperial Royal Army declare the Magyars to be the best soldiers in the Monarchy?

They refused to recognize the stubborn fact that in their little nation of twenty million, over half, almost two-thirds, consisted of ethnic stocks other than Magyar, the dominant element, as is the Anglo-Saxon in the United States. What a terrible price would history exact for this blindness!

We saw the legless, armless, blind, crippled veterans of previous wars everywhere. But they had medals on their chests, special uniforms, and caps. They lived in impressive, well-landscaped asylums to the end of their lives, and we venerated them. They were our heroes, even though most of them had been willing tools of the Habsburgs against the Italians who also had fought for their freedom against the Habsburgs.

Once a year, on August 20th, we observed Saint Stephen's Day. He was the first king of Hungary, who united the warring chieftains and tribes into a strong nation, converted his nation to Roman Catholic Christianity, and gave a western direction to the new nation. True, the conversion was rather crude and superficial, for whole villages were driven into nearby streams and christened wholesale. To this, some missionaries added the magnetic power of martyrdom. Such was Saint Gellert who was nailed into a barrel, that was studded with nails and rolled down the hill of Buda into the Danube. In my childhood, his statue still graced Mt. Gellert in Buda, not far from the royal castle. As a reward for his labors, Stephen received from the Pope a crown and the only title of its kind, "Apostolic King" of Hungary. Some centuries later he was beatified.

The highlight of the celebration on Saint Stephen's Day was a gorgeous procession of medieval splendor when his miraculously preserved right hand, so we were taught, that had done so much good, was carried around the streets of Buda while we looked on in awe; impressed by the legend as well as the overwhelming beauty of the event. The military was out in all its splendor. Generals, long lines of altar boys, priests, bishops, and the Cardinal Primate preceded and followed the Sacred Hand; surrounded by the palace guard of halberdiers in resplendent uniforms and silver helmets, the court and the King in all their magnificence and the Hungarian aristocracy in their famous medieval costumes of silk, velvet, gold and jewels, turban-like hats with gorgeous feathers held in place by jeweled clasps fashioned centuries ago, and their ancient, curved scimitars encased in velvet and gold or silver at their sides. An unforgettable sight, crashing military bands, chanting, military flags, the national tricolor in red, white and green with its significant national coat of arms; the three highest peaks and four rivers of Hungary, and the beautiful religious banners from the churches. How could anyone not be a fanatically loyal patriot with all his senses filled with these symbols and reminders of the glorious history of a thousand years?

And Budapest, the lovely city of my birth! Years ago a traveler was asked to compare Budapest with the other capitals of Europe. Of his reply, I recall only this, "Paris reminds one of a grand dame of the world, Vienna of a merry widow, but Budapest, oh Budapest, is like a lovely, young virgin."

I have never dared to boast about it, but everyone I met who saw my native city before the two world wars and revolutions were inclined to agree. Not very long ago I heard of a sculptress who had traveled in Budapest. I met her at a party. After the introduction, I cautiously ventured: "So this is the lady who has seen the city of my birth!"

"What city? Budapest? Ah Budapest, the most beautiful city I have ever seen!" And she went into raptures about its location, the royal castle, Margaret Island, Lanchid, the first suspension bridge in Europe, the houses of parliament, the cafes with their gypsy music and so on. From that time I had a new and high status in the eyes of all who heard it.

She might have mentioned *Andrássy út* (Andrássy Avenue), the loveliest route into the city park *Városliget*, the semicircular ring on the site of the old wall that once surrounded the town of Pest, the spotless cleanliness of the streets. I keep searching my memory for pictures of a slum but I cannot find any, yet my parents were poor and we never could afford to live in the better districts. I only saw something of these on our excursions and when I went on special walks to the famous confectionery in Belvaros (where they made their matchless creations for the King's own table) in order to buy broken pastry — a special treat for us children.

My parents were too poor to send us to a show or concert of any kind. Certainly not to the opera. The only drama I remember was *Janos Vitez* (Sir John), a rather tragic story of a popular fictional hero played on little outdoor marionette stages in the City Park. We compensated by putting on shows of our own, like Kalman in his father's workshop, to which we charged entrance fees of a penny or two. Almost daily in good weather we girded on our wooden swords and put on our paper *chakos* (military caps) and marched in step through the streets with stern martial expressions, sometimes following one of the military bands that happened to pass. It amused our elders, but to us it was a deadly serious matter.

We played the usual games: tag, hide and seek, scissors, stuck, etc. The latter was a game between two with a soft ball, one child against the wall ready to cry "stuck," meaning hit, when the other had hit him with the ball. If the mark successfully evaded the ball, he took the place of the other. In the summer we also took walks to the *Lukacs furdo* (Luke's Bath), a free municipal institution where we spent hours in the big pool. On one occasion, Steve, my brother a year and a half younger, and I engaged in a wrestling match. A part of our technique was to keep our competitor under the water until he was ready to give up. This time neither of us would and we were almost done in when we separated. We barely made it to the edge of the pool where we sat coughing, holding our heads; very miserable indeed. We never tried it again.

Then sex reared its head. Boys of our peer group began to discuss their new sensations and adventures with girls, wondering about the mysterious world of adults where sex apparently played a very important part. All about us were suggestions that romanticized sexual adventures, like the Polish girl of thirteen who would quickly raise her skirts and drop them to show us a well-developed pair of legs and buttocks. Latrine inscriptions and drawings stimulated some fantastic notions, but no self-respecting parent considered sexual instruction of their own children decent. Prostitution was a legal institution, and every day we saw these unfortunate women sitting in front of their houses in negligee waiting for clients, sometimes shouting after a passing male, "Hey John, I haven't seen you in two weeks!" Some of the more adventurous boys boasted of climbing up on windows at night and viewing unspeakable scenes. Perhaps they did, although I doubt it. It was common knowledge among us that in respectable houses the window curtains were hung inside, while prostitutes hung theirs between the double windows, then in general use.

About this time I went to my first confession at the church in the 9th district of Ferencvaros. I was troubled about my new emotions and thoughts and asked my father-confessor for advice on how to overcome them. He suggested that I say an Our Father, a Hail Mary, and a Credo, and assured me that my mind would clear. It worked for quite a while. Also, I was haunted by considerable anxiety about confessing all of my sins in order that I did not take the Host, the body of my Savior, unworthily.

Then came the great celebration of confirmation. I was dressed in my new sailor suit of expensive blue material, carried my new silver watch and chain, a great treasure for a poor boy like myself, the gift of Uncle Gregor who stood behind me as my confirmation-father. Down a long line of boys and girls came the bishop, arrayed in gorgeous vestments, superhumanly tall in his high miter, surrounded by lesser priests, acolytes and altar boys. Striking me gently on the cheek with his two forefingers, he mumbled something in Latin that I had learned previously meant, "Are you ready to suffer persecution for the Master?"

Awed, I timidly answered, "yes," in Hungarian. Then, dipping a finger into holy oil, he made the mark of the cross on my forehead and passed on. I had been dedicated as a full-fledged son of the church by my "voluntary" decision.

Certainly, the pageantry of the church, especially where it is the state church, is very impressive and the doctrinal conditioning very thorough. Reverence for the priesthood and the fear of damnation predispose the faithful devotee to attitudes scarcely to be found among Protestants and less often among Jews, with the exception of very pious Orthodox Jewry in Eastern Europe.

Sixty years later I can still hum a haunting melody from a mass. It was sung just before the elevation of the host as a solo accompanied softly by an organ up in the loft in the back of the church. Sung by a priest with a good voice, it awed the worshipper and prepared him for the miracle of transubstantiation. Now and then I still sing a hymn of adoration that was sung by the congregation when the priest held high the sacrament, the host enclosed in a monstrance sparkling with rays of gold and precious stones, so sacred that the priest had to wear a special shawl to handle it. It is a beautiful melody and the translated text is somewhat as follows:

This is a great Sacrament in Truth.
This we worship above all.
Thee we bless and worship, Lord,
In the great Sacrament of the altar.

How could a pious, well-conditioned Roman Catholic stay away from Mass, where the miracle of transubstantiation took place at the magical incantation of the priest, so that the Divine Son, second Person of the Trinity, took on flesh again and was sacrificed by the priest for the sins of the worshippers? No Protestant minister handles such a Mysterium Tremendum, and it is useless to accuse Catholics of divine cannibalism — eating the body and drinking the blood of their God.

Mother was a faithful Catholic, but father was not. He seldom, if ever went to church, but never discouraged us from going. Nonetheless, he was a loyal husband, a devoted father, the very soul of honor, and a gallant gentleman who always acted with chivalrous respect toward women. He relaxed on Sundays, puttered around the house, cleaning up things that the others were unable to do. After a good Sunday dinner, he had a brief nap and then went to his favorite tavern for a few hands of cards, usually for very small stakes, that he claimed added zest and excitement to the game. He would interrupt the game to function as secretary-treasurer of a little credit union in a brief business meeting of the organization. Then perhaps a light supper and home to his family.

That was his weekly recreation. Only many years later did I find similar credit unions in America. They were new in this progressive land.

An outstanding memory of those days was a certain Father Hock, called "the priest with the golden mouth." His church was crowded with worshippers whenever he preached. He was a leader in the People's Party, a kind of Catholic Party, eloquent in describing the needs of the common people, the misery of the poor and the need of Christian concern about such matters. My mother and her forelady friends in the cigar factory were his great admirers and seldom missed an opportunity to hear him. However, he was a great exception. Most of the priests and the hierarchy were staunch supporters of the status quo. How could they be otherwise when the church was the greatest and wealthiest property owner in Hungary? It was supported by taxation and its religious orders worked for low wages. Here and there one heard faint grumbles of anti-clericalism.

One very vivid memory is of a visit by Andor, a cousin of mine who was a student at the University of Budapest. With great enjoyment, he told my parents and grandmother about the embarrassing trick they had played on two of their professors. These were priests. Jesuits, if my memory serves me correctly. They found them at an amusement spot where priests were not supposed to be. They were without their distinguishing clericals but Andor and his friends recognized them and, lifting their hats reverently, called out in a loud voice the customary greeting to priests, "Praised be the Lord Jesus Christ."

Embarrassed and blushing they had to reply, "Forever, Amen." Loud and prolonged laughter by all followed his story.

I was rather a puny boy in youth and received a lot of teasing and punishment from the bullies of the neighborhood. Occasionally I was surprised by a bit of dramatic justice. One day a boy, older, bigger, and much stronger than I, living on the same floor in the apartment house, began his customary baiting game. This time it was too much. Infuriated, I knocked him down. He jumped up with great astonishment on his face. I can still see him run into his apartment. He never bothered me again.

Coupled with my puniness was a certain tenderness that made it difficult for me to inflict suffering on anybody else unless I was possessed by great anger. I do not remember torturing animals — a pastime among my playmates. Perhaps this unusual sensitivity and empathy with sufferers, both human and animal, predisposed me to the philosophy of nonviolence to which I am now dedicated.

Grandma was the one who looked after us, cooked, and cleaned. Poor old lady, nearing sixty and her legs continuously inflamed, she must have had her hands full with seven youngsters, aged two to eleven. Sometimes her anger made her physically ill and I still see her leaning against the doorpost vomiting bile. Yet she tried not to tell on us to papa, too often in order to save us from a well-merited caning. My brother Steve had a maddening way of avoiding the worst of this punishment by shouting right after the first or second blow "Oi, papa, I will soil my pants."

"You pig, you!" exclaimed Papa with a final blow, "To the water closet with you!" After a few times, however, papa discovered the trick and Steve no longer escaped, even at the risk of an accident.

But to return to Grandma. We were very poor and my parents were beginning to talk about America, the hope and haven of all the poor, discouraged, and hopeless people of Europe. Grandma was not eager, I am sure, to leave the Old Country at her age, even with her grandchildren, and begin life all over again in a foreign land with its strange customs and impossible language on the other side of the world, braving the terrors of the ocean in the bargain. In her anxiety, she hit upon a scheme that might give her a bit of security if the rest of us embarked on such a hair-raising adventure. She began to save some pitiful *Hellers*, a fifth of a cent in value, on her shopping. Whenever she had one hundred of them she changed them to a *Korona*, equivalent to about twenty cents, and hid them in her trunk. Somehow Papa became suspicious. Perhaps she saved too hard on her purchases of food and once when grandma was out he looked through her trunk. He discovered her pitiful little hoard of 15 or 20 *Korona*. A bitter and violent scene followed in which papa called her some terrible names. He himself was the soul of honor, and above all, he despised slyness, disloyalty, double-dealing, and deceit, so poor Grandma was guilty of the supreme crime in his eyes. My heart went out to both, torn by my affection for them, and wondered about this tragedy that is especially a temptation of the poor.

Slowly my parents felt life closing in on them. There were seven of us now, ranging from one to eleven years of age, and they saw no possibility of increasing their earnings. Father often worked fifteen to twenty hours a day, and attacks of rheumatism tortured him more and more frequently. But his employer, who had a lovely little shop on one of the main boulevards in an elite business section in a privileged area, claimed that she could not afford a healthier location.

Sometimes the shop was filled with dust as Papa worked on a bench equipped with sharp metal fingers, loosening the horsehair until it was soft enough to be stuffed into mattresses, divans, or chairs. Two tiny windows could not carry off the dust fast enough and papa inhaled a great deal of it. I still wonder how he escaped tuberculosis. He could not have worked harder than he did and he already had the best paying job in Budapest at his trade.

Mother had advanced to the top position open to women in the cigar factory — that of forelady. Not informed about contraception, and perhaps with horror about interfering with the processes of nature, not to mention the church's prohibition of such practice, considered immoral and sinful, the family would continue to grow and this would mean poverty. Father already filed a notarized certificate of poverty to provide continued free education for me. The future looked dismal indeed, and rather frightening.

The one ray of hope was the good news from "The Promised Land," America. This ray was greatly magnified by the flamboyant posters of steamship companies and by boasting letters from compatriots who often covered their disappointments and heartaches with glowing reports of life in "The Promised Land." The greedy maw of American industry was doing its share to entice cheap labor. Mother had several friends, cigar makers in New York City, who were earning very well indeed, four times as much as they had received in Budapest. However, they were not foreladies in New York and to my proud mother, her position had meant a great deal. But for the sake of her children, she was willing to make any sacrifice.

I open a window on memory and still see her and father sitting at the table in our big room by the dim light of an oil lamp, turned low to avoid awakening their sleeping children, heads close together, talking in whispers way into the night until I too fell asleep. This went on for a long time, for the contemplated step seemed like a wild adventure indeed. In a distant foreign land with its strange customs, across the trackless Atlantic, with its terrible storms, when passengers were locked below decks while the ship staggered from an abyss to the top of an enormous wave and down again for days at a time and sometimes sank.

Naturally, Papa wanted to come first. But he knew no one in America, had no idea of the methods they used in his trade, how he would go about finding a job, or how much he might receive in wages. And they had already heard that around presidential elections there was apt to be a good deal of unemployment. If father came first they would have to borrow funds, perhaps for two or three years, not only to pay for his trip but until he had saved enough from his earnings to send us the money for our passage. Mother did not earn nearly enough to provide for the family's living in Budapest.

On the other hand, if mother came first she was assured of work through her friends in one of New York's many cigar factories where they worked or had acquaintances. And, Mama argued, "You know, Papa, elections or not, American men must have their cigars, so I would have steady employment. Grandma can do the necessary work around the apartment, cook, and look after the children. Your wages, with a little skimping, could cover the expenses. And if I can earn what Mrs. Haas and

Mrs. Laufig earn, I might be able to send for the rest of you in two years, or earlier, if we borrow a part of the fare."

It was all very logical and true, Papa had to admit, but his masculine pride stood in the way. Men always went first and provided for the rest. How could he face his friends if he allowed her to reverse this and put him to shame?

However, mama argued, she too was sacrificing her pride in giving up her position as a forelady and her security in losing her governmental pension, for, as stated before, tobacco was a government monopoly and she was a civil servant. Month after month their inquiries, discussions, and arguments continued. Bless their hearts, moldering in a grave along with a grandchild of theirs, Victor, in a Long Island cemetery. At last, they arrived at their decision. Mother would come first and the family to follow as soon as possible. Since they had no savings, they had to borrow the entire sum at a high rate of interest from one of the several women in the factory who were also professional money lenders, and from Papa's credit union.

The evening mother left us is indelibly etched on a special tablet in a sacred chamber of my hall of memories. It is one of the most painful and inspiring pictures in my mind that always puts me to shame when I permit fear or discouragement to rob me of strength and zest for living.

All of the children but I were asleep in their beds. Mama in a long grey traveling cape, a grey cap-like hat on her head, silent tears rolling down her handsome face, went from one sleeping form to the other, embracing and kissing them goodbye. Perhaps forever. Most often returning to the year-old baby Vulko, from whom she could not tear herself away. Finally, father took one arm, a friend another, and they led her from the room.

It was ages before we had a letter from New York informing us of her safe arrival. It took twelve days to make the trip from Antwerp. A very stormy passage so she spent all but one day in bed. Ruefully she remarked in a letter: "They made a lot of money on me. Papa had demanded that she must travel second class, not steerage, and in this, he had his way."

After that, the letters came with fair regularity informing us of her slow progress in the land of promise. She had no difficulty in finding board and lodging with a friend from the Old Country and almost immediately found work. Her cigars were models in their beauty but she was slow in mastering the "hurry-up" technique and her wages were discouragingly low. She was very lonely. She missed the affection of her husband. She was surrounded by strangers all day and she couldn't even hear that outlandish English tongue for she was surrounded by Czech women. So in America, she learned Czech first, and I am told by those who can judge, that it was a beautiful Czech she spoke.

One day, about six months later, Grandma came to me and showed me a photograph that, she said, came from a friend. She wondered if I could guess who it was. No, she was a total stranger. I had never seen her. "Oh, but you do know her," Grandma said. "Look at it again." I gazed at the photograph and shook my head, wondering why grandma should bother me with a stranger's picture. "Why, it's your mother!" She cried with indignation, "You don't know your own mother?"

Once again I stared at the photograph. "No, this is not my mother! My mother is a beautiful young woman." In the end, however, she convinced me that it was my mother. I wondered how six months in the "promised land" could change her so.

Later when I joined her where she had lodged, her friend told me how over and over again, she and her husband were awakened at night by her soft, subdued sobbing. When she could not stand it any longer, she went in and tried to comfort her. To her question, "What is the matter?" the answer was, "Can you ask? My husband, my children, my baby!" Then I began to understand.

Among my parents' papers, I found a letter, the only one I saved, written in those terrible days by my father to his wife in America. They will forgive me, I am certain, if I share it. Some of the endearing expressions are approximations of the special mixture of German and Hungarian that they developed in their very private relationship.

My sweet, precious wife: My everything in this world!

Broken in body and spirit, without joy and enthusiasm I seat myself before this letter. I should like to write but I cannot find the proper words to express my thoughts; my head is so confused.

The information Mrs. Haas brought exceeded my worst expectations. So then, in return for all we have risked, yes, sacrificed, we have achieved only that you, my Beloved, my sweetheart, worry, work, and despair unto death! O my love, what have we done? And I, I alone am to blame that this happened to us, and chiefly to you, my poor Love! O how often have I cursed my share in this matter, for it was only my determination to hold fast to our previously formulated plan which has cast us into this sea of pain, loss, and suffering; for you, my Love, even that last day would have remained here with us, your loved ones. Your sweet heart felt already what was before you.

Still, my complaints profit us nothing; it is done; let us, therefore, gather all our strength and endure our present plight as well as we can.

My sweet Love, there is this one thing that weighs heavily on my heart; that you have lost your assured, certain bread for your old age. My beloved, sweet wife, do not oppose me when I say that from now on I alone must provide for all of you; and this will double my strength for my labor; and who knows what good may result from your return. Evil seldom overcomes one without some compensating good.

Look, even now, that I have given expression to my complaints, my mood is no longer so black, in fact I must even laugh over Vutkos, these pencil marks are his, he sits on the table next to me and I have to play with him in order to be able to write a few lines. There are evenings when he simply will not fall asleep. I put him in his carriage and he cries, I pick him up and he laughs and is full of fun; so nothing is left but to get up and play with him. What good fortune is such a sweet little child! As I wrote about him the entire heavy pain lifted from my breast.

Your Faithful Ludwig

Mother's increasing and unbearable loneliness finally compelled our parents to make another break in the family. They decided to send Eddie (myself) until the whole family could be united again. So they scraped and borrowed until they had gathered the sum for my fare. Father took me with him to the cigar factory to meet a woman who made a business of lending money. I recall a well-dressed woman of middle height, shrewd, penetrating eyes, a set face, and thin lips firmly pressed together, with whom my father discussed the terms. The interest she demanded was quite high. Well, she took risks and we needed the money. Finally, the financing of the trip was assured.

For some time father had been inquiring carefully, secretly about someone with whom I might be able to make the long trip across the perilous seas to the new world. Finally, he found a woman who was going to rejoin her husband in America, who had emigrated a year or two before. She was to take me as her son and we were assured it would be quite safe.

There was another difficulty, however. The question of a passport. The Hungarian government had an agreement with the Cunard Line to shunt all emigrants to America into Flume and issued very few passes to other lines elsewhere. Agents of these lines, however, succeeded in selling tickets to the few who somehow evaded the secret service men at the frontier to embark elsewhere. Nobody relished the twenty-day trip from Flume to New York but preferred the nine to twelve days from other ports.

My last day in Budapest dawned and I rose early. It was a sunny day and the city of my birth never looked lovelier. Cautiously, I kept glancing out of the window hoping to get a final glimpse of Agnes Manyoki, only a year older than I, a healthy apple-cheeked, tomboy sort of a girl to whom I had taken fancy only a few weeks before. It was one of those sudden, unaccountable infatuations of early adolescence, and I was quite unhappy not to be able to see her once more. In fact, I shamefully recognized that it was more painful to leave her than Papa, my brothers, sister, and Grandma. Only papa and Steve accompanied me to the station where my new "mother" was waiting for me. Even as I write I feel a sinking of the heart, seeing before me Steve's pitiful face, with tears trickling down as I waved goodbye from the window. But I did not cry, perhaps because of the great adventure, perhaps because I was on my way to Mama, or perhaps I was relieved to leave school. Who knows? Probably, as always, the reasons were manifold and complex. Certainly not amenable to analysis by a twelve-year-old.

We were on our way. Now my "mother" confided to me that we had no passport. All who lacked this, and also the many hundreds of young men who were trying to escape their three years of military duty, faced the possibility of arrest, an uncomfortable shipment home, and imprisonment. It was with considerable fear that we awaited the approach of the frontier. We could hardly eat, though we were well provided with good Hungarian food.

At last the detectives boarded the train and began the questioning of the passengers. My lady, my "mother," caught the roving eyes of their chief, a dapper little man with a military bearing and a well-curled mustache. She was a very handsome woman in the European sense; buxom, a fine figure with plenty of curves, flashing black eyes, black hair, and very white skin. The chief settled himself on the seat beside her and soon they were engaged in animated conversation. He was eager to buy presents for me but I was too frightened to enjoy or accept anything. At the border, many of our unfortunate fellow passengers were taken off the train, but we stayed on. The chief, with a click of his heels, a salute, and a "kiss your hands, gracious lady," that he proceeded to do with considerable warmth, left us. Were we relieved!

In a short time, we arrived at the German border town of Ratibor (now *Racibórz* in Poland). My "mother" quickly established herself in the station master's office. It became our drawing room. We went in and out freely with never a care for our baggage. At noon, we went to a cafe where a number of businessmen and military officers were having lunch. Soon they were ogling my lady, twisting their mustaches and casting inquiring smiles in her direction. She looked at them haughtily, and they kept their places, greatly to my relief.

While this was going on and we were waiting for our meal, I noticed a strange condiment on the table, bright yellow in color, that I had never seen before. I was determined not to betray my ignorance. While the lady gave a special, long look to somebody, I quickly dipped my spoon into the yellow, butter-like paste and stuffed it into my mouth. It was very sharp and had an unpleasant flavor. I swallowed it quickly and started gulping water to control the burning in my throat and mouth. I did not enjoy the meal. This was my introduction to sharp mustard.

Soon we were on the train again, headed toward Hamburg. The station master had carried our baggage and made the customary salute and a hand kiss to "my gracious lady." Slowly I dozed off. When I awakened in the middle of the night, I discovered a swarthy gentleman sitting very close to the lady. Kissing her hands and arms passionately. She nudged him and motioned to me. He ceased his courting and drew to his own side. I was devoured by curiosity and somewhat disgusted by their behavior, but in spite of their carrying on I soon fell asleep.

In Hamburg, the lady showed me some black and blue spots on her arms caused by his passionate bites. She showed me his picture. He was the leader of a gypsy band and they had an engagement in a cafe in Hamburg. He looked very handsome and looked quite the musician, holding his violin, yet rather silly because the photographer had etched a medal on his lapel, so poor a job that even my boyish eyes recognized it as a fake. She insisted on visiting the cafe where he would play. To my relief, he was not there and after leaving a message and our hotel address we left. We never saw him again.

But the lady carried his expensive photograph all the way to New York, where she asked me to keep it, for her husband was to meet her and take her to her new home in Philadelphia. Poor man, I often wondered what happened to them. My loyal mother must have been horrified when I explained who the gypsy was, but she said never a word.

Even though we traveled steerage the band welcomed us aboard the *SS Blücher*, or so I thought. Now I am inclined to think they played for the first- and second-class passengers. Soon the ship's unforgettable, deep, mournful horn gave the signal, and as the band played, the passengers and their friends on shore shouted their last farewells, threw their kisses, and wept. The *Blücher* moved majestically away from the dock and headed for the New World. Budapest seemed so far away. I think I wept that night for the first time since the morning I left my beautiful city, but I fear it was more for my new but forever lost fancy, Agnes Manyoki, than for my family.

3 - First Impressions of America

The following day we left the channel and caught sight of the limitless ocean. The waves of the Atlantic gave me a queasy stomach and I went to my bunk early. The next morning, I awakened to pandemonium. Nearly everybody was seasick, or so it seemed. There were at least two hundred people in this enormous cabin, lying in double bunks, one over the other and arranged in long rows with a not very broad passageway between them. It was slippery with vomit, that the crew was bravely trying to clean up by spreading clean sawdust on the floor. I thought of getting up but was discouraged when I saw the spitting and vomit from lower and upper bunks threaten the passersby. For two days I clambered down only when absolutely necessary. Children cried, women and old people prayed, and men cursed as they tossed on their bunks or ran about with a sharp eye for the malodorous shower. The sights and smells were enough to bring on the sickness even if the rolling of the ship had not. Each day those able to walk at all were driven up on deck while the large cabin was cleaned and fumigated.

The third day, I went on deck. The sea was fairly calm. Still, I had to make a small sacrifice to father Neptune, and rushing to the rail gave up a thin bitter stream to the fishes. After that, I was a good sailor.

The food was adequate, even good at times but not to the taste of the Hungarian passengers, for our cooking is quite superior. It was flat, oddly seasoned, and did not appeal to our palates.

One day, the lady posing as my mother accosted the captain, a stout giant of a German with a ferocious mustache and goatee, and complained about the food served in the steerage, calling it fit only for pigs. He promised to inspect the food in person at least once a day. He was as good as his word and came to the kitchen in the steerage and had a couple of spoons full of every dish. He found it quite satisfactory. My disgusted companion then made a connection with a second cabin steward and promised to pay him well if he brought us fowl or pork or beef from their kitchen. After that, we lived fairly well. I especially enjoyed the roasted duck.

Then we ran into a fierce storm and for two days nobody was allowed on deck. For poor landlubbers who had never even seen the ocean, this was a terrifying experience. Anxiety was clearly etched on most faces. Children and old people cried. Parents tried their best to conceal their anxiety. Most of us were seasick again. Some cursed the day they had heard about America. All in all, those were two very unhappy days. As most of my readers know, seasickness is almost never fatal, but one who has it feels sure he'll die or wishes he would. On the third day, however, the sun came out, the ocean quieted and we felt like living again.

On the ninth day of our trip we awakened early. We missed the steady hum and vibration of the engines and the gentle swell of the waves. Out of the morning fog, a gigantic statue slowly materialized, then the world-famous skyline of New York. The statue represented a lady, holding high a torch. We speculated on its meaning. Clearly, it was not a historical person. It had to be an allegorical, symbolic figure. Was it America welcoming us? Was the light the symbol of freedom and opportunity? Nobody told us.

Slowly, majestically, the *Blücher* veered away from the impressive skyline, towards Hoboken, New Jersey. Soon we caught sight of the pier, crowded with relatives and friends. After some delay, the first and second cabin passengers marched down the gangplank into the new world, but not us in steerage. The only explanation available to us was that they had enough money to pay cabin fare, and this entitled them to this special privilege.

The next day, we too marched down the gangplank, but not into the new world, but onto barges with benches around the sides. They looked more like cattle barges than anything else. A tug took us in tow and chugged us to that place of terror for the immigrants who spoke no English — Castle Garden on Ellis Island.

On landing we saw some flower beds, which cheered us. Then we were led into a vast building with classified cages where the immigrants sat with their pitiful belongings — duly examined and about which we were carefully quizzed. Years later I read about a Hungarian peasant who was being "processed" (to use a modern word). The customs officer was curious about a little canvas bag, quite heavy and asked through an interpreter what it contained. "Oh my son," said the shy peasant, "it is only a little of the soil of Hungary, so that if I die here they can place it under my head in the coffin and I shall sleep so much better in a foreign land."

Sitting on my pitiful little baggage, I stared around me. A vague astonishment filled my mind, for this was the gateway to the wonderland of the world, America. Ellis Island was within sight of the fantastic skylines of New York. Here we were in an enormous cage with perhaps hundreds of men, women and children staring at each other and at the officials who came and went through the gate, with interpreters asking questions, probing, demanding information about our past, destination, resources, relatives and friends in America, and possible employment.

I was only twelve and did not speak the strange language of the new, foreign land. I hoped everything would go well. The lady who had sneaked me past the guards on the boundary of Austria as her son would now tell the truth. She was bringing me to my mother in New York who was employed as a cigar maker in one of the many cigar factories in that vast city, and was well able to provide for me. Would they believe her? When, oh when will mother come? Eagerly, expectantly, I watched the stream of people flowing past the cage to claim their friends and relatives.

Suddenly I was startled from my dozing. Who was that woman who had just passed the cage? The erect figure, the determined walk, the handsome profile, for an instant it looked like my mother! It was only a glimpse, however, and I could not be certain. Then an official came and called a name. Not mine. She was not mother then! The official came and went again. Finally, with a paper in his hand, he went to every group. They peered at the paper and shook their heads. He came to the lady and to me. Why, that was my name, Kautz Odon! I pointed to myself and the lady nodded in approval. The official beckoned us to follow. A hundred pairs of eyes kept us company. We were out of the cage. With outstretched hands came a lovely lady and in a moment, I was in my real mother's arms.

Away from the cage, along endless corridors of the enormous building, on to the deck of the ferryboat, away from that place of joy and sorrow, tears and laughter, hope and despair, Castle Garden, and on to New York City!

There it was, easily recognized because of its unique skyline. As we landed, I observed a peculiar structure overhead. I had never seen anything like it. Tall, oblong, hollow pillars connected at the top by girders holding up some tracks. Steam trains, like the tiny trains of my boyhood from Budapest into the countryside, overhead? "You can travel all over New York with them," my mother informed me. How I wanted to try those trains with their puffing little engines! But my mother dragged me away to a horse-car under the elevated train. I could hardly believe my eyes. Why, in his poor little country of Hungary, in the capital, electric cars ran along the Ring. And here, in rich America, they still had horsecars? Unbelievable!

So we started our journey home, to my American home. It was a slow journey up the East Side along Avenues C, B, A, First Avenue, so I remember it. Perhaps not quite correctly. I was all eyes. But all I remembered in later years was the overflowing trash and garbage cans, papers and filth everywhere, unimpressive tenements, and no sign or promise of any of the wonderful things I'd heard about America. It was odd to see the policemen with their helmets a foot high, clubs instead of clanking swords at their side, walking along the street at an easy gait, unimpressive compared with the dignified and fierce-looking guardians of the law in Budapest. We passed two or three dead animals on the road. I began to wonder if they used them for milestones in this strange city! I grew increasingly despondent. I remembered the beautiful city of my birth, Budapest, the Queen of the Danube, and I was depressed, though comforted now and then only by the pressure of my mother's hand on mine.

Then I remembered my father and five brothers and sister, still in the Old Country, and grew sad again. It was on Sunday. Gradually we became aware of the clean new look of children, the boys in blue serge, black shoes and stockings, the girls mostly in white, and I recalled that in my native city, only the children of the rich dressed like that. Then, I did not mind the filth so much.

The day before, my mother had cooked a special meal for me — Hungarian food. She was a wonderful cook and I gorged myself on it. As a special dessert, she placed a large lovely yellow fruit before me. It was long and gently curved. I had often seen the stewards carry great bunches of them on their shoulders across the deck of the *Blücher*. Sometimes one or two dropped to the deck, and the steerage passengers made a dash to retrieve them.

"This is a banana, an American fruit, and delicious," my mother informed me while peeling it. I took a generous bite. My mother watched me closely. I felt that if I swallowed it my wonderful Hungarian dinner would inevitably come up. Sudden inspiration! I rushed to the sink for a drink of water and accidentally dropped it.

"Never mind my son," she said, "I'll peel you another."

"Oh no, mother, thank you. I'm too full anyhow. I'd enjoy it more tomorrow." It was only after several others had been dropped into the sink "accidentally" during the next few days that she caught on and wasted no more of them on me. It took me several years to develop an appreciation for their flavor. Now they are a welcome gift at any time.

Life in the "promised land" and in glamorous New York City did not begin with much promise or glamour. We lived on E. 44th St., between 1st and 2nd Avenues. There were two or three private houses in front of which the sidewalk was swept regularly and washed occasionally. However, the sidewalks along the tenements that predominated were swept only now and then. Overflowing garbage cans stood in front, and quite a few tenants did not bother to take their dirt down but wrapped in paper to throw out of the window, sometimes their night soil too, for the water-closets were in the yard, one to each floor. I soon learned to cock an eye on the upper-story windows and an ear for their opening. How often I thought with fierce longing of my spotless native city, Budapest!

The American children, very often themselves the offspring of immigrants with the usual lack of understanding and thoughtlessness of children, made fun of the greenhorn kid, easily singled out by my sailor jacket and stiff, high collar, who looked bewildered when they spoke to him, and could only mumble in a queer tongue. Soon I learned a few words, but what an accent! I always pronounced two as "choo", for in my own language, there was no such sound. There was always "da" or "di" for "the" and only years later did somebody show me how to take my tongue between my teeth in order to pronounce the impossible "th."

We had a special game to which we caught on rather quickly. A boy would put a piece of wood or stone or some other object on his shoulder and gestured that I knock it off. I didn't understand the words, but the sweeping motion of the hand was clear. Quite puzzled at this inscrutable action I brushed the thing off and then the boy punched me in the belly or on the head. When they discovered that I was a shy, peaceful sort they made me do this over and over and over again, standing about me in a circle, laughing merrily at my puzzled and hurt frowns. Later I learned about the American ideal of sportsmanship, but not from these boys or the adolescent gangs who were never troubled about standards of fairness, but attacked in numbers without provocation.

So I, the foreigner, the greenhorn, the despised one, now had to go back deep into the past of my own people, the Magyars, to find a sense of worth and courage that my peers here found in the wealth and power of America. The need gave spurs to my imagination, and identifying with the great ones of my native land, I felt equal and superior to the young hooligans[1]. Then there came to me a surge of self-esteem and pride in my forebears that could not be spoken to my American tormentors but was felt deep, deep within. "Wait 'till your nation has lived through a thousand years of tragedy," I thought. To make matters more interesting, my torturers would pelt me now and then with stones and stuff from the garbage cans. In general, I had a very unpleasant time of it.

The next day, another Hungarian boy, little Frank Kerekes, who lived in the same building, guided me to a public school at 1st Ave and 51st Street. Soon, I found myself in the first grade — called the "baby's class" in Hungary. To be degraded from the sixth to the first grade was humiliation almost beyond endurance for me. But what could I do? With fierce determination, I settled down to study this abominable language, with fierce protests by my tongue that struggled bravely to master the new sounds, but my ear did not always register the sounds very successfully.

With my Hungarian background of discipline, respect for adults and general courtesy, I soon won over my teacher, Miss McKenzie, who had a glowing mass of red hair and a temper to go with it. She needed it. With unrestrained slaps to the face and pulling the ears and hair, she soon had those wild East Side youngsters cowed, and we began to learn. Must I confess to the unholy glee with which I viewed this bit of poetic justice? The young terrorists were terrorized. I am not at all certain however that this endeared me to them.

After three months Miss McKenzie gave me a note, said farewell, and sent me to the second-grade teacher. The same day my new teacher sent me to grade 4A. Here, Miss Ward, dark, tall, and slender, always immaculate and of a calm, even disposition, was in charge. Only

---

[1] Here in the original manuscript began a four-page digression into Hungarian history. It has been moved to Appendix A.

someone of an identical background can understand my shock when one day she gently reprimanded a rather big boy. As she turned and walked away, the boy reached over to the blackboard, picked up an eraser and flung it at her, hitting her between the shoulders. I expected the building to collapse and bury us, or see him beaten to death, as it was actually reported once in the Old Country. But she, with unruffled calm, returned, took him by the arm and led him to the front where he stood facing the blackboard for the rest of the period. Why, if this had happened in Hungary, not only the boy but his whole family would have been despised for such an act to his teacher!

In a few weeks, Miss Ward gave me a card of introduction to a branch library nearby. The librarian made out a card for me and waving toward the books suggested that I choose one. I looked about me and viewed the immense treasures on the shelves (only about two thousand volumes). For the first time in my life, I could gorge my hungry mind. In Budapest, my parents were too poor to pay the library fee, and here it was free. I am sure no man who ever found a gold or diamond mine could be as rich. "Oh blessed America!"

Next semester, I was transferred to another school, where Miss Waters was my teacher in 5A. She will forever stand in my memory as a symbol of America at its best. One day some of my schoolmates and I were playing tag in front of the school. Out of nowhere, a delivery wagon dashed upon us. We scattered but I was not quick enough. In a moment I was on the ground and the wagon wheel passed over me. In fright and pain, I jumped up, ran into the building to our cloakroom on the second or third floor, and pulled the shoe off my right foot. Immediately the ankle swelled to twice its normal size and I simply could not pull the shoe back on.

Frightened, perplexed, and in great pain, I trembled as I stood there on my left leg, which was also aching above the knee. The stricken face of Miss Waters appeared, and picking me up in her arms, she carried me down to the teacher's cloakroom, placed me gently on the couch and covered me with her long cape. Soon the ambulance from Flower Hospital arrived, the doctor looked me over and the orderlies carried me down. Miss Waters came to the ambulance, spoke cheerfully, smiled, and pressed my hand as she said, "goodbye."

My poor mother was quite disturbed when she reached home that evening and I was not there to greet her. For quite a while her inquiries had no results. Finally, she learned from a boy in our block what had happened. Only today, as a parent and grandparent, can I begin to feel what she must have felt that day, alone with her fears, facing the unknown and wondering what she will write to her husband.

The next day probably everybody in the ward had visitors. I knew that I could not expect mother since she could not leave work, for we needed and saved every penny so that the rest of the family may come soon. Perhaps, if they had visiting hours that evening, she would come. Physical pain, the ache of loneliness, gnawing envy at the good fortune of others, I was wretched indeed.

Suddenly, as the visitors began to leave, the tall figure of Miss Waters appeared in the doorway. She quickly glanced around the room and discovering her suffering pupil, walked rapidly over to my bed, and with the unerring instinct of a true woman she leaned over and kissed me. Never will I forget that kiss, here or hereafter, for her lovely blue eyes were filled with tears as she gave it.

Mr. Murray was my next teacher in the fifth grade — a tall, handsome man with deep blue eyes and a black pompadour. In various ways, he indicated a genuine interest in "the immigrant boy." One day when I was already in another class, he stopped me in the corridor, showed me his silver watch, and said: "Kautz, if you make it to the head of your class, I'll give you a watch like mine." Kind, generous Mr. Murray! But I was responsible for five brothers and a sister from seven in the morning until after five at night. Perhaps I did not have the ability. Then, again, I was never motivated adequately by gifts, nor am I now. Anyhow, I did not get the watch.

My last public school teacher was another Miss Ward, sister of my fourth-grade teacher: tiny, blond, blue-eyed, and with a lovely figure and very feminine. I was almost fourteen by then and I must have had a crush on her. She trusted me implicitly, and frequently had me monitor the class when she stepped out. I must have done well for none of my classmates accused me of unfairness. One day, when the vice principal wanted a reliable boy to control the exit in a special unscheduled fire drill, she recommended me. But the other monitors had not been warned and they paid no attention to me, but simply, by main force, pushed me out of their way. The vice principal gave me a severe dressing-down.

I was heartbroken because I was not at fault and because Miss Ward would be disappointed. The next day, Dr. Po appeared in class and asked for me. When I stood, he apologized in front of the whole class. He was a real man and Miss Ward was happy. But I am afraid I was too proud and too hurt to show or feel much satisfaction.

My teachers — my blessed teachers! How can I ever be grateful enough for those early days when they were the only ones who gave me glimpses into the heart of America. It is my hope that my later life justified them somewhat for their faith in me.

Not all immigrant children were so fortunate. Thirty years later a youngish deacon in one of my mission churches told me his story. Like most immigrants, his family lived in a quarter inhabited by their own people, Hungarians. They did so in order to find some emotional security and mutual help among their own kind; storekeepers and others who spoke their language. His mother had nine children and had but little opportunity to mingle with Americans of the older stock, nor did the latter care to mingle with foreigners. They spoke Hungarian at home and in the little Hungarian quarter with the result that the children spoke only a very inadequate and ungrammatical English with a heavy accent when they entered school.

"My teacher called me a stupid Hunkie," my deacon said, and his facial expression and tone of voice still registered the deep hurt and insult he had suffered about thirty years before.

His son is a general in the Air Force now and was attached to the missile group in Washington. Well, all occupations have their share of ignorant, prejudiced, and stupid people. I have found them in the trades, business, teaching, and the ministry just to mention a few. Most immigrant groups had to make their way up the American ladder of opportunity against efforts to hold them down, to keep them "in their place."

Our block had a half-dozen saloons on it, and weekends were boisterous and noisy. Perhaps it was here that my first stirring of resentment against the liquor industry was born. Our apartment consisted of two rooms that we shared with a Polish-Hungarian woman and her 12-year-old son Frank, and a Hungarian girl. Cigar makers shared the same bedroom and bed. Mother and I shared a bed in our common sitting room that also served as a kitchen and dining room and bathroom for all of us. It was a cold-water apartment and we heated all the water we needed on a kitchen stove, that also kept our apartment warm in the winter but made it uncomfortably hot in the summer.

On weekends we took turns bathing in a round tub while the others went out or shut themselves into the bedroom. Our latrines were in the yard, one to each floor, marked with the number of the floor, in a row. Unhappily, there were numerous holes dug through the wooden walls at various levels that made for some embarrassing situations, so the more modest and shy individuals carefully chose the time for their visits.

One evening during those days mother had to go somewhere. She instructed me either to not lock the door or not go to sleep. I faithfully promised. As the evening wore on, however, shadowy fears crept into my mind. I was all alone in the apartment, for the others too had gone out. I was alone in the big, bad foreign city of New York, longing for my five brothers and sister and friends in Budapest. If I locked the door no one could threaten me, but strange noises seeped through from outside and I locked the windows too. Still, my melancholy deepened, and finally, I laid down on the bed, fully dressed and determined not to sleep, but sweet slumber promised forgetfulness and a free trip back to Budapest. I startled awake once or twice and this only seemed to prove that I could awaken if I needed to.

The next morning, my poor mother told me the rest. She came home, knocked and spoke my name. No response. She knocked louder, and louder finally shouting my name and pounding on the door. Our next-door neighbor, a Swedish dentist, came out and offered his help. Then he stepped out on the fire escape on which a window opened from both apartments and tried to open our window. Locked. With a kitchen knife, reaching between the frames, he forced the lock open and let mother in through the door. She picked up a small pillow and beat me in the face, but I never awoke.

Periodically, we gathered at the homes of friends and acquaintances to drink wine or tea with rum, sing our beautiful but sad folk songs, and discuss our mutual problems, the trials of our common immigrant life, and our hopes for the future. Sometimes a well-dressed white collar criminal from the Old Country, who had absconded with other people's money, joined us, and after a few drinks would give rings and other jewelry as a present to some of the girls for favors expected, and the next day called on them to reclaim his gifts. On Sunday, we went to the Hungarian Roman Catholic Mass on East 14th Street, held in the basement of the Polish church. It was good to take part in the familiar ritual, to hear a sermon encouraging us, to sing the old hymns, and mingle with our own kind. Life was easier after that.

One Sunday, though, perhaps because our service lasted too long and our Polish hosts wanted the basement for a business meeting, their priest came in immediately after the words of dismissal and made some angry remarks to our priest in Latin. It ended in a furious argument and mutual recriminations that not even the mysteries of the sacred language could hide from our astonished eyes and ears. Soon after we moved our services to another church. Sadly I recalled the glorious days centuries ago when our two nations made common cause against their enemies and even had the same sovereign in the person of a Hungarian prince.

Our neighbors were interesting folk but we never got to know each other very well. On the same floor there lived an elderly German couple who frequently treated me to delicious potato pancakes, the first I ever tasted, and never again so tasty. I don't know what they did for a living for they seemed to be at their windows all day long, enjoying the panorama of our crowded, busy street, doubtlessly knowing more about the lives of the people who lived there than we suspected. One of their jokes told of an immigrant couple. When asked the age, the woman said, "He's dirty and I am dirty too."

An Irish family lived below us, whose boys never made any trouble for me, which was rather strange for I have the impression that most of my torturers in those early days were wearers of the green. The mother was very dark with frizzy hair and I wondered where she had come from.

A ladies tailor lived in the same house. A very proud, conceited male who strutted about his customers with a leer, twisting his mustache. His wife a short, squat figure of a woman, utterly unattractive in face or form, waited on him like a slave, jealous and ever watchful for signs of a new attachment on the wing. A fascinating couple they were to me, forever quarreling, which frequently ended with a beating for the wife. Why didn't she leave him? Always the same answer: "I love him!" Yet she was not above the same sort of thing, for a young man complained about her warm brown eyes watching him through a hole in the latrine wall.

The Kerekeses, a Hungarian family, good friends of my mother, lived on the ground floor. He was a painter and was regularly employed by the North German Lloyd, I believe, as one of their painters to give the ocean liners a new coat of paint before returning to Europe. They were a quiet, happy couple, quite satisfied with their progress. I can't forget the enormous self-esteem displayed by his carriage, the way he pressed down his throat, and the proud expression on his face.

A middle-aged Czech couple were the janitors. He worked regularly at his trade while she attended to the janitorial duties. I recall her as a very strict and stern woman who kept her sixteen tenants in order, a kind friend to my mother until the rest of the family arrived when seven new, happy, noisy children were added to her tenement population. I can never forget the cloud of dust that swirled through her apartment every Saturday, and through the open door and windows as she swept her red, wall-to-wall carpet with great vigor. I almost had an attack of allergy as I recall it.

The fire escapes provided cool balconies in the summer heat, filled with people after supper. Girls were not always careful to cover up and provided some interesting scenes, though not so generally as college girls do today, every day, in their classes.

Greenstein was our grocer and owner of a delicatessen store. It was a tiny place filled with merchandise so that he could hardly move about with a half-dozen customers present. He was a short, very stout, nice, but not very clean gentleman, eager to please and very successful with my mother who was not insensitive to flattery. We bought our goods on credit, and he wrote the prices in a cheap little book for us as well as in his own big ledger. On payday, mother would make a payment or clear up our account entirely. The little store was always filled with the pungent smells of cheese, meat, herring, spices. It was a nice and cozy though rather dirty little place. We remained his steady customers as long as we lived in that neighborhood. He had his reward, for our big family of nine bought most of our foodstuffs from him.

One little friend has an honored place in my memory even though I cannot recall his name. His parents came from Hamburg but he was born in New York. When he discovered that I was a greenhorn he kept me company on our way to school, acted as my interpreter and often took me to their apartment. He had a little mandolin harp that he was learning to play. Soon I induced my mother to buy me one and I enrolled in a school to learn to play it.

Endless push carts with innumerable flies, policemen with their tall helmets looking like giants and twirling nightsticks, torchlight parades at election time, the marchers singing songs that still ring in my ears. There were cartoons about a muscular fighter with sparkling glasses and a ribbon flying behind him, teeth clenched in a smile, sometimes in a Prince Albert, sometimes in a kind of wild west uniform with a big stick in his hand, whacking away at enormous corpulent figures in formal suits wearing high silk hats and a dollar sign on their shirt bosoms. As I learned later, it was Teddy Roosevelt trying to make the trusts behave. I easily recall the terrifying noise of firecrackers on July 4th, Mrs. Horak rushing out of the tenement with a scream and belaboring three young men on the porch with scathing words. One of them had thrown a giant firecracker under her skirt that might have set her dress on fire. Many other, unrelated pictures flash upon the screen of my memory as I pen these words.

With a sinking heart, I recall the long days between mother leaving for work at seven in the morning and her return after five at night, with so little to draw me to the streets and so much to deter me because of the mischievous, thoughtless, cruel and petty persecutions of the kids. But also, I had the support of my pride as I remembered the glorious history of my native land. Wait, I said to myself, until your nation has come through the disasters of a thousand years with centuries of oppression by mightier empires, yet living on, bloody, broken but proud, ever rising to new greatness!

And how we saved every penny, buying only stark necessities and allowing ourselves no luxuries, for we were eager to have the rest of the family with us as soon as possible. A pound of chuck-steak for ten cents with a couple of bones thrown in for good measure with a few pennies worth of vegetables gave us enough soup for two days. Mother would buy the cheapest black and overripe bananas for her lunches, or dry bread and soak it under the faucet until soft and flavor it with salt and paprika. She was earning $20 a week, a princely sum for us, and before another year was up, mother had saved and borrowed enough to bring the others to the "promised land."

We waited for a word from Budapest with new excitement. If I were home I would dash down to meet the postman. After several weeks he handed me a letter. I rushed upstairs and slashed it open, something I had never done before, and scanned it. With every line, my breathing became more difficult and, at the end, I was stiff with fear. It was a letter from Aunt Mary, my mother's sister, informing us that father was down with typhus and not expected to live. If mother wished to see him once more she must return at once — perhaps he might still be alive. Utterly bewildered, I only felt I must give mother and myself time. Crushing the letter, I threw it into the farthest corner of our wardrobe and made a fierce resolution to look unconcerned.

I had just set the table when mother came in for lunch. With a tremendous effort, I smiled. She kissed me and went to the sink to wash her hands. The usual, inevitable question:

"Any mail today?"

"No, mama."

After a while, "Did we get any mail today? It's time papa wrote us when they are coming."

As before, "No mama."

Then she looked me full in the face: "Come, Eddie, Mrs. Horak told me that there was a letter for me."

With a cramp in my stomach, I fished out the evil letter and handed it to her without a word. She sat down at the table and read and wept silently. No sobbing, only those terrible, silent tears rolling down her cheeks into her food and mine as well. We did not eat much that noon, nor that day, nor for quite a few days. Poor mother prayed unceasingly to the Virgin Mary, Her Son, all the saints she could think of, particularly St. Anthony, the favorite of poor people, and to the God who is supposed to watch over all. Her beautiful prayer book of blue velvet with golden clasps was in her hands every spare moment. And we had each other.

After a few days, her decision was made. She wrote to papa:

I know how much you wish to see me once more and you know how I long to see you. But I am certain that for the sake of the children you would rather have me stay and carry through with our original plan. I am going to stay.

My poor brave mother! Not even I, who was with her through those terrible days, knew what this decision cost her, although I am able to feel the agony of it more keenly now that I have had children of my own and experienced the torture of waiting for good news from my beloved; thought to be at the point of death.

Once the decision was made we endured the pangs of anxiety better. Our nights were restless, feverish, our conversations painful as we tried to hit upon subjects not fraught with the concern ever on our minds. Like during her first six months alone in America, my poor mother aged years. Letters did not come regularly enough, and usually took two weeks to reach us. Always there was the gnawing worry about father: what happened during the days the letter was on its way to us? All we knew with the arrival of each letter was that father was still living when he wrote it. But there was no income and they were using up their fares to America for food, medicine, and rent.

If only Dad got better! The money did not matter, even if it did matter very much. We began to hope and continued our prayers, especially to St. Anthony, with renewed fervor and faith. After weeks of uncertainty, the doctor's remarks were less discouraging. However, father would not be able to work for quite a while. How long? He did not know. Moreover, he must have good, nourishing, and of course expensive food. Finally, he was sufficiently recovered. But there was no income and they were using up their fares for the trip. The sea voyage would help greatly to restore his strength, said his physician.

By now mother's little nest egg was less than $100. Once again she went the way of the weary, and to her proud, galling, humiliating round of friends and acquaintances to beg and borrow the few hundred dollars — a veritable treasure to us. Our future, our hope, our all. At last, she had it! I don't know where she hid it during those days and weeks, perhaps somewhere on her person. She did not trust the banks because there were too many that cheated greenhorns or folded up altogether. I believe this treasure went by international postal money order.

Thank heaven there was no hitch. In due time we received a long love-letter from father giving us the name of the steamship line, the ship, the dates of sailing, and expected arrival in New York. It was too good to be true. Anxiety stayed with us until they arrived.

4 - Beginning Again

The clock rang, and we jumped out of bed. I put the coffee on the little gas hot plate and warmed the milk while mother washed and dressed with feverish haste. For this was the day when she would call back for the family at that place of horrors for immigrants, Ellis Island. Giving me final instructions about cooking an unusually rich beef soup for our loved ones, that would be most welcome after their steerage meals, she left.

How the hours dragged! I cleaned out our two rooms with great care, scrubbed the floors, washed the windows, dismantled and dusted the mantelpiece, brushed the kitchen stove until everything in our two-room apartment was spotless. Still, they did not come. Was one of them ill? While mother hurried to our loved ones I stayed on to worry. She looked like a queen and I was proud of her.

I reviewed the weeks and months since the terrible news of father's illness. How slowly, in driblets, the letters from Budapest informed us of father's crisis, turn for the better, a slow convalescence, full recovery and the consent of the doctor to the long trying trip to far off America. But all the money mother had skimped, saved, borrowed and sent was used up. Once again she made the weary round of acquaintances to borrow and beg until she had enough for the family's trip. Well, it did not matter now for they were here, about an hour's ride away.

Mr. Fried, the ladies' tailor, came in and asked if I would be so kind as to bring him some stamps from the corner drugstore. Locking the door and slipping the key in my pocket, I rushed out. I ran all the way there and back. Only a few houses from ours I caught sight of a group I thought I knew. Yes, it was our family, mother leading the group, with a bag in one hand and holding baby Vulko, now four years old, by the hand. His hat came down over his ears — he had lost his on the ship — and the others following her, each one carrying some item of baggage, and bringing up the rear with a large bundle on his back — was father. Then it happened: One of the street kids, a fourteen-year-old boy, himself the son of Czech immigrants, ran up, jumped on father's back, gave him a blow on the head and ran away. That was my poor father's welcome to the Land of Promise. I could have killed that kid.

Soon, however, this was forgotten in the joy of reunion, tales of the trip, the story of mother's experiences and mine, in the satisfying smells and flavors of a Hungarian dinner. Then I played my mandolin harp, as Steve, a year and a half younger, looked on with shining eyes. Within a few months, self-taught, he would play better than his big brother. Ultimately, he became an excellent pianist and a good violinist, largely self-taught, and musical director of a traveling Hungarian theatrical company.

We sang our songs of the homeland and one or two Viennese tunes: *Die Alte Uhr* (The Old Clock) and *Weist thu Mutterl Was Ich Traumt Hab?* (Do You Know What I Dreamed, Little Mother?). Rather sad songs but full of feeling. Mother's fine soprano led us and father's tenor provided harmony. Evening came all too swiftly. Exhausted by the excitements of the day we did not object when mother put us to bed, all of us children in our single bedroom, in the one large bed, across its length, close and snug like sardines in a box. Father improvised a bed on the floor of our living room for mother and himself. Soon, regular, deep breathing was the only sound, happy music to our sorely tried and exhausted parents.

The next day I was left in charge of the children while mother went to work and father began his search for a job. With my pitiful store of English, we read the advertisements, asked a neighbor for directions, and father too left. Then it was my turn to guide the children to school. Yes, the children, for I was now a kind of prematurely responsible parent substitute, with definite and stern instructions to keep them out of mischief and to see that they were properly guided to school, registered, and led home again.

Some of the American boys discovered us — how could they help it in our European clothes? — and saw an opportunity for exciting sport. They started to bait us until Steve, who always had a short and fiery temper, launched a one-man attack in our defense. If those kids knew no Marquis of Queensberry rules, Steve certainly had never heard of them either. He hit, punched, slammed, kicked, and scratched until our tormentors broke and fled from this one-man army. Not much trouble after that. Steve was a born fighter, vicious when aroused and utterly reckless. He protected or avenged all of us, including big brother, who was a rather shy, sensitive, and physically not very strong or brave chap.

At home, though, Steve was not so great a help. He was only a year and a half younger than his big brother, and since he had been the eldest after I left for America it was not easy to take a subordinate position. Once he threw a sharp knife at me, another time he had a seizure on account of his temper, and fell to the floor unconscious, frothing at the mouth. Frightened and desperate, I rushed for mother at her cigar factory on the corner to see if Steve needed a doctor. We brothers still loved each other, and Steve continued to protect the others, including me, his big brother, against the hellions on the street. I was responsible for all of them, and for seeing that our tiny apartment was kept clean, the dishes washed, the beds made, the supper started, and the children kept reasonably quiet and off the streets. Mother did not want her children to become discourteous, unmanageable, and wild youngsters like too many "American" kids were. Out of this difficult situation, a few fights arose until my necessary supremacy was established.

The almost impossible demand of our parents was that we stay off the streets and yet stay quiet in that rickety old tenement. How could seven of us in two small rooms achieve that? With increasing frequency, the janitress, Mrs. Horak, complained to mother about us and expressed her ignorant astonishment at how two such fine people as my parents could have such hellions. Yet, as far as I can recall we did not damage property, and were duly respectful to her, for we had been conditioned for years to give due respect and reverence to our elders in general. She was a sensible person, very fond of mother whom she admired immensely, but middle age and noise made her nervous and complain. But how could even normal healthy children always behave in such close quarters and not be at least noisy sometimes? In truth, she'd had enough of them. Both sides were victimized by the forces of life.

One afternoon we had a particularly good time in our two rooms. The woman in the apartment below us resented this, although she herself had six children. As I grow older I can appreciate the fact that the noise we made could not have been very enjoyable for her. She complained to the janitor. In a lull of our play we suddenly heard the heavy steps of that *czarina* (empress) of the tenements, our janitress, ascending the stairs. Quickly I ordered them under the bed next to the wall and instructed Rose to meet the janitress with an innocent smile and disclaim all knowledge of our whereabouts. Mrs. Horak pushed past Rose, looked everywhere but failed to see us in the dark under the bed and flat against the wall. She left puzzled, scolding with a stern command that we keep quiet — now a rather unnecessary injunction. Crawling out, we sat in perfect stillness for some time, then stole out one by one down the stairs into the street. Fortunately, she did not see us and our parents never learned about our escapade. Indeed they did not about quite a few others.

Hitching uninvited rides on the back steps of ice wagons, slow-moving horse cars, and big, fast trucks were some of our favorite amusements. As we learned English the little branch library became a refuge. There were no playgrounds. The nearest spot of green was Central Park, almost a mile away, and we had to cross five busy thoroughfares to get there. Once there, we had to stay off the lovely green lawns or be chased off by policemen.

Daring Steve made hooks out of pins for himself, bound them to a string, and did some fishing in the lake. Once he brought home several goldfish that I cleaned and fried. We never had such delicious fish. But our parents warned us that we had broken the law and if caught were in danger of imprisonment with bread and water. Did they really believe this or did they carry over some of the legal restrictions of the Old Country? I don't know, but it put an end to this enjoyable diversion.

Still, Central Park continued to be a place of refuge and refreshment, and we negotiated the half mile from our tenement home as often as we could to escape from the wilderness of stone and the threat of traffic. It took us quite a while to discover the Metropolitan Museum of Art, both because no one ever told us about it, and because of the added distance. We gazed open-mouth at the beautiful pictures and statuary, its archeological treasures, among them the mummy of an Egyptian priest uncovered enough to see the gash in his side, used for the embalming process. His features were so well preserved that I could have recognized him had I known him alive 3,000 years ago. Some years later they stored him elsewhere, away from the wondering eyes of adults and children. What a pity! I often wonder where my shy mummy reposes now, safe from the curious stares of us moderns. Will the hydrogen bomb leave such memorials of our age, or indeed of any curious visitors in museums?

This lovely oasis was also a place of peril. I met a girl about my age there one day, shepherding her flock of about as many brothers and sisters as I. We were drawn to each other by mutual sympathy and shared our mutual predicament as young substitute parents. It soon became apparent that she was interested in sexual contact, that at the time was thoroughly distasteful to me, and I soon found that we had to leave for home.

Years later, still an adolescent on a walk in the park by myself, I met a man who stared at me in a peculiar way. I felt quite uncomfortable and hurried on. Suddenly I found him coming toward me again. He had run ahead of me on a bypath. He looked nervous, walked fast and eyed me with a curious, insulting stare. This happened several times until at one point, I retraced my steps, found a bypath and hurried home. Poor oddball hound. I wonder what became of him.

On one of my lonely jaunts in later adolescence, on a Saturday or Sunday afternoon, I suddenly came upon a great number of people on the mall in Central Park, sitting on benches around what looked like an open little summer house. About the same time, strains of music reached my ears. I listened. I was very fond of music, but this, these outlandish sounds, what was this? Marveling at the hundreds, perhaps thousands who listened with apparent enjoyment, I found a seat. There must be something to this! But I found no pleasure in it. Still, I sat. It was toward the end, and soon they played the last number. I can still see number 10 on the board. Well, now, this was something I could appreciate. It was a medley of popular tunes, many of which I knew. I too clapped heartily at its close.

From that time on, since other recreations were expensive, I found myself on the mall listening to Goldman's Symphonic Band. Always I waited with eager expectation for the last number. Here and there, however, there were welcome stretches of sound whose melody and harmony charmed me. After two or three years I developed sufficient appreciation to enjoy most of the symphonic music, and in the end cared not if they had omitted the last number. I shall ever be grateful for that opportunity and the visions of beauty, the challenge, the relaxation and peace that have come to me from good music through the years.

Many years later, during my pastorate at the Sandusky Street Baptist Church in Pittsburgh, Pa., a friend presented me with two tickets to the Pittsburgh Symphony Orchestra. Fritz Reiner was the conductor, whom my brother Steve knew quite well. Under his direction, they played *Beethoven's Fifth Symphony.* Its beauty and challenge proved overwhelming, and before long I broke into uncontrollable sobs. Ever since my favorite, I always thrill to the call of destiny in its opening bars. To what destiny did it call me? Had I a destiny?

At about the same time a new, fascinating show-house opened on Sixth Avenue, the Hippodrome. It had a vast stage for those days on which hundreds of men with horses and elephants fought battles and hundreds of dancers, or so it seemed, appeared in a ballet. I attended two or three times, standing in line for a long time in order to secure the cheapest, twenty-five-cent seat, away up in the last rows of the second balcony. At that distance, any unattractive features of the dancers were blurred and a boy's imagination had free scope in adding beauty where it may have been lacking. I watched the fighting with mounting excitement and was transported out of this world by the beauty, rhythm, and singing of the ballet, and the dance of the flowers and birds. Among the gorgeous plumage of the latter, I especially noticed for the first time in my life, the refined elegance of the swallows with their lemon colored breasts and black wings. I developed quite a crush on the ballerina and returned again only to see her, and more than once she visited me in my dreams.

The East River was only a block or two from our home, and Steve soon paddled about in its dirty waters (not quite as filthy as today), learning to swim long before the rest of us. One day, from the window of a friend, I observed a gang of boys swimming and having a great deal of fun. After a while, they gathered about a fire they had built and engaged in masturbation. This finished our trips to the East River.

In the winter we had snow fights, of course. I invented a new confection consisting of clean white snow, powdered sugar, and rum. We always had a pint or so of the latter using it a teaspoonful at a time in our cups of tea. I am not aware that our parents ever discovered this experiment in homemade confectionery.

After a few months, we were asked to move. After considerable searching, we found a new apartment on 56th Street between Second and Third Avenues. It consisted of four large rooms and a toilet, but we still had to use our big round iron tub for bathing, and heat our water in an old-fashioned wash boiler. Mother and father took turns at doing the laundry. Slowly, laboriously, rubbing the clothes on a washboard and lifting the heavy boiler on and off the stove — a backbreaking procedure. But we lived on the ground floor now with only the cellar under us and felt much freer to romp around in the apartment. Seldom did the janitor have reason to scold us.

Father was not very happy at his work of upholstering. He was a meticulous worker, really an artist at his trade and his boss was quite pleased with its quality. But he forever pestered father with "Hurry up! Hurry up! I can't make money on this if you take so long." Father was disgusted. Was this what they wanted in America? Just slap things together and make things appear right? Well he couldn't, he wouldn't do that! He had to live with himself and he would lose his self-respect.

"But Papa," my mother remonstrated, "I too had to learn to work like that in cigar making. Otherwise we cannot support the family, still less pay off our mountainous debt."

Grumbling, father conceded this and struggled on, changing jobs whenever it depressed him too much. Years later, when he became crippled with rheumatism, he found appreciation at the hands of the sisters in a Roman Catholic Orphanage on Third Avenue. The Mother Superior had only the highest praise for his work. He took his own time, had rest periods, and in general was his own boss. He worked there for years. It was a real asylum for him until he became quite incapacitated by his illness.

As quickly as possible the children found odd jobs, selling newspapers, running errands — all of us leaving school at fourteen and securing our working papers, finding a job, and adding to the earnings of the family, for all of us gave our earnings to our parents while receiving tiny amounts for our spending money — never more than 5 to 10 cents.

On reaching my 14th year I applied for working papers and started looking for a job. This was a rather general state of affairs. It was very unusual for children to continue in high school. This, coupled with our poverty, indebtedness, and a growing family made earning our own keep imperative. Then, there was the general, still observable lack of interest in schooling at about that age, that undoubtedly had its effect on me.

All in all, I was not sorry to quit school and go to work, and it relieved me from my "parental responsibilities." I started work as an errand boy for an artist, receiving the munificent salary of $3 per week for 40 hours of work. In a few weeks, at the insistence of my parents who wanted all of us to learn a trade, I began to work in a stained-glass shop where this was promised. I remember taking a homemade sandwich and a pint of milk on my way to work, with a fruit now and then, and ten cents for carfare. For a nickel, I rode down Lexington Avenue in a crowded streetcar to 32nd Street, sometimes barely hanging on by my toes, once caught by strong arms and drawn up to safety as I missed my jump onto a car that would not stop.

After a nine-hour day, sometimes standing a good deal of the time, I walked home to save the other nickel in order to have a little money in my pocket. With such longing that 14- 15-year-old boy looked at choice fruits, confectionery, and candy in the store windows, not succeeding always in swallowing my saliva and turning resolutely away from temptation. Once I had about five dollars saved, the result of inhuman efforts at self-denial for about four months.

On one occasion, we were sorely in need of funds for making a payment at the grocery store. Looking at me sadly, my father asked, "Eddie could you help us with a few dollars? We need it badly."

Quite shocked and angry, I replied, "How can you ask me? You gave me only lunch and carfare. Where would I get the money? I don't steal."

Patiently my father explained the situation. "We were just hoping that you might have saved a little."

Ashamed, for I knew how hard both of my parents worked, I drew my hard-saved five dollars from my pocket and gave it to him. But it was with real pain.

"We'll pay it back as soon as possible," he assured me. Indeed they meant it, but I knew better. I never got it. They never had that much saved.

Later I discovered that mother regularly inspected our pockets, but I could not blame her, for temptations about us poor kids were many, and we did not always tell her what she needed to know. In this way, she could check and follow up whatever clues were available. As I grew, I became very self-conscious of the large paper bag I carried with milk, a large sandwich, and a fruit and prevailed upon my parents to give me ten cents to let me buy my own milk at noon. This I seldom did, preferring to save it and have a little money of my own and be able to buy a little candy, a fruit of my choice, or confection.

Even so, father, Steve, and I had but one Sunday suit among us, bought at one of many stores dealing in used clothing on 3rd Avenue — and a second-hand suit at that. Consequently, the three of us had to space our social appointments very carefully. Fortunately, we did not share friends, and so were saved from embarrassment and humiliation. My shoes, for years, were also bought in a similar store. That was true of all of us until several of us children were working and we could afford new things to wear. Our feet suffered, as did those of many others who also had to wear second-hand shoes. But my tanned shoes took a high polish and I wore them with considerable pride and satisfaction, if not comfort.

It was our good fortune that mother was an excellent bargainer. She could higgle and haggle better than anybody else I ever knew. She found more things wrong with items that she wanted to buy than several other buyers in combination. The merchants were eager to please her too, for she had a large family. She always took several of us along until the size of the family, nine of us by now, was firmly established in several places. In addition, mother could be a very delightful person. She was very handsome, and she enjoyed haggling and gossiping. It was a game at which she had a wonderful time. And it seemed that because she enjoyed it, the merchants did too.

Often it became a very embarrassing situation for us. Unable to agree on a suitable price she rose with dignity. She had a queenly figure, and with firm steps marched toward the door followed by us. Before she reached the door, however, the merchant would call to her, and we marched back. More haggling and once again we marched. This time out into the street. But the merchant was at the door calling us back. In we went again to more haggling. Out again into the street and walked past one or two adjacent stores before the merchant caught up with us and begged us to come back. In again, and to mutual agreement but not without the merchant complaining about the ruinous bargain, with mother pointing out how impossible it was to clothe a family like ours in any other way.

Later, when several of us were working, she slowly relaxed her haggling and there came a time when she paid a tailor generously to make a suit-to-order for me. But until then, oh how our faces blushed!

I must not fail to tell of the great relief of our parents at learning that there was no compulsory military service in America. In Hungary each of their six boys would have had to give three years of their lives to his majesty Francis Joseph I. They loved their adopted country all the more. I often wonder what they would say now. Probably, they would feel that since it is the Russians who threaten us, whom they had always feared as the "Russian Bear," our posture was right, and since they were not pacifists they would endorse our military preparations.

They spoke about the "Yellow Peril" too. Also, they had retained some glamour for the uniform if only as a symbol of masculine fitness. They were proud of me when I visited them periodically as a soldier during World War I. I had a proud bearing, straight as an arrow, head held high and a rapid stride. The doughboys on the streets of New York took me for an officer and often saluted, which I returned with relish. In perspective it would also appear that my father Ludwig took a special pride in his son since he himself had been declared *untauglich* (unfit) when examined for the army of Francis Joseph I. I must not fail to mention their oft-repeated exhortation: "Children, love America, for you could never have had your opportunities in the Old Country." We did. We saw only a few uniforms and only on the police and firemen.

In those early days, six or seven Hungarian families gathered together for relaxation every Sunday afternoon in the large back room of a saloon on East 63rd Street. It was good to exchange experiences and share each other's joys, sorrows, and problems in a foreign land and in a language that had no problems for us. We ate, drank a glass or two of wine or beer, had a European game of cards, danced to the music of a few gypsies, and returned home rested and renewed by this fellowship.

On weekends too, mother had opportunities to do some special cooking and baking for us. Hungarian cooking is very tasty anyhow, and she was a wonderful cook. Even at this moment I can almost taste the extraordinary hamburgers made of pork and beef and rolls with finely chopped onions, a touch of garlic, paprika and a little black pepper; or the stuffed ducks, geese, chickens, green peppers and "pig-in-a-blanket"; not to speak of the delicious strudels with cheese, apples, nuts, poppy seeds, and even sweet cabbage filling. My wife was persistently and, at times vociferously, resisted my pleas and pressures to produce some of these dishes. She claimed Hungarian cooking was very time consuming and fussy, and I must admit that it is.

Later on, as we learned English and discovered open areas not too far from home, we made excursions in the summer, usually to Spuyten Duyvil, now, alas, covered by apartment houses. After a leisurely breakfast, we took the subway train to 207th Street and soon were among the trees, chasing butterflies, reveling in the grass or just running about, surrounded by birdsong and sunshine, taking a whole day's rest away from the hurry and problems of our working days. Mother Nature took us to her bosom to soothe and renew us. We gathered daisies, buttercups, black-eyed susans, clover and branches from flowering bushes — large armfuls to beautify and perfume our poor tenement. As soon as we left the subway and the city children saw us, they followed us in a crowd begging for some of our wildflowers. "Give me one, just one, mister," they often cried. They shouted with glee when they received a spray or two and rushed home to show their parents. And for several days we had the fragrance of nature in our dark rooms.

One of our friends bought an old motorboat that was forever breaking down, leaking, in need of repairs of one kind or another and chugging along at the dizzying speed of four miles an hour. When he allowed Steve or myself to steer it, we felt like pirate captains or admirals of the fleet. The poor at least had this sometimes, if they could afford it, to give color to bleak lives. Once again, as in Budapest, I saw myself in the rich blue uniform of a naval captain with plenty of gold braid, a shining sword at my side and spy glasses glued to my eyes. With deep gratitude, we often recalled Mr. Lappi. For him, too, this was a welcome recreation, even though he spent most of his time tinkering with the engine. Sometimes we went fishing with him and caught a few small flounders, but what a heavenly treat when mother transformed these into *halpaprikás*, a kind of fish soup made with plenty of onions and paprika.

Soon with acquaintances at work and friends among fellow "Hunkies" and other greenhorns, we discovered Dreamland Pier at Coney Island and other places where we could indulge our newfound, manly sport of fishing. One cold Thanksgiving day, Steve and I went out to the pier to try for a good catch. This was important for it not only provided us with recreation but could save us a considerable sum on food. It was very cold. The older experienced fishermen had their bottles of strong drink with them to supply them with the persistence each needed and the illusion of warmth. Steve and I had a cup of coffee, each costing only a nickel a cup in those good old days, half of which we spilled before our shaking hands could carry it to our lips. We could not afford another cup.

From ten in the morning until around five in the afternoon, we never had a bite. Every time we pulled up our lines it was clear that fish — if any came around — didn't even smell our bait, nor anyone else's. We ran up and down the pier, flapping our arms to keep warm, and took refuge now and then behind a wooden wall with hands in pockets and pulling our caps low to shield as much of our faces as possible and drawing our bodies into the smallest possible bundle to conserve our warmth.

Adding to our misery were the visions we had of ourselves going home with empty bags and everybody along the block asking, "What luck?" "How many did you catch?" "What did you get?" We would be objects of derision for days or until we redeemed ourselves with a really big catch. If only somebody around us would catch enough to sell us a few, a deception engaged in generously by unlucky fishermen. Whenever I think of that experience I can understand better the feelings of poor, hungry, dispirited Esau who sold his birthright for a mess of pottage.

Then it happened. In one hour's time, we caught twenty-six lyngs and whitings, one to two pounds each. We forgot the cold, hunger, and the long wait. Proudly, we marched down the street from the streetcar to our home replying to the eager questions of our would-be tormentors, "Yes, we had fair luck, we only caught twenty-six lings and whitings," and when they asked us for a look at them to see how big they were, we opened the bags and said deprecatingly but with a note of victory and exultation, "Only twenty-six one and two pounders." Needless to say, our reputation as fishermen reached a new high on the block.

Although I was relieved of the grind of daily attendance at school and homework and quite enthused over earning a living, I felt uneasy about not finishing grammar school. Following the advice of teachers and parents and the demands of my hungry mind, I registered at night school. I attended for two years, taking various courses, without the benefit of counseling, trying this and that in a blind, unconscious effort to find myself.

I remember only one of my teachers in night school, and with gratitude, for he was interested in me in a warm, personal way. He was a short, slender man with stooping shoulders, almost a hunchback, but with the kindest face and luminous eyes. How like a careless youth to forget his name! He stopped me one evening as the class was leaving the room, and drawing me to one side, asked me about my goal in life. With some embarrassment, I confessed that I had not been able to decide.

"Have you thought about sociology?" asked the teacher.

"No, sir."

I had never even heard the word and did not know what it meant.

How did that extraordinary teacher see in the immigrant boy, so ignorant about life, particularly life in American society, the makings of a social scientist? Forty years later I became a sociologist and a very successful university professor.

Later I enrolled in a bookkeeping course in the International Correspondence Schools, but after a few months gave it up. I had no interest in figures or business, and it was a lonely and discouraging with only a bulky textbook for a teacher. A representative of the school called again and again, insisting that we fulfill the contract and pay for the course. In the end, we did so, receiving the necessary texts that we ultimately gave away.

In one of my night classes, I became acquainted with a very attractive youth. Let us call him John. He too was trying to discover what he was best fitted for. He had hit upon palmistry and astrology as aids in this self-discovery. We spent hours studying these pseudo-sciences but discovered only the vaguest matters, some of which were close enough to the truth to give us encouragement for continuing. Among these were the faint lines below the palm of my hand, that indicated poor vitality. I certainly appeared to have that. But the five or six violent love affairs and marriages indicated by lines under the small finger and other similar predictions were never realized. However, it was a fascinating exercise to try to peer into the future and find some guidelines for our lives, so totally lacking in our environment.

About the same time, I had an unusual dream that had a profound impression on me, and during those uncertain years gave me considerable courage in my times of depression that would increase in number and intensity. I dreamed that I was in a rowboat with some of the boys working in the shop. We landed on an island where one of the boys got out and left us. We continued rowing. Suddenly it became apparent that the boat was moving ahead under the impulse of an inner force over which we had no control. I took my position on the bow, leaning on it and peering into the foggy distance. To my horror, the boat then left the water and continued on an elevated structure that rose out of the water, hopping from crossbeam to crossbeam, and ever higher until the people below looked like ants. Then, to my great relief, I awoke. I pondered the dream and concluded that I was a child of destiny carried by forces beyond me.

But this did not stop me from ceaseless reading in many fields, including fiction, drama, history, science, socialism, and religion. If I was a child of destiny, I certainly was not going to depend wholly upon it. The library became my haven amidst the vicissitudes of life, a source of new ideas, a place of dreams and of adventure. This, however, was only a vague feeling — not a clearly formulated purpose and decision. As I look back upon that dream, I believe that I had a feverish desire to be somebody — to rise from the ranks of nobodies, as if from one grain of sand on the seashore, or one of the teeming millions of New Yorkers, to become someone who counts for something. And the dream was the fulfillment of the desire that seemed an impossible realization in life. Certainly, it gave me hope, inspired me to renewed efforts, and saved me for years from despair.

John became a palmist — a fortune teller at Coney Island in a year or two. He had a curious combination of a naive belief in palmistry and a shrewd calculating attitude with respect to his clients. He told me how the palmists in his tent used to fight each other for the privilege of telling the fortunes of the simpletons they had learned to recognize at first glance.

He had a lovely family: a sober conservative father, a kindly mother, and two beautiful sisters. However, for some reason his family was not the moral anchor mine was to me. One evening he was rather restless and he did not want to talk when I called on him as we usually and endlessly did. He said he was going downtown. Would I go with him? Where to? Oh, he went down to see his woman every few weeks. She was careful and clean — no danger — and not too expensive. My stomach turned.

"But, John, do you think of your mother and your lovely sisters?"

"Sure, but what did that have to do with it?"

No, I was not going. However, our friendship continued along with our interest in palmistry. From time to time I called to his attention the sickening exhibits on venereal diseases and begged him to quit visiting a prostitute. John laughed at his fears and assured him that it was quite safe.

About a year later John again asked me to go downtown with him. "No, thank you." But John was going to a venereal clinic! You can't forsake a friend in trouble, and he was in it deep. How deep we did not realize. Some time later he entered the venereal ward in the municipal hospital on Blackwell's Island. I saw him once or twice on his visit home. He railed against his luck, cursing the woman, blaming God, fulminating against everybody but himself.

By that time, I had a thorough conversion and became a committed follower of Jesus. I pleaded with my friend to turn to God, but in vain. Leaving a copy of John's Gospel with him, I left my friend in deep gloom. On my next visit months later, his broken-hearted father informed me that he was dead.

I knew another young man who was greatly concerned over a persistent dripping. Without adequate knowledge or counsel, he became quite concerned and developed anxiety about having caught a venereal disease somewhere, somehow. He visited one of the quacks who offered free examinations to people with a venereal ailment. Their lurid advertisements appeared in the daily papers. He was impressed by the atmosphere of secrecy in the office. The "doctor" examined him and said that he could not give a diagnosis until the initial the fee had been paid. The young man, quite poor, had no such money with him and promised to return.

Fortunately, he somehow got in touch with the Y.M.C.A., where a competent physician examined him and assured him that there was nothing wrong with him except an extremely sedentary life, and if he joined the "Y" and took regular exercise, that annoying though harmless dripping would disappear.

Today, with far less prudery and much more instruction about sex and the miracle drugs, we still have a growing rate of venereal disease among adolescents.

5 - Puzzlement

I left the stained glass shop on West 33rd Street off 5th Avenue and started to walk home. After nine hours of standing at work, I was tired and did not feel like walking, but I had to save my carfares because my hard-pressed parents would not be able to provide me with much spending money. Oh, I might have insisted and pressured them into giving me more, but that would not do. How could I, in all decency, ignore mother, who was the chief breadwinner now along with me. Father stayed at home to cook, clean, and do all the necessary housekeeping chores.

As I walked up 5th Avenue in the crush of rush hour traffic, I thought of my father. What a gallant gentleman he was! Conditioned to a man's role in Europe — head of the household, provider, disciplinarian — he was reduced to a woman's subordinate role by rheumatism. Sometimes he took thirty aspirin pills a day to keep the pain under control. Sometimes an exciting game of *tarok* (an Austrian card game) would give him relief. Only when the pain gripped him with a new intensity would he exclaim in his favorite modified cuss word, *Krucinezer!* At times he would walk the floor for hours while all the rest of us were asleep. Yet he was up before all of us to prepare our breakfasts and lunches and see to it that those still in school left on time, properly dressed. He did his work at home efficiently and with dignity. And he was respected everywhere. He became an excellent cook — as good as mother at everything but pastry. It had been a bitter change for him, but he accepted his lot without complaint, with a sweet spirit, and was a source of encouragement to all of us when something went wrong at work. Each night he waited on mother, took her shoes off, and sharpened the special knives for cutting tobacco leaves until they were like razors so that she could roll more cigars than ever before. He continued as a tender, affectionate lover, giving mother the emotional support she needed.

Only that day Gus, one of the men at the shop, told me how foolish my parents were to have so many children — there were nine of us now — and sacrifice themselves for their welfare. Well, he was right in a way, but measuring them alongside this pleasant and pleasure-loving fellow, married but forever flirting with women everywhere, and going to houses of ill fame, I felt that my parents were rather superior.

Yes, we were poor but considerably better off than we had been. The three adult men in my family had their own Sunday suits now and the rest of the children had fewer clothes and shoes bought at second-hand stores. We had finally paid off our debts and even had a few dollars in the bank, never more than one hundred, but it seemed like a treasure. Even I had started a savings account at the Ten Cents Saving Bank and had almost $20 on deposit! Steve and Rose were working, too. In a few years, we should be fairly comfortable. We had a five-room apartment now on East 77th Street — still a bit crowded for eleven of us — but it had a bathroom and a separate kitchen. We had to have a double bed in the front room and put a mattress on the floor for the night, but we were quite comfortable and had a dining room, that served as a sitting room as well.

Yet as I walked up 5th Avenue toward home I noted with a pang, as so often through the years, the splendid equipages with their coachmen. Laughing men and women, "bejeweled and bejowled" dowagers in the carriages, and bitter feelings clouded my mind and emotions. My parents worked so hard, my father was a physical wreck, and nothing but hard work was ahead of us without vacations or much recreation. Here were the rich, many of whom did nothing useful for a living but exploit the poor and enjoy gorgeous parties at the Waldorf and in Newport, while their secretaries clipped coupons for them. The Sunday supplements of the *New York American* and other newspapers made all this abundantly clear and vivid. Evidently, even in America justice did not prevail.

I reached Central Park. I decided to walk through the park and feast my eyes on the lawns, flowers, trees, lakes, swans, birds, pigeons, and squirrels. After a while, I sat down on a bench to rest my feet and to think.

What's the meaning of existence, of the never-ending struggle to make ends meet, of the obscene contrast between poverty and wealth, the difficulties in finding worthwhile friends? I read, read in every spare minute: fiction, poetry, religion, economics, and philosophy, but I found no satisfying answer.

I had finished with religion years before when I read a biography of John Hus, the reformer of Prague. I had drawn this book from a branch library near my home, and with my vivid imagination and tender concern for human suffering, lived the horrors of religious persecution that finally burned the reformer alive; and in the pyre, his own faith in his church and in God was consumed, apparently forever. Those devils, calling themselves servants of God, were capable of burning a man alive for not agreeing with their creed at some points! But, perhaps there was no God at all. How could there be, with so much injustice and suffering in the world? Curiously, some years later, I looked for the same book — or another biography of Hus at the same library — but it could not be found. Did a bigot also find the book and destroy it?

In my agony at losing the support and security of my faith, I turned to my father for help. We took a walk in Central Park, and I still remember the bench where we sat and talked. "Well, son," he said, "religion is for women, children, and weak-minded people, and I am glad you are maturing." Then he told me about his own experiences as a boy. His father was the sexton of the church in the village of Hadres, near Vienna. Father often took his place as ministrant at the altar, where to his horror, he sometimes saw the priest drunk or sacrilegiously handling the sacred symbols of the faith and intoning the sacred words. Often he accompanied the priest to the bedside of a dying man to administer the last rites while ringing a bell all the way. In New York the kind sisters in the orphanage where he worked almost made him believe in a good God, but who could tell in a world so full of evil and injustice?

Day after day I was surrounded by men with foul and unprintable conversation filthy even in the context of our permissive, progressive era, as four-letter words adorn literature that, in my childhood, I found only on the walls of outhouses. They vied with each other in telling filthy stories of their sexual adventures, even though some of them may have been highly colored by their imaginations. All these stories and obscene pictures were a continuous provocation to cheap, animalistic sexuality. No, we must be fair to the lower animals. They don't have the imagination to conceive the depressing perversions practiced by "homo sapiens." It all made me sick in the stomach and yet kindled my desire to taste the intoxicating yet poisonous fruit of their adventures and exploits to find out if these were as sweet as they claimed. Was I missing something important in life?

My initiation began a week or two after I started to work in the stained glass shop. One of the foremen sneaked up behind me and felt my genitals. Shocked and humiliated, I whipped around to find him and the men nearby laughing. I rushed out of the shop, down a flight into the office where, in tears, I protested against such insulting treatment and offered to leave at once. The boss sympathetically assured me that this would not happen again so I went back to my workbench. Soon, the foreman came and asked if I had said anything in the office.

"Sure!" was the answer. "If you do it again, I'll knock your block off!"

I was frightened, of course, but I stood by my statement. Nobody else, during the eight years in the shop, repeated that performance. And I learned that in order to prove a match to those muscular men, I needed to develop a weapon of singular power, with which I was blessed: my tongue. I did so with such effect that a sarcastic remark or two would throw those strong men into a rage, but I escaped physical punishment.

Fred, a fellow apprentice who later became my friend, assured me that this was not that bad and advised me to take it in stride. He told of his friend who had worked there when they employed girls also. He was a very handsome boy and paid no attention to the girls. One day they set upon him and despite his struggles pressed him to the floor and exposed his genitals. For two or three years after that, no girls were employed, and later, only in a separate department on another floor.

My shop experience, with the exception of the above, started pleasantly enough. About fifteen boys were employed for errands and copperers. Lampshades of many pieces of colored glass were in style. These pieces were cut according to individual patterns, their edges covered with very thin copper, assembled on wooden blocks, and soldered together. The copperers stuck strips of copper, waxed on one side, on the edges of these pieces of glass, preparing them for the solderers.

It was a happy group of boys under the oversight of Charles, a youth, four to five years my elder. Charles was a person overflowing with physical and mental vitality, interested in science, art, music, fencing, physical fitness, photography, and whatnot. He guided our conversations into these fields, whistled beautifully arias from operas he had heard, and kept our minds off the cheap, vulgar, and filthy aspects of the constant sex talk of the men around us. He bought boxing gloves and fencing foils, which he taught us to use, and led us on excursions to the seashore where we rowed, fished, swam, boxed and fenced. At work he was strict but kind, and the day passed rapidly in the stimulating atmosphere he created.

We sat around a single long workbench within seeing and hearing range of each other. The men called Charles "King of the Kids," but under the sarcasm there was an undertone of respect. He treated them always as a gentleman. The group constituted a little oasis of wholesomeness in the shop that I sorely missed when I became an apprentice. I always felt a deep gratitude to Charles for those happy days. Oh, they had their quarrels, petty envies, jealousies, and misunderstandings, yet a general good feeling prevailed and made reconciliation and cooperation much easier. I marveled at Charles, for he had missed affection, understanding, and fellowship on the part of his father, but the glory of the memories of his grandfather, one of Napoleon's generals, provided a substitute inspiration. I was also very fond of his simple, unassuming mother — a good homemaker. Years later, Charles revealed to me that through those years he was an earnest reader of the New Testament, which he never revealed to the group, and we could not have guessed it because, to our knowledge, he was not a churchgoer. His interest in photography carried him into the field of commerce and travel and establishing a well-known business of his own.

The men and boys represented a cross-section of the city both geographically and nationally, religiously and morally. We had a few religious men who compared favorably with the others but only smiled apologetically when the others spread their filth in words or actions. One of their pastimes with apprentices was for two or three of them to throw a boy on the bench, draw down his pants and expose his sex organs. I hear this is still practiced in the schools of some fine residential areas. They call it stripping. Some of the churchgoers were as lewd as the others and sometimes more so. This hypocrisy confirmed my anti-religious attitudes.

Our shop, on one of the top floors in a tall building, gave glimpses of intimate living through the windows of hotels in the neighborhood. Sometimes all of the men crowded to the windows to see the sights — more intriguing no doubt in this time when the body was well covered even at the beach, and the peculiar dressing habits of some women, one of whom had her picture hat and corset on before putting on anything else, marching back and forth with a jaunty air. Many, if not most of the men, were regular visitors to houses of prostitution. They tried their best to introduce the apprentices, and succeeded most of the time.

Some of these men had beautiful children and I often wondered why this did not have a more restraining effect on their fathers, for some of the loveliest children had the foulest fathers. However, there was a code that tabooed lewd conversation near a man's immediate family. One of the men was pouring some filth into my ears one day. I turned a disgusted look on him and said, "Frank, how would you feel if I talked like this to your son?"

Visibly shocked, he replied, rather lamely, "I'd punch you in the nose," but never finished his story.

All of them enjoyed their alcoholic beverages — mostly beer. Every noon the apprentices gathered the beer cans of the men and went to a nearby saloon to fill them up and buy sandwiches for their lunch. The latter were well seasoned and thirst-inducing and so increased their consumption of beer. The apprentices often had their fill while waiting for the cans to be refilled, and only infrequently did the bartender discourage this practice. At lunch, I was often treated to a glass of beer by one or another of the men eating at the same bench. Of the forty men in the shop, only two were hard drinkers. Cookie always had a red nose turning purple but was an excellent worker. Herbie had the unhappy habit of spending his week's pay at a saloon unless his wife was on hand to take his pay envelope. He too was an excellent and conscientious worker and apparently kindhearted and happy.

During his apprenticeship, I developed severe stomach cramps that sometimes doubled me up at the bench. These would be particularly severe mid-morning and mid-afternoon. Neither patent medicines nor a physician's prescription helped much. The causes may well have been psychosomatic and rooted in the tensions of daily living. They ceased with a happy marriage some years later.

It was during the early days in the shop that I found a friend in Tom F. He was a clean-living, wholesome boy, although with a touch of snobbishness because of it. His parents were devout Roman Catholics and Tom was an altar boy. I spent hours of wholesome relaxation in the clean atmosphere of this home — so different from the foul air of the shop. I felt safe, comfortable and expansive in this oasis of friendship. But one evening after a few minutes of conversation Tom ordered me out of the house. But why? He would not say but repeated the command, adding, "and never come back!" In a daze, I left the apartment, stood helplessly before the door trying to recover from this unexpected shock, this inexplicable behavior, and I slowly walked home. An intensive search of my mind revealed no clue to Tom's strange behavior. We never spoke to each other again. It puzzled me for years. I now believe that this was about the time when my doubts about my religion became serious. I probably spoke them quite frankly to my friend as about everything else. I must have told his parents about it and they brought pressure on Tom to break the friendship they considered deleterious to their son's happiness and a mortal peril to the salvation of his soul. The agony of the experience was a spot of pain in my memory for years.

Despite all, the men were uniformly kind to me, willingly helping me to master the intricacies of their artistic trade; covering up my mistakes and encouraging me in my efforts. However, I lacked the necessary manual dexterity to become a good glass-cutter, and never mastered the difficult art of cutting around an intricate pattern in glass of varying thickness and with soft pliers of various shapes, instead chewing into the indentations. How many lovely pieces of glass, carefully selected from 50-70 racks, and blocked out around the paper pattern broke in my hands? But the fellows with whom I worked were never harsh.

Two of the men, one of them my foreman, were witnesses at my examination for citizenship. They made a fine impression on the judge, whose questions dealt only with everyday matters and not with civics, on which I had so carefully prepared. My application approved, I was sworn in and left the courtroom glowing in my new dignity as a citizen of the United States.

Like my father, I was a perfectionist. When I soldered a lampshade together I wanted the soldered lines to be perfect: nicely round and free from air bubbles. Frequently the shade foreman remonstrated with me, "Hurry up Eddie. We don't want to lose money on this. Look how much faster Mickey turns these out."

Hurt and indignant I complained: "Yes, but look at his work. Flat lines full of bubbles. You can see that it's slapped together."

But the foreman had the last word. "Don't be so particular. When the shades are plated, nobody will notice them especially on the inside." So, I tried to hurry it up, but without much success.

At my insistence, the last year of my apprenticeship was in the window department. I had an eye for color and probably would have made a good selector. Putting the windows together was not too difficult but needed considerable practice. Cutters were always needed, but my lack of manual dexterity was an apparently insuperable problem. Selecting was the top job and took years to learn well, and because of the competition, was difficult to achieve.

Yet to work at making beautiful things was very, very satisfying. Some of our lampshades contained over one thousand pieces of glass, each piece carefully selected. Some of our windows, mostly American stained glass, were extremely beautiful. It was esthetic satisfaction of the first order to see these taking shape and the loveliness that delighted the eye. Still, the uncertainty of employment — for our trade was also exposed to the vagaries of fashion — and the uneasiness at my inability to become a master craftsman of the first order, efficient and speedy, made me increasingly dissatisfied and unhappy.

Once, I was out of work for a whole month and had to go to Bridgeport, Connecticut to find a job. But when one has spent years learning a trade it is difficult to change, even in America, where economic and social mobility is so prevalent and accepted. And the margin of security for such a large family was too narrow for experiments with new occupations.

There was a lot of laughter in the shop. On the whole, the men were a happy bunch. Whitfield — what a name for a humorist! — was particularly adept at the parody of Salvation Army services, Sunday school, and religious hymns, to our vast amusement. Yes, ours, for my bitterness concerning religion had made me a militant atheist, far more so than anybody else of my acquaintance. I railed at God and religion on the smallest provocation. Long before I heard it from communist sources I believed and preached that religion was the opium of the people. Most of the men in the shop were rather easygoing and tolerant in such matters.

One of our favorite jokes was to sneak up on a fellow and tie a fire pail to his apron strings at the back while another or several others held his attention with a story, a joke or an argument. All of us watched eagerly for the next development. The longer the wait, the greater the relief when the inevitable happened. If the wait was too long, somebody would call him or he would be summoned to the telephone. As soon as the man took a step or two he pulled the pail of water on himself. Shouts of protest and of glee filled the shop while the poor victim sent maledictions in every direction.

Sometimes one of us hung a little coffee can above a fellow's head while he was away from his place, and rigged it up in such a way that a quick jerk by someone out of sight would tip the can. Suddenly the man jumped as cold water poured down his neck and called the culprit the foulest names he could think of, while everybody looked at him in astonishment and inquired with poker faces what the trouble was or if they might help him in some way.

On a hot day, a solderer ran to the washroom to freshen up and glanced into the mirror to find black marks all over his face. Somebody had smeared some black powder on the handle of his soldering iron and he had rubbed it all over his sweating face. When he returned, everywhere about him there were loud observations of his clean face and how well he looked. With blazing eyes, he examined their faces for signs of guilt but without success. And he had no peace until he played his little joke on a person he suspected or disliked. But there was little malice in these practical jokes, and the foremen entered into the game heartily, but were never the victims.

Then there were the singing sessions when two or four of the men gathered in a corner and sang a popular song with excellent barbershop harmony. Around Thanksgiving and Christmas, just for fun, a turkey was raffled off. We had a jackpot on the world-series in baseball with the lucky number collecting all. We played pinochle and had arguments and fistfights, but I don't remember a single serious one.

The stained glass workers had a union covering Greater New York with its membership. It had regular meetings at which anyone with a grievance could have the floor. For every five journeymen employed for a full year, the boss had the right to engage one apprentice. This limit was imposed in order to prevent the crowding of the trade with more workers than could be employed, for such a situation would weaken the union. We elected officers regularly and our meetings were always orderly.

However, there were pace-setters in the shop whose efforts determined the approximate time a certain job ought to take. Frank was one of these. He was very efficient and speedy, and his work was as good as it was fast. Nobody turned out their work in the same time, but this was allowed for by the foreman. And there was Fritz, something of a goat for the foreman. If a job took too long, the foreman would give Fritz a scolding that the firm was losing money on it. Poor Fritz would break his neck to please the foreman and establish a new record to which other workers were then held.

The foremen, however, as good union members, looked after the welfare of the workers as well as profits for the firm. This was very difficult sometimes and resulted in practices easily condemned when viewed from the outside or by an efficiency expert. I recall an occasion when our foreman in a conversation with Frank casually dropped the remark that in the office they had orders for only two more weeks. Frank slowed down and quietly passed the word until all of us learned about the situation. One of the men came to me and asked, "Ed, do you want to work yourself out of a job?"

Greatly astonished at such a foolish question, I replied indignantly, "Of course not! What's the big idea?"

He passed along Charlie's remark. We all slowed down. Fortunately, new orders came and we were glad to return to our former rate. I have often told this story in my college classes when we studied economics and asked how many would work themselves out of a job in a similar situation. No one volunteered.

All through my period of adolescence, I had some unpleasant experiences with gangs. They usually loafed on street corners waiting for an "easy mark" to come along. This might be a greenhorn, an abnormal person, a "rube" from the country — anybody who looked or acted differently. I had a high visibility because of my erect carriage, almost leaning backward. A fast walker, seldom did anybody pass me, but I usually passed all others, eyes always front, clothes impeccable, and shoes polished to a mirror finish. One evening I was walking along 1st Avenue around 64th Street when a group of six or seven young adolescents, twelve- to fifteen-years-old, attacked me. I was not particularly brave but I had to defend myself and turned on them with fury. They scattered and in a moment about as many 18-year-olds joined the fray. Almost immediately I was knocked to the ground. Just as I got to my feet a truck came along and they scattered to get out of its way. I was not fast enough and a wheel passed over my foot, but I took to my heels in unconscious approval of the Hungarian proverb: "*Szegyen a futas de hasznos*" (Running is a disgrace, but useful).

The Sunday funny section of the newspapers provided considerable entertainment for me and for all of the family. I particularly remember Buster Brown, who got into all sorts of scrapes and whose mother always finished it off with blows on his buttock, administered with a hairbrush. Lulu and Leander were a devoted young couple of lovers, with enormous heads, handsome features, and soulful eyes, whose passion always ran into heartbreaking difficulties, but whose love conquered all. Then there were the Katzenjammer Kids, much as they are today — long and lanky Mutt forever victimizing shorty, chunky Jeff and others. As I recall, these were all rather crude in comparison to the comic sheets of the Old Country but they were not difficult to follow for greenhorns, printed in color, full of drama and conflict, and a good deal of it dealing with the experiences of childhood.

The Horatio Alger stories provided vitamins for our struggles up the American ladder of opportunity. In the papers published for immigrants, there were stories of our own kind who had become rich and powerful even though very few became millionaires or great leaders in politics. In New York, a few were lieutenants or non-commissioned officers of Tammany Hall. They aided the immigrant in his problems with the law, citizenship, illness, and unemployment. The grateful immigrants turned in their votes for their benefactors. Too bad the good solid citizens and the old established churches did not match the cohorts of Tammany with equally weighty good works. Perhaps the half-century of corruption in our great metropolis might have been made shorter or escaped altogether. And there were the colorful marches around election time — a band leading a group of torch-bearing citizens, or bums, singing popular marches or satirical songs about the other political party, sometimes translated into unprintable language by the immigrants.

One political figure of those days remains indelibly printed on my mind by the many cartoons I saw. It was a very muscular man of tremendous vitality in a Prince Albert coat with a black ribbon flying from flashing glasses, wielding an enormous club, attacking large corpulent men with tall silk hats and a dollar sign on their chest. I learned that this was Teddy Roosevelt, the poor man's champion attacking malefactors of wealth, breaking up the trusts and their tremendous concentration of riches and power. It made the poor immigrant youth feel very good indeed.

Father was determined to become an American citizen. Night after night he was in school learning English and, later, citizenship. Night after night he fell asleep in class.

"Why do you torture yourself like this, Mr. Kautz?" inquired his kind teacher. You work too hard during the day. Stay home and rest.

"Ah but I want to be a citizen." And almost thirty years later he won his citizenship certificate. Dear old Papa! If all his children would have had his persistence! What could they have become in this blessed land!

Then there came a vision of loveliness into my life. On a Sunday morning there came a knock on our door, four flights up, in a tenement near the East River on 76th Street. Mother opened the door and there stood Margaret in a tight-fitting white dress under a black coat, big black eyes flashing from under heavy eyebrows, crowned by a big black hat from which an enormous black ostrich feather swept to her shoulders. She was beautiful.

Who was this lovely creature? She worked in the cigar shop and mother had taken a fancy to her and invited her to visit us. So here she was. Of how long she stayed, what we talked about, and what else happened, I remember nothing, but only an overwhelming impulse that I had to see her again, soon. Next evening I walked about a half mile to the house where she lived with her two sisters, hoping at least to catch a glimpse of that peach-and-cream complexion and flashing black eyes. Somebody in the family noticed me as I walked back and forth in front of the house and invited me upstairs. Their little tenement apartment was on the second floor but for me, it was close to heaven. We continued to see each other with increasing frequency.

One Saturday afternoon we were alone. We sat beside each other on the couch. She drew me to herself. But I idealized her too much and I pulled away. Sometime later I learned that one of her sisters and she were going to visit their parents in Hungary. I was heartbroken. On the morning they were to leave, I went to her house to catch another glimpse of her. As I arrived, they came out of the house to enter a cab, that was to take them to the ship, and invited me to come along. Overjoyed, I accepted. When the liner left the pier and sailed out to sea, it carried my heart with it. I wept bitter tears, and boarding a streetcar arrived late at the shop.

But why did everybody on the car stare at me? I discovered that there was a disgusting yellow streak running down my suit and I remembered that I was carrying two eggs in my paper bag to be boiled for lunch. The cup of my wretchedness was full. But the shame of the yellow spot distracted my mind from my heartbreak.

Cards and letters came with fair regularity. They were having a gay time. Even the two younger priests of the village church came and danced with them frequently. I had my suspicions and they were not pleasant. Certainly, they did not increase my love or reverence for the church. Not long after they returned home, our affair broke up. Something much more important had come into my life that I have reserved for the next chapter.

Adolescence came with its full impact on me, with its dreams, hopes, ambitions, fears, and disappointments. The fresh breeze of new ideas and experiences, increasing clarity of vision as I looked upon life, and matching confusion as I saw great and shining goals and experienced the uncertainty, hesitation and the slow, torturous approach to them. There was the feverish haste to reach them, the fear of failure, of remaining a nobody, and the recklessness and timidity in my trials and errors. There was the indefinable, inexpressible, often unconscious *weltschmerz*, the feeling that something was terribly wrong about life in this complex world.

My imagination had been fired by the legends of heroism and stories of true greatness in the thousand-year-old history of my native land. Added to these were the inspiring lives of the Founding Fathers of my new, adopted homeland, America, and the modern stories of success against great odds of such men as Edison, Carnegie, Ford, Rockefeller, and others. I, too, wanted to be *somebody*, not just one of the unknown living in the vast anonymous multitude of the Metropolis. I longed for greatness, not just fame, wealth, or power. I felt that only a noble success could satisfy me. But I was an infinitesimal grain of sand on the shores of time. I felt the stirring of potentials inside and their pressures to find fulfillment in comparable deeds. But how? What? When? Where?

I had no competent counsel to guide me. My experiences at night school and the lonely study of bookkeeping at home bored me to death. My father accused me of a lack of sticktoitiveness which was true enough, yet later on, when I had found worthwhile goals to which I could dedicate myself, I became admirably persistent. Even though I derived joy and pleasure from working at my trade, I faced the probability of becoming a second-rate journeyman because of a lack of manual dexterity. Nor was there much security in my trade except for a comparatively few men — the best. But I had to stick to it because I had served a five-year apprenticeship to arrive, and with the deterioration in my father's health, I became the chief breadwinner of the family — a large one of nine children and two parents. This, of course, precluded marriage for some time to come, and if I married and had as many children as most people I knew, why, the situation could become quite desperate.

Then there was the slow deterioration of our family. In the face of temptations for immigrant children in New York, drawn and torn, as they were, by two cultures, the sacrifices and fine example of the parents sometimes proved ineffectual. One of the boys left home at fourteen years of age, working on a coal barge that sank in a storm off the Virginia coast. Then he enlisted in the army. Another also left home and enlisted. A third, rebelling against the obligations imposed by a large family and blaming his parents for having so many children, left home and never returned. Two of them made early or hasty marriages that my parents, particularly my mother, strongly disapproved of. Later disciplined and mellowed by the lessons of experience, all but one returned home, growing in appreciation of their parents for the rest of their lives. But these were years of bitter disappointment for my parents. Father took it more easily. He had the lovely *gemutlich* (easy going disposition) of his early Viennese conditioning. He expected his children to make a decent living honorably and raise a family. He had no earthshaking ambitions and did not press his children to take advantage of their educational opportunities.

For mother, however, it was a continuing source of humiliation and resentment that not one of her children wanted to continue schooling, which she herself had so unjustly missed. For in her childhood the village priest had come to her father and told him what a gifted daughter he had, urging him to give her an education. But her father, a mason and bricklayer, protested that only a wealthy man could afford that. He had a very limited and uncertain income, not at all like bricklayers in the United States. Finally, the good priest offered to provide the necessary expenses if the father consented. But the latter closed the conversation with the statement, "I am but a poor man, your Reverence. Let her remain poor, also." It was not a rare attitude among underprivileged people everywhere. Perhaps he hoped also that Rosa might soon add to their income, which would certainly be lost for a number of years if he consented.

How often mother told this story, always with deep pathos in her voice, hoping that her children might be inspired to continue or return to school! How glad she would be to make additional sacrifices for them if they were to give up their income. She told it for the last time to me just a few hours before her death at the age of 72 with echoes of the old heartache.

I read and read and read rather indiscriminately for escape, which I found in Dumas' historical novels, Jules Verne, and H. G. Wells fantasies. I was driven, too, by the need to make something of "the vast bumbling confusion" that was life. Socialism, with its emphasis on the good life for all and protest against economic injustice, was a strong attraction, and the hope it offered for achieving a better world was a precious star in the darkness that surrounded me. Astronomy both soothed and depressed me as I contemplated the awe, wonder, and beautiful order of the stellar universe. I began to doubt my atheism as I pondered the problem of creation without a creator. But it depressed me also, for how could there be any meaning for an infinitely small speck of animated dust. Myself, carried along at inconceivable speed on a mere speck, the Earth, from where to where? Surely I was not important in that vast perspective. Only much later did it occur to me (or I read it somewhere, which is more probable) that a speck which had the capacity to think, dream, imagine, compose music, conceive a system of philosophy or ethics, measure the vast distances in space, and weigh the distant suns was indeed the greater, for no giant star, molecules or atoms had the capacity to do so.

I read in spiritism and became acquainted with a man and his adult daughter who practiced it. She was a medium, and when "possessed by a spirit," drew remarkable pictures of beings on other planets. But the seances exhausted her and she became rather sickly. In addition, she and her father had a peculiar, unearthly look that made me uneasy — afraid, perhaps. This dabbling in spiritism ended soon. It only added to my confusion and my feeling that there are areas in life that elude the sober search of science.

I had no use for religion and missed the sense of balance, the hope it engenders, and the strength it brings in the crises of life. In fact, with many of the most religious people I encountered, much of all this was conspicuously absent. I resented the closed worlds in which they lived, their fear of new ideas, their slavery to dogma.

I condemned the church for its persecution and killing of those who questioned its doctrines, its frequently baleful influence in political and economic affairs, its support of privileged exploiters of the poor, the sophistry of its thinkers, and the all too frequent low sexual morals of the priesthood, especially in situations where it was the state church.

Not all of this could be as clearly enunciated as these words may indicate, but this was the fiery content of his nebulous, thoughts and feelings. Therefore, I was a militant atheist, fighting always against the blight of religion. Under the impact of astronomy and spiritism, as well as my dire need for new sources of inspiration and strength for living, my atheism mellowed into a suspicious agnosticism.

The social injustices, even in America, my disappointment in friends, the tragic death of John caused by venereal disease, the inner tensions of sex and the continuous stimulation regarding sexual indulgence in the shop, the outer temptations to release, and the perilous satisfaction brought on a state of anxiety. Thinking of my parents, I found that I could only despise myself were I to practice what apparently all the men indulged in. My father had taught me to respect women and to treat them kindly, considerately, as the weaker sex. My mother represented the sex that others used as cheap means to their degrading pleasures. As old fashioned parents, however, they never had a frank talk with me on sexual matters. So I stumbled about in sad confusion tinged with despair.

6 - A New Direction

The family sat at the table after a delicious dinner, relaxing and chatting over the events of the day. Mother told about two extraordinary women she'd met in the shop that day. They too were Hungarian, very pleasant but different from the others. They never engaged in telling off-color stories, filthy jokes, cursing, or swearing, nor in the gossip, often malicious, that kept nerves on edge and gave expression to the envies and jealousies that arose in competition for the foreman's or superintendent's favor.

Those two could make the life of a cigar maker very unpleasant indeed by finding fault with her work, throwing out cigars, scolding the worker or allowing themselves liberties resented by decent women but welcomed by others who sought an easier life. These two women were unfailingly gracious and wholesome — not attractive physically but with very winsome personalities.

Some days later mother discovered that these women were Baptists, a Christian sect rather weak in numbers among Hungarians but strong in faith. They took their faith very seriously and endeavored to recapture the spirit, fellowship, and simplicity of the age of the Apostles. They read their Bible daily, engaged in prayer before every meal, punctuated the day with prayers, and went to services every Sunday. They kept themselves separate from the world by avoiding the usual amusements of dancing, reading novels, theater-going, and drinking parties, as well as the greater physical sins of fornication, adultery, and drunkenness. They were a sober, serious, but friendly group — not very scintillating but concerned about the high ideals of Jesus and seeking earnestly to incorporate those in their own lives.

Soon I found myself visiting regularly at the home of these two women, where we engaged in serious conversations about the meaning of life. Margaret, the fourteen-year-old daughter of one of them, was a sweet, silent girl. A pale face and big black eyes were an added attraction. They invited me to church. It turned out to be a tiny Hungarian mission of twenty members or less, holding services in a basement room of the Second Avenue Baptist Church in New York City. I found nothing attractive about their worship. I missed the gorgeous altar of the Roman Church, the rich decorations, and the music. I missed the splendid robes of the priests and the mysterious ritual. I still remember a particularly beautiful solo by the priest to a subdued organ accompaniment in one of the masses, just before the "elevation of the host." There was nothing churchly about their room with its folding benches, a simple table with a maroon cover, and a Bible on top.

The little congregation sang a number of hymns led by the minister who picked out the tune with one finger on a not well tuned square piano. He called on various male members to lead in prayer, give testimony or read a passage in the Bible. Then he preached in a halting, stuttering manner with an indefinable, repelling air, a sermon that made no impression on me at all. Very seldom did I return to their worship.

My aggressive atheism, by now mellowed into an equally aggressive agnosticism, must have been very trying to those good people, but they endured me, hoping, I suppose, to convert me to their faith. Only their winsome kindness kept my anti-religious impulses in check. The fact that only they, among my acquaintances, were willing to discuss life's serious meanings, kept me visiting the women in their little two-room basement apartment. They avoided debate or argument. That was fortunate, for I had read many more books than they, and could have run circles around them, easily entangle them, and make them look foolish, leaving me disgusted with them for my easy victories.

They wove into their conversation quotations from the Bible, particularly from the Gospels and Paul's letters. In time, these intrigued me enough to ask them for the loan of a Bible. They were glad enough to do so. However, they only had a large family Bible that weighed about five pounds. But I wanted to read it for myself, so I did not mind lugging it home. Eagerly, they wrapped it in a newspaper and I carried it home, walking about a mile in order to save a precious nickel.

That very night I started to read their holy book. The more I read the more I wondered how intelligent people in this enlightened age could believe stuff like that! A tissue of legends, impossible stories, tales, and myths. So now I introduced my reactions to these into our talks. I suppose they felt rather helpless and called on their new pastor, an earnest person and a clever, fluent speaker. He could not help me but made the services more attractive, and I attended sporadically. He even introduced me to a visitor from Hungary — the outstanding leader of the Baptists in Hungary. With astounding naivete, this bearded gentleman, a professor in their seminary, simply asked me if I loved the Lord Jesus.

"Well, I respect him and admire him, but hardly love him."

He smiled sweetly and turned away from me.

One Saturday afternoon, I visited the new minister. He had asked me to do so and bring with me the Bible references that puzzled me and he would try to explain them. We spent nearly two hours on these and at the close, I spoke simply and crudely.

"Sir, this is all a lot of foolishness to me."

The shock registered in his face, but he recovered quickly and countered with the answer. "Well, the wisdom of God is foolishness to men but God will catch the wise in their own wisdom. So the Scriptures say."

Curious, I asked, "Where?"

Opening his Bible, he said, "Right here in First Corinthians, the first chapter," and he pointed to verses 18-25.

This challenged me and he noticed it. "Do you really want to know the truth?" he asked.

"Sir, I'd give my life to know it!" I replied with deadly seriousness, for I was at the end of my resources — toying with the idea of suicide.

"Then," he said, "ask God to show you the truth."

I pondered this all the way home. Was I to throw away my mind, my reasoning powers? That seemed utterly foolish and dangerous. These were simple people with little knowledge of the accumulated treasures of human achievement. But I could not argue away their attractive personalities or their lovely lives. On my walk all the way home I pondered this puzzle. Was it possible that meaning and truth come in other ways also?

After dinner that night I withdrew into our sitting room home. I picked up the Bible and a cigar, long and thin, specially made by my mother for me, but instead of lighting it I put it aside and made a funny little prayer.

"Oh God, if there be a God, show me the truth."

I no longer recall what portion of Scripture I read. I only knew that for the first time it gripped me. Here was something real, something for a modern, something for me.

From that night on I read the Bible in all of my spare time. I bought a pocket Bible and read it on the streetcar on my way to work, even at lunch in the shop. I became the laughing stock of the men around me. I could not care less for I was on the trail of some meaning, something precious, perhaps a way out of my despair.

I went to the little mission regularly now. My new seriousness impressed the members and they began asking when I would join them. Annoyed, I flared up at a little ladies tailor. "Look here, when I am ready I will let you know. Now stop pestering me!" He stopped. Slowly there came the conviction that this was what I needed. But why not return to my first faith, Roman Catholicism? No, my historical knowledge of its persecutions, its bloody extermination of heretics, its centuries-old support of the wealthy and powerful, its vast riches and neglect of the poor and underprivileged, and many, many other things made that impossible. I never found in that splendid old church the vital spirit I experienced among these simple people. But to join that group would offend my mother, still a devout Catholic, even though she attended the Baptist services with me.

One Sunday afternoon, coming home from church, I stood on the steps leading into the house. I looked up at the sky where the clouds were breaking up after a storm. There was a large rough circle where the sky was showing through. In my confusion, a prayer escaped my lips.

"Give me a sign, Oh Lord. If this be the right way let a bolt of fire light up that space." In a moment many little branches of fire filled the spot. With tear-filled eyes, I rushed into the house and gave thanks.

However, the real decision was still some weeks away. One evening after I had read the Bible and all were asleep, I knelt alongside my bed and prayed.

"Lord take this tangled-up life of mine and make it what it ought to be." No vision or dream followed this commitment, no ecstasy, nothing extraordinary. In those early days, however, such experiences were not too unusual. A deacon in the church in Trenton, N.J. told me about his.

He had been attending the Baptist services in an Ohio town and read his Bible regularly. But he belonged to a Christian church. There, however, the minister never preached on conversion and a new life. One evening as he read his Bible he became greatly concerned. He dropped on his knees and in his bewilderment cried out.

"Lord, show me, which is the right road!"

A blinding light filled the room and there stood Jesus saying, "Follow me," and disappeared.

This he interpreted as divine guidance to the new faith. Years later when I knew him he was a dedicated leader in his church and a sincere follower of Jesus. Everybody admired him. Until he told me his story I could not have imagined that he would have such an experience. He was such a calm, unexcitable fellow.

Soon after, I became conscious of new power to withstand temptation, new courage to declare for clean living and proclaim my Christian convictions. There was a new sense of direction and assurance and meaning to life and its struggles. I decided to ask for membership in the little group of believers even though it meant giving up a lot of things: the theater, of which I was very fond, dancing, for which I did not care, movies and the reading of worldly books, both of which I was addicted to. We only read the Bible and religious literature.

We gave up Sunday excursions and all "vanities." The latter included a fancy vest that always made me self-conscious, and a boutonniere, which was plucked from my lapel by a "sister" with a serious look, and the word, "vanity." It meant not working on Sunday, which was the Lord's Day, and living in such a way that others should not have to work on my behalf. Accordingly, I always walked to church on Sundays, back home and everywhere else. It meant not eating in restaurants on Sundays or buying anything except in extreme emergencies.

I gave up smoking, which was not too difficult. Many years later a specialist informed me that I was allergic to tobacco smoke. Alcoholic beverages were renounced. This came to me in a rather dramatic fashion. By now the entire family except father attended services at the little mission regularly. One of my brothers, about twelve, came home from Sunday school as I was sitting down to supper and pouring myself a glass of beer. They'd had a vivid and impressive lesson on the evils of alcohol. Gripping my arm he pleaded, "Eddie, don't drink any more of that vile stuff." I looked at him and noting the intense seriousness of his gaze, I poured the beer back into the bottle and replaced it in the icebox. Then I asked him to explain his request. This he did and I was glad I had acceded. I never touched the stuff again although I was very fond of it. This gave a new angle to the baiting of the fellows in the shop, but it did not matter.

It was understood that a member of the mission was not to marry an "unbeliever," but only a Baptist — preferably a Hungarian or European

Baptist — for American Baptists were considered too "worldly." The decision would also mean a dulling of one's critical sense in reading the Bible and accepting a rather literal interpretation of it. But my need was great and, like a starving man who is not particularly concerned about the dish in which life-saving food is offered to him, this did not worry me at all. The new significance of life and the strength and courage for facing it relieved me of critical scrupulousness for a time. The narrowing of life had its compensation, as the sprawling shallow river into a deep canal, that then becomes capable of carrying big ships.

My father, however, was deeply troubled. For him, this was a retreat from life, as indeed it was in a sense. One Sunday, after I had told him of my decision to give myself to God and join the mission, he looked up with deep pity in his sky-blue eyes and sadly warned me, "You are giving up all the joys and pleasures of life. One day when you reach my age you will say to yourself, 'What a fool I have been.'" My father was wrong. I never regretted my decision.

My mother did not stand in my way, for she herself was approaching the same decision. In any case, did not the Master say, "Whosoever loves father, mother, brother, and sister more than me is not worthy of me?" Above all else, I was determined to be worthy of Him, for like one of His first disciples, I felt, "Thou hast the words of Eternal Life." At the prayer meeting that week I stood up and asked for baptism. After examination before the church, I was immersed. It symbolized that I died to the old life and started anew with Jesus Christ.

Curiously, it was the Roman Catholic Bible that finally convinced me about baptism. The Protestant Bible was clear enough on the mode and meaning of baptism. But I had been sprinkled as a baby. At my request, one of the members brought a copy of the authorized Roman translation in Hungarian, of the imprimatur of the Cardinal Primate of Hungary. Eagerly, I turned to Romans 6:1-4. I read the text on the upper half of the page. The wording was practically identical to that of the Protestant version. It referred to the commentary on the lower half of the page. Here I read: "Baptism means what its ancient and original mode of administration meant: the burial of the old man of sin and the resurrection of the new man in Christ." That settled it. Even the Roman Bible affirmed the Baptist practice. What right did they have to change it?

7 - War On Satan

Life had become a very exciting thing. We were agents of the Eternal, soldiers of Christ engaged in daily battles against evil, both in our own lives and in our environment. Every one of us carried either a Bible or a New Testament with him, the "Sword of the Spirit," always. I read it on the streetcar going to work, at noon when eating lunch, and after supper at home. In talking to others we quoted or read from it liberally and we gave our witness everywhere. On the street, if we heard somebody speaking Hungarian or carrying a Hungarian newspaper, or reading one on a streetcar, the elevated or subway train, we had a tract handy with the address of our meeting place.

We set up our soapbox on various street corners. We sang, prayed and preached, all in Hungarian. There were five such places on Manhattan Island, including the entrance to the Second Avenue Baptist Church where our regular preaching services were held. These outdoor congregations varied from a dozen to five hundred people. Not infrequently, we were pelted with stones, over-ripe fruit or garbage and doused with water — sometimes dishwater — by the "congregation" or by tenants of a tenement.

We had special difficulties on East 65th and 79th Streets at 1st Avenue, where the newer, cheaper apartment houses were inhabited by skilled workmen. Most of them were atheists. The reason for this was that all over Europe, self-conscious working men knew or felt that the church was on the side of the aristocracy and wealth, so in turn, they despised or hated organized religion and all it stood for.

When we started our meetings on the corner of 79th Street and Avenue A, where we held meetings five nights a week, five hundred shouting, jeering, screaming men, mostly atheists, surrounded us night after night, making it impossible for anyone to hear our message. They called us Rockefeller's missionaries (John D. Sr.), for wasn't he a Baptist and a conscienceless millionaire? How much were we receiving for this despicable service of stupefying honest workmen with the dope of religion? How much would a convert receive from Rockefeller's unlimited resources? The guesses went into hundreds of dollars each. We were hurt, of course, and we protested, but to no avail; for, they said, how could we give away such trade secrets?

We sang, prayed, and read from the Bible, but no one listened, and when our pastor stood up on the box to address them they howled like a pack of wolves. This continued for two weeks. Then Pastor Dulity had a saving idea. He asked me to sing a solo. I had a fairly good voice at the time, a sweet, sentimental tenor (that later cracked somewhat under the strain and stress of open-air preaching). Quickly finding a hymn and the scale, I stood up and sang. The poet was right. The savage breasts were soothed and they listened in astounding stillness. As I finished our pastor jumped up and told a joke. They laughed. Then he told a story. Something about a poor struggling immigrant perhaps. The ice was broken. From that night on they listened.

We still had disorderly meetings. One night I was knocked down and I ran for my life. Over and over again we were drenched by showers from tenement windows. One Monday at breakfast my mother told me of the meeting at 79th Street on the previous Sunday evening. She was wet from head to her feet by the time the service ended, but she said, "Never have I been so happy in my life!"

Some of the women made lewd remarks about how handsome the minister was and how they would not mind baptism if he held them in his arms. The men would start discussions among themselves in small groups just to draw the attention of the crowd away from us.

Some of us wanted police protection, to which we were entitled. The pastor felt that the sight of the police would only enrage our atheist friends. It would be reminiscent of the suppression of agitation and free speech by the regime in Hungary. No, let us suffer patiently as did our Master and win them by the power of love. But how can you love such wild animals? I protested some and stayed away from these meetings.

In spite of everything, though, there was real worship on those street corners, not the aesthetically satisfying worship of a cathedral. No great music, no impressive pageantry, no well-trained choir, no carefully composed, eloquent sermon with its splendid flights of oratory, only fervent prayers and brief, heartfelt testimonies to God's goodness.

Fortunately, our pastor was a man of wide experience, lively imagination and a good sense of humor. His talks were informal, entertaining and dealt with the world they knew, reminiscent of the days when he too earned his living as a working man, and ending with a spiritual message. He smiled and laughed a great deal while slapping his thigh in merriment, and became acquainted personally with their leaders. After a while, he had the crowd with him even though they had no use for God.

From that time on he would single out a troublemaker and shout in his direction, "Isn't that true, sir?" There was a man among them, conspicuous because he wore a cap while the others wore hats. Repeatedly our minister would shout in his direction: "Isn't that so, my cap-wearing friend?" Everybody stared at him and laughed. Embarrassed, he would mumble something and try to make himself less visible by standing behind taller men. But soon, as he made himself obnoxious the pastor called on him again to affirm something he had said. After a few days, our cap-wearing friend seldom made trouble.

Much of this went on during the feverish days of World War I when foreigners were suspect everywhere. In Chicago, the women of the German churches were frozen out of the Baptist Association. The head of the Czechoslovak Seminary said to a young woman who was later engaged to a Hungarian, "You, whom I used to carry in my arms as a little girl? I'd rather have you marry a Negro!" And Negroes did not stand high in his estimation. The time came when our motherland, Hungary, also lined up against the Allies and America. We, as immigrants and most not yet citizens, were enemy aliens. But the authorities allowed us to carry on our work, and to preach freely in an alien, enemy tongue. Oh blessed America! Where else could this have happened?

There was a vacant lot near the East River on 79th Street. It was used as a dump by several in the surrounding tenements for their trash and garbage. The Evangelistic Committee rented the place, fenced it in and, after we had cleaned it off, installed some benches, a platform, an arc light, and a projector, and we continued the meetings.

We had children's services with Bible pictures and hymns on the screen, which was usually crowded, followed by an adult service where sometimes we also used the screen. These meetings were more orderly, but we still had troublemakers who usually stood outside the fence. Sometimes, during the night the light was smashed, the fence, benches, and piano damaged, so we had to hire a watchman full time.

All our efforts yielded but one middle-aged washerwoman, Aunt Julia, who became one of the most dedicated, sacrificial spirits in the mission. However, we attracted quite a number of children and young adolescents and when we ended our outdoor gatherings they came to our Sunday school.

We were deeply moved when little Zoltan, aged twelve, brought his five brothers and sisters on a cold winter day. His overcoat buttoned over his arm, crippled by tuberculosis. His father was a drunkard but his distraught mother somehow held the family together. She found new strength at the services of the Mission and in the pastor's visits. In another family, there were five lovely, fatherless children.

The mother was a working woman who had a hard life providing for her brood. Periodically, she entertained strange men overnight. Here a devoted grandmother hovered over the children, fed them, washed their clothes, kept house, and led them to Sunday school. Ultimately, she too joined the church, followed by several of her grandchildren.

A gypsy family also came to the services, and in a little while, the eldest son became a Baptist. He was the breadwinner in the absence of a father who had died or disappeared. One of the most faithful Sunday school scholars was a girl of thirteen. One day we discovered that her mother sent her to the drugstore for contraceptives.

There were, however, several families with a wholesome climate from which we had no problem children. These, too, were attracted by the services on the "dump" and their parents encouraged them to come. Two very handsome and vivacious boys were sent to us by atheist parents because I had invited them. They were our neighbors and trusted me. Years later, the boys joined a Baptist church in upstate New York. Apparently, most of those who did not join the mission became useful citizens and good fathers and mothers. It was only possible to follow up on a small number of those with whom we worked. Ten years later, the Rev. Dulity baptized two of our atheist Jewish friends in far-off California.

From fall until the following summer, a few of us went calling for children. Wherever we heard of a Hungarian family, or children speak the language on the street, we invited them to our services and Sunday school. A few of us went an hour earlier every Sunday before the school began at three o'clock. Within a year, we had an attendance of one hundred thirty, although our membership was still small at around forty. We had moved our services to the Central Park Baptist Church on East 33rd Street, which was nearest to the center of the Hungarian population. Here the large Sunday school room could be transformed into a basketball court.

Soon our pastor and two young laymen played basketball with the boys who came to our mission. In this way, we learned to know them, their problems, hopes, and fears quite well. They received a great deal of personal attention along with their families. Not often did they become members of the church, for they had too much to give up and had inadequate spiritual support in their homes. Frequently, they fell by the wayside after joining the church, for the temptations and pressures at work and elsewhere proved too strong. Some, however, became staunch members after they had their "fling in the world."

One of the important people in the group was an attractive, ebullient miss, about nineteen years of age. Full of vitality, laughter, and the joy of living, Miss Lukacs was a center of attraction everywhere. Also, for a time, she was a person of mystery. Invited by a couple, she came to our Sunday school, sang heartily, followed everything with big shining eyes, and disappeared when the school closed. We discovered that she was a faithful member in the Slovak mission but attended our school because they did not have one.

One Sunday, during opening exercises, our minister announced that there was a young Slovak Baptist girl in our midst who would make a good Sunday school teacher. "Miss Lukacs, here is a group of six girls, please come and teach them." Overcome with astonishment, she accepted, but after the class she broke into tears and said that she had never taught a class and had no material. "Never mind, my dear," the pastor assured her, "we'll provide you with everything you need." Fearfully, yet not without joy, she accepted the assignment.

At about the same time, the pastor gave me an equal number of boys to teach. Half of them were my younger brothers — not an enviable situation. The two classes competed with each other in growth and attendance. In a year she had thirty girls in her class but I had only twenty-five boys. This friendly competition has continued ever since, usually ending in her victory.

Miss Lukacs had an extraordinary combination of religious fervor, commitment to the cause of Christ, and joy. Her enthusiasm was irresistible, infecting everybody else, including serious and gloomy deacons and ministers, young people in the church, and children on the street corners where she told them stories as a part of the outdoor service. She was quite different from me, whose commitment equaled hers but whose life had been less protected and, as evidenced by most of the foregoing, who had seen so much wrong and evil that it had embittered me.

I had shed most of the bitterness, but I was always conscious of the evil around me, which made me terribly serious and even gloomy. God would win some day, I had no doubt about that, but it was self-evident that God was not winning overwhelming victories in the present. I could not be happy in an evil world except when repentant sinners gave themselves to God. I tended to emphasize the terrors in store for sinners here and hereafter rather than the winsomeness of the gentle Jesus, meek and mild. I was engaged in a holy crusade against sin.

One evening, I had preached on the death of Jesus, surely a melting subject. But I had concentrated on the wickedness of sinners, dwelling vividly on sins practiced generally in the Hungarian colony. An enraged sinner accosted me after the service and told me, "If it had not been for you I'd have knocked that young so and so off the platform."

Rev. Dulity replied, "Now you must not do that. The young man is full of zeal even if he does not always use good judgment, he'll learn. I am sure he did not mean to insult you."

My "Gloomy Gus" of a Christian was irresistibly drawn to happy, enthusiastic Miss Lukacs, who was equally devoted and serious yet bubbled always with the joy of living. She wept over her wayward Sunday school scholars, but she also laughed more merrily and heartily than any of them. They loved her, followed her everywhere, and drew other girls into their charmed circle by telling about their wonderful Miss Lukacs.

Yet she had known troubles and heartaches. Her parents were the first Baptists in the little village of Stara Tura, Czechoslovakia — then part of Hungary. It was situated in one of the lovely idyllic little valleys among the pine-clad mountains of the Carpathians. Later it became a tourist paradise and a spa. She loved to tell of its beauty and the three rivers that flowed through it. One day, in a more realistic and unguarded mood, she told about the ducks stirring up the mud as they paddled across. Amused, I kindly refrained for years from twitting her about the rivers that had shrunk to a creek with its two branches.

Her mother was a businesswoman who sold goods bought in Vienna to villages in Austria that were far from shopping centers. She usually had a female servant, big and muscular, to carry the heavier bags and packages. Usually, these trips were quite profitable but the long season away from home and among strangers made her quite homesick at times.

One summer, to assuage her loneliness, she took Ann with her and entrusted her with a special tray of odds and ends to sell. Everybody took to the happy child, for she was only twelve years old with a quick tongue and beguiling manner. They bought her things whether they needed them or not, and then she helped her mother sell the goods she had reserved for herself. It proved an unusually prosperous season.

Next year, however, Mr. Lukacs wanted to resume his place on these business trips. He had gone regularly until little Ann was born. Even then, one summer they took the baby with them. But little Ann became ill and had to be taken home. She told me that she cried all the time until the other passengers in the train begged the father to throw her out of the window. When they reached home, the father bought two milk-goats and raised the baby on their rich milk, giving her coffee suds when this brought on constipation. She did well, for when the mother reached home that fall, she was astonished and delighted to find a healthy, happy child with cheeks like "dawn in those mountains." It became a family joke to remark whenever she became too lively: "The goats are jumping!"

But what to do with little Ann and her two older sisters? Katherine, who was crippled, and Mary six years older. Well, mother had a newly married sister up on the hillside, about four hours walk from their house. They had no children of their own yet and would surely care for the three, especially in view of the fact that mother practically raised her sister and always showered her with gifts. Yes, they promised faithfully.

Mary, twelve years old, took care of the cattle in the pasture. Katherine, ten, and Ann, six, would play together. The girls were duly installed in their summer home and the parents left feeling secure that their little ones were in good hands. How sadly they miscalculated! The little ones were set to work and kept at it all day. They were fed very little and poor food. Uncle was bound to surprise the parents by teaching tiny Ann to read. With a newspaper in front of her and her uncle standing over her with a stick, she was told the words and expected to recognize all of them, once told. Whenever she did not recognize one, whack, down came the stick. Finally, concluding that she was a dull child, he gave it up.

In the same way, if the children didn't care to eat something, uncle picked up his stick and sternly commanded, "Eat." One day while the two sisters were herding the baby geese, it occurred to them that the geese ought to grow faster and therefore eat more. Standing over them with a stick, they commanded them to eat. When they would not, down came the stick. They all died. Never did uncle discover what happened to them.

One day Katherine and Ann washed dolls' clothes in a tiny puddle that flowed down from a spring. This infuriated the uncle and he dragged crippled Katherine by the hair, for he did not dare to beat her, but Ann received a terrible beating that left blood trickling from her buttocks. The aunt wept bitterly and tried to stop the infuriated husband, but in vain.

When the parents arrived home, the aunt sent the children home. Katherine very sick and the other two full of complaints. The uncle said to the parents: "Ann is a dumb child; I tried my best to teach her to read but not a word stuck in her brain." Christmas came and uncle and aunt came to visit them. Father, determined to show off "the dumb child," had his little daughter read a section of the Bible to the uncle. Never again did the parents leave their children with anybody.

"I'll stay home; nobody is going to beat up my children," said the father. But Ann loves to tell the story of the geese, enjoying the bit of dramatic justice she now, as an adult, recognizes in the story.

Shortly before Ann's birth, her father had an unusual conversion experience that led him into the Baptist faith. He happened to be in Vienna, sitting on the steps of a rather modest church, listening to the sermon. The minister was preaching on the text, "Know ye not that ye are the temple of God?" It gripped this stranger who knew German well enough to understand the sermon. He could not shake off the thought: "I am the temple of the holy God! But if I am, I must live a different kind of life." Occasionally, he had gotten drunk, made his wife unhappy, and did things he ought not to have done. He took his bottle of brandy from his coat pocket and threw it into the canal nearby.

Then to his honest, simple mind, the question came, "But how can God live in a smoky house?" He dearly loved his pipe that had given him so much comfort. If only he had heard the sermon after he had smoked the new package of tobacco that he had scarcely started. After a struggle, out came the tobacco, which followed the brandy into the canal. Soon after, he presented himself for membership in that German church where, after they had heard his story, they received him with great joy. The Word of God had its effect even when they knew nothing about it.

Then Mr. Lukacs wrote a letter to his wife informing her of his experience and the new life begun in the Baptist church. They were Lutherans, and knew nothing about the Baptists, not even the meaning of the word back home. She showed his letter to friends and neighbors. They shared her consternation. He was out of his mind, they thought. She must be very careful, for a madman may do anything.

She awaited him with fear. From the time he arrived home, she watched him, his every word and every movement, day and night. Yes, he was a changed man, but he was a better man — much better. After six months of this new life reading the Bible and praying with him, from the heart and not from a prayer book, she too "saw the light" and became a Baptist Christian.

Now the village turned against them. They wanted nothing of the new faith. Persecution followed. Stones were found in the room where the children slept. Once, some neighbors waited behind a tree with axes for the father, determined to exterminate the new faith. Fortunately, they lost their nerve. But when a little brother died, the villagers and the Lutheran priest did not permit the little body to be buried in consecrated ground. It was kept in the Hus Tower, then finally buried outside the cemetery fence.

When little Ann was ready for the Slovak school taught by the Lutheran priest, and she appeared for registration, he asked, "Are you a Baptist?"

"No, but I expect to be when I grow up."

He took her by her hand, led her to the door and literally kicked her out. She ran home, told her father, then asked with shining eyes, "Is that suffering for Jesus, *drahý tatíček* (dear father)?"

"Yes, my child," replied the transported father, "Yes indeed, you suffered for Jesus."

Such was the new faith, powerful, vital, and life-changing. No wonder that soon there was a little chapel for the growing little mission. The Lukacses often entertained visiting preachers, who were enthralled by the merry little girl who was such a devout Christian at twelve. But her life too had changed, most vividly symbolized by the fact that she no longer stole flowers from graves in the village cemetery and in consequence, no longer had to fear the ghosts who came after her at night to make her behave. Nor did she steal the neighbor's fruit.

8 - Liberating Perspectives

"Have you ever thought that God might want you in the Gospel ministry?"

Soon after my conversion, this question was asked over and over again. But how could I consider it seriously since I was the chief breadwinner of the family? For the first time, all of us had new Sunday suits instead of second-hand, with new shoes and dresses. I looked forward to the time when mother could be relieved from her daily burden of cigar making in a stuffy, noisy, stinking shop. However, my pastor, the professors of the Hungarian Baptist Seminary, and others kept stirring up my conscience.

One morning, I started for work and I found myself compelled to go to the pastor instead of work. Rev. Dulity was surprised indeed at my early call. He sensed a crisis, invited me in, and offered breakfast.

"No, thank you. I have something far more important on my mind. I need your advice. I feel God is calling me into His service."

"If that is so, you had better obey."

"But how can I when they depend on me at home and really need me?"

"That I cannot tell you but you must trust and obey."

"It would mean years of schooling and I have no money. We never had even a hundred dollars in the bank until recently. The family can't support me. They will have it hard enough to get along without my earnings."

"Come let us talk to God about it," and kneeling, the pastor led me in a long fervent prayer, telling God about my predicament and entreating Him to grant me faith and courage if indeed this were His will.

As we stood up, my pastor took my hand and, looking deep into my eyes, said earnestly, "If God really wants you He will find a way to make this possible."

I went home. My father, who took care of the housework including the laundry and cooking the meals, looked at me astonished.

"Are you sick, Eddie?"

"No, dad."

"Then what is wrong? You should be at work."

"I know, papa, but I can't. You see God wants me to be a minister."

My poor father! He was speechless. I thought he would have a stroke. In fierce indignation, he lashed out at me in bitter words.

"Here I am, crippled with rheumatism, unable to earn the daily bread for my family, and my eldest son has a crazy dream! And what about your poor mother? Have you no heart for her? Just as I predicted, religion has driven you mad. Do you realize that you are setting the family back to where we were ten years ago?" He went on and on until the agony in my own face stopped him. How could I blame him? He could not understand me. I had faith to buoy me up in this crisis, but he was an atheist or an agnostic. Poor father. It was bad enough for me with my faith!

I went into one of the bedrooms and spent a long time grappling with God. Then I went out into Central Park where I had my painful meditations previous to my conversion. I had no idea how I could break this terrible news to my poor mother even though she, too, was a Baptist Christian by now.

It was a long, bitter evening. Supper was delicious but I had no appetite. To the troubled inquiries of the family, I could answer only in non-committal monosyllables. As I went to bed I called mother and said that I had something very important to tell her. She settled on a chair by my bed and waited, but I could not bring myself to speak. Gently she urged me and finally, I blurted it out.

She gazed at me in wonder. "Was it this you found so hard to tell me?"

"Yes, mother, for I realize full well what my decision means for the family's welfare, but especially for you in that stinking factory."

She placed her hand on my brow and said: "My son, if God has honored me so by calling you into His service, who are we to stand in His way? Have no fear. The same Almighty God who brought us to this blessed land in spite of the frightful difficulties and has seen us through every crisis will stand by us now and provide. Have faith and obey."

I have often wondered about this crisis and tried to analyze it. As in all choices, there must have been several unconscious as well as conscious forces pushing me in this direction. Certainly, I was not conscious of them at the time. Only in the perspective of the years, with added self-knowledge and experiences, do these choices emerge.

In the microcosm of Hungarian Baptists, the ministry carried with it an aura of dignity and holiness that only those who belonged to such a "come-outer" group can adequately appreciate. He was the proclaimer of the divine Word, a shepherd of God's people, the counselor and exemplar to the followers of Jesus. The drama of the pulpit had a great appeal. His position of importance was neutralized only by the strong feeling of democratic equality. He was the first among equals.

Over against the "worldliness" of the shop characterized by the smut, rough behavior, and unlimited cursing of an all-male society, the church was the clean, wholesome, and gentle society of the followers of Christ. To be with them was a relief — the breathing of fresh air, inspiration and strength for living on a higher plane. Yes, I wanted to get out of the disgusting moral climate of the shop.

Undoubtedly, I was ambitious, as revealed by the dream previously reported. I wanted to achieve something admirable and worthwhile, to prove myself, and to make real the possibilities I felt surging within me.

While various aspects of the stained glass trade gave me deep esthetic satisfaction, my lack of manual dexterity made the cutting of glass, especially of intricate pieces, torture. How many lovely, carefully selected pieces I broke! Then the men with whom I worked had to spend a long time hunting through the racks to find another to replace the one I broke.

Often this was only second best. They were usually patient with me but this did not lessen my disgust with myself. Also, like my father, I was slow — driven by my passion for perfection. Then periodically we felt the curse of unemployment. Once I trampled the streets for a month looking for another job, any job, for every week's pay lost meant mounting debts at the butcher, the grocer, and from friends. Finally, I left the city and went to Bridgeport, where I found employment for a few weeks until recalled to Duffner and Kimberly in New York.

Now the die was cast. Materially, my lot would be harder. Most of the pastors were receiving considerably less than I had earned, although the salary came regularly. Mentally, spiritually, perhaps even socially in a limited way, the benefits promised deep satisfaction. I waited for developments.

My pastor escorted me to the offices of the Baptist City Mission Society and the American Baptist Home Mission Society. Doctors Sears' and Brooks' executive secretaries questioned me, were apparently satisfied, and set the wheels in motion to prepare me adequately for my new task. Dr. Brooks wanted me to enter the Hungarian Baptist Seminary in Cleveland, receive a minimum of preparation, and get to work as soon as possible. He was possessed a strong bent for evangelism and was eager to have me at work immediately among the immigrants. Even the three years necessary for this minimal training program were too long for him.

Dr. Sears, on the other hand, insisted on the best education possible. He saw the need for an educated ministry among immigrants in the near future. "You must get your high school first," he insisted, "then go to college before you enter a first-class seminary."

I had my first pangs of discouragement. The program he outlined stretched to eleven years and I was twenty-three already! And I had to leave at the end of the sixth grade in grammar school to help support the family. True, I spent two years in night school, but the courses I took had been a potpourri of various subjects only distantly related to preparation for high school.

My pastor, an unusually perceptive and wise man, encouraged me to follow Dr. Sears' advice. They glimpsed something promising in me that I myself had not discovered.

Dr. Sears promised to try to get me into Townsend Harris Hall, the preparatory department of the City College of New York, where they offered a three-year college preparatory course. How high and exacting the standards were I fortunately did not know, or I may have given up in despair.

Day after day for two weeks, I sat in the outer office of the principal, a big, stout, impressive man with a flowing mustache, who scarcely ever looked at me. Finally, I was summoned into his august presence, granted permission to attend, and was sent to the registrar. I have often wondered what went on behind the scenes during all that time.

My first class was Latin I with Dr. Senftner, a man of small stature with a little mustache and flashing black eyes. Immaculately dressed, he glanced up at me with a severe expression as I presented my registration card.

"You're two weeks late! How will you ever catch up? Well, take a seat. See me after class, and we'll see what can be done."

The class, many of them only twelve-year-olds, looked at me — at this big, adult, ignoramus, starting so late and not even knowing enough to enter in time. I was speechless as always when I suffered injustice. I could have wept with hurt and shame, but I settled down as well as I could and tried to understand what was going on. After class, I went up to the teacher's desk and explained why I was late, told my age and indignantly assured him that I was not there for fun but to work. Well, by the end of the semester I was earning a good grade. Dr. Senftner, this peppery little man, was reconciled. He was strict but fair — an excellent teacher even if inclined to be a martinet.

Then there was Doctor Klein, my excellent professor in English. He dressed formally and always wore a cutaway — or was it a Prince Albert coat? His face reminded me of Shakespeare with his pointed beard. He was an excellent reader and dramatized *A Tale of Two Cities* so that it has lived with me ever since. *Rip Van Winkle, The Sir Roger de Coverly Papers*, and *The Oregon Trail* by Prances Parkman were almost equally interesting. The sufferings of the latter because of a stomach ailment impressed me tremendously. Here was a man who in the face of tremendous odds in illness covered the Wild West and wrote its important story. What an inspiration.

Dr. Shapiro came over from the college, I believe, to teach us Ancient History. He carried a cane, wore pince-nez glasses, and lectured informally with a leg draped over the side of his chair. He was always interesting!

Never had I been a good scholar in arithmetic. Consequently, I dreaded math, but Dr. Schuster was the teacher extraordinary par excellence! He went from student to student, stopping behind each one, and if stuck or on a wrong track he would lead us to the solution. To this day I don't know how he did it. He did not tell us what to do or how to proceed, yet his questions started our minds in the right direction. Neither before nor after have I had such a teacher in mathematics. Bless him! The following year I flunked plain geometry with another teacher who was kind enough, but he could not teach as Dr. Schuster did.

One day, as he was explaining the beauty of mathematics to me (utterly repulsive to me until then), he drew on the blackboard the graph of an algebraic equation. Suddenly, like a light from heaven, it dawned on me the wonderful order of mathematics. I whispered in awe to myself, "God is here!" Seldom, if ever, have I had such a revelation in any other class — not even in the seminary.

Dr. Perl was my professor in Latin II. For some reason — perhaps he too had an immigrant background — he manifested a special interest in me that was very encouraging.

And how could I ever forget another of my instructors, who came as a substitute for only a few days, to teach us *The Ancient Mariner*. He was a short, stoutish person with light blue eyes that shone gently through rimless glasses, and not very impressive or inspiring until he started to read. Not even Dr. Klein had been able to make me forget all else — to almost hypnotize me with his reading. Every class session was a trance. It was a rude awakening when our regular teacher, not Dr. Klein, returned. Heaven forgive me, but I have forgotten his name.

Never again in prep school, college, seminary, or university did I have more inspiring teachers than at Townsend Harris Hall, and seldom as good! My gratitude to them is immeasurable. I can only hope that later on I too meant something like that to my students now and then.

In connection with my hopeless struggles in geometry, I recall two of my classmates very well. Little Reese, who sat on one side, and little Parker on the other — both of them about twelve years old with minds as sharp as razors. They helped me very willingly when a problem seemed insoluble. In their eyes I saw compassion and wonder, and the unspoken question, "You poor, big dumbbell. What are you doing here?" I loved them both and still feel grateful to them.

In free periods between classes, I used to study at the City College Chapel. Again and again, I did not study much because of the glorious music that flowed from the organ under the inspiring touch of an unknown organist. The lovely memory of one especially beautiful chorale still haunts me, perhaps because in church we sang a hymn to the same tune.

Once I saw an academic procession. What dignity, what color, what significance! I watched eagerly for the dear familiar faces of my professors.

It was a hard yet happy struggle. I'd been out of school for nine years and inadequately prepared for high school, especially for Townsend Harris Hall with its high standards and the regular four-year course squeezed into three where they simply threw you out if you did not measure up. I had to study day and night. I remember rising at five and retiring at eleven, but I had a shining goal and an adult appreciation of my opportunity.

Every afternoon on my walk home after classes I made it my business to pass the brownstone front home of my Ann on 120th Street near Lenox Avenue. She lived here with her foster parents who loved her dearly. Mrs. Burkhardt took special pride in dressing her and claimed credit for my falling in love with her. In truth, she deserved considerable credit for it. Ann sat in a window on the third floor waiting for me but coyly disappeared as soon as I rounded the corner. It did not matter. My fatigue disappeared and I continued the long trek home walking on air.

We were engaged by now. We had worked in church and Sunday school together, attended the open air services, suffered persecution together, and attended teacher training classes at Columbia together. Perhaps it was inevitable and surely providential that we developed a noble friendship and genuine affection crowned by the ever-new miracle of love. I had watched her tell Bible stories to children at the street meetings. They crowded around her, spellbound, listening to every word and staying by her until the meeting ended. Her enthusiasm and devotion apparently had no limits. She visited women with incurable diseases until they died. Everywhere she went she brought cheer, hope, and a sense of the presence of Eternal Love. When I hastened after her, she would hurry to the streetcar line and attempt to catch a car for home. The rascal! How I ran to have the privilege of escorting her! It was only after our marriage that she confessed that she had been a schemer. Yet more than once I was offended by her spontaneity, informality, and mischievousness. After a worship service, collecting the tiny glasses used in communion, instead of going around by the partitions from one bench into the other, she simply hopped onto a bench and over the partition, one to the other.

"Why, Miss Lukacs!" I exclaimed in horror at this irreverent behavior.

Once, as I sat at the piano leading the choir, I suddenly found the piano tilting over me. Astonished and frightened, I stood up only to discover that the girls were pushing the instrument. They burst into laughter. It did not help my wounded dignity to learn that my Ann had stirred them up to it. A stern and cutting remark restored order and the rehearsal went on.

After a prayer meeting, Miss Lukacs and her friend pressed an attractive package into my hands. Pleased and expectant, I tore it open to discover only orange peels, but the culprits had vanished. On another occasion after prayer meeting, I found the room full of the smell of perfume. Since this was one of the worldly practices we had been cautioned against, I made inquiries but was unable to find the culprit. I was the last to leave, and as I put on my winter coat it reeked of perfume. No one had to tell me who perpetrated this unseemly joke on me.

"Miss Lukacs," I pleaded the following week, "Please don't play a trick like that on me again! Everywhere I went, every street car I entered, people stared at me wondering who I was. I smelt like a walking perfumery." Those enormous grey eyes looked at me so penitently, yet with a glint of amusement. Then she broke into her merry laughter, which to this day is my best medicine, and I could no longer be angry.

I was escorting her home one evening when I asked her to marry me. It was soon after I had given up my job and started high school. I told her frankly how hopeless my situation was, my education stretched out for seven or eight years ahead. I confessed that it was reckless and wrong of me to ask her to wait for me but I could not endure the uncertainty. Did she care enough for me to give me hope? Could we become engaged? Perhaps she also might go to school, and the years would pass more quickly knowing that we were together in this.

"What would I not give, Brother Kautz, to have you do this in my parents' home in the Old Country! But as my father used to say, 'and she looked at the stars.' The stars are the windows of heaven, and God watches us through them. Let us ask His guidance in this important matter."

I bowed and uncovered my head and both of us prayed earnestly right there on the street that His will be done, and hoping with aching hearts that our union was His purpose indeed. Then she consented to accept and wait for me, but in order to honor our parents, we should ask their consent and blessing as well. Accordingly, I wrote to her parents which she translated into Slovak. Soon their consent and blessings arrived. My parents were fond of Ann already and gladly gave their blessing.

They were horrified, however, to learn that we did not intend to marry soon — perhaps not for years. And Ann go to school? What for? Women did not need an education to keep house, bring up children and do women's work! We should marry soon and use what resources we had to set up our home. Everywhere we found this reaction to our plan, on the part of church members and ministers alike. Idealism was all right but this was foolishness! Nor did Hungarian Baptists approve of long engagements. They were realists, and were aware of the perils.

Only our pastor approved. He knew from observation and experience what an educated wife can mean to a minister. He spoke to Dr. Sears who also approved our plan. But the closely-knit spiritual family of our mission church was offended. They were about to summon us to explain how we had dared to proceed so far without consulting them. Our pastor kindly and tactfully explained this to us, assuring us that he himself did not agree with them, yet how nice it would be if we asked for their forgiveness and consent in a few words. This we did and the church approved, aided no doubt by our pastor's wise efforts behind the scenes and his reminder of our devotion and constant good work in the life of the church and the loss the mission would sustain if they excommunicated us, for our English-speaking brothers would be only glad to welcome us.

My Ann was a very courageous girl. She had left her parents at fifteen with the eager adolescent spirit of adventure, full of ambition to succeed in the new and wonderful world, America.

"Why, *tatíčko* (daddy) and *mamička* (mommy)," she consoled them, "in a few years I'll be rich and come back to take care of you."

But it was a heartbreaking experience for them. Of the nine children, she was the only one left at home. Seven had died and Anna's older sister was in America and not getting rich at all, no, not at all. Papa Lukacs threw himself upon her as the carriage stopped at the railroad station and wept bitterly, "Jacob had twelve sons but only one Joseph. I am losing my Joseph. Woe is me!" he wailed.

In New York, she had a difficult time. She had the stature of a child of eight and no one wanted to employ her. Finally, the brethren found her a place in an Irish family on the west side. The mother was mortally ill with cancer and they needed somebody to wait on her while her grown children were at work. She soon fell in love with this merry child, taught her English, and made her son — who worked in a bank — fan her burns caused by an accident in their home, when he came home. But sometime later the old lady died and little Anna had to find another home.

Providence watched over her, she is certain, for she soon found another home with a German-Swiss family. Here too, because of her sunny disposition, hard work, and winsome ways she soon became a daughter to Mrs. Burkhardt. Both Mr. and Mrs. Burkhardt took great pleasure in feeding her and dressing her. In fact, Mrs. Burkhardt sewed for her and even had naps with her. Whenever she saw pretty materials for dresses she bought them, and being a clever seamstress, made them for Anna. Soon she was the best-dressed girl in the church — healthy and strong with round rosy cheeks and intriguing dimples. In her new home, she learned to read English by means of the daily newspaper — a slow, tedious method.

But now she was readying herself for another flight — another adventure. She had always wanted an education and now came the opportunity. Dr. Sears saw to it that she was accepted at the Baptist Missionary Training School in Chicago. But now, she too had to fight her American foster parents. Didn't she know that home missionary pastors were poor as church mice? She would live in poverty for the rest of her life. And so many things could happen while she and I were separated by one thousand miles for at least three years while she received her training. And, at five feet eight inches tall and weighing only one hundred twenty-six pounds, they'd thought I must have tuberculosis. Was she going to spend the slowly accumulated savings of five years on schooling and start her married life on nothing? A girl owed a dowry to her betrothed. Why not stay with them and continue to save until I was ready to marry her? We would have a better start financially, at least.

Thank heavens, the urge to know, to advance, to keep pace with me was so strong that she could not be discouraged. The Sears' were delighted.

"You know Anna, the first time we saw the two of you in the Hungarian church, we said to each other that you belong together and hoped that you would marry each other." Such an insight from discerning and important people strengthened our decision, and we fought off, not too easily, those who would have disheartened us.

It was a very depressing experience for me when I said farewell to her at the Erie station. I wept bitterly and so did her foster mother. But not Anna, for she was off to school, for the first time out of New York City, thrilled to see new places, away from the humdrum daily routine of housekeeping and eager to see more of America.

She had a wonderful time on the train. Everybody was so pleasant and kind to the little foreigner. An Adventist missionary attached himself to her and gladly shared her food. Her new country seemed boundless. For twenty-four hours the train triumphantly puffed its way on the shining steel highway up and down lovely mountains, which reminded her of the Carpathians — the crossroads, rivers and fertile plains where everything grew in abundance, such as she had never seen before. Friends in Buffalo took her to see a great miracle, Niagara Falls. Finally, she arrived at the great metropolis, Chicago, on the inland sea — Lake Michigan.

She plunged into her studies with the same dedication that she carried into everything. How she needed it! She had only six years of schooling in Hungary and here she was in the same classes with high school and college graduates. She had to take a special course in English to learn grammar and composition, which she had never had. By the end of the first year, she was proficient enough to earn the praise of her president, Dr. Behan. In other courses, there were kind friends who gladly shared their class notes with her, two other girls, one American born of Slovak parents and the other a Czech graduate of the University of Prague who helped to interpret the unusual vocabulary and style of textbooks. In the life of Christ she received the highest mark. The teacher confided to her that the dean lectured her on such "impropriety, for how did it look for a foreigner to receive the highest mark?"

One day the three Czechoslovak girls visited the seminary nearby where young men were trained for home missionary work in America among their own people. As she was introduced to the president, he looked at her curiously.

"I knew a family with that name in the Old Country," he said, "and you remind me so much of Mrs. Lukacs, your rapid speech, your mannerisms."

She laughed merrily. "Yes, she was my mother."

Then one of her friends whispered into his ear, "she is engaged to be married to a Hungarian."

President Kralicek's eyes blazed. "Hungarian? This girl whom I cradled in my arms? Why, I'd rather have her marry a Black man than a Hungarian!"

She was thunderstruck. A Christian leader spoke these words! Her simple, unschooled father was a far better Christian. Did he not write her, "I do not care if you marry any man, only be sure he is a Christian!"

For the next few weeks, her two friends argued with her every day, trying to make her break her engagement to a hated Hungarian until she threatened to have nothing more to do with them. Only then did they desist. About ten years later one of them spent a couple of days with us. Ann asked her, "How do you like my Hunkie husband?"

She replied, "Find me another like him and I'll marry him tomorrow."

The Fundamentalist-Modernist controversy in the Northern Baptist Convention was at its height even as in other Protestant bodies. The

Fundamentalists held to a literalistic and unscientific interpretation of the Scriptures while the Modernists were committed to an acceptance of the findings of science and insisted on treating the cosmology of the Bible as out of date and fitting the time in which the Scriptures were written. The controversy was complicated by application of the teachings of Jesus to a modern industrial society, the "Social Gospel," that threatened the unconscionable profits and autocratic management of industry that many Modernists espoused. The Fundamentalists were always fighting and calling names, fighting for "the faith once for all delivered unto the saints." On the other hand, some Modernists went to the other extreme and had but little faith left. It was a struggle of great complexity — very bewildering to the average church goer who was strongly swayed by the ancient phrases and theological language to which they had been accustomed from childhood. Churches were split, students walked out of schools, new seminaries were founded, families split, missions suffered, and a feeling of mistrust poisoned relations between Christians, much as Americans mistrust each other now because of the fear of Communism.

This evil spirit struck Ann's school too. Because a professor taught that the Old Testament story of creation was not to be taken literally, students marched out and continued their education elsewhere. While Ann sympathized with them because of her own very conservative background, she admired her teachers and the president too much to doubt their Christian devotion. Her own heart was broken as she looked at the sad face of her beloved President Behan. Perhaps, unconsciously, she was helped by the remembrance of her father — a simple, unschooled Christian reading Darwin. It may also be that in her subconscious there still lurked the doubts of her childhood, when she saw some scattered bones buried in a common grave, knowing that in time they would turn to dust. How could these bones be assembled again on Resurrection Day? "Nothing is impossible to God!" her fundamentalist friends replied.

At any rate, she stayed, but we still treasure the agonizing letters we exchanged about the new teaching, the new Bible disciplines, and the new trends in theology. They were not very learned discussions but they were earnest, painful, and determined gropings of Christians trying to adjust to what new world science was revealing to mankind.

She learned to play hymns on the piano — mainly, she said, to be able to accompany her fiance, who was something of a singer and made good use of it through the years in many other and varied situations.

9 - Life in a Prep School

It was dark when I got off the train in Mountour Falls, NY. Since no one was there to greet me, I asked the station attendant about the way to Cook Academy. Leaving my trunk and carrying my heavy valise, I began my rather long walk to the school, stopping often to rest my aching arms. I met no one and it was a lonely walk up a tree-lined road amidst the mysterious whispers of their branches and the unaccustomed sounds of nature — crickets, frogs and who knows what else.

It was September, and above me stretched the vast vault of the heavens. Under city lights one never saw this, and a sense of awe rose within me, adding to the mystery all about me. I was afraid. Soon, however, I reached the academy building. I climbed up the steps into the gloomy hallway wondering where I might eat or sleep that night, then heard faint echoes of human noises. Carefully picking my way in the darkness, I slowly made my way toward the sound. At my knocking, a short, slight, balding man in his thirties opened the door, recognized a new student in me and invited me in. It was Principal Hanke who became one of my staunchest friends.

"Welcome to Cook Academy. Why didn't you write us when you were coming? You are a day early."

"Yes, sir, I know, but I thought I had better come earlier to get adjusted a bit before classes begin. It was rather spooky for a big city boy walking through the dark streets, but I did not want to inconvenience others."

"Well, well. Have you had your supper yet?" Without waiting for an answer he called for Mrs. Hanke. "Could you get supper for a hungry man?"

She did, and soon I was telling them the story of my life. Then they led me to a guest room and, although the deafening silence of the countryside kept me awake for a while, I finally fell asleep.

The next day — or was it two days later — the others arrived. Many of them were older boys, although none quite my age, about twenty-four, except Crawshaw, who was around thirty. Consequently, I felt more at home even though we had a few twelve-year-olds, both boys and girls, for this was the public high school for the town as well.

Quite a few of the older boys had religious vocations in mind. The resident group generated a strong moral and spiritual climate along with the principal and professors, nearly all of whom were faithful church members. It did not take long for about eight of us to form a group that met on Saturdays for a Bible study and prayer. We usually had ten to twelve at our meetings, inviting others who might be interested. After a brief meditation on a Scripture passage by one of us and voluntary comments by whoever desired to ask a question, tell an experience, or add further words of explanation or exhortation, we dropped on our knees and spoke our individual prayers as we felt. Then we went around the circle, shook hands with each other with a fervent "God bless you," a custom imported by me from the Hungarian Baptist Mission. All of us were benefited and kept these meetings going for the entire year.

One day a young man from Venezuela joined us. He spoke very poor English and came to Cook in order to brush up on it. He did not know how long he would stay. We invited him to our informal worship, had our brief ritual as usual, and left. At his request, we invited him the following week also. As we were about to rise from our knees, our South American friend broke into a torrent of words. Though we did not understand a word, we were deeply moved, for we felt that they came from the heart. And as we stood to shake hands, he rushed from one to the other, taking our hands in both of his, thanking us, informing us that he was a Roman Catholic and never had an experience like this. He also told us that he was a newspaperman and that he would write an article for his paper on his experience and our replies to his questions. After a few days, he left the school but the thrilling memory of this never faded from my memory.

The local pastor, who was a kind of chaplain for the Academy, once came to visit the students. After several knocks at the door, he entered the room where he found one of us on his knees, praying out loud for his fellow students. He quietly closed the door and left, but the following Sunday he wove this experience into his sermon with great effect.

A few boys were sent to our school by their parents to be protected or straightened out. They were placed with older, more stable students who unobtrusively watched over them and guided or helped them with their studies. One of them was sent by missionary parents on foreign field. He was a nice, friendly chap, but incurably lazy and sleepy all the time. It mattered not that he was awakened by his roommate. Then, the morning bell rang. He never came down to breakfast. One morning his roommate simply turned the bed over. The sleeper never appeared. After breakfast, several members of the Senior Governing Board went to his room and found him lying on the floor with his bed on top of him. Pitchers of cold water and a good paddling failed to cure him. Finally, they carried him in his sheet at midnight to a bathtub filled with icy water and dipped him repeatedly until he screamed his pledge to reform. He was better after that. Poor fellow! Was he ill or homesick or an escapist from the demands of school life? I never discovered.

We had a playboy also, whose parents paid all of the school expenses for his roommate, who tried to keep him out of bad company, available even in a little town, and to inspire him to prepare his homework.

Another chap never took his shower with the rest of us. After a long time, he revealed to one of the group that he was a hermaphrodite and that his mother made him promise never to undress before others. His oddities were easier to understand after we knew this. We kept his secret. He came from a fine Christian family and their boy's condition must have been a terrible burden to them.

There was little Stefi, about five feet three inches tall, about my age, short-sighted and wearing a pince-nez with thick lenses. He was slow of mind but possessed terrible patience and persistence. He and I often did our lessons together. It was a trial for me because of my nimble mind, and for him as well, on account of my bursts of impatience. One evening I exploded, "Stefi, you are so stupid!"

Gazing at me with his patient, kind eyes he responded, "I know, Kautzie, I am sorry."

I could have crawled under the table for shame. The incident haunted me for years. In reality, it was the old story of the hare and the tortoise, for he achieved what I never did, becoming a physician with an office in the Medical Arts Building of Omaha. I still have not earned a doctorate. His career was a credit not only to him but to America as well, for he was an immigrant boy, and to home missions, for it was a missionary who became acquainted with him on the street near Mariner's Temple in downtown New York and invited him to Sunday school. He had no parents, but lived with an uncle whose child he cared for and wheeled about in a baby carriage all day. This missionary discovered a real spiritual and mental hunger in the ragged boy and befriended him until, as a Christian, he found himself at Cook Academy. Later, at Colgate University, he cleaned bushels of potatoes every day and attended several furnaces all through the bitter winter of the Chenango Valley, where snowstorms stopped rail traffic and the thermometer went down to 30 below zero. He did many other odd jobs to make ends meet. And when he had done all this, he found time to come to our house and help my wife with the stove and with our baby. A Prince of the Kingdom was he, my simple, unassuming, slow-moving, hard-working, and laboriously-thinking Christian brother. His memory is enshrined in our hearts.

One individual in our intimate circle had an agonizing problem. He felt God's call to the Gospel ministry and decided to obey. At the same time, he was in love with a girl whose father was a minister, but who never caught the vision of Christian service. She resented her family's poverty and the abuse of her father by inconsiderate members lacking in understanding and kindness. When she learned that the boy intended to become a minister, she told him plainly that they were through unless he changed his mind. Many an evening did the two of us slip away from the others into one of the classrooms and pour out our ardent prayers for guidance, courage, and strength. The Lord's will prevailed. The boy became an important minister.

In view of all that the Academy meant to me physically and spiritually, it is very rude of me, and I greatly regret to state that the faculty was inferior to that in Townsend Harris Hall. They were earnest, compassionate, hard-working men but apparently lacking in basic potential, skill, and ability to inspire the students. Yet I owe a great debt of gratitude to one of them who enabled me to do two years of Latin in that one year by giving me the extra time for the second course in the evenings. It was a small school, limited in its financial resources in spite of the aid it received from the state for opening its doors as a high school for that district.

Cook Academy was a military school with a daily drill in the chapel, which doubled as a gymnasium as well. World War I was on and President Wilson was readying the country for the awful plunge into the fiery abyss. One morning, in the absence of Principal Hanke, our vice principal led the daily chapel service. He was an ordained Methodist minister and an eloquent speaker. His name was Wilson unless my memory fails me. Using Scripture as a point of departure for his sermon, he began with a splendid appeal for fuller dedication to Christ and ended with a fiery appeal for self-sacrificing patriotism. We were only days away from a declaration of war on the Central Powers. He informed us and told us how the President needed the assurance of every American's support. Then he suggested a motion to the effect that we send President Wilson a telegram assuring him of our support in whatever our nation faced.

My mind raced through the implications of this act and my heart beat wildly as I realized that I would not be able to go along. I was a follower of Christ and, as such, it was inconceivable that I could approve of war and the slaughter of His brethren, for whom He died.

The motion was made, the question put, and a standing vote taken. It was unanimous, almost. I sat. Mr. Wilson glared at me and made a still more fiery speech, denouncing all who come to this country and do not appreciate it. At least they could show their respect for America, by saluting the flag and singing "My country, 'tis of thee." I did not hesitate for I loved my adopted country and was profoundly grateful for the opportunities she had given to me. Now I was a marked man in the student body and was challenged daily to explain and defend my point of view. At two weekly YMCA meetings, I had to debate with the student body and faculty the position of a Christian in wartime! Had it not been for the little fellowship of prayer, I might not have had the courage to struggle through this, but they knew me well, trusted me and encouraged me even though they did not share my views.

Soon after, I felt driven to the decision to give up military drill. I turned in my rifle and informed Student Lieutenant Lightfoot of my decision. He was very stern, refused to deal with me, and sent me to Principal Hanke. Refusing to obey orders may mean expulsion. What would I do then? How would I face all the good and important people who were making my education possible, one of them, a Mr. Treat, in far-off California? But there was no honorable way out so I went to see Principal Hanke. He was very kind and tried to reason with me.

"Did you know that Cook was a military school?"

"Yes, I did."

"Do you think it is fair to suddenly defy the school rules under which we accepted you?"

"Apparently not; but I did not realize all they involved."

"What do you propose to do about it?"

"I do not know. I only know that even by the wildest stretch of my imagination, I cannot picture Jesus plunging a bayonet into a soldier, who probably was the least responsible for the war."

"Didn't God take sides against His people's enemies in the Old Testament?"

"It certainly is so declared."

"Are you superior to God?"

"Indeed not, but Jesus gave us a different conception of God, and I am a follower of Jesus."

"Don't you love this country that adopted you?"

"Yes, well enough to give my life for her but not well enough to engage in wholesale, undiscriminating slaughter for her."

"The school may have to dismiss you. Are you ready for that?"

"It would break my heart and I am willing to work my head off if I am permitted to stay."

"You pay no tuition. We provided a scholarship and work for you. How about that?"

"I feel like an ingrate, and I could not blame you for expelling me, but God have mercy on me! I cannot continue with military drill because it means supporting preparations for activities that my conscience and Jesus and what the Father of all men condemns."

He dismissed me and for the next few days, I could hardly eat or sleep. Glum looks, challenges, mutterings, and threats followed me to class, meals, to church, everywhere. One of the most winsome Christians who was one of the older students, Phillips, asked me one morning, "Mr. Kautz, if the President himself called on you to join the army, would you refuse?"

"Yes, Phillips, I would have to."

"Then, I don't think you are a Christian," and walked away.

I looked at him in amazement. What a strange conglomeration of patriotism and religion. Where was his supreme loyalty? With his nation or with the Father of all mankind? I could have laughed and cried.

Poor Principal Hanke was on the spot. He and his wife were of German descent, and like so many of our best citizens, under suspicion because of the fevers generated by war. Everything they did or said was viewed through the dark spectacles of suspicion and fear. Nor was malicious prevarication omitted. For instance, in the accusation that he raised the American flag upside-down! It was ridiculous, for this daily ritual was carried out by our student soldiers. He had to spend a major portion of his speech at a festive social occasion defending himself against the accusation of prejudiced super-patriots. And now he had me on his hands, a young man of Hungarian birth, whose native land and America may soon be at war! Fortunately for me, calm and Christian voices on the Board prevailed and I was permitted to stay.

We had a fine football team, mainly I suspect because of the higher age and greater weight of our boys. We had our celebrations, hikes up Havana Glen, Christian youth conferences, and periodic rough-housing, that did not always spare our professors. One day, thoughtlessly, they all went to a party. In no time, the ringleaders, among them some of the best boys, planned a raid on the professors' rooms. They shifted their furniture around, sometimes exchanging pieces in the various rooms, hung their belongings on chandeliers, folded sheets so that they could not get into bed, placed thumb tacks on chairs, scattered salt and flypaper on the floors and screwed loose the light bulbs. These were some of the tricks they played on the unsuspecting faculty. When they arrived, none of us were to be seen; lights out, all of us in bed. Soon we heard mutterings, the noises of moving furniture, hurried steps in the hallways and whispered conferences. Suddenly, from next door a raw oath ripped the silence. Our math professor had stepped on flypaper. Bedlam broke loose as our professors rushed in from one door to the next demanding the names of the culprits and finding only yawning, innocent, and ignorant students who in turn inquired what all the excitement was about and joined the faculty in restoring a semblance of order to their living quarters.

10 - The Challenge of College

Among the rolling hills of central New York in the Chenango Valley lies the town of Hamilton. Its tree-lined streets, well-kept houses and gardens, the pretty square or commons, the Baptist church with its impressive gate and little gold-domed tower keeping guard over the morals of the inhabitants, and finally the hill, crowned with the buildings of Colgate University, made a pretty college town. It appealed to me at first sight and as we made our way over the willow path by the pond and up the hill to Eaton Hall I felt the challenge of a new life. This building, Colgate Seminary, was referred to humorously, if not with a touch of contempt, as the Angel Factory by the other students.

Once again Dr. Charles H. Sears, executive secretary of the Baptist City Mission Society of New York City, prepared my way. I was aching with desire to begin my vocation, for I was almost twenty-six by now and I resented the apparent necessity of spending at least seven years at college and seminary in preparation for my task. Many others in the Northern Baptist Convention must have felt the same way and were entering Bible Schools with their shorter courses and more extensive studies in the English Bible. Also, seminaries were increasingly suspect because of their courses in "lower" and "higher" criticism, and their efforts to come to terms with science. But my confidence in Dr. Sears and his mediation for a scholarship and the experiment at Colgate University with a new course degree, that would take only four years, led me to enter this school.

The new course was established in order to attract young men who otherwise might enroll in Bible Schools. It offered a Bachelor of Theology degree, comparing in scholastic value with a B.A. or a B.S. The course offered a broad introduction to the major areas of our culture:

history, economics, science, psychology, sociology, literature, music, debating and oratory with a major in theology. I found it adequate. It drew some very capable men, at least one of whom at this writing is dean of one of the oldest and best theological institutions, Harvard Divinity School.

Practically all of us were dependent on the scholarship offered by the Baptist Board of Education of New York. Very few of us were married and our modest stipend was just about enough to see us through if we were frugal.

All of our non-theological courses were taken in the regular college classes, with no such advantages as football players could lean on. I recall, with gratitude, Dr.. Brigham in geology, Dr. Smith, nicknamed "precisely" because of his constant use of that word, Miss Ingersoll and Myers in public speaking, and a dapper professor with an officer's well-kept mustache who taught us economics.

Soon the findings of geology and biology came into a head-on collision with the pre-scientific world view of the Bible; I ran into no end of trouble. Which was right? Science was supported by all the techniques and laboratories of science and the great men who sought to find objective answers to the phenomena of our vast universe and of the no-less-wonderful world within us. But the Bible was the revelation of God, Creator of it all. How presumptuous to question it? And if one questioned parts of it, could the rest be accepted? If parts of it were not to be relied on then what became of revelation and consequently of one's salvation? Yet my own personal religious experience was a fact too, a fact of tremendous significance for it had saved me from despair and had given me new hope, new strength, new courage and new significance to my life. Perhaps my theological studies would straighten me out. In the meantime, uncertainty, doubts, and bewilderment were taking possession of me and mine was an unhappy state indeed.

Dr. Sterrett was our professor of theology. His was a mind of the first water: logical, consistent, and profound. But as I listened to his lectures my consternation increased. It is not possible to describe what happened. I can only say that his lectures were a series of quakes that made me feel there was no firm foundation for anything I believed in. Fighting for my very life, I fiercely challenged his statements. I knew my Bible well and I challenged him at almost every point in his lectures, throwing Bible quotations at him. Some of my classmates became very impatient with me and did not hesitate to express their disgust at what they considered to be my obstructionist tactics. Not so my wise, kind professor. He listened to me with unfailing patience. Coming off the platform, standing before me and trying over and over again from various angles to explain and make palatable this new teaching. In the end, I considered him to be the most inspiring teacher at the seminary, but the end was a long way off. In the meantime, I was a terrible gadfly.

My introductory course in the Old Testament was of no help. It only multiplied my problems and sharpened them to an unbearable degree. A few of us, three or four, decided to have an informal prayer after these two classes asking for divine guidance and, with the best intentions, pray for our professors as well. One of us, a converted rabbi, used all his rabbinic logic to confound these heretical professors without effect. He decided not to risk his faith and left the school.

It was my good fortune that, in the Dean of the seminary, Dr. Vichert, I found a conservative Christian whom I could trust. He was thoroughly sympathetic to the new disciplines but rooted firmly in the Christian faith. He was kind enough to invite me to his home where we had a long talk. I told him that I was almost at the point of leaving because I did not wish to lose my faith that had meant so much to me.

"Have you stopped praying?" he asked

"No, sir."

"Have you stopped reading your Bible?"

"No, sir."

"Well, I have no fear for the men who continue to pray and read their Bible. If you can be patient with us, I can assure you that in due time your faith will rest on broader and deeper foundations than before. Stay on with us if you possibly can. I am sure you will not regret it."

I stayed. The worship services in the local Baptist church helped me a great deal. Here were no questions of criticism, "low" or "high," but great affirmations of the Christian faith by the eloquent interim minister, Dr. Lawrence, who had known personally that spiritual and homilitical giant, Charles Haddon Spurgeon of England. It was a delight to sit in his class and listen to his recollections, experiences and wise advice. Once I asked him if it was necessary to feel nervous before a sermon and exhausted after it, or was this simply a matter of the neophyte's inexperience? In reply, he told us about having Spurgeon preach in Dr. Lawrence's famous church in Brooklyn, NY. After the service, they had dinner together. In the course of the conversation, Dr. Lawrence told him about his own nervousness when he faced his congregation, sometimes verging on panic, and asked this world-famed preacher if he was afflicted that way.

"Have you noticed my foot on the chair in back of me, while I was preaching?"

"Yes, and I wondered about the reason for it."

"Well, it is simply that it has a tendency to tremble so that I need to put my full weight on it. Oh yes, I feel as you I do about facing a congregation."

"So," continued Dr. Lawrence, "don't expect an easy time. True preaching takes something out of you and if it costs little it is not worth much."

Since then I have learned that it is not only preachers who have this experience but singers, actors, politicians, and all who I face the public. A certain amount of tension before a public appearance is necessary for success.

I wonder if I was the first Hungarian student at Colgate. Another boy from New York City, the offspring of a fine ministerial family in the Reformed Church of Hungary, entered during my second or third year. Poor fellow! He was not a ministerial student and received no aid. His mother was a poor widow and he had a terrific struggle to earn his living. He soon developed a nervous twitch. Finally, a breakdown compelled him to leave. Poor boy! He did not have the backing that I enjoyed.

While he was still with us, our home was open to him for relaxation and an occasional meal. One evening he invited me to go to a movie with him. I was immersed in my studies and asked him to take my wife instead, especially since she was tied to the house most of the day with our newborn baby. They left, had a good time, and, on their return, I invited him in. Soon we were engaged in an animated discussion. I did not hear the restlessness of the baby two rooms away but my wife did. She actually rushed in on another occasion because she had heard a safety pin open! She became increasingly unhappy. Finally, in a stage whisper and in Hungarian, she blurted out, "Why don't you tell him to go home? Don't you hear the baby?"

"Thank you, Mrs. Kautz," Zoltan replied, "I am going."

She blushed furiously and apologized. She had forgotten that he was Hungarian and had indulged in our customary tactics among our American friends. He was a good boy and readily forgave us.

One day, I was invited to a church function to give an address on Hungary. It was a challenge. I drew upon the glorified, rather chauvinistic history they had taught me in Budapest, even as we still do in this blessed land, and delivered my speech with flaming enthusiasm. The next day, President Bryan greeted me on his daily walk with, "And how is the glorious Hungarian this morning?" For a week or two after, Dr. Burnham, our famous Hebrew scholar and a dignified gentleman of the old school always in formal attire for his class, stopped for additional information about the history of Hungary. At my suggestion, he finally bought the only history available, *The Story of Hungary* by Dr. Vambery, the famous scholar. I confess it was pleasant to rise from anonymity to a recognizable personage.

Slowly, I began to see light as I traveled through the long tunnel of doubt and bewilderment. Dr. Anderson, nicknamed "the mystic," and Dr.

Estes, both in the field of the New Testament, constructive and positive, were of great help. Dr. Crawshaw's lectures on Wordsworth, Tennyson and Browning were like infusions of new blood into my spiritual veins. They too had struggled with the doubts arising out of science and the new humanism and had achieved victory over them. I still treasure my textbooks on the great poets, underlined and scribbled on many a page, preserving "Craw's" wise and pungent remarks, witticisms and warnings. What a teacher! His lectures on Shakespeare held me enthralled. The class sessions were always too short. He read extensively from the great plays with great effect. Not until then had I realized the splendors of the English language. It was a revelation, but we had playboys and roughnecks who came to his classes because he was famous and it was the thing to do. Sometimes "Craw" had a difficult time quieting them down for his lecture. On one occasion he shouted a thunderous, "SHUT UP!" and in the startled silence, he continued the line from Shakespeare with a twinkle through his gold-rimmed glasses. He had used the Bard to call his class to order. He wiped his Shakespearean mustache and beard and continued. His classes kept growing until only the chapel was large enough to hold them. Now some of our ambitious young men lay down in the back benches for naps to make for the sleep they had missed the night before. I often wonder if "Craw" ever discovered them.

In view of my present interest in economics and history, I do not understand my lukewarm interest and almost no recollection of these courses. We used Richard T. Ely's new text on economics, rather radical for that day, but in view of my own bitter reactions in these areas during my adolescence in New York City, I was not impressed.

In history, I have only a vague recollection of a disorderly class in which our short, stout, unimpressive teacher stood up front and talked fast to keep us busy with note-taking and to keep the class from talking and cutting up. He was very kind to me personally and gave me two of his own books that I kept for years. My lack of interest in history applied to both the sacred and the profane. Perhaps my professors did not measure up to their opportunities.

Sometimes I think of the "he-men" on the campus as bullocks, full of physical vitality and strength, but with a rather tepid interest in things of the mind. And yet this must be a wrong impression since we turned out a good number of men who made their mark on the life of the nation and the world. However, their class behavior was such that I keep marveling at the patience of our professors. I never saw such behavior at Colgate in a far more permissive age. Was it due perhaps to the absence of the gentler sex?

Such was the situation in my classes in sociology. Our professor stood up front to call the roll, and nobody paid any attention. He too resorted to speed to quiet us and make some impression on us. Was it in this class that one of the boys flung the core of an apple at him? No, it would not be, for the professor caught it in midair and flung it back. The class howled. No, Dr. F. was too mild for that. But it happened! He too was very kind to me. Though my term paper was ten days late, he gave me a mark of excellence. Maybe my essay deserved it, but he should have penalized some for my tardiness.

My very brief experience in public speaking and singing was altogether delightful. My young professor had me on his mind for the debating team but the need to eke out a living over and above my scholarship, especially after my marriage and still in college, erased that opportunity.

Since I was blessed with a sweet, weak, tenor voice, Dr. Hoerner saw in me the promise of a soloist in the church choir and glee club and gave me special lessons. How well I remember his teaching me to run up and down the scale with the outlandish word, "Hnaw, hnaw, hnaw," that he repeated in a strong nasal tone overemphasizing it in order to give me the insight. One day, sitting at the piano doing this and other vocal exercises, my voice suddenly broke into a new dimension of quality I never dreamed it had. I put my head on the piano and wept for joy. I sang a few solos in church, but alas, again the need to earn a living ended my hope for making the glee club. Dr. Hoerner was deeply disappointed and so was I. This double disappointment depressed me for a while, but my calling to the ministry was a source of comfort and strength.

11 - Blow Bugles, Blow

The pistol shot in a god-forsaken little town called Sarajevo in the Bosnian province of the Austro-Hungarian Monarchy that killed the heir to the throne, Franz Ferdinand, and his wife, had very faint reverberations in this blessed land. Our newspapers cashed in on it as usual, emphasizing the drama and giving little insight concerning the total situation. One crown prince less in this world — who cared? Not I, certainly. It was good to be away from the caste-like class distinctions of the Old World — its militarism, its prancing aristocrats and generals, its worldly ecclesiastics who were the spiritual support of the status quo, its armament races, and its poverty.

Not even our history teachers in college told us that we were living in a new world that had shrunk so much that distant parts of it were closer to us than Boston to New York during our revolution, in terms of communication. They did not teach us that our world was now like a vast bowl of jelly — touch it at one spot and quivers run all through it.

The pistol shot exploded the accumulated political and economic rivalries of the European empires and the explosive grievances of oppressed nationalities. In a very few years, the horrible magnet of war drew helpless human beings by the millions to distant fields of battle to fertilize alien soils with their blood. But everywhere the soldiers departed to the frantic cheers of the people who pelted them with flowers and to the stirring marches of military bands, with flags flapping bravely in the breeze, numberless bayonets gleaming in the sun as, rank upon rank, they marched happily through the excited multitudes. It was a splendid show to the civilians who were sure that their brave men would soon return as victorious heroes. Then came the filth and blood of the trenches and in "no man's land" the rotting carcasses of homo sapiens, the unforgettable stench and horror, and the periodic enervating boredoms that slowly drowned out the pomp and glory.

We had mixed feelings about it. This was not our war. Europe was three thousand miles away. Why should we interfere? Didn't President Washington warn us to keep free of the imbroglios of Europe? Anyhow, if they would have had enough sense to unite, as we did, they could have solved their problems peacefully.

But the powerful, probably irresistible forces of our shrinking world tugged at us, pushed us, forced us into this world conflagration. Not the least of these forces were the dreams of our adopted citizens from Europe: Poles, Czechs, Slovaks, Romanians, Serbs, Croats, Slovenians, Latvians, Letts, and others. They longed for liberation, freedom, and union with their compatriots while separated by artificial boundaries and foreign states. Their longings coincided with our ideals of democracy, consent of the governed, and justice. Their leaders here and abroad started movements to aid their struggling compatriots and influence our statesmen in their favor. The Czech, Slovak, and Moravian cultural societies, for example, called a meeting of their people in Pittsburgh, Pa., and under the leadership of Masaryk drew up a constitution for the new state of Czechoslovakia — a state that had no previous existence. Dr. Masaryk won President Wilson to their side, and a new state was born — a European state in far off America!

Nor were Americans impervious to the blandishments of military glory. Our Revolutionary War, the unending wars with the Indians, the Mexican War, our Civil War, the Spanish-American War, and the consequent "destiny" to expand, not to speak of Dollar Diplomacy and its implications, all conditioned us for the adventure of war.

And there was our great president Woodrow Wilson. His eloquent pleas for "war against war," "to make the world safe for democracy," "the self-determination of the people," to mention a few of his ideals struck fire in our American hearts along with a deep sympathy for the English people whose traditions enriched our nation so much, and for the French who aided us in our struggle for independence. We inevitably drifted into war.

Our enthusiasm for war matched that of Europe a few years previously. It was a lark — a picnic — a high adventure. We "forgot our troubles and smiled, smiled, smiled." We sang our war songs and, while certain of victory, marched jauntily "with the Cross of Jesus going on before." We were going to turn back the beast of Berlin and avenge the atrocities of the Huns on women and children. There was a high vision, a glorious purpose, and the fiery zeal of a Crusade.

I suppose I shall never forget the great parade up Fifth Avenue with its countless bands filling the avenue with martial music, neat attractive Red Cross nurses and their clean, inviting lorries. The rhythm of endless lines of marching bayonets sparkling in the sun led by gallant officers sitting erect on their prancing horses. The dashing cavalry, rumbling cannons, flags flapping proudly in the breeze, and the prophet of the New World with gleaming glasses and broad smiles, tipping his high silk hat to the ecstatic crowds. Oh, it was a brave, never-to-be-forgotten sight — the pomp and the glory!

How could I help but feel the tug of all this on my emotions? My adopted country automatically excused me as a seminarian from serving in the armed forces. As a Christian pacifist, I was glad at first. But I loved the land that had adopted me and was presenting me with opportunities scarcely to be dreamed of in my native land. Gratitude was always a strong motive with me, and now that America was in peril I could not deny the obligation to serve her in some direct and immediate fashion. Waiving aside the objections of my Christian conscience, I decided to waive my theological exemption and volunteer for service in the Medical Corps. When the draft board called me, I explained my position and asked to be enlisted. The captain or major on the board was annoyed. Why didn't I avail myself of the exemption rather than put them to some extra trouble? I tried again to explain my devotion to Christ and my love for America, but they indicated neither understanding nor sympathy.

I am no hero and I have my normal share of fear and cowardice. I wanted, however, to share the peril of war with those who did the fighting by helping to save lives instead of destroying them, and the enemy soldiers were my brothers, too. I realized, to some extent, that mine was not an ideal solution, but a compromise, for I would still be part of the war system. Whatever my own motivation, the army was interested in patching up the wounded and sending them back to the slaughter as soon as possible. So what was I doing? What was I accomplishing? How often was I to face this conflict of loyalties in various forms and be frustrated to the point of despair by my inability to break out of a vicious circle?

Then came the day. We met at the draft board, said farewell to loved ones who had the courage or the need to see us off, and were marched to the ferry at East 23rd Street. Father stayed at home but my brave mother was there, not crying or sobbing but standing very still with a determined look on her face. My Ann was there, fiercely grabbing my arm and warning off a drunk who was dragging his little dog along with a spiked helmet on its head representing the Kaiser and with an endless stream of profanity declaring what we would do to the Kaiser.

Only a few nights before, the church gave a farewell party for me, at which I sang the new Gospel song I had just translated into Hungarian, *I Trust in God Wherever I May Be*, and my Ann accompanied me on the piano with tear-filled eyes. It was a splendid and inspiring evening with warm, encouraging words, fervent prayers for my safe return, and much weeping.

We finally arrived at Camp Upton, Long Island — an embarkation camp. Evidently, we were not to be detained for lengthy and thorough training but hurried across where the commanders of decimated armies were clamoring for the strong fresh youth of America. But we had to receive our medical examinations and shots against various diseases and to assigned to units, etc..

For a month, we lived in tents, quarantined four to a tent.

It was not a pleasant situation. Some weeks later, I heard the sergeant in a barracks tell an officer, "That's the toughest bunch they ever sent down from New York" — corner toughs, gamblers, gangsters, as well as some innocents like myself. The former had a lot of fun baiting us, and when they discovered that I was a student for the ministry they improved on the usual profanity and foul stories for my special benefit. Years ago, the shop had been pretty bad, but nothing like this. And I was no longer accustomed to this filth and vapid talk all day long from early morning into the night. Nor could I escape from it all, except for brief walks up and down the alley between the rows of tents.

One evening after supper, there was a glorious sunset. The sky was bathed in rose, pink, blue, gold, and green as the flaming red sun slowly sank below the horizon. As I watched my soul expand, I thrilled to the vast canvas in awe, and a deep peace filled my being. All this beauty was proof of the Eternal Loveliness behind it and I went back, with comfort, to the confinement of the tent and its flesh-bound occupants. I wondered how the spotless Son of God accommodated Himself to the situations of His earthly existence. By contrast, it must have been much more difficult. But (sobering thought) He felt more at home among the subversive tax-gatherers, the prostitutes, and the roughnecks, than among the clean, educated, pious but hypocritical religious leaders. I have often pondered this without discovering an adequate explanation, but the mystery did not lessen His challenge to be compassionate to similar types of people.

Now and then, very infrequently, I had a glimmer of hope and encouragement. One day a chap came into my tent, one of the gadflies, for a talk. I have forgotten the content, but in the end we knelt by my cot and I prayed with him. So my example counted for something after all.

One day, we had our inoculations — a triple shot in the chest. It wasn't very painful and we marched back to our tents jauntily. Then we lined up for "chow." While waiting, several of the men keeled over and dropped to the ground in a faint. It was a source of no little pride that I was not one of them, although I could not boast of a strong, athletic physique.

The authorities drew men from our group whenever a unit about to embark lacked its full complement. Twice they did this and twice they passed me by. The third time they included me. Then I received word that my Ann, now a missionary among the Hungarians in Bridgeport, Connecticut was down with "the flu." Only those who lived through that terrible period can imagine and feel what such news meant. The mortality rate was so high that the sheer news became equivalent to a sentence of death.

The boys in camp came down with it one day and a few days later were dead, especially the big, husky-framed boys from the West. The base hospital was filled with them. Terrified and hysterical relatives made confused telephone calls to find out about their loved ones. One day I answered such a call from a mother in a western state who wanted to know how Jim was.

"Jim who?"

"Don't sass me, young man; tell me about Jim."

"But I must know his full name."

"Never mind that, just tell me how Jim is," and she threatened to tell the commanding officer. I transferred her to the Major's telephone at once. On another occasion I watched two elderly parents, who had traveled for days from a far western town to see their boy only to be told that he had died and his body was on the way home. They crumpled under the blow. Night after night as one passed the numerous wards there came the awful sound of boys coughing their lungs out.

And now my Ann, my lovely, merry Ann, my joy and my love was down with this dreadful disease. And that very night they would transport me to the vast slaughterhouse of Europe. I sent a telegram to her foster mother and one to my own mother, begging them to look after her and bidding them farewell. In the agony of my soul, I composed a poem to say farewell to her, one of the very few and very faulty poems of my life. It was a night of horror and the gray dawn was welcome.

As we lined up for roll call, the sergeant informed me that along with some others, I would not embark. The colonel refused to let us leave without overseas equipment. I was both disappointed and relieved. I wanted to prove myself a brave medical corpsman and a loyal son of America. But even as condemned men are relieved when their death sentence is commuted, so was I. But these experiences, jammed into just a few hours, left me weak.

Instead, I was transferred to the receiving office of the Base Hospital where the continuous duties kept my mind occupied with other people's troubles, and made the long wait for news about my loved one considerably easier. I learned from the two mothers that for weeks my Ann had rushed from one home to another, from morning until night. Carrying her home remedies with her, she nursed the sick, prepared food for them, cleaned up where necessary, and sometimes did it all in homes where everybody was ill. Finally, it proved too much and she herself succumbed to this dreadful contagion. Fortunately, my "Tiny Tim" was tough, and slowly, oh ever so slowly, she recovered.

It was impossible to arrange for a visit, although my superiors thought highly of me. The entire camp was quarantined for over a month. Then one day, by grapevine, came the news that the quarantine would be lifted in a few days. I immediately filled out a form requesting leave to visit my fiance. I was on the first train out of camp and within a few hours with my love. After a few joyful and feverish hours, I rushed to New York to visit my family and report to her foster mother.

Once more after that, I was able to steal a couple of hours to see her. I was sent on an assignment to escort a boy to his parent's home in Connecticut. He had developed a mental illness and was unfit for further military service. Ann suggested that the only privacy we could find would be in the lovely cemetery nearby. So we spent some precious minutes in that spot. Here we were safe from interruption and protected by the silent ones, deep in their last sleep.

Only weeks later did I learn of the vast disservice I did to Ann. At a church meeting, one of the deacons called the shocked attention of the members to the fact that their missionary had been seen walking in the cemetery with a soldier. Soldiers' morals both in the Old Country and the new were not particularly admirable and Ann was called on to explain. What kind of an example was this to the young people of the church? Surprised and taken off guard, she simply said that the soldier was Brother Kautz, whom they all knew as the faithful Christian who had preached in their pulpit with acceptance, and who was her fiance and they had done no wrong and nothing to be ashamed of. But they said it was wrong for a missionary to be engaged, especially for such a long time. Well, they knew this when they called her, she reminded them, and they did not object.

Then the minister took her aside and said, "Now look, Miss Lukacs, why don't you just say you are sorry you got engaged, and everything will be alright?"

"But how can I? I am not sorry and if I were I would have to be honest and break our engagement."

"What will it cost you to say that you are sorry? Only three words! Is that worth quibbling about?"

However, my Ann has an adamant will once she makes up her mind. The meeting closed.

On the way home, one of the men asked permission to escort her home. On the way, he acted nervous and troubled. Finally, in agitation, he blurted out, "Sister Lukacs, forgive me."

"Forgive you? For what?"

"Well," said the young man, "I am a gravedigger. I love you. And when I saw you walk about with a soldier I almost went out of my mind with jealousy! Please forgive me for the suffering I caused you."

"I forgive you and I pray God will," she replied.

But the overzealous, narrow-minded, and rigid members of the congregation could not forgive their missionary. Ultimately, she resigned.

Suddenly the war came to an end. People went mad with joy and relief. Out into the street they poured with every noise-making contraption they could find. Factory whistles blew everywhere.

Locomotives informed the passengers on their trains with loud blasts, so did ferry boats and ships in every harbor. Anxious parents, relatives, and friends embraced and kissed each other and pumped each other's hands in inadequate expressions of release from tensions. Believers dropped on their knees and poured out their fervent thanks to the Ruler of the Nations for the end of the Holocaust and the dawn of peace.

So my Ann rushed over to the minister's house and exclaimed,

"Brother G., come. Let us thank God!"

"What for?" He inquired with a blank face. She knew what he meant. All through the war, following the fundamentalist trend, he had preached on the imminent coming of Christ. The war was the prelude of Armageddon when the Lord, followed by the hosts of heaven, would return, wipe out evil and evildoers, and set up His Kingdom. Even the dramatic and suggestive time of the Armistice, the eleventh hour of the eleventh day of the eleventh month, no longer gave him any consolation. God had let him down. The event gave the lie to his preaching. He feared for his prestige among his people and for his faith in who failed to carry out the prophetic word to his servants in the Bible. He had considered all earthly things vain and futile. One day, as my Ann and he started on their calls, she called his attention to the little son who was waving and calling goodbye.

He looked at her in dismay: "Why, sister, all this will pass away! Let's hurry about the Lord's business." And somehow he never connected this with the fact that he was responsible for the coming of seven children in quick succession into this vain and evil world.

Little Johnnie was a cute and lovely child with his blond ringlets, big eyes, and bandy legs. Once, during the war, I preached in their church in uniform, which rather emphasized my barrel-stave legs. They must have fascinated the boy, for upon reaching home he cried out gleefully, "Mummy that uncle soldier was bandy-legged just like me!"

I was eager to get back to school and continue my studies, so I lost no time in making my application for a discharge. Only six months did I have in the Army, but it was enough — a life where every hour, almost every minute, was directed by others with little opportunity to exercise one's own initiative. In a few weeks, my discharge papers came through. I returned to civilian life.

12 - Back from the War

While not easy, it was by no means as difficult for me to get adjusted to civilian life as for those who had been in the armed services longer and under more trying conditions, alternating between the terrors and horrors of combat and boredom, and the letdown in resting centers with their excesses of sex, gambling, and drinking in order to forget.

Soon I was studying hard once more at Colgate University in order to make up for a semester's loss. One of my friends of the good old days at Cook, that already seemed a generation away, worked at the library. He called my attention to a new book. The title has faded from memory but the author was a newspaper correspondent, Bass by name, who revealed what went on behind the scenes at the peace conferences in Versailles and Trianon. I drew the book and stayed up all night reading it. Toward morning, I slammed it shut and exclaimed in the silence of my room, "Dear God in Heaven! If this is true, we'll have another war in twenty years."

Then I dropped on my knees and pleaded with the Eternal Goodness to save the next generation from the inevitable agony. It was a despairing cry, for how could the injustice, hatred, and ignorance, revealed by the book, issue in peace? And I did not know that the League of Nations' "grand and beautiful concept" would become a holding company for the victors rigidly insisting on its pound of flesh from the living body of the defeated nations? Nor about the vacuum of power in place of the Austro-Hungarian monarchy that could not be filled by the little, weak successor states. Nor had I heard about the insult to Japan when she asked that the equality of races be written into the covenant of the league, and the threat of the British statesmen to make trouble for Wilson in the South if he insisted on race equality. The subject people, mostly colored, might get ideas!

When summer arrived, the Evangelistic Committee of New York City called me into their service again to preach the Gospel on the city streets. With another student from the Hungarian Baptist Seminary, we gave our testimony to the love and power of God on a different corner each night. He played his trumpet until a group gathered, then I jumped on a small collapsible stand we carried with us and spoke until the group dispersed, or seeing some interested hearers, we closed the meeting with a prayer and mingled with the crowd distributing tracts, answering questions, inviting people to our Sunday church services, or not infrequently engaging in a hot debate with atheists.

One evening, I saw a woman stop on the edge of the listening group. She was worn, haggard, and deadly pale. Her eyes glowed like live coals as she listened to the message. She had a baby carriage in front of her and a child holding on to her skirt on either side. Eagerly, she held out her hand for a time and left. She was back each night thereafter on that corner, and when the street meetings ended, she brought her children to Sunday school and before long joined the church. With her little brood and a scapegrace of a husband, who gave her five dollars a week to live on, she struggled on for years until her children were grown.

Once, at the insistence of my mother, I called on her. Several times I turned away from the door of her tiny three-room tenement apartment. What could a young chap like me say to a woman in such a desperate situation? Finally, ashamed of my lack of faith, I knocked on the door. When she saw me, her face lit up, and soon I was seated in the kitchen where she was mending the laundry and pointing out the wash she was doing for somebody else. Her tale of woe burst from her lips in a flood of words. I could only listen and pray with a breaking heart for a family so hopelessly enmeshed by the forces of life. At last, I asked, "Does it make any difference, since you found Christ?"

"Blessed be the evening when I found my way to the first street meeting," she replied. "You know, I was thinking of going to the East

River and drowning my children and myself. Then I discovered that we have a loving God who cares. Now, when it seems I cannot endure the struggle any longer, I shut myself in the bedroom, get on my knees with my Bible in front of me and, as I pray, new strength and courage fills me so that I can go on."

In college and seminary, where the impact of new, strange ideas, novel concepts and abstract speculations often tend to make faith in a good, overriding Providence difficult, if not impossible, that poor woman's experience was a blessed corrective. Others like it along with my own conversion reminded me through the years that behind the changing, often contradictory phenomena of our human existence there is a blessed reality, with its own resources of inspiration and power available to sincere, earnest, humble seekers.

In the forenoons we had Daily Vacation Bible School. It was advertised by a big poster on the wall of the church. The word was spread by personal contacts with as many children as we could find in an area of several blocks around the church. The sessions lasted from nine to twelve with a varied program of secular songs with a message (yes, there were a few like that, and very effective, too) and religious hymns, Bible and character stories, prayer, memorizing important Scripture passages, and handwork.

It was a joy to work with these children, five to thirteen years of age, and receive the thanks of the parents at graduation for taking their boys and girls off the streets for five weeks. But it was exhausting too because some of them were quite unruly, boisterous, and tough. Our discipline had to be very gentle yet effective and our contacts winsome in order to charm them into somewhat regular attendance. But the charm and challenge of childhood was a rich reward. Certainly, our salary of $15 per week was not.

My Ann was engaged in identical activities in connection with the Czechoslovak mission nearby. It was a joy to be so close to each other after an engagement of almost four and a half years. She tackled this new job with her usual enthusiasm, but if the difficulty in her former field was a certain fundamentalist fanaticism, now her effort was neutralized by a modernist pastor. Apparently, he had a social passion, for on hot Sundays he would say, "Let us take these poor people out into the park. They have sweated and sweltered in the hot tenements and streets all week."

Then he would take her class and lead them to Central Park. She invited him to call in homes where only men were at home. He either ignored it or responded, "Oh you work too hard! And what do they pay you for it? A measly $60 a month. Why, I earn $50 an evening with my singing! Come I'll treat you to a baseball game." When she begged him to put a placard on the side of the church announcing the Daily Vacation Bible School, he kept putting it off until it became evident that he did not wish to become involved. This work for the underprivileged children of the East Side did not appeal to him. Was his social concern anything but a sham? When I saw her desperation I hung her sign. He came and watched. In my anger, I blurted out, "You don't deserve a missionary!"

He demanded an apology. "What, for telling the truth?" He could complain to the executive secretary. Let him. And I took Ann to my home for a delicious lunch.

Through no fault of her own, to outsiders, she might appear a failure. She made an attempt to explain the situation to the supervisor of missionaries. But the minister's wife was a fine seamstress and sewed dresses for her and they frequently had her for dinner. And so, to the supervisor, the fault was clearly Ann's. Years later the truth came out, but too late for Ann.

Why not get married? We had waited long enough, although neither of our daughters thought so, until they were ready to marry (then even a year was too long for them). I wrote a carefully composed letter to Dean Vichert, explaining our situation and asking that my scholarship of $30 per month be continued. Married students were not especially welcome in those days and I was afraid. However, Dean Vichert was very understanding and assured me that I could depend on that amount.

Then I wrote to Vernon, where I had preached a few Sundays the previous spring when their pastor had entered the chaplaincy. They replied that I would be welcome but they were not able to pay more than $13.50 per weekend and for that I would be expected to conduct prayer meeting on Friday evening, visit members and friends on Saturday, preach at morning and evening services on Sundays, and be present in Sunday school and youth meeting. This would be an impossible schedule now, but we were young, vigorous and dedicated. We did not mind the work, but could we live on an income of $58 a month? I had no savings at all and she had a secret nest egg of $200, of which I knew nothing. Her foster mother's prediction was being fulfilled. We were almost as poor as church mice. Fortunately, we needed no clothing. But our rent would be $20 per month and we still had war prices on some goods. Sugar was twenty-eight cents a pound. Ann made it quite clear that we could not have more than a half-pound of meat a day for the two of us, and I was a great meat eater! My brave Ann figured and figured. Finally she concluded, "If you will be satisfied with my management and the food, I can get along. I would be satisfied with anything if only we could be united after our interminable engagement."

Our hearts were set on a simple, private wedding. No formals, no dinner, very few flowers, few guests. But my mother would not hear of it.

"What my eldest son marrying surreptitiously? I won't have it!"

"But mother, we can't afford it otherwise."

"In that case, I will provide it."

"But how can you? You have no savings."

"No, but I still have friends. I'll borrow $50 and make a dinner to which I want you to invite a hundred guests. I'll make it better than any caterer!" She did, too, for she was a wonderful cook.

Accordingly, we included mother's pride in our plans but only in a way that would save our own self-respect. We would consider the cost of the dinner only as a loan from her to be repaid as soon as we were able. Out went the invitations. Flowers were sent to us from Vernon friends and a Hungarian Baptist woman working in upstate New York. Dr. Hazzard of the City Mission Society filled his car with autumn branches, brought them to the little church on 80th Street and made a tiny arbor in front of the pulpit where the vows would be made. When we stepped into the sanctuary, it was filled to overflowing — people standing, even on window sills. We had not realized we had so many friends.

In his excitement, our pastor committed a serious error. He included in my vows "the pledge to obey," while omitting the same from Ann's vows. It has embarrassed me ever since! Every argument could end with a reminder: And what did you promise? Well, the good man, a friend really, has gone to his reward. I hope the great Judge did not take him to account too severely for it.

When the guests had left, Ann went up to mother and embraced her saying, "Here is another daughter for you, mother."

But my poor mother to whom I was much more than a son, a loyal friend, could only look at her with cold restraint, icy in her determination not to break down and unable to accept gracefully the fact that, hence, another woman would be first in the life of her son. Yet, she had made it very clear that Ann was the one she approved of for me. I stood by helplessly, feeling the heartache of both. I took Ann to her home at the Baptist City Missionaries' quarters and returned to my own home.

The next morning, we took the train to Hamilton, New York, where Colgate University is situated and found quarters for the night. We put on a brave front like an old married couple and were somewhat mystified when our hostess inquired the next day whether we had married recently. We were certain that our behavior had been correct. To our inquiry, she responded, "I found some rice on the floor."

Within a day or two, we found a nice little furnished apartment with an elderly couple where we shared the kitchen and laundry facilities. They were a very kind couple and made our stay very pleasant. He was considerably older and pitifully devoted to her. When she went on a visit, even for only a few days, he propped up her picture on the table in front of him. Our own love was strengthened and beautified by their devotion.

Like most students, I had outrageous study habits. Beginning at nine o'clock in the evening and closing sometime after midnight. Mealtimes were irregular, missing, or postponed when "very busy" or too lazy to go out. I still weighed only 120 pounds although 5' 8", a tall, cadaverous youth who looked like a tuberculosis candidate. My "love" was determined to change all this for my benefit and, although I admitted the need, I was not eager to change. Her affectionate, patient, sometimes humorous coaxing, coy pouting, and impatient scolding along with my joy, my eagerness to please her, and the security of our new home and our marriage were idealistic commitments to make our marriage succeed, and brought about the necessary change.

She was so eager to please me with balanced meals, setting the table just so, with flowers, even if they had to be wildflowers or weeds — "lilies of the field" we called them as our Master had done — keeping our apartment spotlessly clean and in order. It was a lovely change for me, coming as I did from a home situation where nine children and at least two adults shared the cramped and crowded quarters of five rather small rooms in a tenement apartment in which it was quite impossible to have everything in order in individual closets or dresser drawers.

She arranged my linen carefully, and when I thoughtlessly and carelessly pulled out something, upsetting it all, she patiently rearranged them again. One day I came home from class and found my things on the floor. Was she putting them in order again? No, she was not. She sternly informed me that I was to put them away to suit myself and keep them that way. Love is wonderful! I meekly did as told, though once in a while she still has to remind me.

Ann endeavored to continue her education, and attended a class or two every day. At home, I read some of my assignments in literature, history or religion while she prepared our evening meal in the kitchen. It did not seem fair, however, that she spent so much time on preparing course dinners for me. Even if, in view of our stringent financial situation, they were not as elaborate as might be imagined.

She bought pecks and bushels of potatoes, which I usually avoided at my mother's table. Also carrots, turnips, and onions, all of which were ignored, if possible, in favor of meat in my parental home. We had turnips so often that if we were in better circumstances or served in the homes of our friends they would blush in embarrassment. We always had a little sweet dessert: pie, cake, or jello, and very inexpensive.

A few years ago, she suggested making a one-egg cake such as she used to in the early days of our marriage. "Oh please don't," I pleaded. But she thought it might be interesting to recall the early days of our marriage. I consented but, alas, most of the cake was consumed by the birds. Most of the time, when we settled at the table and I looked at my lovely, happy wife, I didn't know what I was eating, only occasionally noticing the vast difference between my former reals and the experimental dishes of my young wife.

One day, I shyly suggested that she cook a simple dish, something that could be prepared in a single pot. However, she knew of no such dish. A bit fearfully, I suggested a favorite food of mine that we often had in my home. She listened eagerly while I gave the recipe: "slice and brown a large onion in fat, then cut up six to eight green peppers into it, a medium-sized tomato, and a half pound of frankfurters, salt to taste and simmer slowly."

I was sitting at my study table when she came to me, and sitting on my lap, offered a taste of the new dish. But she kept blowing and blowing it, because it was so hot. At last, she offered me the spoon. I thought I put live coals into my mouth. But I swallowed it bravely and in a hurry, and out of a loving heart, lied. "It's delicious."

"I am sorry darling," she said, "I added black and red pepper to your recipe, hoping to make it better."

When we sat down to eat she had the nerve to ask me to return thanks for our evening meal. I did. After all, God did His share well. Then as I was about to serve her, smiling sweetly she said "Please don't give me much, I'm not very hungry."

"You rascal," I said to myself. "I know you, but I'll show you. And I served a generous portion to myself. I had to devour a half a loaf of bread to get it down to the accompaniment of continuous blowing of the nose and wiping of eyes."

"Never mind dear," she consoled me, "I made some delicious cocoa," and proceeded to pour it.

But oddly she took the first cup, which usually was mine. It poured into my cup to the sound of plop, plop, plop.

"What have you there, my Love? Is it cocoa a-la-lump?" I kept forcing the rubbery stuff down my throat. "I'm so sorry. The milk curdled." So I had to console her.

Today she is a splendid cook, so my patience and her persistent efforts to atone for those early days have brought rich dividends in palate satisfaction.

Ours was a home for lonely, discouraged, homesick, fellow students. They were always welcome. One day we found one with his head on his arms on the piano, fast asleep. We let him rest. When the commencement came, we arranged a party, sometimes with dinner for their relatives and friends. It was our privilege to share their joys, sorrows, victories, and defeats.

13 - A Village Pastor

"I am taking this yellow rose from my garden and giving it to her if I approve of our little minister's choice. If not, I'll not give it to her." Mother Latham was the speaker — a big, husky New Englander, eighty years old but full of vitality and one of the outstanding personalities in Vernon, where I had spent a weekend the previous spring. I had invited Ann to come with me to meet those good people. They too fell in love with her, and Mother Latham gave her the rose.

In the fall, we took another trip to Vernon, hoping to be called to serve the little church. Reverend Filson had stayed in the army and his efficient wife had taken his place but was eager to join him. It did not take long to agree on conditions because we had no other choice. They offered us $13.50 per week and living quarters from Friday evening to Monday morning. Of this, we had to spend $13.50 for railroad fare and planned to give $1.50 per week to the church.

Vernon was a little town of about six hundred inhabitants with about four hundred more people scattered around the countryside. I learned that most of the families had migrated from New England, although most of them were two or three generations removed. Not until we ourselves settled in New England forty years later did we hear again "e..yah" for "yes" as we had in Vernon. Our little church had about sixty members: active and retired farmers, some mechanics who worked at Oneida Community, a silverware factory, two people working in the local bank, the school principal and a teacher, a milking machine manufacturer, and two nurses — a group very representative of the community.

There were three churches in all: A Methodist, which had the largest membership, about one hundred fifty in all and a modern slant; a

Presbyterian, which had most of the wealth with about one hundred twenty members worshipping in a stately old church with stained glass windows and a fine organ; and Baptist, with the smallest and least attractive building but very warm and home-like inside and with an earnest, dedicated membership that sent four into full-time Christian service. The highest record in proportion to membership as far as I am aware.

At the first Sunday morning service, we had a congregation of about sixty. In the evening, thirteen of us were scattered about the little auditorium — an awful letdown for me! I remember how, in our little Hungarian Baptist churches, our congregation in the evening was always larger than in the morning. My heart sank and cried to the unseen God, "Lord help me, I can't stand this." Something happened, for almost immediately our congregations began to increase so that by after a year we had eighty to one hundred people present every Sunday evening.

We did not spare ourselves. Each week from the time we arrived until we left, our efforts, thoughts, and prayers belonged to our little church. Mother Latham watched for our arrival by train, and by the time we turned the corner of her street that led to the church, she was in the doorway of her house, even in a snowstorm, and called us in.

"Come in children, and have a little bite and a hot drink before you go to the prayer meeting." Usually, it was a generous supper. She and her daughter Eva, a trained nurse, hurried to put on the food and told us about the happenings in town since the previous Sunday. We were warmed through and through, body and soul, by their welcome. Meanwhile, the wind howled outside and a snowstorm slowly enveloped the town. It was easy to go only a few steps away to the church and into the little upper room with its hot stove and ten to thirty people waiting for us.

In the intimacy of this small fervent fellowship it was easy to give a Bible exposition and engage in prayer. It was conservative Christianity at its best. Almost never did we hear malicious gossip or carping criticism, although we were told years later that there was quite a bit of it in the little town. We were astonished.

The next day, we rested late and dear "Aunt Ella," our hostess and "Uncle Jesse," her husband who took care of the furnace, kept as quiet as possible. After breakfast we started on our pastoral calls. Soon we had the village proper covered and needed a quicker way to get about than on the "steeds of the Apostles." Uncle Jesse came to our rescue with a pony or a gentle horse so that our calls reached farther and farther into the countryside. In the winter we had a sleigh. The merry tinkle of the bell on our horse and the clop-clop of its hoofs as we sped over the white landscape was quite a romantic experience to us city dwellers.

At noon we provided our own lunch, but not for long. Soon we were regular guests at Father Cox's home — the kind, proud, honest, village cobbler who had stopped going to church some years before, disgusted over the unchristian conduct of a minister. Mother Cox was rather stout and moved about with considerable difficulty and pain because of a dislocated hip suffered with the birth of her last child. She had a lovely face, kind as well as pretty, and when she came to church Sunday on the arm of her husband, one would have thought of them as newlyweds, though they had been married thirty years. Many a generous meal did we have at their table — bless them! One day we wondered how many chickens they had broiled — there were so many legs! Greatly amused, they informed us that it was rabbits not chickens that day.

One day, we arrived a little earlier than usual, and as we entered the shop, we found Father Cox at his bench smoking a big cigar. Ann burst into tears. This kind, noble man smoking! It was not in our Hungarian Baptist tradition. As we served those good people in our English-speaking church, we discovered that, while they had some traits like smoking we believed were wrong, they also lacked some of the weaknesses and unchristian traits in our own Hungarian Baptist fellowships. It was an education in understanding and Christian tolerance.

After a brief rest in the afternoon we continued our calls, occasionally in the evenings as well. More often after our supper in our quarters, we prepared for Sunday. There was but little opportunity for this during the week. My studies were exacting, scholastic standards high. I carried as many courses as possible, twenty-three hours per week for one semester, so my preparation for church services took place on the trip to Vernon and on Saturday and Sunday preceding the services.

Our people must have appreciated the burdens we were carrying. Nearly always I arrived in church as our bell gave its final peal. Often I was late — once or twice very late. But the choir waited patiently, albeit anxiously at times, until I was ready to march on to the platform with them, and no one ever upbraided me except my long-suffering wife.

Nearly always, we were invited to dinner on Sunday and excused immediately afterwards to get our rest. Then once more I plunged into my preparation for the evening service, making some brief, hasty notes, and arriving just in time, but not always. One Sunday, my poor Ann begged me, as usual, to be on time, and I promised faithfully. During my preparation, however, fatigue and sleepiness overcame my determination and I threw myself on the bed not to sleep but only to snatch a brief rest. Suddenly, I heard our church bell only a minute's walk away give its final clang, clang, clang! I jumped up, dashed some water into my face, cast a hasty glance in the mirror, and rushed out. I was already preaching when I fully came to and realized where I was. I was frightened as never before or since. I had announced and led in the singing of several hymns, prayed twice, read the Scriptures, made the necessary announcements, and had started my sermon before I was fully awake!

I have always enjoyed preaching. It was during the sermon that I was at the height of my powers, at the peak of my vitality. However, I always felt drained of all my strength afterward. My prayers in that little church were always extemporaneous, not as carefully planned, composed, and written out as in my later years, yet the people thanked me about as often for them and for the sermon, which has not happened again until many years later. I enjoyed freedom in preaching, using only scant notes, secure in the love and confidence of my congregation.

But dear old Father Tufts was nettled sometimes. Was it some theological point, or a poor illustration, or an extreme statement to which enthusiastic preachers are prone — especially young ones? I no longer remember. He was thoroughly at home in the Bible, an intelligent and thoughtful person whose criticism, always kind, I received in good spirit. I still see him in his pew, head bent to one side watching me with keen eyes, which expressed sympathy too. Suddenly, he lifted his head, looked startled, bowed, and shook his head. I had again wounded his sensibilities. Fortunately, those wounds were but scratches and sometimes there was a twinkle of amusement in his eyes and a smile upon his lips that he could not always conceal between his mustache and goatee. We remained devoted friends.

Ten years after we left the church, we made our first visit to see our Vernon friends again. As he bade us farewell, Father Tufts, struggling to keep his emotions under control, said to me, "Mr. Kautz, I want you to know that there has not been a day since you left us that I did not pray for you."

If I have achieved anything since it may be attributed in significant measure to his earnest prayers. He has since passed on, as did most of the adults. He was a retired farmer, president of the village, and very conservative in his habits and attitudes. Especially in the matter of church finances, but as a true democrat, he always went along with the majority. He was deeply devoted to his fragile little wife and their devotion to each other was a continuing inspiration to us — especially when we spent a weekend in their home. One evening, we found him sitting on a stool with his head in her lap, gazing at her with a rapt expression as she read a letter from their daughter, a professor in a mission college in far-off Burma. Before we retired that night, Ann and I renewed our vows of devotion to each other.

Uncle Jesse Perris was a good foil for Father Tufts. He was a milking machine manufacturer. An ambitious, enthusiastic, successful, smiling businessman, in the prime of life, who could always be depended upon to push a new idea or at least to give it his unprejudiced consideration. His enthusiasm was tempered by his calm, soft-voiced wife Ella, who would warm him now and then with a patient smile and "Now, now, Jesse," and he would make a sober correction or smile sheepishly.

It was during these days that the larger Protestant denominations of the North united for the first time in an extraordinary, ambitious financial campaign. The country was prospering but the contributions of church members had not increased proportionately if I remember correctly. The Northern Baptist Convention set a goal of forty million dollars for home and foreign missions and education to be raised in five years. It took our breath away! Other denominations set similar goals. There were large interdenominational mass meetings addressed by outstanding laymen as well as missionary leaders and outstanding ministers. The one we attended with a delegation from our little church was held in Syracuse, New York and addressed by John D. Rockefeller Jr. — a truly great man and a Christian gentleman. My wife was very eager to see him and, in her enthusiastic manner, kept saying, "Where is my John D? Where is my John D.?"

A gentleman sitting next to her spoke up: "Lady, I believe he is married."

For a moment my Ann was speechless. Recovering, she showed the ring on her left hand and replied, "I am too."

As the presentations continued, my imagination pictured vividly all the good that this enormous sum could do all over the world, for in those days it was a vast sum indeed. And I wept in deep sorrow over the suffering of the vast majority of God's children throughout His good earth. We returned to our little church determined to do our share, and more, in this glorious enterprise of all Christians in the United States.

For the next few months, we worked feverishly at the task. Every sermon dealt with the challenge of this great adventure. After a great deal of discussion measuring our resources and possibilities, we set our goal

— an impossible one, all of us felt — but only a few would admit to. The Sunday for our canvas was a feverish one. Long past the hour for the reports, we did not know whether we would reach our goal or not. Just before the evening service Uncle Jesse rushed into the sanctuary to the blackboard and wrote upon it the amount pledged, rather above our hopes. We stood and sang "Praise God from whom all blessings flow." This tiny church, usually giving $120 a year to missions, had pledged ten times that amount!

This success, however, led to searching of hearts, for their minister received a salary of less than $900 a year. Among themselves, they began to discuss diverting some of the money pledged and add it to the minister's salary. Finally, one of them told the pastor how unhappy they felt about the situation and what they were planning to do. The minister was aghast at the suggestion.

"No, no! That was impossible. It would amount to raising money under false pretenses. Was all my enthusiasm for the cause to carry with it the suspicion of personal financial profit? Never, never could I consent to such a dishonest thing. The money pledged for missions could never be used for anything else."

It was really not necessary to emphasize this so vehemently, for they were honorable people whose given word was kept even at a loss to themselves, and they were uneasy enough about what they were proposing. The word went out that the pastor could not accept the proposal and that he was right. The brother of Uncle Jesse, not a member of the church but a faithful attendant since the coming of the young pastor and his wife, offered to give an extra two dollars per week if it were added to the minister's salary. Father and Mother Cox pledged another dollar with the same stipulation. Within a week or two, my salary was raised by fifty-eight percent to an annual $1208. Their joy was full. So was ours, for they had responded in a marvelous way to our leadership and made clear in a very tangible fashion their appreciation of our efforts.

Nor was this all, for they often brought us gifts of food in garden produce, fruit, and baked goods, and we never ate such sweet delicious corn and peas before or after! One never-to-be-forgotten weekend, one of the ladies whispered to my Ann, "I baked apple pies for my family today and I thought of you and I baked one for you."

The next morning the eldest boy, about eleven, of a large and very poor family was at our door, "My mother sent you this meat pie," and before we left for Hamilton on Monday we had received six pies of various kinds. All of our friends who called on us that week were treated to a generous piece of pie. How they enjoyed it and marveled at the Kautz's new prosperity! Many, many times we were dinner guests in the homes of our people. In fact, we had few meals by ourselves — usually breakfasts.

How often did those dear people drive us home and sometimes bring us to Vernon! When our firstborn arrived around Thanksgiving day they drove me home, with two other cars full of people, right after the Sunday evening service to greet the baby and to bring to the mother the greetings and best wishes of the church and community. A month later, a devoted friend, not even a member of the church, came for us in his open touring car — a Ford with side curtains only and no heater — and took us to Vernon. The thermometer stood at 17 below zero when we arrived, but the little one was warm as toast wrapped up in a blanket between two pillows with her uneasy mother groping in every little while to make sure she had not smothered the baby. Dear Yokeys probably never had their house as warm as during this Christmas vacation. We were transported home in the same manner. Never again did we enjoy the love, the appreciation, the devotion of a church to such an extent, nor the success.

In three years the membership increased by one third, the Sunday morning congregations doubled, and the evening attendance increased sevenfold. But more, the spirit of the church was wonderful for its brotherliness, willing service, and lack of cliques and snobbery. One day, the wife of Mr. Ward the bank treasurer, Aunt Ella the milking machine manufacturer's wife, the minister's wife, and the village nurse Eva, and Mother Latham's daughter packed their car with pail, broom, mop, groceries, meat, vegetables and fruit, and drove to a poor house on the outskirts of the village where the mother of five children lay sick in bed. They cleaned up the house, cooked the day's food for the family, cared for the sick mother, and promised to continue their care until she was well again. It is no wonder that the parents soon joined our church and became faithful members and the children became regular attendants at Sunday school.

Our prayer meetings on Friday nights were a great source of joy and power. Our attendance varied from one-third to three-fifths of the membership. And oh how they prayed! One year, while studying the Gospel of John in Greek, I took them through that book, basing my exposition on the Greek text I had with me. I have not dared to do anything like it since. Choir rehearsal followed. They sang with enthusiasm but not always in harmony. We had a few fine voices, but they were often drowned out by a few raw ones. Their singing grated on my ear, and not infrequently at Sunday Worship I had to make a special prayer to recapture my inspiration after their singing.

Young, enthusiastic, and foolish, I had the temerity to ask one to retire. She did, but all through worship she sat right in front of me looking hurt and insulted even though she "forgave" me. This led her daughter the organist to refuse service at the organ, and a few others also made clear that I had made a sad mistake. In our little church the unhappiness was palpable. I was sorry, made due apologies, called on my hurt folk, and tried to heal their wounds with kind words and prayer. Ultimately, it was patched up, but even the best patches do not look too well. I learned to keep out of choir problems.

Things were going well. One Saturday morning the Methodist and Presbyterian ministers dropped in for a friendly chat. I soon discovered that they were concerned about a few of their members who attended our services now and then, particularly on Sunday evenings. They had an agreement between themselves not to steal each other's sheep. Would I join them in this? Of course! They were greatly relieved, but I read in their eyes not entirely free of their doubts.

Willing or not, we were competing for the attention and support of the community. Clearly, three Protestant churches were too many. I spent my last year working for a union or a federation of them. With our combined membership firmly organized into one church, we could have been the most powerful influence in the community. However, my colleagues were not very enthusiastic about it, and although the official boards of the churches discussed it, the narrower parish royalties and the opposition of the Methodist District Superintendent made even the initial efforts hopeless. Many unhappy things have happened there since, which might have been prevented if the followers of Christ had listened with open minds and hearts to the prayer of the great Head of the Church "that they might be one ..."

My last and greatest dream and effort to serve the cause of Christ in this community failed and it was the cause of great sorrow for me to realize that the churches missed the crest of the tide that might have carried them on to a wonderful new adventure. In essence, though certainly not in magnitude, it was what the prophets of the Old Testament must have felt again and again as they failed to impart their vision to their people and the consequent doom.

And, my own church was as guilty in failing to measure up to this opportunity as the other churches. It may even be that the very successes achieved in those three years gave our church a false sense of achievement and security, blinding them to the necessity of this new adventure demanded by the needs of the community and by the weakness of a divided church.

How I should like to add to the list those others to whom we owe a heavy debt of gratitude: Peppers, Clutes, Yokeys, Mummeys, Robertes, Hoags, Mrs. Gates, and others, some of whom were not even members of our church. May they all be granted the knowledge that in the heavy trials ahead of us, recollections of their kindnesses brought strength and courage for years to come.

We were deeply disappointed in our failure to win Mother Latham for membership in the church. We knew that she loved us dearly and trusted and admired us. She was the grand old lady of the village, 86 years of age but young in spirit, with great physical vitality, a fine mind, and living wisdom that shone in her face. Finally, one day, I found enough courage to tackle her.

"Mother Latham, I know that you love us and you know how fond we are of you, also. How is it that, to all our pleading that you come to church, you turn a deaf ear? Is there something you hold against us after all?"

"No, children," she replied and her face became very serious, "When I was a girl of sixteen, back in New England, my mother stood up in a church business meeting to give her views on a matter of importance. In those days women almost never took part in public discussion, and the men were not slow in reminding her of the injunction of the Apostle Paul that women keep silent in church. I knew that my mother was as smart as any man in that church and, in addition, had much more common sense than most of them. I made up my mind right then and there that I would never go to church again."

We saw that our pleas would be in vain and ceased. But we could not help reflecting, with a little bitterness, how the wisdom of another age reached into ours nearly two thousand years later and caused tragedies. This had happened in the little mission church in New York and was going to happen again and again in our lifetime.

Sometimes I wonder just how often in my youthful zeal and enthusiasm I was unnecessarily cruel, even as in the choir. Auntie Price, a widow, entertained us regularly over the weekends during our first year. She was always dressed in mourning for Cecil, an adopted son, who was killed in World War I. She was always sad and referred to him often in tears. We comforted her, prayed with her, read the Scriptural promises, but all in vain. The black cloud of her sorrow would not lift.

Years later, on our first visit to Vernon, she came to me after worship and said, "You know, Mr. Kautz, you helped me most when you told me one day that I must stop feeling sorry for myself."

I was shocked and protested: "Did I really, Auntie Price? How could I, when you were so hurt already?"

"I am glad you did," she assured me with her sweet smile. "You were right and I thank you for it now, even though it shocked and hurt me at the time."

And so the goodness of Eternal Love made recompense for the errors and follies of zeal then and thereafter.

My mother spent a brief vacation with us one summer. After several weeks she asked me one day: "My son, are these people real Americans?"

"Indeed, mother. Many, if not most of them, had their ancestors in New England."

My mother thought for a while, recalling the people she had known in New York City, mostly first and second generation Americans with the peculiar snobbery of those who preceded others in the New Country by a few years, and without the consideration and courtesy of our Vernon friends. She said, "You know, I think I like them very much." They liked her too — her winsome smile, flashing eyes, lovely face, and motherly spirit.

One winter day I visited a home where a girl was putting a log in the kitchen stove. She was about fourteen, had a round baby face with a peaches-and-cream complexion, and big brown eyes that stared at me. She was very attractive, and as the flames lit up her face I felt a desire to possess her. Frightened and ashamed, I left as soon as possible. I realized then that even dedicated and very happily married ministers were not immune to temptations of the flesh. It did not occur again, but once was quite sufficient. I learned to be very careful with my members of the opposite sex.

Years later, the wife of somebody I knew very well confessed to a similar experience. She told of going up the steps between her husband and one of his friends. "Suddenly, unexpectedly, we touched elbows and a thrill went through me," she confessed. "I was ashamed. I love my husband and I am chagrined that I should have a sexual thrill because of such a passing contact."

I explained to her, as I did to my marriage classes many years after, that this is part of the mystery of sex. We do not know why some members of the opposite sex attract us. We can never know when this may occur. Is it only the pull of sex? Why only that in itself, may be powerful enough to cause one to forget his mate, children, future, God, heaven, and hell. We may learn to recognize the danger signals, be on guard, and reduce the opportunities that provide fuel to the flame, but infatuations may be sparked by beauty, and the many-sided, indefinable quality we call glamour, by artistic or musical gifts, by conversational gifts and charm, by physical beauty, and by mental or spiritual gifts. I myself, through a very happy married life of over forty years, have repeatedly found myself on the brink of infatuation, but was able to resist its blandishments and its corrosive influence. Probably it was easier, even much easier than for others, because of the charm and loveliness of my Ann, her loyalty and devotion to me, her kind consideration of all my needs, and her helpfulness in the difficult trials of life of which we had our share. Nor do I claim any credit for that deep sense of loyalty that I either inherited or learned from my parents, as I experienced it in their dedication to each other and the family. How well I recall my mother's puzzled wonder when she heard about somebody's separation and divorce!

"My son, you just don't understand these people," she said one day. "I can never forget the solemn moment when I stood before the altar, in God's presence, and pledged my vows of fidelity to your father." I learned early that what an older marriage counselor called "idealistic determination" is the most important element in a successful marriage.

Undoubtedly, our basic commitment to a just and holy God of love to whom all His children are precious had a great deal to do with our devotion. We could never say of each other what many of my girl students felt many years after in my marriage courses, "I wish boys would not think of me only as a female, only as a body to be explored and exploited, but as a person."

Less often, but no less positively young men expressed the same sentiment concerning some of their girlfriends. We respected, nay, revered each other, and this was rooted in a deep conviction of the dignity of each child of God, with the stamp of the Eternal upon him and a spark of the deity within him. When this was reinforced by a deep love, eagerness to give, to please, to sacrifice for the loved one, it lifted and transformed the natural, instinctive, and basically selfish drive of sex to a new human, and perhaps even superhuman level.

It was not easy to achieve this nor could the high level demanded by this ideal be maintained without slips, stumbles, and failings but always our commitment recalled us to this higher life. We had our petty quarrels and we jangled a good deal, but as my wife approvingly quotes a Texas architect's wife, "I often felt like choking him but never like leaving him."

All this reminds me of a story by a very dear and trusted friend of mine, a fellow pastor struggling in a little village parish as I was that tested him to the point of a nervous breakdown. One of his members was a simple, uneducated man with a very pretty wife and two little children. One day he called his pastor in great agitation and asked him to come at once to his place of work. When the pastor arrived he was walking up and down in the warehouse like a wild animal. With flaming eyes, he poured out his troubles like a volcano. The village physician had taken a fancy to his wife and he was going to kill him. How did he know? His wife had told him about suggestive remarks made by the doctor. Well, perhaps she was only flattered by the attention of a prominent pillar of the community. Oh, she was flattered all right, but he was going to kill "the bastard." Did he know anything more than the boasting of a vain woman? Indeed he did. He had sneaked into the basement under the doctor's office and listened to him praise her beautiful body and make remarks with sexual overtones. He could hardly contain his rage and had to rush away to not kill him at once, for he had a revolver with him.

It took quite a while, a lot of patient listening, continuous inner prayer for guidance on the part of the minister, and a soothing remark now and then as the poor maddened husband stopped for breath. Then the pastor pointed out that the peace and happiness of many more people was involved, not just his own. Did he love his wife? Yes, to distraction. Did he care for his children? What a question! Of course! Well, what will it do to them if he were hailed before a court as a murderer and executed? And that scoundrel of a physician, unworthy of his calling, he too had a family. Had they hurt him in any way? No. Was he going to destroy their good name, brand their loved one a moral leper and destroy their home? Oh, for someone to horsewhip that bastard out of town! But his innocent family was his shield. Did he know it? Then a woman in the congregation complained of unwelcome attention by the doctor in his office. But she too was a vain, empty-headed, though well-meaning person, and she would not tell her husband for fear of a tragedy. My poor friend was at his wit's end. At last, he stumbled upon the story of David's adultery with Bathsheba and decided to preach on it the following Sunday evening when the husband's work kept him from the service, but the wife was usually present with her children.

That evening, he recalled, he preached as never before. He pictured vividly how temptation begins and conquers a willing person, how a selfish and gross thirst for pleasure, a sheer animality of sex, and the blindness of infatuation debases a great King and a vain, careless, foolish woman, and leads to murder, public denunciation, the judgment of God, and sexual rottenness in David's own family.

He contrasted the calculating treachery of the King with the pitiful but true and lovely loyalty of Bathsheba's husband. He was disappointed, however, at her reaction. She betrayed no sense of guilt either in her words of appreciation or in her look as she shook hands with her pastor after the service. She only asked for the Bible reference of the story.

Yet, he concluded, there came an awakening of some sort to the woman for she read the story at home, told her husband about the sermon and stopped seeing the physician. The pastor thanked God. He had saved two families and forestalled a scandal that might have torn the little community into fragments.

A black cloud suddenly cast its frightening shadow over the sunlit skies of these happy and successful days when the affection and admiration of our people surrounded us with a deep, calm security. It was the Homestead Steel strike hundreds of miles away, in which so many workingmen, mostly immigrants, lost their lives. They worked twelve hours a day, seven days a week, and often when the day and night shifts changed places, they stayed on their jobs for twenty-four hours next to the hot, fiery furnaces. It was an inhuman situation and no one would dare even to try to justify it today. Only fifteen years later did I actually visit a steel plant in that area and get a firsthand physical experience of the heat in which these men had to work.

Probably for the first time the leadership of the Protestant denominations was also deeply disturbed. So much so that they sent an able and competent committee of clergymen, seminary and college professors, economists, and sociologists to investigate the situation. They found that the workingmen were justified and recommended various improvements. Among these, the most important was the eight-hour workday with three shifts instead of two.

When these findings were published, Mr. Elbert Gary, president of U.S. Steel blasted the report as impractical and impossible, and blasted the committee as "a bunch of reds."

My passion for justice and humanity brought on a fierce revulsion, such as I had known years before when I walked up Fifth Avenue after work and compared the parade of luxury and conspicuous consumption with the poverty of the tenements. I preached a fiery sermon indicting both the nation and the Christian churches for such a shameful situation.

Although the press reports played up the red scare, the eminence and integrity of the committee commanded attention and respect. But the strike was crushed and "the fear of God" beaten into the strikers by the company police. The deputy sheriffs hastily recruited from among the street corner loafers and bums of our big cities. These left their mark of terror on the steel communities for many years, as I discovered during my pastorate as a home missionary much later.

The summers in Vernon were pleasant indeed. A large section of the parsonage garden was placed at my disposal where I raised vegetables for our table. I discovered how sweet and tender Golden Bantam corn can be if picked immediately before cooking. Tomatoes too had never tasted so good, like the ripe peas of which we received generous portions for a few cents from the farmers on their way to the canning factory! But we paid the price later, for seldom, if ever, could we enjoy fresh vegetables from stores again. They never tasted fresh.

There was no vacation for us, not even a few brief days. Yet, relieved from the heavy grind of studies, much of the day spent in the open air under sun-filled skies, the relaxed attitude made possible by the affectionate concern of our people, all of them our friends, summers were real vacations after all. Walking home on the dark road, our arms about each other, we did not suspect that our members caught glimpses of us, and we were rather embarrassed when we learned about it. But our members loved us even more for that.

One summer in 1920, when we were expecting our first born, my mother was our guest for six weeks. She also brought with her my two sisters, Margaret, twelve, and Mary, fourteen. Naturally much of our conversation centered on her expected new grandchild, on child training, and on our hopes and ambitions for him — or her. Ann was determined to present me with a boy, and of this "Grandma" approved. Somehow, it did not matter much to me, in spite of the strong prejudice in favor of the male in the Hungarian culture.

Neither Ann nor I had received any sex information in our homes, but picked it up wherever available. Much of it was wrong, inadequate, and most of it on my side, rather smutty and foul. Now with our little one on the way, we were determined to give such information ourselves consisting not only of facts but of ideals and right attitudes as well. My poor, old-fashioned mother, conditioned through the major portion of her life by Roman Catholic teaching, was horrified.

"What? Parents themselves giving their children such information? Scandalous!"

"Would you like to hear how I'll tell him?" asked Ann.

"I certainly would!" she replied with emphasis.

"Well, it will be something like this. When God created mothers, he also created within them a little mansion through which He will work the process of creating His children. Each month there is a house-cleaning in this mansion, but also a magic egg is put into it and only a magic key can open its gate and unite it with the magic egg. When these come together God puts the life into it so that from that time this life grows — develops into a little baby. For nine months this little baby is in the mansion, sheltered from all harm, fed through magic tubes coming from the mother, the most comfortable place he will ever know during his whole life. The baby grows and after nine months it is big enough and strong enough to adventure into the wide, cold outside world. He begins to go through a narrow dark tunnel to the little gate. This gives pain to the mother and when he comes to the gate he begins to knock, knock. Each knock also gives the mother pain but he insists as if he could say, "please open the gate so I can come out." Often, in fact almost always, the doctor helps him to come through the gate safely. He pops his head out, then out he comes. Everyone rejoices and welcomes him except he himself and he begins to yell announcing that he has lungs and that he is here. He is not happy — why did he have to leave that comfortable place and flop into this cold world where it is so hard to breathe at first? But that is life and that is the way you came to us. Oh how happy we are! It is God that sent you to us, and we are grateful."

There was a long silence. Mother's eyes were filled with tears. What her tongue was unable to say, the warm glow in her face did, "I had no idea it could be so beautiful." Never again did she object.

With the coming of fall, we moved back to Hamilton. The football season crashed into the quiet village. The Red Raiders of Colgate were a famous team, usually much better than such small colleges possessed. We regularly played giant Syracuse on Thanksgiving Day. We did not care if we lost every other game but that one. Everybody in the village had but one thought: Beat Syracuse! At the final rallies before the big game, the bigwigs, who included the administration and favorite professors, addressed the student body and faculty, calling on all to fight as one man. "Beat Syracuse" was the refrain. Long before we left the town, the enthusiasm generated by the rallies, cheers, and fighting songs was at fever pitch. On the day of the match, almost the entire village boarded the long special train to Syracuse. When we arrived, we formed a column with our band in front and marched through the streets of the city roaring our defiance and shouting our songs, "For we will fight, fight, fight for dear old Colgate!" The Colgate crowd looked pitifully small in comparison. No matter. We had the fighting spirit, win or lose. Our squad ran out and was greeted with a roaring "Co-o-o-olgate, Co-o-o-olgate, Co-o-o-olgate! Rah! Rah! Rah!"

And if we lost, reformed our marching column with the band in the lead, shouting, cheering for our team, and roaring our challenge to giant Syracuse. We marched to the steps of their city hall, held an impromptu rally, and marched to the train. Only on the train did I we give way to our disappointment and gloom relieved by the memory of proud moments in the game, and the determination to win the following year.

My Ann was an enthusiastic fan. Never did I dream that my gentle wife could develop such a wild determination to win. She cheered and cheered. We seldom missed a game, and a deep sadness settled on us when we lost that was difficult to shake off.

We started our trips to Vernon again. About midway, we had to change from a train to a large electric coach. This was quite a trial on cold winter days, for there was no station — only an open shed at Clark's Mills. One Friday evening my Ann, always friendly, noticed a little hunchback waiting too. She engaged him in conversation, much to my disgust, for I had not yet overcome my big-city reserve, nor an unreasonable jealousy. I made my displeasure quite clear, but my sensible, tenderhearted wife wisely paid no attention.

In the coach, the conductor called out each destination as he took our tickets. "Vernon," I heard him call. I glanced back and saw the hunchback give the conductor his ticket. Mortified, ashamed, conscience-stricken, I wondered how I was going to preach the Gospel of love in that little town where everybody knew everybody else after the way I had acted and felt.

Some days later, on the way home from Sunday morning worship, Ann developed one of those strange cravings of pregnant women. She asked me to step into a garden we were passing and pick a few apples for her. I protested in horror, "What? You want me to go into a stranger's garden and steal? And on the way home from church?"

"But I must have some or I'll be sick!"

"Don't you see that they are green? You'll get sick if you eat them."

By the time I reached home, I was worn down. Picking up a paper bag I humbly went to the back door of the house where we had seen the apple trees to make this silly request of the strangers who lived there. I prepared an apology and an explanation as I hurried over. When the door opened it was our hunchbacked friend! I blabbered my request and apology in great humility. The apology he kindly waved aside and filled my bag.

Returning home, I washed those green apples thoroughly, accompanied by many a headshake, and fearfully set them on a chair alongside the couch wondering what would happen next. I watched her eat them all, a dozen or more, and waited for the unhappy, inevitable results. To my astonishment, she got up and prepared dinner with no ill effects. I was discovering how unpredictable women are, especially pregnant women.

About this time she also developed a periodic, great insecurity and fear for the future that she was unable to dispel no matter how hard she tried. She loved our people dearly, and she knew they loved her and showered us with gifts of food and invitations to meals, but periodically she resented our small salary and wished they had kept their gifts and paid us more. Later, she was heartily ashamed of it, but at the time, she was powerless. Oh pregnant women!

I was very uneasy on weekends when it was no longer advisable for Ann to accompany me. We could not afford a telephone, and living in a house by ourselves with no close neighbors handy and our first child on the way, I was consumed by anxiety until I reached home again. Finally, we secured Mrs. Gates, a trained nurse and member of our own church, to come and be with her while I was in classes and away on weekends. But the blessed baby took its time and arrived only two weeks later. Fortunately, I too was at home and saw the wonderful miracle of human birth. I held her hand through the process. The doctor, perhaps feeling uncertain about my possible reactions or maybe feeling sorry for me, sent me to the drugstore for something I'm sure he did not need, but I ran all the way and arrived home to see my little daughter emerge. "Slap her, slap her," said the doctor, then the welcome little cry. "You have a little boy," said the doctor, but the little mother responded with indignation,

"Don't try to fool me! I heard you say 'Slap her!'" The nurse placed her in my arms and we wept for joy.

With all our idealism we are also quite realistic, and we saw nothing beautiful or even pretty about our tiny baby. In fact, we thought she was rather homely with her very white face — from all the apples? She had jet black hair and stick-like arms and legs. But she was our own, and when our physician left, we wept again as we gave thanks to God and pledged our best to the challenge of parenthood.

Our kind nurse stayed with us another ten days and, with many apologies, charged us only $50 for the twenty-two days. My Ann had it all ready for her under her pillow — good old days and wonderful people! Our doctor's fee was equally considerate.

The following Sunday, the church made up a convoy of three or four cars and took me home immediately after the evening service, bringing gifts of love for the baby and her mother.

Then came the exciting and great day of Commencement. The impressive pageant of the academic procession, the eloquent addresses, and the happy faces of relatives and friends, and the slow, majestic music filled the chapel. The new dignity of achievement in the bearing of the graduates with their diplomas in hand, rolled and secured by maroon colored silk ribbons, made this an unforgettable occasion for us, even if some of the faculty and administration may have found it boring, as I and the faculty did later at the university where I taught. Bachelor of Theology students, about fifteen of us, also had a separate service in the seminary at which two students spoke. The greatest thrill was undoubtedly that of my mother. Years of hardship, prayers, and hopes were rewarded in that overwhelming hour of realization that her education, that had been made impossible by the limited and perhaps selfish vision of her father, she gloriously realized in her eldest son. And to see that he had been chosen as one of the speakers for this occasion, was almost more than she could bear. Tears of joy and gratitude rolled down her cheeks. Nor did I hesitate to lay the laurel wreath of achievement at her feet. And this atoned in part for all her disappointments in her family for whom she had high expectations, perhaps unreasonably so.

But I was also indebted almost as much to my lovely, determined, sacrificial, and uncomplaining wife who carried the burden of our long engagement for four and a half years and the burdens of self-denials and hardships in three years of struggling through college and serving a church. Now the long struggle was over.

We were finally ready to tackle the job we had prepared for — to be home missionaries to the Hungarians in the United States. Our church people pleaded with us to stay with them at least a year or two longer. And how hard it was to say no and to leave our friends, so devoted and loyal, whom we loved so dearly. Never again would we know the wholehearted unanimous support and love we enjoyed in our little country church. It would forever be our first and dearest love. Mercifully, this was hidden from us. But the original vision of service to our own people that had fired and impelled us into the long and hard struggle for an adequate education, was still with us. I was thirty-one and she twenty-eight — adults who had been maturing through the years. It was time to take up our life's work. Our Hungarian friends were determined and worked persistently behind the scenes to have one of the mission churches call us. Finally, the call came from a church actually smaller in membership than our little English-speaking church. It was a tearful farewell all around as we entrained for the daylong trip to the big city of spiritual opportunity. How fortunate that we could not glimpse the future!

14 - A Happy, Hopeless Task

We found ourselves in a pleasant little community — a working-class suburb of Chicago. The tree-lined streets, tiny lawns, colorful gardens, and clean houses made a good impression on me. Ann knew this area very well, for this had been her mission field while at Baptist Missionary Training School. In large part, it was her devoted and successful work there that led their modest church to call us. She was dearly loved here and the people awaited us eagerly. Also, we had been advertised as the best-educated couple in Hungarian Baptist work, and the church looked forward to our ministry with great expectations.

It had been one of the outstanding churches for a generation, and pride in the past never left them — but generated nostalgic longings for a resurrection of their greatness. Alas, the Russellites, now known as Jehovah's Witnesses, brought in their Gospel and split the church. The leadership of the church was an earnest and committed group, but was unprepared to deal with this new doctrine.

The movement was the child of a Baptist minister in Pittsburgh — Pastor Russell. It encouraged an extreme development of Baptist democracy. In the Hungarian churches, too, all members were considered ministers, but they also had their ordained pastors and missionaries, who wielded considerable power because of their office, as well as their personal endowments. Their former pastor, Brother Balogh, virtually the founder, was a rather authoritarian personality who emphasized a strict morality and generous giving through the tithe. In the new dispensation of the Russellites, the tithe was made unnecessary, for there were no full-time ministers to support.

Preaching and teaching once again became the privilege of all, and how those simple brethren loved to preach! According to their teaching, the Savior was already in the world, incognito, preparing His followers for the translation of the saints before Armageddon and the end of history. They were the chosen few insiders sharing in the secret of God's grand design. It was very intoxicating and apparently well-backed by passages selected helter-skelter from various parts of the Bible. Finally, about half of the congregation left the church and formed a fellowship of their own. It gradually disintegrated. A few of the more prosperous or better-educated members left the community and joined other churches.

There were about sixty members left in the little church. We were starting again with a membership with which we had begun our work in Vernon. But no matter, these were our people, torn by "wolves," and discouraged in heed. All this engaged our sympathy, kindled our devotion, and strengthened our determination to give our best.

It was not easy to begin. We were taken in by a widow who lived in a tiny house with four rooms heated by two stoves with simple, inexpensive furniture. As winter came, we were not very comfortable. The walls sweated so that we had to wipe off the moisture, and before long our baby, almost two years old, and her mother developed an infection of the ear.

Four years after World War I, there was still a shortage of housing, but by persistent effort on our part and our church members, we finally located a nice apartment of six rooms. The landlord, however, refused to clean and refinish it so we had to use part of our meager savings to do it. Forty years later we still remember with gratitude our kind Mr. Lovas, a painter and paperhanger with his own little store, who gave us his time freely and materials at a greatly reduced cost.

Due to my Ann's expert financial management, we were able to pay cash for our furniture. We had skimped and saved for three years. She'd had no new winter coat or hat for five years, to mention just two items. For years she had dreamed of her color scheme, that we now proceeded to carry out. Because we bought almost all our furniture in one store, we received a very generous discount. Finally, our new little nest was ready.

We invited our best friend for a preview. He stood in the doorway, speechless, then he said, "I knew it would be pretty, but I didn't imagine it would be so beautiful!"

Three months after our arrival, we had our housewarming. My Ann was determined to treat our simple, poor brethren with the same expansive and generous hospitality as our professor friends at Colgate. Out came our new dishes, finest linen, best silver, gifts of our Vernon church, and the best food served in style.

Our members came and our little apartment could barely accommodate them all. We borrowed chairs from our landlady and friends. We were overjoyed to entertain them. Ann's happy laughter and enthusiastic greeting filled my ears and heart with joy. Only slowly did we realize that our friends were much less enthusiastic. Now and then we caught glances and expressions and whispers that we were unable to interpret. Only later did we awaken to the unhappy realization that many, if not most, of them suffered tortures of envy. Our home and our generous treatment were interpreted as flaunting our possessions, education, and manners. Our joyous generosity was a sad mistake — an error in judgment — but in spite of the inevitable disappointments of life in our friends, we still recall these days with gratitude.

Yet my Ann was entitled to a nice home. She had waited long enough for it, skimping and saving to make it possible. Our church had contributed nothing toward it. Our salary was $130 a month plus no prerequisites such as our premium into the pension fund of the denomination, utilities, rent, convention, etc., yet we came gladly — happy in the privilege of serving God through serving our people. Not until we received our first check did we even know what our salary would be, and most of it was paid by the home and city mission societies.

Our idealism, a gift of our Heavenly Father, came to our aid. We made all kinds of excuses for our simple people — even inventing some.

A very new and dear friend, himself a candidate for the ministry and a member of the church, softened the blow and warmed our hearts with special kindnesses and a recital of the special virtues of various members, and also various unhappy experiences in their lives that might account for their shortcomings.

With undiminished enthusiasm, we continued our work. The little chapel was an architectural gem — not at all like the unattractive structures in most places erected by building contractors without architectural oversight or guidance (it was spoiled later by its elevation on a high foundation to provide a basement for social affairs). The sanctuary had lovely dark-green comfortable pews. The platform was furnished in good taste, and at the back of the pulpit beyond green velvet curtains there was a large Baptistery with a realistic picture of the Jordan River flowing into the pool. Well-lighted, flanked by palms, and surrounded by ferns and flowers at immersions — it was a pretty and inspiring sight, kept very clean by a dedicated sexton.

A small organ and a piano for music, providentially played by a highly gifted young high school student with an unusual feeling for nuances in worship, provided a wonderful complement and background for the minister that rivaled large churches with much larger organs. He led our small choir with equally surprising finesse and listened to the sermons with attention and reverence seldom found in church organists.

Our congregations were quite satisfying. In the narrow, unworldly channel of their religious life, devotion to the church and all its activities flowed strong and deep. Absence from religious services was unthinkable without good reason. Slowly, as new people drifted in, the congregation grew in numbers, and we were encouraged by additions to our membership.

So, it was both a satisfying aesthetic experience as well as an uplifting spiritual one to lead in worship and to preach, but also very taxing. Since all of my education from my twelfth year had been in the English language, I found it necessary to prepare my sermons in that tongue and then translate them into Hungarian.

All during this process I found it necessary to simplify my message so that even my illiterate elderly folk, as well as our American-born youth possessing only a smattering of Hungarian, would understand it. At the same time, I had to be aware that a few of my members had a good education and others had unusually good minds. These might be bored by too simple a message.

I tried my best to meet this challenge, but it played havoc with my dreams of developing a fine style according to the standards implanted at Colgate University. Many years later, a leader in the American Baptist Convention made a flattering reference to the vivid and concrete terms and phrases in my preaching. So, as nearly always, there were compensations too in this discipline. I am grateful, but still often wonder how I might have developed instead in English-speaking pulpits of suburban churches with a well-educated congregation, such as some of my colleagues always had.

My congregation rewarded and inspired me with close and reverent attention. Only one tired businessman would take a brief or extended snooze during sermon time. Almost never did I succeed in keeping him awake to the end of the sermon. It did not take very long, however, to discover that our American-born children and young people were not receiving much from the sermon in what to them was not their mother tongue but a second one. Almost unconsciously, as I noticed their attention wandering, I suddenly swung into English with a word or a phrase or even a sentence or two to make clear the meaning of what I tried to convey. At once their eyes lit up and their flagging interest was revived.

But the adults were shocked. At the next business meeting of the church I had to defend my rude action of breaking into a foreign tongue in the midst of a sacred discourse. I attempted to explain the dilemma of our youngsters as well as my own. Those with children appreciated my endeavor even if they could not fully approve, in view of the strong opposition of other adults. I asked for freedom to experiment — to tell a children's story or make a very brief presentation in English. This was granted, but at the next service, when I launched into English, one of my deacons stood up and, with eyes blazing, stomped from the sanctuary.

It dawned upon us that a psychological chasm was opening between the immigrant generation and their children that boded ill for the families and the church. To build bridges across the lack of understanding and misunderstanding, we established two new institutions — a weekday school for the children and an evening school for adults.

The children met Wednesday afternoons after school and spent about ninety minutes learning Hungarian folksongs about the heroic legends of their Magyar ancestors, the tragic but glorious history of one thousand years, and little Hungary's contributions to mankind. The main purpose was to dispel their sense of inferiority arising from their ignorance of the parents' backgrounds and to instill in its place a certain pride for the land of their ancestors. We hoped that this might draw the children closer to their parents despite their parents' poor knowledge of the history of their adopted land.

Among these children was a very unruly group of four from the Kral family. They were restless, lively, and undisciplined but lovable children. We could never predict what might happen in an unguarded moment, such as climbing through the church windows. One day I met the mother on the street.

"Oh Mister Kautz what are you and your wife doing to our children?" she asked.

Somewhat taken aback, I parried with another question, "I have no idea. What have they done?"

"Well, recently they have been spending more time with us and asking questions about life in the Old Country. And you ought to hear them sing some of our folk songs."

I explained to one grateful parent the purpose and program of our Hungarian school. But this did not save me from resentful questions by my elderly parishioners who demanded an explanation for the impious act of teaching folk songs in a church — an utterly worldly procedure on the part of their pastor. Despairingly, but patiently, I tried to explain, but without much success.

One Wednesday afternoon, Charlie Kral was waiting for me at the church. Excitedly, he explained how his public school teacher remarked to him that day after he had told her one of our hero stories — that his parents came from a great nation. Evidently, Charlie was no longer ashamed of his ancestry.

For our adults, we set up a school in Americanization consisting of two classes: beginners, who would learn to converse and to read and write English; and the advanced, who would learn about the history of the United States and prepare for citizenship. It was gratifying indeed to note how their understanding and appreciation of America grew as we shared with them its ideals and the struggles and sacrifices of its people, the idealism, and the unbelievable success stories not duplicated elsewhere.

One day, I told the story of the Boxer Indemnity Fund. In reaction against foreign exploitation and the grabs of Chinese territory by European powers, the people, led by the fanatical patriots called Boxers, rose against the White settlers, merchants, and missionaries, and slaughtered thousands of them. The foreign powers in concert sent in their armed forces, crushed the revolt, and sent heavy bills of damages for the lives and property destroyed to the Imperial Court. In due time these were paid. When the share allotted to the United States was paid (about twenty-five million dollars) our government returned the money. The surprised and grateful Chinese, in turn, used these millions to establish an educational fund whose income was used to send thousands of Chinese to study in America.

As I told this heartwarming story, I noted a peculiar expression on the faces of the men and women before me. Its meaning slowly dawned upon me. They had a difficult time believing my story, for this was not the kind of America they had learned to know in the mills, mines, and steel plants. Their bosses and employers did not have such attitudes.

Clearly, their pastor was carried away by his idealism and enthusiasm for his adopted land and unwittingly exaggerated something he'd read somewhere. Nevertheless, there came a new appreciation for and new confidence in the New Country even though they had suffered injustices, and many workers had been exploited mercilessly by their employers.

One of the infrequent visitors at church services was a young bachelor — a self-confessed atheist and Red Communist. We rather liked each other even though our philosophies clashed whenever we met. All my endeavors to interpret Christ or America fell to the ground. Then one day, rather unexpectedly, he made a confession. "You know, I work in that coal yard over there. We work pretty hard sometimes when rush orders come in or we fall behind in our deliveries. When this happens, the boss comes out of the office, rolls up his sleeves, and shovels the coal along with us. Now, can you imagine a boss in the Old Country doing this?"

"No, I can't," I assured him.

"Well," he continued, "I see now that America is very different after all. I'm glad I am here."

One day, a ten-year-old boy came in while the Sunday school was in session and began to distribute some leaflets. Glancing at the leaflets, I noticed that it was Russellite literature. Promising him that I would distribute them myself after class, I took the leaflets and he left. In a little while he was back again distributing his leaflets. Scolding him gently for thinking me a liar, I took away his literature and asked him to tell the people who sent him not to disturb our services, for I had caught sight of some adults with him outside. He did not return.

At the close of the Sunday school, I announced what had happened and gave the leaflets to two adults at the door and asked them to distribute them. Some of the older members, who had been through the terrible days when the church lost quite a number of its members, including some prominent lay leaders, turned pale and rushed up to me protesting this outrage. I stood my ground. In any case, the church lost no more of its members to the Russellites.

It is with sad misgivings that I pen the following lines, for I loved these people. Yet I feel I ought to do so for the light it may shed on our common lot. Slowly, unwillingly, I was forced to realize that about a tenth of our members, all of them adults, suffered from serious mental disturbances. (Gladly would I have given all of my language courses for more psychology! Those I had in college and seminary in 1917-1922 were of no help at all.) One of those was the mother of six children or more, very proud and very gifted, but most of the time caught up in emotional turmoil. She was one of those consumed by envy at our housewarming.

When she gave birth, my Ann waited on her, washed the diapers, cleaned the house, and helped in every possible way. Some time later I made a pastoral call. She paced the floor and engaged in endless denunciation of nearly everybody. When I knelt to pray, she continued, and as I was leaving she blurted out, "Why does your wife have only two children and I so many? Why don't I have a good husband?" I thought her husband *was* a good man. When she was inspired in church during the congregational singing, her voice arose clear and strong in a pure mezzo-soprano of lovely quality and perfect pitch. With proper opportunities and training, she might have become one of the great singers of our time. Perhaps this bottled-up potential, unceasing childbearing, and the hardships of immigrant life all conspired against her.

Occasionally, there was a touch of humor in our situation. One day in the course of a visit by my Ann, the wife of one of our deacons remarked, "You know, it's so lovely to hear your husband address you in such endearing terms."

"Doesn't yours?"

"No, he does not."

"Do you talk to him like that?"

"The old fool? I should say not!"

Both of them were around forty-five.

One summer we went to a little town in Michigan for a week's vacation. Several of our members lived there, and we hoped for accommodation at a rate we could afford. At one of these homes the family had "gone native." The place was dirty, and the people went about barefoot in soiled and spotted clothing with unkempt hair and unwashed faces. This was very strange, for our people were usually very clean. At once we sensed a certain hostility, confirmed when they proudly informed us of their humility, for they did not show off in fine clothing and went about barefooted as did Jesus and His disciples.

We retreated as quickly and gracefully as possible and knocked at the tiny cottage of another family, a man and his wife who were uneducated peasants from Hungary. Their home was poorly furnished, with only benches instead of chairs, but everything was spotlessly clean including their persons. They gave us a warm welcome, made us sleep in their own bed, and they themselves slept on a mattress on the floor.

Then there was the very masculine "he-man" who treated his shy, obedient wife with condescension and commanded her about as his slave. In their case, the term *uram* (my Lord), used by women as the equivalent of "my husband," literally meant just that. Their children came in quick succession. She soon wilted and perished. Sure of his masculine glamour, he remarried soon after. To be certain that he would find a woman of the Old World culture whom he could manage, he went back to the hometown in his native land. This time, however, he met his match, and soon after, the new wife was his boss, to everybody's satisfaction and amusement.

It reminded me of an ancient story when the lord of a manor arrived to find his home looted by Tartar raiders. He caught a glimpse of his wife on the saddle in front of the bandit chieftain and sighed, "Poor Tartar!"

After a few months, our unprincipled landlord sold the house and we had to move out of our lovely apartment. Fortunately, we soon found another, right next to the church, clean and large but dark. However, right over the fence on the church's property was a garden where our sexton's wife grew vegetables and lovely flowers. Our little daughter, about three years old, had a wonderful time with the elderly lady. She often played there with her little friend Lily.

One day, Lily fell out of her crib and died. We felt that we ought not to hide the realities of life from our child, so we took her to see her little dead friend. "There are the inevitable questions, and we hope adequate answers," my Ann said.

We were now expecting our second child. Ann came regularly to our daily Vacation Bible School to play the piano and tell a story. Our missionary, Miss Knopf, was of great help, and thanks to her persistent footwork we had a large attendance of children of many creeds and nationalities. The parish priest from the nearby Catholic Church took a walk every day past our chapel to see if any of his children attended. They were duly warned off, the parents notified, and not a few were able to keep them away from the heretics.

One day, one of our members, Mrs. Paul, made an unexpected call on Ann. Her flushed face, fiery stare, clenched hands, and general demeanor betrayed extreme tension. To Ann's greeting and questions, she gave excited and incoherent answers. Did Ann know where her husband was? No. She rushed into our bedroom to look around and then ran out and down the street. Ann quickly locked the door and sat down trembling. Unfortunately, I was out making pastoral calls. What was wrong? Some days later, Mrs. Paul confessed that she was very jealous of her husband and was driven to desperation by suspicions of his affairs. She hardly knew what she was doing and had to rush out before she'd attack Ann physically. It is a wonder that this utterly unjustified action did not bring on the premature birth of our second baby.

My amazing wife, however, was present at the birth of Mrs. Paul's next child. She waited on her, washed the diapers, bathed the baby, cleaned up the apartment, and helped in every way possible. The husband was always respectful, appreciative, and kind. He had a little trucking business, that often took him away from home. He was a winsome, happy-go-lucky chap, and in the course of his business had many contacts with housewives. I never came across any misbehavior on his part to justify her unceasing jealousy. He was a faithful attendant at worship, always paying close attention to the sermon, and very appreciative. We never saw him misbehave.

Ann had made careful preparations for our second child. Her obstetrician was a woman who'd been her school physician. The approximate date was set, and a place reserved at the "Lying-in Hospital" — or so we'd thought. One night Ann awakened me with the news that her pains were increasing and occurring every five to ten minutes. Would I call up her physician? We discovered she was on her vacation. Somehow we got hold of her vacation telephone number and called her. She calmly informed us that she would call the hospital and make all the arrangements. We need not worry. She'd have a competent colleague take charge. So I quickly called a cab and dressed in record time. We were barely ready when the driver rang our bell, and we hurried out as quietly as possible, leaving our three-year-old asleep in her crib. The cab driver took one glance and sized up the situation. We blessed him ever since, because he drove ever so carefully, avoiding many bumps and holes on the poorly paved streets.

When we arrived at the hospital, we discovered that, despite what we were promised, no arrangements had been made. My poor Ann was thrown on the mercy of a cold, unsympathetic intern. How we longed for Dr. Bebee, whose blessed hand relieved her of much suffering when our firstborn arrived. I thought of Mrs. Schuetz, the midwife who assisted my mother at the birth of the last two of her twelve children. More than once my mother had remarked, "Her hands ought to be plated with gold, they help so much."

But my poor Ann suffered more with our second child than with the first. After an interminable wait while I sat helplessly by and walked up and down the room, they took her to the delivery room. I rushed to the telephone and called up our good missionary, informing her of our plight. She dressed quickly and hastened over to our apartment, fortunately finding the baby still asleep. Then I went back to my wife, who was wheeled out of the delivery room exhausted but smiling bravely. We had another healthy little baby — a blonde this time. I too must have looked a scare, for with great pity in her big eyes, my Ann asked me to go home and rest.

Some weeks later, we called on one of our elderly members, a very devout man bedridden and mortally ill with cancer of the stomach. For years before coming to America, he had been one of the colporteurs of the British Bible Society in Hungary. He had suffered not a little for his faith and was highly regarded by the church even though he no longer was in religious work. As we stepped into the sick room to pray with him and bring what comfort we could, he suddenly sat bolt upright in his bed, his face distorted by passion, and pointing his finger at my poor wife, shouted, "Out, unclean, out!" We almost collapsed. There was no explanation, but later we learned that he was upset because my wife had not observed the period prescribed by Moses when a mother is considered unclean after giving birth.

To make matters worse, two or three women in the church were persistent centers of gossip. These scandal mongers invented the most unbelievable but juicy morsels of gossip and kept the church in constant agitation. The church was an increasingly ingrown group, with very few accessions, away from the main center of Hungarian immigrants living a very restricted life. This created a situation where they rubbed elbows constantly, knew each other's faults too well, and, instead of trying to win others, always tried to reprove and improve each other. And, being human, they all had a generous share of common frailties, plus some special ones generated in such situations.

Then, to top it all, one of our deacons went wrong. He had made advances to a fifteen-year-old child, daughter of his wife by a previous marriage. They covered up his sin for quite a while until they could not bear it any longer. The man confessed and was ready to make atonement in whatever way the other deacons and the church decided. His wife would no longer live with him. The decision was made that he return to the Old Country, leaving his house and furniture and bank account to the family and taking only enough for his passage and for self-support until he found a job. We had a last prayer together on our knees in my home, then I escorted him to the street, and with a heartfelt grip of his hand bade him farewell. My heart broke when I said goodbye to him. We wept. I can still see him, a bent and broken old man, half-blind, deprived of an industrious life's rewards, going down the street and out of our lives. Occasionally, I still wonder sometimes if at heart he wasn't better than some of his judges. He was almost sixty years old, had lost an eye in the shop, and had been a faithful member of the church for years, generous in giving and fervent in prayer.

This shook the little group to the depths. Recriminations and accusations followed. Blame was heaped upon the pastor and the officers of the church. How could such filth go on for so long undiscovered? But apparently, until his wife told me the story, nobody suspected his involvement with her child. It became increasingly difficult to trust one another. The business meetings degenerated into such loud quarrels that the windows had to be kept closed. Sunday services could scarcely be edifying under such circumstances. I have always been very sensitive to the reactions of my hearers before they were expressed, and on one of these agonizing Sundays, as I was preaching, the psychic wave of hostility was so powerful that I almost collapsed. With supreme effort, I stayed upright and successfully brought worship to a close, but now it was evident that we could no longer stay. In addition, even more seriously, Ann's physician warned me that she would die within a year unless I speedily took her out of that poison-infested atmosphere.

We invited the city mission secretary to dinner and informed him fully about our circumstances. He was exceedingly sympathetic. He trusted us and was very fond of both of us. In the little mission churches among the German settlers of the West, his father had found similar conditions and, if I remember correctly, suffered much as we did. He assured us of his own confidence and of God's concern, and promised to stand by us whatever happened. Then, as we knelt about the table, he prayed for us, thanking God for the honor He extended to us by calling us to such a difficult field, and asking that His Will be done in our lives. We received a new infusion of strength and determination to stay on longer.

Soon, however, another scandal broke. An adult son from one of the families that had been a center of evil gossip suddenly left his wife and disappeared. I have no doubt that his relatives knew where he was, but in this case they were not very eager to talk. Belatedly, we learned what had happened, and I had another firsthand experience with the peculiar social forces in our country, for this man went a distance of not more than sixty miles, over the border of his own state to the next state, and set up a new home in another town.

He had made careful inquiries and then acted on them. Fulfilling the legal requirement for residence, he inserted an advertisement in a regional newspaper asking for information concerning the whereabouts of his wife. Nobody who knew her, of course, ever read these items. Finally, he appeared in court with his lawyer asking for a divorce. The judge in all good conscience had no choice but to grant it. So, in one state he was a bigamist liable for prosecution, and in the other he was legally married.

In my spiritual agony, unable to sow and nourish the seeds of a healthy spiritual life, I planted a half dozen trees in front of the church property, which helped to maintain our sanity. The fragrance of their blossoms in spring and their shade in the hot days of summer still symbolize our hopes and efforts for the spiritual life of that church. Alas, others followed us — choice spirits with commitment and sacrificial devotion, wisdom, and broad experience — but in vain.

Still, there were joys and satisfactions. There were no further losses to the Russellites, nor to the Pentecostals, both of whom were making determined efforts to capture the church. Then there were a few choice spirits who appreciated our labors and courageously stood by us. Others less brave gave us hidden support by their affection and sympathy. And a very few caught the vision we were seeking to share of a life of genuine devotion to our Heavenly Father without the doctrinal rigidities and the concealed, often unconscious selfishness and spiritual snobbery frequently found among those who claim to be God's chosen.

Shortly before we left, one of those who converted during our stay, an uneducated but gifted man, gave us a testimonial that still warms our hearts and inspires our gratitude. It was after a dinner in his home, one of the last in the community. As we were chatting, he suddenly said, "Do you know what made me decide to be a Christian?"

"No, I have no idea, but I should like to know."

"Of all the ministers who preached in our church, you were the only one who did not try to frighten me into a decision for Christ with the fires of hell. You always emphasized the love of God and how the only adequate response to that was the gift of our love and life in return."

How happy we were! How the angels sang in my heart for days after that! Today, one of his sons is a foreign missionary in Japan.

But no matter how we loved, forgave, and worked, tensions mounted in the church, inside of us, and even in the community, to which some of our own members leaked our troubles. We were at a dead end. The first time, and perhaps the most serious one of several. Finally, we could stand it no more. One Sunday, I resigned, effective as of the next day. Much as this should have pleased them, they were in shock. They listened to my poor sermon in dead silence and hurried out of the church with looks of guilt.

Our city mission secretary was as good as his word. He provided preaching appointments for the next few weeks, kept my small salary coming, and took steps to induce the Home Mission Society to employ us as general missionaries in a tristate area. We moved to another suburb, bought a modest home to serve as headquarters, and looked forward to a new start. Our future was quite uncertain, but the unbearable tensions had been lifted, and we began to plan our spiritual campaign on our new and extended field.

15 - My First Adventure in Teaching

My train was approaching my new destination, the lovely city of East Orange, New Jersey. It had been a long, restless, lonely night. Separated from my wife and our two little girls, two and five years of age, my heart ached for their happy company at breakfast, and I felt very lonely as I contemplated a new and uncertain life among strangers. How welcome would I be?

The school president had been eager enough to invite me. He had come a thousand miles to interview me, and along with two eminent Baptist leaders, brought considerable pressure upon me to accept. But would that be enough to assure a cordial welcome? He had to find someone immediately because the former head of the Hungarian Department had resigned suddenly to take charge of the church I had given up. Undoubtedly, he was better fitted for the pastorate than for teaching. He had no formal education in college or a standard seminary. His students were complaining about his teaching — no wonder, since he himself had no hope for the future of the school. Every church in the convention had a pastor, and these ministers were uneasy about the competition from the seminarians. Only much later did I learn how serious this was when the students complained about the remarks of these pastors, "Where do you expect to serve? Which church can invite you? Whose place do you expect to take?" And these pastors would twit to me, "Did you go to East Orange to bury the school?"

But full of hopes, dreams, and enthusiasm and the conceit of youth, I always replied, "The school will live and thrive as never before." Good-naturedly they laughed at the young upstart. They grudgingly admired my spirit and idealism. They welcomed me to their pulpit. I preached my heart out on faith in God and the opportunities still beckoning in Hungarian areas untouched by the Baptist message.

I wondered about the students. Only eight of them were left, all of them immigrants with little education, and two or three were as old as myself. There were no textbooks in Hungarian, so they had to take down in their slow handwriting my lectures, and these notes became their textbooks. Some simple texts on the Bible and theology would have to be found, but none were available in Hungarian. Would I have to translate the material from English and dictate the texts to them?

By the time my train arrived I was quite exhausted. I stepped off wondering if anybody would be there to greet and guide me to the school. There was no one. For once, I splurged on a taxi that delivered me to the school. My aesthetic sense was delighted with the splendid stone mansion, its parquet floors, marble fireplaces, crystal chandeliers, and well-appointed library, which was the gift of the president who was quite a scholar himself. The classrooms were adequate, well furnished, light, and attractive — beautiful in fact, with their paneled walls, lovely fireplaces with mantels and large mirrors over them. Soon I had settled in a guest room by the president himself, who received me cordially and was eager to set his new faculty member at ease. Then the Hungarian students arrived to greet their new professor. They had been at the station but had arrived a few minutes late.

Most of that night, I slept fitfully, wondering how I would teach seven subjects and twenty-two hours a week, using mostly Hungarian, when all of my own education from the sixth grade on through seminary had been in English. There were no textbooks to teach Hungarian grammar, composition, or literature except for a pitifully small fifty-page typed booklet from which my predecessor had lectured. Immediately, I borrowed such notes as the students had and set myself to keeping a day or two ahead of my students. Fortunately, I had saved my seminary texts and class notes, but it was already evident that I would have to adapt and simplify them immensely.

Even so, within a few weeks, I had a student rebellion on my hands.

My class in the Apostolic Age walked out on me after they read the test questions on the blackboard. They called me inhuman and a slave driver, and informed me that their former professor never treated them like that. Bewildered, disappointed, and hurt, I called in the president, explained the situation, and immediately translated the test questions. The president approved them and assured me of his wholehearted support.

It was evident, however, that the standards of scholarship would have to be raised far more gradually than I had imagined. Not very happily, I proceeded to do just that. I also cultivated my students socially, played volleyball with them, attended the daily devotions, never failed to pray, told stories of my own struggles and failures in school, and gradually established a good relationship with them.

The president recognized the impossible demands they had imposed on me and soon secured the editor of a Hungarian newspaper — a graduate of the University of Budapest — to teach the Hungarian cultural subjects.

The most fertile soil for the Baptist message had been the new immigrants who needed sympathy and encouragement, plus moral and material support. All this was gladly and plentifully given by the members of the Hungarian Baptist churches and missions. At the close of World War I, new federal legislation greatly reduced the influx of Hungarian immigrants. This affected other immigrant groups as well, especially those from Southern and Eastern Europe. This generated a feeling of pessimism among all of them concerning their future.

This pessimism invaded the Hungarian Baptist Union and reached its climax at the annual convention in New Castle, Pennsylvania. The secretary of the Union delivered a report that was utterly dark and hopeless. It sounded like the death knell of Hungarian Baptist Missions. The sanctuary of the Welsh Baptist Church, where they were holding their meetings, was decorated with black crepe for the funeral of an important member. With a flair for the dramatic and for extreme statements and something of a "ham," the secretary was not a person to miss a cue. Pointing to the black crepe on the walls, he shouted in anguish, "There, brethren! Even Providence is pointing to our future in these unplanned, unexpected funerary preparations."

Impenetrable gloom settled on the convention and enveloped its decisions in an atmosphere of defeatism.

It was in vain that I made an impassioned plea for faith and courage. I told them of a sapling I had observed in the Orange Hills, which had split a rock, wound itself around it, thrived, and grew into a large tree. Life had achieved the impossible. If plants could do that, how much more could be done by those who carried within themselves the divine life?

On my unending visits to the churches, I spoke on the future of the convention, challenged them to educate their youth, to use English whenever necessary in Sunday school, to instruct them in the glorious history, traditions, and culture of the Old Country, and to prepare immigrants for citizenship. I pointed out that they could not, indeed ought not, expect to maintain Hungarian islands in their adopted motherland that gave them the wonderful opportunities not to be found in the land of their birth. Let them remember how the undigested, alien islands in their own native land led to the dismembering of Hungary in the city of Trianon.

Americans had a right to be concerned about the forty million foreigners in their midst. He called for a gradual and grateful merging of their forces with those of their new mother, America — so ready to adopt us and grant to her adopted children the same rights, privileges, and opportunities that her native sons enjoyed.

I pointed out that to expect permanent Hungarian islands in the ocean of American culture was unrealistic and impossible. Inevitably, the tongue, so dear to the immigrants, would become a foreign language, secondary to English, particularly to their young people. Rural churches in compact settlements could resist the change for a longer period because of their isolation. Immigrant groups living in compact urban communities could also resist the pressures of the surrounding culture for a longer period, even in big cities. Ultimately, all of them would be absorbed.

If, in addition, we gave regular and enthusiastic instruction in the history, music, and literature of Hungary, and so developed an appreciation in our youth for their Old Country heritage, they may learn Hungarian with some enthusiasm and understand it better in our churches, and because of their appreciation, they'd develop patience when they did not understand it well.

About fifteen years later, when I became the pastor of a fair-sized English-speaking church, my daughter expressed a wish to hear a Hungarian sermon. Astonished I asked, "But why? You would hardly understand most of it."

She replied, "But daddy, it sounds so rich, much more so than English."

I also begged parents to send their youth to my school and I would prove to the doubters how the beauty of their tradition could capture their hearts and minds. In time, it might even be possible to persuade colleges to accept Hungarian in lieu of other foreign languages. Surely, school authorities would easily see the rich educational value of such a program.

Alas, neither the educated nor the uneducated immigrants appreciated my suggestions very much, and proceeded to act with extreme reluctance and slowness, but my enthusiasm challenged the attention of the brethren, if only to poke fun at me. I was a good preacher in both languages, so that both old and young listened to me with pleasure and profit, and they listened to my hopeful dreams and challenges. At times, they were enthralled in spite of themselves. As the years passed, they became accustomed to the notion that their churches might last as long as they, and concluded that the situation was less acute than they had imagined.

Once a year, I edited an educational publication of the official organ of the Hungarian Baptist Union. It was twice to six times the size of the regular issue and filled with inspirational articles in Hungarian and English on the need for education, Hungarian culture, descriptions of life at the seminary, including jokes, biographical sketches of religious and missionary heroes, and deep discussions of the Gospel. It was plentifully illustrated and became a sensation in Hungarian America. Much larger and wealthier denominations had nothing to compare it with, nor did the other departments at the school. I solicited advertisements from colleges and seminaries and excerpts from the Baptist Publication Society to illustrate this edition.

Hungarian Freedom Day was celebrated every year around March 15th. It was called "Hungarian Evening," a tradition at the school where our music, poetry, songs, and customs filled a two-hour program of such beauty and inspiration that it became a continued topic of conversation the rest of the year. Attendance grew steadily, and it became our biggest annual event, so had to be moved from Assembly Hall of the school to the First Baptist Church.

Unfortunately, this created a good deal of envy on the part of the other Departments — even in the administration itself, which implied a lack of loyalty and support on the part of the Department for School Affairs. They never acknowledged that they could draw on ten members of the faculty and the administration and the entire student body versus the single head of the Hungarian Department and its students for their one annual program.

One year the students of the Department presented one of the prize dramas of the American Drama League in Hungarian translation. This was given in a number of towns and cities in the East — usually in the churches.

In South Norwalk, Connecticut, the church rented the hall where the Hungarian theatrical companies presented their plays. The local paper reported in glowing terms of the production, stating that it was fully equal to that of the professionals and superior in content!

On another occasion, my class in Hungarian literature transformed the story of Jacob in the Old Testament into a play in Hungarian that they produced at a youth convention. It was generally agreed that neither before, nor after, did the Hungarian youth produce anything worthy of comparison. I directed both plays, and my wife did the makeup and supervised the costuming.

These and other interesting activities, along with the growing enthusiasm of the students, made the school a matter of pride to the churches. Here was a growing, living project of their boys, their girls, and their professor.

Increasingly, the Baptist Home Mission Society turned to me for suggestions when they contemplated changes in the field, but this was apt to be embarrassing, because the Hungarians had their own executive secretary who acted as their official liaison and expected to be consulted on all changes. This was proper, and I had to draw on all my tact to deal with those situations. Not that I had very much of it, but my naive bluntness established a reputation for reliability that others slowly lost because they were too concerned about giving "right" answers to their superiors. I was careful to refer them to the proper authority for consultation, yet shared my own opinion in confidence if pressed for it.

Over and above the impossible teaching load in two languages, supervision of the religious, moral, and social life of the department, the tension of a mediator between our American supervisors and my Hungarian colleagues was beginning to prove too much. In addition, the Old Country inheritance of ethnic rivalries, resentments, mistrust, and even hatred that grew out of World War I made the whole situation much more difficult.

Only Christian idealism tended to ameliorate the cultural conflicts and tensions of the common tradition of the suffering in Europe, of the Baptist sectarians inflicted by the Old State Churches and Confessional bodies, and the strong Baptist tradition against war and violence,. Nevertheless, World War I and the peace settlements weakened the common Baptist tradition, fanned patriotic fires, and caused endless discussions and arguments in their common brotherhood.

Soon after beginning my teaching at the seminary, some of my students engaged in one of their periodic and bitter discussions over the peace treaties with their fellow students from Czechoslovakia. This one ended in a fist fight. I was ashamed and hurt. In a school dedicated to Christian and Baptist brotherhood, the old virus of extreme, vainglorious, narrow patriotism had infected the minds of our students. It threatened to sap the strength, courage, and loyalty born of devotion to Jesus Christ, the Savior of all men, and to serve the divisive purposes of imported, narrow, chauvinistic European patriotism.

I called my students together and gave them a stern lecture on the meaning of the Christian Gospel. "Betrayers of the Love of God!" I called them, "Pagans with a thin veneer of Christianity," "Fools bewitched by the powers of this world, who were helping to cut into fragments the only body that could heal the wounds of war and hold the world together, the Christian Church, the Body of Christ."

Slowly, the climate changed. We even invited the Czechoslovak Department to a meeting of our Hungarian Cultural Society. This they finally accepted, but did not reciprocate until toward the end of the year, and only after repeated prodding by me through the Head of their Department.

Nearly forty years later I met this colleague at a banquet. His first words were, "You know, I had often thought about our harsh words against your people. It was too bad. We didn't really mean them."

But I knew better. Still, it was a good sign that even if belatedly that he spoke as he did. These tensions plus the frequent speaking appointments and my regular work at the school reduced me almost to a skeleton.

The food, by American standards, was fair, even good, but to our Old Country taste very unsatisfactory and, once in a while, impossible. I particularly remember the Thanksgiving dinner that first year. When the roasted turkeys, golden brown and plump, were carried in, the students broke into applause, with broad smiles and shining eyes. We could hardly wait for our first bite. But it tasted like fish. We left it all on our plates, including the first bite. Evidently, the birds had been fed on fish. The president and his wife bravely ate portions of it, but even their example could not revive our vanished appetites.

Before the term was over, severe pain developed in my stomach. Insomnia, listlessness, and irritability made me miserable. I had always been plagued by my limited energy and the need for regular hours for sleeping and recreation, and now I was almost at the end of my endurance.

My mother recognized my basic trouble. She kept saying, "Send him home to his wife and family and he will get well fast."

So it was. Home once again, showered with attention and affection by a loving wife and two happy, chattering little daughters, and free of the pressures of school, I was well again and preparing my summer trip to the churches and my courses for the coming year.

16 - New Achievements and Dreams

Fall came, and we were back together. One year of separation was long enough for all of us. They had been shut in for two weeks by one of the terrific blizzards of Chicago, the children had been ill, and my Ann almost bled to death with an infected tooth. We rented our house for a year, listed it for sale, and left together.

In no time at all, Ann transformed our new apartment, provided by the school, into a lovely home. How happy and proud our students were to have their professor back. They fell in love with my charming wife and beautiful children. They boasted about their professor's home and spent a good deal of their spare time in it. They were often guests on Sunday evenings for a simple but delicious Hungarian supper. Forty years later our daughters still recall with longing those joyous evenings. Full of good food, cheer, and fun, we sang our folk songs, Hungarian hymns, and gospel songs, and closed with a circle of prayers. Since the parents and ministers held us responsible for the physical and spiritual welfare of their sons and daughters, which we felt no less keenly on our own account, we fostered a close relationship with our students. One evening each week, Ann went up to the school and held a prayer meeting with our girls. On Sundays, we usually filled two long pews, and sometimes more, in the First Baptist Church. We held each other to the stricter standards of their families and home churches. It all made for a departmental spirit quite superior to that of the others. This, along with the annual tour of churches by the professor, resulted in a growing registration until the Hungarian students constituted about one half of the student body.

Unfortunately, this developed interdepartmental jealousy. Their professors did not spend the time I invested in recruiting students during the summers. Their attitudes were much the same as that of my predecessor, who saw no need for the school nor any future for it. They were satisfied to get along with a few students, assured of their jobs as long as the school lasted.

Nor was the administration happy with the unbalanced student body and the devotion of the Hungarian students to their professor and his wife. In various, subtle, and not so subtle ways, they tried to undermine that relationship and transfer that loyalty to themselves. Apart from our personal feelings, this was not good since it also meant the weakening of their ties to their homes, their churches, and things Hungarian. Those who responded were granted special recognition and favors, which caused a cleavage in the department.

The desire of the administration for a unified school was not difficult to understand or appreciate. Certainly, it would have weighed heavily with me had I been the president. But our churches sent their youth to our school because they knew and trusted us, and hoped to receive them back again unalienated from their Hungarian background. This was also true of the Czechoslovak, Italian, Polish, Romanian, and Russian departments.

Perhaps the two loyalties were irreconcilable, although I still have a strong feeling that they were not. Certainly, the Hungarian students did their share in all of the school activities and responsibilities. And it was not their fault that the administration with a staff of ten failed to plan and present extracurricular programs that were as colorful, varied, significant, and as well publicized as our Hungarian Nights.

Early in my teaching, it became evident that neither the school nor our churches would continue to prosper unless the school's standards were raised. Ours were not even the equivalent of high school. At the beginning of the Baptist work, adults, often married and sometimes with children, were summoned into missionary service and given a three-year course that included elementary English and rather elementary courses in Hungarian and the Bible. That education was adequate for that time. Those quickly-trained missionaries with their folksiness in speech and attitudes, their closeness to and understanding of the common people, appealed to the immigrants and enabled the missionaries to influence and win them in large numbers.

Even in 1930, the lay leadership in our churches looked with suspicion on an educated ministry. One of the largest churches refused to call a man who was recommended by the Home Mission Society, who suggested that they call a college-bred man. "He's too educated," was their objection, though he was one of their own — conservative in theology, devoted to missions among his own people, and in deep sympathy with their moral and spiritual standards.

But the days of free, unrestricted immigration were over. Young people in increasing numbers went on to high school, and to me it was terribly urgent that we raise our standards at least to that level, and higher if possible, to attract our youth. Instead of the usual foreign languages — not very meaningful to them — they would take several years of Hungarian beginning with elements of the language and on through the history of Hungary and its culture.

This, I felt, would prove far more interesting and vital to them because of their ancestry, and develop an appreciation of their Old Country heritage, thus enabling them to be interpreters of the two cultures to each other. Hungary, with its glorious history of a thousand years, had cultural treasures of great value and significance for enriching the lives of our youth, and through them, American life.

I still remember little Joe, a boy of sixteen, uninterested in schooling, whom his parents sent to us with the hope that we might kindle in him a concern for education in general and for the Hungarian language, and literature in particular. He resented it and sat in my Hungarian class day after day with a dumb, grumpy, obstinate determination not to learn or become interested in the Hungarian courses.

I had discovered a historical novel that I used with beginners. It dealt with the defense of Eger, the last fort to defy the Turkish conquest which swept over the unhappy nation like a tidal wave. Again and again, the heathen hosts attacked the tiny fort, reduced to rubble by the Turkish cannon, but in vain. They had to be driven with whips to the final attack. The decimated defenders fought desperately, and the enemy retreated. Eger was saved, and with it the last hope of an enslaved nation.

My students had to report on the assigned reading at each class session. We discussed it and I read pages to them with all the dramatic power I could summon. They were excited, eager, and enchanted. All but Joe, who sat there day after day with the same defiant mumble: "I haven't read the assignment." I was ready to give up and dismiss him from the course.

One day, for some reason, no one had covered the assignment. Then with a glint of amusement and victory in his eyes, Joe spoke up, "I have read it!" We discovered that, in fact, he was pages ahead of us. He gave an enthusiastic report to the amazed class, which crowded around him at the close of the session and overwhelmed him with congratulations. From that day on Joe not only gave no further trouble but became one of the most enthusiastic students in the Hungarian subjects. "The Stars of Eger" had laid its enchantment on his spirit.

This was repeated in the advanced courses with the more advanced students as we studied the epic ballads of Arany, the poetry of Petofi, among others, and the dramatic poem of Madacs called "The Tragedy of Man," to mention a few. The unsuspected beauty of these untranslated, and perhaps untranslatable gems of Hungarian literature fairly bewitched them.

Only the loose and filthy lives of some of the authors were always an insoluble puzzle to these Baptist students with their elevated moral conditioning. "But, Brother professor, how could these men think and feel so beautifully and lead such rotten lives?" This gave rise to discussions on morality, religion, and esthetics again and again, and on the paradox of beauty in literature and the ugliness in the lives of its creators. Never had I seen such enthusiasm in foreign language courses in high school, and seldom in college.

I mentioned the need for higher standards of scholarship to the president who was duly interested, but not enough to do something about it. I then set to work on the department heads. It took a good deal of persuading to have them take a stand with me in this matter at a faculty meeting and together request an advance in our standards. The president admitted the need, but was afraid that the trustees of the school would turn him down. It was evident that he would do very little, if anything, for fear of losing face. Then we got to work on the teachers in the English courses. After winning them over, we presented a united petition that the president could not ignore or sweep aside. After debating this in several faculty meetings, he reluctantly agreed to present it to the board. To his surprise, it was received with approval, and the way was opened for the reorganization of our curriculum.

While we had an encouraging increase in younger, American-born students in my department, the others did not. From the angle of a significant increase in student enrollment, the new plan was a failure except in the Hungarian Department. But the school was committed and the students approved. Next, I began to agitate for a junior college level, and when I found no encouragement, I started to weave daydreams about the possibility of uniting our school with a Baptist coeducational college of approved standing.

My observations and experiences on my summer trips confirmed my feelings that, in such a situation, I could build a Hungarian department of forty to fifty students, doubling our enrollment. Slowly, the painful truth impressed itself upon me that our president would never consent to it. Too much of his life had been invested in the school, and he could not be reconciled to play second fiddle in a college administration.

Wild and apparently impossible notions began to haunt my nights and days about taking my own department out of that situation and seeking a new home elsewhere. The Italian Department had done so, and they seemed happy in their new environment. Why not us? But I had no such influential connections as my Italian colleague, and I was eager to make this transition with as little unpleasantness as possible. No solution appeared to my fevered vision.

Gradually, a feeling of hopeless desperation settled over me. However, my vision of greater usefulness to my people and to my beloved America drew me on to greater exertions. The black cloud of doom hovered over the school and my plans, but faith in an overarching Providence made its imperious demand that I challenge fate and fight on. I felt that the days of the school, of my department, and of my own future among Hungarian Baptists were numbered. But filled with the inspiration of the heroic legends in the history of my native land and the heroes of the Bible, I fought on.

I covered fifteen hundred miles one summer, visiting our churches at a cost of $75 to the school, using the least expensive means of transportation and begging rides from members and friends of our churches. I was worn out at the end of the trip. Yet the president approved my expenses only after a stern lecture on my recklessness in spending so much. My disgust almost led me to resign right then and there.

Just about this time *Népszava*, the largest Hungarian newspaper in the United States, requested an article from me about the school, and particularly the Hungarian Department. For the first time in the history of Hungarian Baptists, the outstanding Hungarian newspaper was eager to publish a feature article on the despised little sect and their wonderful department at the International Baptist Seminary. Immensely encouraged, but fearful of the school's collapse, I held back but duly reported the new recognition at home mission headquarters. They, too, were greatly impressed.

About this time, an outstanding celebration in the history of Hungarian America took place. It was the dedication of a statue of Louis Kossuth, the great leader of the Hungarian Revolution of 1848 in New York City. It was a gift of the Hungarian government and a masterpiece by one of the great sculptors of the Old Country. New York City donated a choice location for it on Riverside Drive. A prominent delegation of scores of leaders of Hungary's political and cultural life, and of the newly organized World Federation of Hungarians made a special pilgrimage for this event. They brought with them a gift of the Hungarian nation — an enormous Hungarian banner, surmounted by a small sphere containing soil of all the counties of the motherland, and the Hungarian eagle. The tricolor, red-white-green, had at its center the historic coat of arms representing the four largest rivers in the left half, and the three highest peaks of the Carpathians in the right. On either side, a guardian angel, heavenly symbols of divine protection, all of it surmounted by the thousand-year-old crown of Hungary.

After the usual contingent of New York's finest, the band of the elite seventh regiment of the National Guard followed with beautiful and stirring marches. Then came the delegation from the Old Country in their gorgeous medieval costumes, sparkling with gems and old historic curved swords by their sides. Tens of thousands from all parts of America, representing Hungarian life in its totality, made up the procession. Included were the clergy of the various denominations in their ecclesiastical robes and high clerical headgear, the women in the folk costumes of their home counties, men with broad tricolor sashes or boutonnieres, and representatives of all kinds of societies with their flags and church banners floating above them in the brisk and chilly spring breeze.

Never before or since has there been such a multitude of Hungarians assembled anywhere in America as that which surrounded the statue of Kossuth, and they were augmented by many thousands of Americans who came to view the event and wonder at its meaning. The Seventh Regiment Band played the two national anthems beautifully, leading the assembled multitude in their singing. The words of the Hungarian anthem, very inadequately translated, are:

God bless the Hungarian
With good cheer and abundance,
Stretch forth a protecting arm
when he contends with the foe.
Torn by misfortune through an age,
Grant him a gay, happy year,
Since this people has atoned
for the past and the future.

Memories of the millennial tragedy of the Old Country and the pent-up emotions of the vast multitude found expression in tears and sobs until overcome by the pathos of the occasion. It became impossible to follow the correct and lovely rendition of the band. It was lost in a vast, impassioned cry to God for justice and mercy.

17 - Caught in a Whirlpool

About this time I was invited to give an address to the large Hungarian Department of a Protestant College. It included an invitation to dinner at the Hungarian professor's home along with leaders of that denomination and top officials of the college administration. It was distinguished company, and it meant a new recognition for Hungarian Baptists who had been despised by this and other Protestant denominations as an insignificant and schismatic sect not viewed with favor or respect even at this time by many of the clergymen.

It happened during the Prohibition Era, and I was shocked to see my countrymen serve and drink wine. But they were supported by the American religious and educational leaders present. They all drank as if the new law were not a part of our revered Constitution.

With my Old Country background, remembering how wine was glorified in song and poetry, and how even Baptists in the homeland drank wine regularly with their meals, it was not difficult to understand my countrymen. However, this disrespect for the Constitution of the land of our adoption seemed wrong and inexcusable. I felt the same way about the American guests.

It started me on a bit of informal research along these lines, an analysis of the situation, and a consideration of the problems arising from Prohibition. I found that about forty million people in our population, or about one third, were under the influence of continental European traditions. All of these endorsed and glorified alcoholic beverages and used them at all social functions. Many of them, like my father, whom I never saw under the influence of alcohol, used such beverages in moderation, and like our family, always had them in their homes. However, I knew how unfounded it was to say, as the enemies of the Prohibition did, that "beer and wine did not intoxicate," when I often saw the men in the stained glass shop get drunk on these. It was equally misleading to proclaim that Europeans knew how to drink without getting drunk. I knew too many Europeans who overindulged in alcoholic beverages regularly. But I could well understand the indignation of my father and many other Europeans who drank in moderation, for they had come to the land of freedom and their lifelong, age-long custom had been declared a crime.

With so many immigrants and their offspring set against the new Amendment, not to mention millions of older Americans, I could not see how the attempted change by law in habits and morals could succeed.

Millions of Protestants were in favor of Prohibition after three generations of conditioning, education, and agitation in their churches. But the immigrants, largely untouched by temperance education with the exception of Baptists and other small religious groups, consumed alcoholic beverages in large quantities in their homes. I viewed with dismay the failure of the "noble experiment." Beer was the rallying cry, and the saloon was to be banished forever. But thanks to the insatiable hunger for profits, the conscienceless magic of the advertising fraternity, and the appeal of alcohol itself, we soon had taverns, a new name for the old saloon, and an ever-increasing consumption of not only beer but hard liquor as well as a growing number of drunks and alcoholics, not less than we had before, as we had been assured would be the case.

The fact that the use of alcohol was the reason for the greatest number of accidents was, and continues to be, carefully covered up by the Madison Avenue crowd. Also, its unhappy impact on marital, professional, business, and political life in our land. It was seldom emphasized and scarcely ever pointed out that we spent more on alcoholic beverages than on education.

In a feverish election, Franklin Delano Roosevelt was elected to the presidency. Beneath the charm of his personality and the magic of his speech, I found little that was concretely and specifically constructive.

Beer, beer, beer was the emphasis. So, I could not vote for him.

Herbert Hoover, the great humanitarian worshipped by new Americans of continental antecedents because of his concern and labor for the hungry masses after the war, did not seem to be aware of the forces that demanded new vision and programs. In consequence, I cast a protest vote for Norman Thomas, the great critic of both parties, the perpetual presidential candidate of the Socialist Party, a constant affliction of the comfortable, and the persistent gadfly of American Society. I lived to be glad for the election of Roosevelt because of the reforms he carried through.

Came the collapse of the Stock Market in 1929, and with it, the economic system breakdown and a worldwide depression. The income of churches and missionary societies hit bottom, and the necessary financial income of our school reached an all-time low. All missionaries of the American Baptist Home Mission Society were asked to take a ten percent reduction in salary. I was troubled by recollections of the small incomes and large families of some of my fellow missionaries in the Hungarian churches.

Talking it over with my equally concerned Ann, we came to the decision that we would offer to take a larger deduction, say twenty percent or even thirty if the society would withdraw its request from its poorest paid workers. In my letter to the executive secretary, I pleaded that all of the better-paid employees of the society be asked to equal the contribution we were willing to make, and so make unnecessary the reduction of salaries on the part of those least able to bear it.

My wife thinks that this was a serious mistake and that from that time I was a marked man, but I am still inclined to think it was a proper suggestion. In the concluding paragraph, I made a glowing prediction that if this were done, a new, warm sense of Christian brotherhood, devotion to our denomination, and multiplied zeal would result, which would revitalize our denomination and bless all our efforts. The society, alas, never replied to our offer or suggestions, but accepted instead our ten percent contribution.

I discussed this with a prominent minister of our denomination. He pointed out how difficult such a program would be. He himself had planned his life in line with his income: insurance, medical care, clothing, his child's education, etc. Somewhat impatiently, I pointed out that a poor Hungarian missionary brother of mine, with a total salary of one $130 a month and six children, was not able to plan at all, but had to meet his most pressing needs as he was able. Well, that was too bad, of course, but all of us were in the same depression, he said. What a tremendous opportunity we missed for a dramatic expression of Christian brotherhood that might have had widespread repercussions for good. But we were told, sometimes with admiration but mostly with pity, we were idealists and one must be practical in this world.

Teaching the Prophets of the Old Testament, my conscience was often stirred by the injustices and exploitation of the poor in their days. My vivid imagination made it all very real as I not only taught about them but actually lived with them. As I did so, the old resentments of my youth were rekindled, and I found satisfaction denouncing the evils of our times along with the "malefactors of great wealth" whom Teddy Roosevelt had also excoriated.

I discovered that a dedicated Christian could be as radical as dedicated Communists and more so. As I look back upon those days, it gives me some satisfaction that I did not indulge in the cheap eloquence of some of my colleagues who were able to condemn that ancient society and its privileged exploiters with fiery words, but speak softly, in weak generalities, when they spoke about the evils of our time, if at all.

My keen desire for honesty in all this led me to ask how far I myself was involved in the injustices of our time. At first, it was not difficult to disclaim all responsibility, for was I not a poor, uninfluential preacher in a despised little sect and a hard-driven teacher in a third-rate school? Not that I could state it all so clearly — rather it was this kind of feeling. However, one day it occurred to me that my salary, in part at least, came from the Mission Society's invested funds. These dividends, in turn, came too often from the stocks and bonds of our great corporations, which were not famous for their good labor relations.

I remembered the Homestead Steel strike, the strikes in the coal mines of West Virginia and Pennsylvania, and bloody riots often fomented or started by the excesses of company police and deputy sheriffs. Too often these were recruited from among the loafers and criminal elements of our big cities and supported when necessary by the national guard. Certainly, in some measure, my salary was tainted not only by the sweat and deprivation of workers and their families but by their blood as well.

This brought about the horrible realization of my own predicament. It made me sick at heart to discover that while I was teaching about a God of love who has no favorites, but is equally concerned about all his children, and perhaps more so for those who are disinherited and suffer unjustly, I accepted my living from sources that denied that love and generated resentment, fear, and hate.

"Let justice flow like a mighty river," Amos had shouted centuries before. Was I acting in a just manner? I lay awake at night or tossed in troubled sleep. I must be consistent as a moral person, especially as a Christian, and as one in the great tradition of the Old Testament prophets, who wedded religion and morality in indissoluble marriage. It seemed that I must resign. But if I do, will the new professor be as concerned about these matters as I was? Not too many were. And if not, would not my resignation make the situation worse? Would the protest of a little man like me carry any weight for changing those conditions? Apparently not.

One thought followed another in an endless chain presenting possible choices with their probable consequences. After weeks of painful cogitation and subconscious struggles, I finally arrived at the conclusion that the only way to escape the web of involvement in the forces constituting our society would be to migrate to a desert island. But there I would be of no use to anybody, including my family, and tragically unhappy in my righteous and useless isolation. So I stayed on, humiliated and humble, but determined to speak out against the evils of our day as the prophets did.

On one of those terrible days, I was praying for my family. I was pleading for health and strength for myself, and for an adequate income and opportunities to give my daughters a college education so that they might have a rich, full, and useful life. Suddenly, an unexpected question raised its head in my mind: "What right have I to ask God for opportunities for my children — opportunities denied to billions who are equally precious in the sight of God, the Father of all men? Are my loved ones His favorites and entitled to unequal opportunities? Was I trying to tempt the Judge of the Earth to actions I condemned in sinful men?"

Finally, a new prayer formed itself in my mind, about like this: "Forgive me Oh Lord, for my selfish petition. You know it springs out of a deep love for those whose lives Thou hast committed to me in a special way. According to Thy wisdom and love grant us this favor and I pledge my life to the eradication of all those unfair conditions, unjust practices, and evil traditions that rob Thy children of opportunities for a rich, full life. Amen."

Let it be stated in humility that I have tried conscientiously to fulfill that pledge, and even as I pen these words I ask forgiveness in deep humility for the opportunities missed, unchristian deeds, and motives. For I, too, have sinned and I plead for mercy.

My many-sided duties and opportunities as a teacher, preacher, choir leader, drama director, field agent, consultant to home missions, editor of the convention organ, etc. made my life full and satisfying. I am grateful for them, but their multiplicity often made choices difficult throughout my life. Now another duty was added — that of being the pastor of a tiny Hungarian mission in Connecticut about one hundred miles away. This relieved the school, which was hard-pressed for funds as the Great Depression deepened.

My Ann was determined not to let me go alone. She insisted on buying a car and taking the children along. She had had enough of living apart that one year in Chicago. So we bought what we could afford, a rickety, old, big Nash sedan, for which we paid a mere $100. It was in such poor condition, unknown to us, that it almost cost us our lives. Week after week we drove to our new field, Ann doing most of the driving in order to conserve my never-too-abundant energy for the work of the church. As soon as we arrived at our destination, she hastened to the nearest store and hurried to prepare the meal.

With her zest for life, merry laughter, warm interest in people, and a genuine and healthy devotion to God, she brought new joy and vitality to the little church, and all loved her for it. Our little girls with their friendliness, with their genuine devotion, and their recitations at the youth meetings, made an unforgettable contribution. I was blessed with the best little family a minister ever had. How they added to my inspiration and courage in that tiny, constricted parish!

And what lovely people we had to work with! Our host, a middle-aged man, a devout and sincere Christian, with a wife confined in a mental hospital and a daughter with a malformed hand, invited us to share his nice, well-furnished five-room apartment. In turn, my Ann cooked for them as well as for our own family. It made for a precious friendship that endured to his death.

On special occasions and holidays, we filled our car to overflowing with our family and three of our students who enriched our services with music, poetry, and testimonies. My faithful Ann cooked for them all, unless our members divided the students among them.

Two Hungarian men, workers in a local hat factory and members in a large English-speaking church, were attracted to our services and attended regularly, even joining our small choir and making other, significant contributions to the church. They were warm-hearted, outgoing, devout individuals, intelligent and well read, whose religion embraced the totality of life and society, and with whom we had many satisfying conversations. One of them was the superintendent of a hat factory and shared with me his concern about automation, just beginning at his plant, where a machine was about to displace four hundred workers.

Both were Republicans, and during the presidential campaign, which ended with Franklin D. Roosevelt's election, my superintendent friend solemnly informed me that Roosevelt was a very sick man and, if elected, would not last his term. By that time I had learned how political campaigns were conducted in my beloved America. I expressed some doubts concerning his information. He assured me that he had it from an excellent source, but it was highly confidential. It would be well to spread it in order to save the country from a calamity. My memory assures me of innocence in this nefarious whispering campaign. Happily, my friend developed an increasing admiration for the "hopelessly ill" President, as his administration produced some much-needed reforms in our national life.

One of my special problems was the situation in the family of a former minister. I had many wonderful Hungarian meals at his table and was warmed by the affection and admiration of his sons, daughters, and wife. I felt thoroughly at home in their midst and still remember them with deep gratitude. As their trust in their new pastor developed, a deep cleavage in the family was revealed.

All of them were hostile to the father for his inexplicable fits of cruelty — like when he gave his children unmerciful beatings. One of them was growing deaf from a blow received for a minor misdemeanor. He almost hated his father and was ready to leave home. Love of his mother and a noble sense of responsibility, however, kept him faithful. I dreaded meeting them at weekends for fear of finding a disrupted family and the church discredited in the Hungarian community.

I listened, watched, prayed, and waited while hoping for a clue that would help me untangle this mystery. For the father was evidently a sincere man, who had had a genuine conversion, utterly committed to the cause of Christ, devout in a stern fashion that was not unusual in those days, and a good provider. He was courteous and kind to outsiders and observed daily family devotions and prayers before and after meals as was the custom in Hungarian Baptist homes.

One evening, after a wonderful dinner in their home, he and I retired to their sitting room to chat. As we shared memories of our past, he recalled his early youth. He told me how at twelve years of age he was apprenticed to a cobbler. The master had four or five journeymen and apprentices working for him. They all had lodging and board at the master's home as a part of their wages. If the master was in a bad mood, he found fault with the first journeyman who in turn passed it on to the second and so on down the line, and if any of the others were grumpy about something, it was always passed on to those below him. The grievances, scoldings, and sometimes blows always passed down the status ladder to the youngest apprentice. He received the least and poorest food, left over after the others had their fill, the least sleep, the hardest cot, and the fewest kind words. This lasted for years.

"You know," he said, with the echo of a lifetime of pain and resentment in his voice, "I made up my mind to get even with others whenever I would get my chance." Even as lightning suddenly illumines the dark countryside, so this unplanned self-revelation threw light on the hidden mystery of this tortured personality. Not even his genuine commitment to Christ was able to remove or neutralize the deeply rooted hatred against life that had treated him so cruelly. This deep, unconscious, compulsive need to get even welled up under pressure and found expression in violence against those nearest and dearest to him.

Again, as often in my ministry, I would gladly have given all my work in languages plus other disciplines for adequate knowledge of psychology and analysis to meet his terrible need. Alas, I did not, nor did many ministers in America, have such knowledge. He was past sixty years of age. How could I dig under the vast accumulation of the years and perform a miracle? Sadly, desperately, I had to acknowledge my inadequacy.

His eldest daughter, a lovely, sweet girl, had an unhappy marriage, and it occurred to me that perhaps we could begin the remedial process in this tragic family situation through her. Since she too had been victimized by the forces of life, she might possibly find enough compassion in her heart to understand and forgive her father. We met at lunch in an ice cream parlor. Sitting in a secluded corner, I told her my insight about her father.

"My poor father," she exclaimed, and her eyes filled with tears.

I asked her to help me explain this to her brother and the rest of the family, and try to awaken compassion in their hearts. I pointed out that as far as I could see, the family had to carry this burden to the end, but if they had a patient, compassionate spirit and saved the father from all possible strain, perhaps the situation would not be unbearable. I appealed to the love of God in her heart, and in some measure, present in every heart, especially in those who have given themselves to Him. She promised to do so and to share this insight with the others. It is good to report that the family remained united until his death some years later, although we had a very difficult time with the eldest son. However, he found happiness in a good marriage a few years later, and so did the eldest daughter.

18 - Another Dead End

During my stay at that school I was introduced by a mutual friend to a Hungarian Roman Catholic priest who taught the courses in Hungarian language and literature. Wondering if any of the appeal of the church's gorgeous ritual, such as the mystery and miracle of transubstantiation and the manifold impact on sight, smell, and hearing, so strong in my childhood remained, I attended services a few times, but they left me cold even though I still appreciated the beauty of the worship. Without realizing it, I had begun to distinguish between esthetic satisfaction and worship. These are often confused by those who seek ritualistic enrichment of what were considered bleak, unattractive forms of worship. For religious sophisticates, such enrichment may be advisable, even necessary — but I had outgrown it.

I myself had an opportunity to lead divine worship in churches where the loveliness of the surroundings and the dignity of the ritual lifted and inspired me. But I am not at all certain that more or as much of the saving power of the Gospel was mediated through these as compared with simpler, "bleak" forms of worship. I have the feeling that as we approach the more splendid places and rituals of worship we tend not to worship but to view an impressive spectacle, and worship tends to take on the trappings and attitudes of an imperial court rather than the simple approach of children to their Father.

As I became better acquainted with the priest, I invited him to our home for dinner. By now my Ann was an accomplished cook, combining the best features of Hungarian and American cooking. He enjoyed the meal immensely and the vivacious chatter of our little daughters. I explained that we had family devotions after our evening meal, and invited him to join us. He consented readily. We read Scripture, discussed it briefly, and knelt around the dinner table to pray. Each of us, including our daughters, prayed briefly, enfolding our guest in our petitions. Then we stood, shook hands, kissed each other, and said, "God bless you," as was the custom in Hungarian Baptist circles. Our guest was visibly impressed.

Some weeks later, he was our dinner guest again. The meal and devotions progressed as usual. But as we were about to rise after prayers, our guest broke into a passionate, eloquent prayer of his own. It sounded as if an inner dam had broken and the pent-up feelings of the years flowed through his lips in a torrent of Hungarian. We listened in amazement and waited in wonder until the long petition came to an end. As we shook hands, we noted that he was perspiring heavily, his hands damp, and beads of sweat were covering his forehead. He said, "I wonder if you realize, colleague, that this was the first time in my life that I prayed without a prayer book."

That evening he began to tell us about his big problem, which had its beginnings when he was a seminarian at Buda, the hilly section of Budapest across the Danube. The young seminarians roamed the streets of the city, and one day they came to a basement where Baptists were holding a service. Curious about these "heretics," they descended into a plain room with some benches along the walls, and a table and chair in front. They found themselves in a small congregation of about twenty or thirty people. They listened to the fervent singing, prayers, and reading of the Scriptures.

"Colleague," my guest continued, "those simple folk, mostly peasants, prayed more eloquently than the bishop of Budapest. I have never forgotten the experience."

In the course of his studies, he met a girl, fell in love with her, and decided to give up the priesthood to marry her. He confessed his predicament to his bishop whose advice was, "Now, my son, don't do anything rash. If you cannot live without this girl, I shall give you a special dispensation to live with her. But don't leave the priesthood." He followed his bishop's advice and his girl loved him well enough to live in sin with him.

Now they had a twelve-year-old son, and he felt conscience-stricken for him as well as for her. He wanted to legitimize their union and give the boy his name. I met the son and found him a very attractive chap and the mother a charming young patron.

We discussed his problem for several weeks. The only solution appeared to be the original one he had contemplated years before — to leave his vocation. But how would he support his family? His education and experience fitted him only for the priesthood. Would it be possible for him to enter the ranks of the Baptist clergy? "Yes," I assured him, provided his decision was prompted by a new, real dedication to God and a year or two at a Baptist seminary. And to marry the girl. I promised to confer with leaders of our denomination and bring him more certain suggestions.

These conferences confirmed my suggestions, and a prominent pastor promised to find both the seminary and the financial support to make such a program possible. However, at our final conference, he astonished me with the information that he could not go through with it.

"Colleague," he cried in desperation, "I cannot do it. I am afraid of the Church."

I looked at him in amazement. "But you are in America," I assured him. "Here the Church does not possess such power. Moreover, Baptists here are very strong numerically, socially, economically and politically. They are not the despised and persecuted tiny sect of Hungary."

He only hung his head and in deep melancholy murmured, "The Church has a long and powerful arm. I am afraid."

I could only wonder how in this blessed land such fear could exist. But his lifelong conditioning evidently held him in bondage. Later, he was transferred to a parish in another state as an assistant to the priest of a large church. I have no idea what became of him, his son, or the mother. I pray they are well and not too badly crippled by their handicap.

One day, on arriving home from my classes, my wife, in great agitation, informed me that she had a visit from one of our pastors — a dear friend whom we had known for some years and admired as a dedicated, hard-working, winsome, and very successful pastor. He had told her about a scandal that was about to break in his church. Some of his enemies were spreading gossip that he was having an affair with the wife of one of his deacons. But it was preposterous. She assured me, for she knew him well, as well as the woman in question who had seven or eight children. My Ann had worked with him one summer as a missionary and found him a consecrated servant of the Lord, always kind and helpful and loved by his people. He had denied the accusation, but she did not need that for she knew him very well.

"Please go at once to his church," she pleaded with me, "and clear him of this terrible accusation. He told me he would welcome it."

I met with his deacons. They sympathized with him, but could not withstand the swelling flood of suspicion and animosity in the church directed against them as well as against their pastor. The woman had disappeared. The deacons helped the minister to hunt for her throughout the city, wherever she might have gone into hiding, but in vain. Then the minister's wife found an address in his pocket and led a couple of the deacons to that place in a big city nearby, where they found the woman with two of her children. She confessed that the rumor was true, that he had found that temporary home for them and had placed them there. She loved him, and the two children were his.

They appealed to her love for the other five children she had forsaken, to her devotion to God and His cause, and to her love of her church where for years she had been a faithful worker and leader. They begged her to return home with them and save the church from the disgrace and shame threatening them all. But what about her husband? Would he take her back? They assured her that he still loved her well enough to forgive and forget all if she returned to him. She admitted that he had been good to her all through their marriage, a good provider, a tender and considerate husband, and a kind father. She had no complaint against him. They took her home.

The husband received her with joy and assured her that the two little ones, though not his own, were welcome, too. He would provide for them and treat them like his own. After all, they too were victims in this situation. The family stayed together, and unless some cruel tongues later injected the poison of the scandal into their children, they'd grow up into normal adulthood.

But in a closed business meeting, the storm broke. The officers of the church were accused of collusion, laziness, and blindness. They should have noticed long ago that something was wrong. Charges and countercharges flew back and forth, and tempers flared. As in all such situations, there were some who relished discussion of the sordid details, insisted on it and got no little satisfaction from the fact that even a minister was laid low by the sins he, himself, so eloquently condemned.

Other meetings followed that resulted in a rapid deterioration of the spiritual climate of the church until, in desperation, the leaders turned to the secretary of the State Convention. He, in turn, called us and requested me to take charge of the situation. He arranged with the church to call me as an interim pastor, and with the school administration, to release me from some of my duties. They still had happy memories of Ann's service with them, and this would make us doubly welcome.

So deep was the secretary's dejection that he wondered if our foreign language pastors were worthy of his confidence. His trust in our erring brother had been so complete that he had repeatedly praised him in his board meetings without reservation, and in public as well. Now he felt that his judgment in other matters would be jeopardized before the board and the convention. His deep disappointment in the able leader he had trusted and loved drove him to the brink of despair. I had to emphasize that American churches were not free from such scandals, and our pastor from similar weaknesses, nor other secretaries from identical disappointments. His hope and courage returned and the threatened dissolution of the church, which he feared, never took place.

Dismayed and brokenhearted themselves, the officers of the church responded eagerly to my guidance. But as in other similar situations, old grudges and suspicions and unholy desires to get even under the cover of righteous indignation rose to the surface from the murky depths of their unconscious. Shame and humiliation covered them in the light of the ideals they had proclaimed and which, unhappily, they had used to chastise their unregenerate neighbors. Now they were unexpectedly exposed to their derision and counterpoint.

All this and more, coupled with fears for the future of the church, created a very complex situation indeed. The foundations of their spiritual lives were shaken under them in a moral earthquake. What could be done? First of all, we challenged them to be honest and face up to the realities of the situation. The church officers were asked to accept blame in all humility for not discovering in time what was wrong or acting wisely and decisively to correct it.

Many of them wished to resign, but I insisted that they stay in their places and fulfill their duties with increased determination and dedication. It was pointed out that God had not changed. He was still our loving Father and a God of power. These closed meetings were bathed in prayer, directed away from the past to the future that still was "as bright as the promises of God." It helped considerably that I was their professor and head of the Hungarian Department at their seminary.

In closed business sessions of the church, I reminded them about scandals in other churches where open sins were not punished by exclusion, whereas we had excommunicated the sinners. As far as we were aware, outsiders had no knowledge as yet of what had happened. Let us not discuss it with anybody. If the church held together and the members faithfully attended the services, rumors and gossip would subside and die. Victory in our great trial would mean the restoration of faith to the members of the church and their families. It would mean renewal of the Hungarian community's faith in the Baptists and the

Gospel they preached, winning back the trust of our American brethren and the rescue of one of the most important churches in the Hungarian Convention.

We had a series of sermons dealing with the imperfections of the primitive Christian church in Corinth. We ignored and excused nothing in our crisis, but pointed to the inspiring fact that our Heavenly Father is able to build a new church and a new world by and out of imperfect Christians, even as He did in Corinth. Always I challenged them to keep their eyes on Jesus, our great leader, and take them off faulty human leaders and fellow sinners. While depending on the love and power of God, the church could come out of this trial purified, strengthened, and, perhaps, a more efficient agency of the Gospel.

All this meant a great deal of labor in board and church meetings and pastoral calls, and an unusual drain on our nervous and spiritual energy. In addition to the indispensable divine resources, of which we were very conscious indeed, we had the constant aid and loyal support of the local missionary. She knew the people well, had their confidence, and with her sweet, even temper, had a calming effect on all. Her father had been a missionary in the Old Country and frequently entertained in Ann's home. This added the touch of old friendship to our relation, a considerable plus in the situation.

The people recalled with joy and gratitude my Ann's previous summer with them, elicited by her diligence, devotion, and enthusiasm from old and young alike and by her merry disposition and hearty laughter. The unsuccessful service of a male seminarian, almost twice her size, made her work among them even more significant. So they looked eagerly forward to our coming each week, even though she made it quite clear that she could come only on some weekends. Thanks to her training, our little girls with their affectionate disposition, good manners, enthusiasm, and their participation at youth meetings, were quite an inspiration to all.

We were regularly lodged with a strong-willed woman with a hard exterior, given to harsh language when critical of others, yet with a soft and kind heart and a deep devotion to God. She was a "mother in Israel," much like Debora of long ago, with unbounded hospitality and kindness to us. We listened patiently to her sputtering and reproved her when necessary as we would our own mother. She loved our children and spoiled us with her attention, delicious Hungarian food, and endless admiration.

Her daughter, a student nurse in the local hospital, and her youngest son, a high school student, were a constant joy to us. They were leaders among the young people, faithful church members, and devout followers of Christ. The daughter did not hesitate to share her faith with her patients, often pinning encouraging Bible quotations to their curtains. Once I listened spellbound to a brief speech by her at a youth rally.

Her brother, later an outstanding official in the American Baptist Convention, assisted the missionary in the Daily Vacation Bible School, taught Sunday school, helped me in the open-air meetings during the summer, and was my other self during my days at school. The eagerness of brother and sister to learn, our spiritual and mature conversations with them, their unsullied youth, noble ambitions, and their rapt attention at worship endeared them to us forever. For their sakes alone, if for no one else's, I would have preached with all my enthusiasm and wisdom. The brother was observant enough to remark years later, "During the time you were with us I never heard two sermons identical in structure."

As the depression worsened, however, I could not shake off the feeling that our school was coming to an inglorious end. It was not the first nor the last time that my accursed intuition warned me, long before a crisis, of its approach, increasing my anguish by its slow appearance and my inability to take constructive action. However, I always struggled against what appeared to be black, irresistible fate. Although, in the perspective of the years, it frequently took on the brighter colors of an overriding Providence. At least some of its aspects did.

So now I began to review the names of various coeducational Baptist colleges of good standing where I might seek affiliation for my department. I felt I could tap new resources for students through my contacts and offer myself as an instructor in a new Hungarian language department.

However, no such move could be made without a strong recommendation and support by some prominent leaders of the denomination. Since it was clear that our school president would not support such a move, I went at once to the secretary of the Home Mission Society.

"You are right," he stated about our school president, "he won't play second fiddle to anybody."

I presented my idea, concluding, "It's a crazy dream, I know."

He protested, "No! Don't say that. It is not crazy at all." I pleaded with him to make it possible for my department at least.

We discussed it for quite a while, and he dismissed me with the promise that he would think about it. "Now don't give up. That is a great idea. Continue to think and pray about it." But I had no illusions. I had learned from other sources that Rockefeller money had been invested in our school. I felt it would mean a loss of face with that important Baptist family to confess to an error in judgment in recommending the establishment of our institution.

What further steps were taken by the secretary or by the society I do not know. I never heard about it again. By then I was so thoroughly committed to my task, so successful in recruitment, and so deeply convinced that God was in it all, that I simply could not accept the collapse of my plan to save the department.

But as the Depression closed in on us and every possible avenue for advancement was barred, I became increasingly unhappy and nervous to the point of despair in God Himself, who was supposed to be concerned about His work in the world. My anxious Ann sent me off to Ocean Grove to rest and to attend the Tabernacle services there. I walked, bathed, read, meditated, and listened to the preaching of Rodney "Gipsy" Smith, the

British evangelist.

I don't remember a single thing he said, but his sweet, gentle manner, soft voice, and charming personality soothed me and I went back home if not fully healed in spirit, at least on the way to recovery by a new willingness to accept the inexplicable at the hands of my Heavenly Father. It was in those terrible days that I discovered the prophet Habakkuk in the Old Testament and learned again to trust my vision and to discover the new depth of meaning in God's revelation to him: "The just man lives by his faith." This was what I had to do in my situation, too.

The inevitable finally happened. I was discharged — the last department head and full-time professor. From that time on only part-time instructors kept the school open until its life petered out. The Home Mission Society, however, was very kind to me and tried hard to find a new position of importance for me, but the only opportunity on the horizon was the United Hungarian Parish in Pittsburgh, Pennsylvania, composed of three small missions that could no longer be supported separately. With aching hearts, we bade farewell to beautiful East Orange and the school, wondering what the next chapter of our lives would be.

19 - In the Great Depression

"Welcome to Pittsburgh," our host, the Executive Secretary of the Pittsburgh Baptist Association greeted us with a broad, glad smile. "You will stay at our home tonight and tomorrow. I am sorry my family is away on vacation, but we'll manage." It was a lovely gesture and we appreciated it very much. Ann cooked dinner for us while I conferred with him at his office concerning our new field.

He explained that they had drawn together three missions into one field called the Larger Hungarian Parish. These had been shrinking in membership for some time, until there were only about 80 members in all. The two larger churches were about seven miles apart, and the third about thirty miles distant. The incomes of the missionary societies were hitting an all-time low. The earnings of the church members in the field also reached all-time lows, some of them working only two or three days a week, and others not working at all. In fact, each of the two larger missions could pledge only $12.50 a month to my salary. The utmost they and the Home Mission Society could offer me in all was $150.00 including church contributions.

There was a parsonage, yes. An apartment of four or five rooms in the church building where their former pastor had lived for several years. Auto expense? Sorry, no. Pension premiums with the denominational pension fund? They could not afford it. Well, it did not sound promising. Not at all. Yet this was a general situation involving the entire denomination, the nation, and our poor compatriots working in the field. Should we, could we, consider ourselves exempt? The heaviness lifted a bit and I was determined to look at the total situation with unjaundiced eyes and see the hopeful aspects too, for surely some would come into view.

After lunch, we picked up the family and began our inspection trip of the area. Both of the buildings needed painting and renovation inside and out. We were pleased to observe, however, that they were clean. Both buildings were situated well in the Hungarian quarter and very accessible to our people. But one of them was in a slum area with youth gangs hanging around the street corners. The parsonage was situated in this area. My Ann could not control her tears. Was she to raise our lovely daughters, on the threshold of adolescence, in this community where juvenile delinquency was evident even to our eyes? With whom would they be safe while we were visiting our widespread congregations? Her lips set resolutely. No matter how, we must have better surroundings for these tender plants.

The kind secretary immediately recognized the situation and said, "I don't think you should be asked to live here. I'll see what I can do with my board. Still, I do not see how we will be able to pay you more than $125 a month. Perhaps we can rent the apartment and you might find a house elsewhere within your means."

After dinner we felt better and began planning our next move. All agreed I should come back alone and look around for a suitable home or apartment. The American pastors would announce our need in their churches, and our Hungarian members who knew the area would also help.

The next morning after a farewell to our kind host, we were on our way back to lovely East Orange, N. J. We thought of beautiful Oraton Parkway with its tree-lined avenues on both sides of the wide park in the center — clean, without the smog awaiting us on our new field — and once again gloom settled over us. Fortunately, our happy children began to sing their Sunday school songs and soon all of us were singing. As we sped by the lovely landscapes of Pennsylvania over Route 22, rich in curves, and every turn revealing a different view, our gloom lifted and we arrived at home ready to tackle our new adventure in faith and prayer.

I lost no time going back to get acquainted with my new members and finding a house. The kindly pastor of the First Baptist Church found a temporary home for me with one of the deacons. They were sincere Christians with something of the strict standards of our own Hungarian brethren. It was a lovely, restful home for me in a newer suburban development with the elderly couple, who gave me frequent rides to out-of-the-way places lacking public transportation. At other times, my new members gave me the necessary lift.

My meals were provided from both sources by invitation. The rich, tasty Hungarian food was nicely balanced by the simpler American fare and aided by regular afternoon naps that I kept well, in spite of the long days. There was the constant outpouring of nervous energy as I listened to the troubles and heartaches of my people, the three preaching services on Sunday, and three midweek prayer meetings often followed by business meetings. My hosts were very understanding and considerate and never condemned me for late rising and naps. They appreciated my heavy schedule and my need for adequate rest. They almost treated me as if I were their son, and it was very pleasant indeed. My grateful heart sends little prayers of thanksgiving for them even as I pen these lines.

After a great deal of inquiry and searching, I finally found a handsome little house, almost midway between the two main missions, on a hilltop overlooking the smoky valley of a steel town. It was a lovely view, despite the occasional smog. In the back of the house was a little garden and lawn with some flowering bushes and perennials. The interior decorations were in good taste and I looked forward to the coming of my little family with joyous anticipation, eager for the happy surprise on my Ann's expressive face. They came and were as pleased as I. My hosts adopted them also until our furniture arrived. Bless them. My Ann was a heroine to all, for in a day when few women drove cars, she had come alone, with our little daughters of nine and twelve covering about three hundred miles over the rugged hills of Pennsylvania, with its steep roads and horseshoe curves. The turnpike, with its wide, gently graded road had not yet been built.

On our first Sunday, three cars carried and escorted us to our tiny third mission in a coal town of some size, and a shopping center, where we held our services in a one-room schoolhouse. About twenty-five of us filled the school benches and had an inspiring service, singing as only Hungarian Baptists can sing, with all our might, out of hearts full of devotion. Inspired by it all, I preached for all I was worth with never a movement on the part of my congregation to relieve their cramped muscles. After a brief Sunday school session taught by one of the deacons of the mother church, we were invited to a delicious Hungarian dinner, which with the warm happy conversation around the table, refreshed us thoroughly for our trip back to the second mission, where the youth meeting was already in progress. Quite unlike the youth meetings in the American churches, the adults and children were also present and participated with poems, vocal and instrumental music, stories, experiences, the reading of Scripture, and prayers. The handsome and devout young people, with some very good voices among them, and the warm, spiritual climate inspired me again.

In a few weeks, out of our confused general impressions, the formidable problem on our new field clearly emerged. We had to minister to three missions with separate meetings, boards, and affiliated groups, a bare minimum of twelve worship services, and as many Sunday school sessions and prayer meetings per month. Immediately, my Ann insisted on taking the longer trip with me, to relieve me of the driving, and of teaching Sunday school at our tiny third mission. With thanks for her rugged vitality, her excellent training, good health, and fervent missionary spirit, I consented.

We had to learn how to drive on the steep and very narrow roads, especially hazardous in winter. One of our deacons sat with Ann as she drove home one slippery Sunday afternoon on a very narrow road and shouted as she started to slow down on a treacherous upgrade, "Go on, sister, step on it, never mind if you skid a bit from side to side, step on it!"

She did. We passed a car so close that we scraped it in passing, but we did not stop or slow down. Neither did they! It was a close shave.

Several times on the way home in the late afternoon and early evening we drove with our heads out of the windows, through the fog, and so found ourselves driving on the wrong side of the road. With faces glued to the windows, our daughters waited for us with considerable anxiety and welcomed us with joyous relief. After a quick meal and a very brief rest, we were on our way again to the evening service at the third mission. Once, we had a blowout, fortunately near the church and in front of a firehouse. While the girls and I hurried to the church, the kind firemen changed our tire and Ann arrived later.

We were rather uneasy about our children also, for we had to leave them all alone in the house. Several adolescents of our church volunteered to stay with them but we had been warned about their questionable behavior and dared not trust our daughters to them. Somehow we were able to give adequate reasons for our refusal, such as preparing their homework, which they accepted, and so we gave no offense. So, for four years through the school terms, they had to stay by themselves.

The parent mission was permeated by a pride that always insisted on first-place and special consideration in all matters. There was some justification for this because of superior energy and endowments on the part of some of the officers. They were also more independent. All the same, these admirable qualities gave rise to friction among them. However, they managed to close ranks and present a united front in all matters concerning their own group. The other two groups were less domineering, less argumentative, more cooperative, and kind — probably more Christian in the deeper meaning of the word. Their youth had been deeply influenced by the missionary of another denomination and were notable for their devotion and high moral standards.

Much later, we learned that an unholy competition, generated and nurtured by their pastors through the years, had created resentments and suspicions from which we still suffered. One of the deacons of the parent church unconsciously illustrated this with a story in which he was a participant. It happened on an Easter Sunday evening at the home of the minister of the parent mission. They'd had wonderful congregations and a large number of baptisms. In an expansive mood, the pastor said to this deacon, "Call my brother (a pastor in the other mission) and tell him how many baptisms we had. Let him bust with envy!"

Making every allowance for his vivid language, it nevertheless betrayed a spirit that poisoned the life of his church and the relationship between the two missions. Years later we were still reaping the bitter fruit. Now when a shrinking membership and income made the utmost cooperation necessary, we were constantly impeded by mutual suspicion, pride, and resentments.

By the end of the first year, it became clear to me that the only way to save these missions was to unite them into one organization, one center, and one building. We planned and carried out an all day conference on a Sunday at the parent-mission at which I proposed a few forward steps, including a similar planning conference at the other, bigger mission the following year. One hundred twenty were in attendance, staying together for worship, Sunday school, youth meeting, dinner, and supper. The church was practically filled. The singing almost lifted the roof off the building. A hastily organized choir sang inspiringly, and I preached my heart out on the unity of Christ's followers that we must manifest to the world. Our youth meeting revealed again the many splendid gifts in the three missions, and the program participants outdid themselves because of the large congregation.

Three large and beautiful flower baskets added to the festive air, gifts from the tiny mission, plus the rich Hungarian meals. The afternoon discussion, about the immediate and more distant future with a plain statement by myself of the tremendous difficulties we were facing, was concluded in a spirit of amity, even enthusiasm as we were enjoying the uplift of our first significant cooperative action as I drew a glowing picture of the possibilities. We parted late that night with a warm glow of success and a feeling that we had entered a new phase that promised well for the future.

Alas, as their enthusiasm cooled during the following months, and as I continued to explain the need to the officials in private conversations, and to picture the glorious possibilities envisaged by the conference, they began to pose all kinds of problems that could not be met at this initial stage of our planning. At the second conference, held at the second and bigger mission, only a fraction of the parent mission's members and officers appeared. It was made clear by them that all others would have to join the parent church and hold all services there, even though its location was at one extreme end of the larger parish.

I continued to explain patiently, and paint as vividly as I could, the hopeful possibilities of a central location and the dark probabilities of dissolution in their present situation. It was useless. Well, I could have gone on as long as my strength had held out, but how long would that be? So we stayed and continued to struggle. There was nothing else we could do, yet we continued to hope that the ever-deepening depression might force them to see the light and infuse a humbler spirit. They gradually used up their savings — and with it the opportunity to educate their children. They were having increasing difficulty in meeting the mortgage payments on their homes. Their women and children had to find work, for even the pittance they earned helped. Slowly, inevitably, the majority of the population in all three towns had to ask for relief, including most of my members — a galling experience to the proud Hungarians. But the parent church was adamant. Their children owed it to them to come back home and unite with them.

Curiously, they had no pride accepting gifts sent for the needy poor by the larger American Baptist churches. There was an elderly missionary on the field who had learned through the years, long before the Depression, that when she could not attract children to her sewing and Sunday school, little gifts to them or their parents would keep up the attendance, make a good impression on visitors and supervisors, and enable her to write good reports to the missionary societies. Generous gifts to the members and the pastor had assured their cooperation and silence. Now such gifts were doubly welcome. It was depressing to see how the self-esteem of some had crumbled. Acrimonious discussions broke out as the boxes were opened and the contents distributed. Once, one of the women, a warm, lovable person and a devout follower of Christ, even brought a cheap little necklace to my Ann that she indignantly refused.

Soon after our arrival, our elderly missionary lady asked Ann to help her in her work: the sewing school, visitation, Sunday school, and youth work. She volunteered to pay someone who would look after the children. It was unpalatable to Ann to neglect her own in order to engage in formal religious work. Ann's children were her first God-given responsibility. We also had a suspicion that our missionary wanted to harness Ann's enthusiasm to the task that should have been her first obligation.

She was getting old, but was unwilling to give up or loosen her control for fear of financial insecurity, or for loss of status in the church and community, or of boredom, or for fear of all these together. The poor old lady even had a gold medal from the national missionary organization for many years of faithful service. Our deep sympathy was with her, but we simply could not take on her work too. She tried to win Ann over with gifts sent to her by the churches, but Ann politely refused. It did not seem fair. They had not been sent to us.

"You stuck up?" she rasped. It proved impossible to convince her by courteous explanations. She had practiced this for years.

She injected herself into our work with the youth and the women in the other mission, had her picture taken with them, and was able to interpret these to the Mission Board as new angles, new advances in her work. It was totally unnecessary, unsought, and largely unappreciated. It only convinced us more firmly against taking on her work, too, at the parent church.

Finally, a few years before her death, she began to drop hints here and there concerning an inheritance she was leaving for her friends. Her relatives had passed on. She would even show a few precious objects, such as a ring and a watch and give the impression that one or another would receive it on her death, and asked them to hold it in confidence. In consequence, she had more attention and service than ever before. When she died, she had an expensive funeral, a bronze casket enclosed in a large wood coffin lowered into a grave carefully lined with thick cement. It was the largest funeral in the community that year, for she had distributed her charities to many, and many more heard by the grapevine, of the wealth to be distributed after her death. The funeral was a splendid occasion, one she would have enjoyed, as she doubtless did planning it.

First carefully, then feverishly the expectant "heirs" began to look for a will and her possessions. There was no will and only a few pitiful possessions of little value. They began to suspect each other and wound up accusing each other of filching them.

"She promised this to my daughter," cried one.

"But she told me that *I* would have it," rejoined another.

So it went, and even her landlady who had been unusually kind and considerate to her, and to whom she owed a considerable sum, was left without compensation. It took the church members quite a while to recover from the experience and to discuss it all with some wry amusement. I am tempted to psychoanalyze the old lady and her friends, but I'll forbear.

However, in order to forestall wrong conclusions about "rice Christians" on the home mission field, I must hasten to add that I knew of no such flagrantly wrong practices elsewhere. American churches were eager to share their resources with mission churches, largely composed at this time of immigrants with very limited means who lived in run down, underprivileged areas. They felt that the Gospel of Love had to be expressed in such tangible fashion. Certainly, such concern was welcome on the part of the recipients, although proud Hungarians often refused such aid. However, self-esteem was greatly undermined by the ever-deepening depression, the increasing unemployment, the exhaustion of modest savings, the loss of homes, and the hopeless dirge of fourteen million pairs of feet pounding America's streets and roads in a futile search for work.

And, however glibly privileged college students and professors may argue the necessity of winning converts to the faith by pure ideology, teaching, and preaching, Christians follow a Master who met all types of human needs through generous actions.

Hearts possessed by a divine love simply must express it in an effort to help their fellows. What a false concern it would be to proclaim the love of God in mere words and lovely thoughts to people who need much more than that.

I have heard the most fantastic arguments in my sociology classes against such actions which appear to have some validity in the rarefied atmosphere of ivory towers, but little or no force in the harsh situations where poor and underprivileged people must live. Sharing is a divine necessity for the Christian. Beginning with President Truman's *Point Four Program* and coming to full fruition in President Kennedy's Peace Corps, even the much larger number of non-Christian, as in our government's foreign aid program, are participating in a similar concern and sharing on a global scale. We fervently hope, therefore, that some of the silly thinking in ivory towers will undergo a change, too.

Also, it can, and no doubt does happen, perhaps more often than we like to think, that the recipient of the kind deed exploits the giver and does not respond in kind to the love expressed. This also happens to parents, friends, and others whose concern, kindness, and love are abused. Also, selfish motives may poison the kind action. It may still be beneficial to the recipient. So what? Shall we always expect noble, perfect human beings? Are the faultfinders so perfect themselves that they are justified in pointing a finger at or condemning others?

In order to please the parent mission and make them more hospitable to our suggestions later on, we registered our children in their Sunday school and participated in their morning worship. Following the service, they sometimes entertained us at dinner. Afternoons were reserved for the tiny mission in the coal town. Always, these were our hosts at a delicious evening meal — a happy social occasion as well. Then we rushed home to pick up our daughters and went off again to the third mission for youth meeting and evening service. Since I could be at only one Sunday service, deacons and laymen took their turns at leading the service and preaching at the two larger missions. My Ann found it very trying to listen to them, even though she admired them for their Christian courage and devotion. Since they took very seriously the "priesthood of all believers," they did not hesitate, and the drama of declaring God's will was an inspiring, exhilarating experience for them. Also, Hungarians are born orators, I am told, and I am inclined to believe it. If true, it made preaching far easier for them than for others endowed with a lesser "gift of gab." But too much of the sermons consisted of exhortation and pointed fault-finding — a weakness to be found in the ranks of educated American ministers as well.

The exclusive use of Hungarian made for some real difficulties in teaching the children and young people. Our daughters were taught by an enthusiastic layman who had not completed the equivalent of grammar school. He spoke in an unending torrent of words, looking at various spots and corners of the ceiling, then suddenly transfixing a scholar with his gaze as he propounded a question to him. Our daughters were amused or bored, but seldom, if ever, inspired. Their mother, with the excellent preparation she had received at the Baptist Missionary Training School, was eager to take over and teach that class, but the leaders of the mission lacked the insight and humility to ask her, and of course, we would not force our judgment upon them.

Finally, Ann decided to take things into her own hands. She had been requested to teach a youth class in the other Sunday school. She accepted, and in no time had an enthusiastic group that she taught in English. However, the superintendent, a retired elderly gentleman quite active in Hungarian and community affairs, was offended by the introduction of English. When his objections proved unavailing, he resigned. The mission, aware of the new enthusiasm of the class and delighted by what they learned, accepted his resignation and made her their new superintendent. By degrees, she introduced what she had learned in her school. In a few weeks, she had so transformed the school that when a prominent denominational official visited her class, he declared it to be the best he had seen. He was especially delighted with her class because they did not spend precious minutes on school gossip or news of sports and athletics, but discussed the Scriptures and the meaning of the Christian life. Their eagerness, thanks to the influence of another missionary, was in lovely contrast to that of the Sunday school group in the parent mission, for years under the influence of their own missionary, mentioned previously.

To the protesting brethren of the parent mission, I simply pointed out that, since they were not eager to avail themselves of a trained missionary's services, but the other mission was, it was hardly fair of them to object. We could not expect them to admit this, but at least they finally accepted the accomplished fact.

In each of the two larger groups, I trained a mixed choir of about fifteen voices each. They enjoyed singing and followed my leading very well, with unusual nuances and expression. When the great Baptist Youth Convention was held in Pittsburgh our united choir sang at an evening meeting in Hungarian costume and was broadcast on the radio to the delight of Baptists and Hungarians everywhere. Not long after that they also sang at the Hungarian Baptist convention. We were acclaimed the outstanding choir in the convention, and ours was the first to appear in robes (I borrowed from neighboring American churches). Later, we sang several times at Hungarian celebrations and it was sadly admitted that the choir of the Baptists was superior to those of the far larger Catholic and other Protestant churches.

These were vivid illustrations of what we might achieve if our efforts were united in one organization and centered in one place. I did not hesitate to point it out. But the mother church was adamant.

Our achievements were equally happy and significant in the field of religious drama. We presented a prize drama of the American Drama League in both English and Hungarian. Christmas and Easter plays brought large congregations that were moved to tears by the inspiring presentations. Our actors were chosen from the two larger churches. My Ann did the makeup and costuming and secured the simple props we used while I was director and producer. It was hard work, but also a great joy. Once again, the glorious possibilities of closer cooperation were clearly shown — but in vain.

These activities led to a new appreciation of the Baptists by the Hungarian community. An increasing number of invitations came from various churches and organizations to participate in programs and celebrations. For the first time, the Baptist minister was invited to other pulpits and was the orator on significant Hungarian holidays. All this was immensely gratifying to my members and to myself.

20 - Churches On Trial

Our contacts with the American clergy were gratifying. The mission secretary gave me a wonderful introduction to the large Baptist Ministers' Conference of Pittsburgh. They repeatedly asked me to lead in worship, which led ultimately to a series of worship services at a summer conference of the Baptist ministers of Pennsylvania. This resulted in an engagement a year or two later to lead in worship at the summer conference of the Baptist ministers of New York State.

For the first time, I was completely accepted by my American brethren, and we met them and their wives on equal terms. The pastor of the neighboring American church made it his habit to call for me on Mondays and drive me to the weekly Baptist minister's conference, at a welcome saving to me. He was the leader of the fundamentalist group with a sweet cooperative spirit and often invited me to their special meetings that they held at the close of the general meeting. I could not refuse in view of his fine spirit and many kindnesses, even though I found the rigid, creed-bound atmosphere somewhat stifling.

The majority of the big-city ministers were of liberal persuasion, possessed of a social concern missing in the other group, but in some instances, lacking the emotional enthusiasm and evangelistic zeal of the conservative brethren. Usually, they were more intellectual and, on the whole, had a more rigorous and complete education. I was welcome in both groups and felt that beneath the theological and philosophical differences was a real devotion to Christ in both.

I had quite a surprise one day when I visited my kind Brother who was my volunteer chauffeur on Mondays. He was sick in bed. We chatted, and before leaving I asked him if he would like to have me pray with him. A fervent "yes" was his answer. As I bade him farewell there were tears in his eyes. He thanked me and said, "You know, brother Kautz, you are the first minister to pray with me, though several had called." That included his fundamentalist brethren! I went away wondering.

A year or two later, I had a similar experience with a Hungarian pastor of another denomination. A few years after that, I had another such experience with my superior, the executive of the Home Mission Society, and I began to wonder if this was a general practice among ministers. I am not happy over this reaction to the earlier, often cheaply pious attitudes. Must we forever be swinging from one extreme to the other?

The luncheons following the Monday conferences were particularly enjoyable because of the relaxed atmosphere where we freely shared our victories, problems, or defeats, joshed each other good-naturedly, and discovered that we had similar or identical problems. This developed sympathy and understanding that in turn resulted in a cooperative, brotherly spirit I seldom enjoyed anywhere else.

I recall a very joyous trip to the Easter Convocation of my seminary with one of the younger ministers. All the way, we discussed theology, so much so that on our return we once found ourselves lost and had to retrace our drive twenty-five miles before we were on the right road again. He was an extreme liberal with many doubts, and I still have a poignant memory of his prayer at a worship I conducted: "I believe, Oh Lord. Help Thou my unbelief."

He accepted nothing for the trip, while a fellow minister to whom we did a great favor and was conservative charged me generously for an identical trip, even though his salary was twice as large as mine. My generous friend invited me to fill his pulpit on Sunday while on vacation, and at the centennial anniversary of his church invited me to be the first speaker at the opening meeting. The other one never did.

We now entered our third year on this field. A rumble of serious labor struggles filled our ears. The Steelworkers Union, C.I.O., had been organized and was invading every steel mill in the state to organize the workers. In self-defense, the management also began to organize their workers, hoping to control their programs and activities. One of our young men in one of the missions became a company union organizer and officer. He was an ambitious chap and proud of his new achievement. I discussed the situation with him and warned that his union would not have freedom of action. He disagreed and resentfully rejected the idea of a labor union.

What did clergymen know about labor anyhow? I pointed out that I myself had served an apprenticeship in a union shop and later became a member of the decorative art glass worker's union of New York City. Consequently, I knew about labor. I had preached on the bloody Homestead Steel strike while still in college and kept in touch with the struggles of workingmen. But the heady wine of recognition by the big boss in the plant effectively prevented him from recognizing the facts.

Since practically all of my members were blue-collar workers and a large percentage of them in steel plants, I was aware of the growing tension and feared a repetition of the violence in this area twenty years before. It haunted my dreams and I wondered if a "little guy" like myself could do anything to prevent it. Finally, at one of our Monday luncheons, I shared my concern with my fellow ministers in the Baptist Association asking their advice. There was a silent consensus that nothing could be done.

Perhaps the situation was not as serious as I imagined. Some of them had no steelworkers in their churches. Wasn't the whole movement inspired and spearheaded by communists? And those who had members in the steel mills were usually located in steel towns where the total situation was under the control of steel corporations like Homestead, where the Carnegie-Illinois Corporation dominated the life of the town. Our extreme fundamentalist brethren felt that the church ought not to meddle in economics and politics, but stick to its task of preaching the Gospel, and that we ought not to take sides for there were good and evil men in both labor and management.

The ministers in Pittsburgh proper, largely liberal in their leanings, appointed a committee to wait on Mayor MacNair and discuss the situation with him. They specifically requested him not to allow gangsters, ex-convicts, or bums to be brought in and appointed deputy sheriffs, as had been done in Homestead and many other places where the workers struck for better working conditions and higher wages.

"Will you accept appointments then as deputy sheriffs and induce other respectable elements to do so?" The Mayor asked.

The committee was staggered by this challenge until Reverend Louis Holzer bravely promised his cooperation. This encouraged similar replies from others, and in turn, the Mayor promised to keep questionable elements out of the city's law enforcement agencies. This was a heartening report and indicated that a united stand by ministers, and courage to do their share, could result in constructive action. Fortunately, the big strike did not materialize, and our concerned gentlemen of the cloth did not have to make good on their pledge.

At subsequent luncheons, I kept pressing my fellow Baptist preachers for continued action, especially in areas where the steel companies appeared to be in total control, but without success. Finally, one of them said, "I don't think you'll get any farther with this group. But I happen to be president of the Liberal Club of Pittsburgh where we have representatives of the clergy of various denominations, women's organizations, educators, and reporters. I'll call a meeting, and you give a report on conditions and the outlook as you see it. Be ready to answer questions, and I'll see to it that a good report is published in at least one of our dailies here in Pittsburgh."

"But will the words of a pastor of three little missions carry any weight? I'm willing to share my impressions and ideas with one of our big guns. Let him present it."

No prominent pastor volunteered, and I accepted the role with fear and trembling, for it was perfectly possible for steel management to bring pressure upon my members to get rid of me. At the same time, I had a strange relief. At least I would be doing my bit to forestall a bloody conflict.

So I made my report to an influential group of about fifty people, reported the next day in two columns on the second page of a big Pittsburgh daily. I read the article with considerable satisfaction, which was rapidly displaced by anxiety. Around nine o'clock, a call came from the paymaster of Carnegie-Illinois Steel. The head of the plant wished to see me. Rather cockily with courage I did not feel, I replied that I knew no reason why I should see him. I too had my work to do. Well, they had read the report of my address in the paper and wished to discuss it with me.

I refused at first. They knew very well what the issue was. And I was not going to excuse, explain, or justify my stand. Was I not in the succession of the Hebrew prophets who demanded social justice for the workers in the name of the Most High? Nor did I like the pressure he used in demanding an explanation to the big boss in his office. Yet I had to admit that it was not a wholly unfair request. Would I give them the opportunity to present their point of view? I could not refuse that. I went to the mill.

The paymaster was somewhere in the plant and would return in a little while. In the meantime, would I take a look at the polling place where the men would vote on whether or not to join the company union? It was well arranged, with fair privacy for the voters, and decorated with little American flags. Since the gentleman who requested my visit was not present, I went home, no easier in my mind in view of possible consequences.

Next Sunday my young company union enthusiast tackled me right in church with considerable worry and hot indignation. His "friend," the superintendent, had demanded to know "who this man Kautz, his pastor, was? By what right did he interfere in the affairs of management?" And he made clear to my young friend that his pastor needed a good dressing down and made to stick to the Gospel. With a tight control of my tongue and temper, I kindly tried to make clear that when I was concerned about injustice and possible violence I was indeed acting in the spirit of Jesus, a working man as well as our Savior, and that of the Old Testament prophets. He was not convinced, and from that time not very kindly disposed towards me. Had I not undercut his efforts to rise?

I was more successful with another blue collar worker in the same plant. Alec was a happy-go-lucky sort, smiling even when worried about feeding his large family. He was faithful to his church, helpful, and kind-hearted, sometimes to the detriment of his family. He was enterprising, and established a poultry business in McKeesport at the depth of the Depression, going as far as a hundred miles or more into Ohio for his chickens, which he brought home on his decrepit truck.

His wife, the mother of six lively children and excellent cook and housekeeper was a true helpmate, who with her saving habits balanced well his easy spending and generosity.

She was not well educated nor a woman of high potential, but had a generous amount of common sense. She was thoroughly devoted to her family, giving her children plenty of love and hovering over them like a hen over her chicks. Christian faith and devotion to the church kept their family together during the trying days of the Depression when others fell apart. We were often entertained at Sunday dinner in their home, and it was a joy to be with them even though our conversation was rather limited in scope and depth.

At one of these Sunday dinners, after grace, Alec turned to me and said, "You know, brother, I appreciated your sermon this morning. I realized what you were talking about." (My theme had been the Kingdom of God and I had made some strong and vivid applications to the problems of our society, especially those of our economic system as revealed by The Depression.)

"Did you, really, Alec? Tell me about it."

He did. At the age of twelve, he started to work in a coal mine in West Virginia with long hours and a long week. At eighteen, he joined the National Guard and was called to serve at a time when they had one of their bloody strikes, telling me, "Repeatedly our officers commanded us to fire on innocent people. We got together and agreed that the next time such an order was given we would turn our guns on them. Somehow the top command heard about this and the following day we were marched to the railroad station, entrained and taken to the border of the state, given a year's pay, and told to stay out of the state for a year. Yes, I know what you were talking about, yes indeed."

I looked at him aghast. This had happened in my beloved America, not in czarist Russia. As we continued our conversation, I understood why gruff, dictatorial John Lewis was revered by the miners. Only his ruthless approach could stand up against the ruthlessness of the mine operators. This was confirmed by two members in my coal-town mission, one of them unable to walk upright because of an injury in a mine, and the other in constant pain so acute, at times, that the perspiration ran down his face. He had held up the ceiling of a collapsing mine while his buddies escaped. They taught me to admire their fearless union leader. Thereafter, I never hesitated to say a good word for Lewis.

Alec's children fairly worshipped my Ann. "Lady Kautz," they called her. Whenever their mother made her delicious Hungarian cakes and cookies, little Joe stood by the table and pleaded, "For Lady Kautz, too, mummy."

His mother replied, "But Lady Kautz can bake her own cookies."

The little fellow persisted, "No mummy, she only plays the piano and tells stories," referring to his Sunday observations.

When their mother was hospitalized with a very serious illness, Lady Kautz took them into our own home. Later, as the eldest daughter developed rheumatic fever, she too was taken into our home for weeks of convalescence. No wonder they loved her.

One day, little Joe misbehaved in Sunday school, slapping other children. So Lady Kautz led him out and challenged him, "All right, Joey, now see which of us can hit harder," and held out her hand. He came down on it, while she came up from below to meet it.

After a few blows he desisted, protesting, "Not so hard, Lady Kautz, not so hard!"

Sometimes, in Sunday school, Lady Kautz, carried away by her enthusiasm, was a bit careless about her English or relapsed into the German accent she picked up from her Swiss and German foster parents. One of the girls in our Eloise's class would imitate her to our daughters' embarrassment and disgust. One Sunday after the service, as they reached the street, Eloise put up her fists and cried,

"All right, Ruth. Put them up and let's have it out." Looking into those blazing black eyes, Ruth promised not to poke fun at Eloise's mother again and the affair was settled. This happened very seldom, for the children and young people fairly idolized my Ann. She thrived on it and became more charming and radiant than ever. It was a happy time all around in that mission.

While the U.S. Steel Workers, C.I.O., was organizing, a delegation of the local union called on me and asked to head up a community-wide organization in Homestead to support the union and counteract the propaganda of the steel companies. I informed them that such a movement at that time appeared doomed because of the tremendous power of Carnegie-Illinois Steel and the fears of the entire community of their power. However, it should not be too difficult to organize a community forum at which we could discuss world, national, state, and community problems and advise such action instead.

After deliberating for some days, they returned and requested that I head up such an organization and set up a committee representing the various elements of the community. Assuring them of my willingness to work for the cause, I pointed out that success would be far more probable if they won over one of the prominent ministers in town to give it status. They tried, pleading in turn with the pastors of the big and influential Presbyterian, Methodist, United Presbyterian, Lutheran, and Baptist churches. However, my colleagues would not tackle even such a thoroughly American institution as a community forum. It was a great challenge and I accepted.

At the next meeting of the town's Ministerial Association, I presented the need for such an institution, asking for the endorsement of the Ministerium, which represented about a dozen Protestant churches, and the Polish National Catholic Church. I offered my plan for a broad representation of the various elements in the community — Religion, business, labor, and management. After considerable discussion, they went formally on record supporting such an organization. Then with considerable and painstaking effort, we established a large committee of about thirty to plan the meeting. The pastor of the First Baptist Church of Pittsburgh, Dr. B.C. Clausen, was to be our first speaker. He was an eloquent orator and an eminent clergyman. A question period was to follow his presentation, at which the audience could not only ask questions, but take issue with the speaker.

A few days before our first meeting, I received a telephone call. Had I seen the latest issue of the local newspaper?

"No, I had not."

"Well, you better take a good look at it, for it contains an article with a banner headline on page one, warning everybody to stay away from the newly organized, communist-inspired and supported community forum."

I could hardly believe my ears and lost no time calling the president of the Ministerium. He was very angry, "Why, the editor is a member of my church. He knows the ministers approve. Let's go and see him."

We did. The pastor introduced me as the chairman of the forum. I tackled him head on. Didn't he know that the ministers of the town were in the movement from the beginning? Did he imagine we, ministers of the Gospel, were communists or their dupes? Was that his opinion of his own pastor? Halting and stuttering, he made a half-hearted apology claiming that his information came from an "unimpeachable" source. He would not name it, however, and humbly promised to print an apology. He did, a week later in a small paragraph buried on the inside pages. Poor fellow! He was in a tight spot between pressures from the steel interests and their cohorts, and the Ministerium.

In spite of his slander, we had good attendance and collection for expenses at our first meeting. But the original slander and continuing malicious rumors had their deadly effect. Advertising posters, prominent speakers thoroughly respected in their home communities, outstanding local citizens acting as chairmen at the meetings, continued announcements in the churches, and personal invitations failed against the underground pressures of the corporation and the memories of the bloody strike about fifteen years before.

One day, I met the priest of the Polish National Catholic church. He too was a member of the Ministerium. We were friends and greeted each other heartily. I expressed my disappointment at not seeing any of his parishioners at the forum meetings. He looked up and down the street, stepped up close to me and in a low voice, almost a whisper, he said, "We are with you, colleague, but my people cannot forget what happened in this town during the last strike. You know, they couldn't even lounge on their own porches, they were chased into the house and were even beaten by the thugs of the steel company carrying the shields of deputy sheriffs."

I looked at him in bewilderment. Again I was made aware of lawful deserts of lawlessness in my beloved America. I was angered — fighting mad. And helpless. Was there any other way for labor and for citizens with the American passion for freedom and fair play to rectify the situation without violence? Could I blame them if they did resort to violence? On the other hand, the majority of the workers were immigrants of various nationalities, and it was easy to brand them "reds" and "commies" and, therefore, to look upon and treat them as enemies of America. The best-paid jobs were held by Americans, who were apt to look upon "foreigners" as competitors for their jobs, and so tended to side with management. That was one, if not the chief reason why the previous strike had been lost. Could they ever get together? They did in subsequent years when the Americans discovered their need for the "foreigners'" support. Later, the "foreigners" developed anti-Negro feelings as they, in turn, feared their competition for jobs. Oh, my beloved America!

This anti-foreign feeling seeped into churches and schools, too. One day, I was visiting in the home of one of my younger deacons and talking about "the good old days." He described the struggle his parents had had with a large family. Long hours in the steel mill left his father little time and energy to study English or to prepare for citizenship. His mother was tied down by the unending tasks of her large household. In their tiny Hungarian colony, knowledge of English was not necessary. Consequently, they continued to use their native tongue almost exclusively.

"When I entered the first grade of public school," explained my young deacon, "I spoke English very poorly, and there was a great deal I simply could not understand. I remember well the embarrassment when my teacher repeatedly called me a 'dumb Hunkie' in front of the class."

There was pain in his voice and in his face as he told me this. I wondered if his halting, stuttering speech was a penalty he was paying for the stupid impatience of his teacher. How much more fortunate I had been as a little greenhorn kid, with my public school teachers in New York City. And as I write, I am reminded that his elder son is now a colonel in our Air Force!

In my naivete, I imagined that in view of my open and rather courageous espousal of the cause of labor that workingmen, especially those of Hungarian background, would come flocking to my services. Alas, I had to discover that a courageous stand for the exploited is not always rewarded by them. Ah well, right was right whether rewarded or not. Was I not a successor to the prophets most of whom were killed for their efforts? I was escaping rather easily.

And, at about that time, John Ramsey, an official of the steelworkers union, came to Pittsburgh with the purpose of organizing a Religion and Labor Fellowship. Only a few of the clergy cooperated, but to know that even a few were with me was a source of strength at this time. But I was soon immersed in other problems.

21 - A New Opportunity

"I am happy to present to the congregation our new pastor, The Reverend Mr. Kautz and Mrs. Kautz, who come to us from abroad, and their lovely daughters." In this impressive manner, a prominent attorney of Pittsburgh introduced us to our new congregation of the Sandusky Street Baptist Church.

I was nervous. I looked out at my new people in the beautiful sanctuary, with the sunlight pouring through lovely stained-glass windows. It was about six times the size of the biggest mission church we had left, with a membership over four times and a congregation more than twice that of all three of my previous missions Seated in their comfortable pews on red cushions was a sprinkling of dignified men who looked like pillars of society with their handsome, intelligent ladies, and quite a few eager young people. Though I had prepared carefully, the sermon was one of the poorest I ever preached in that church, so my wife informed me years later, which some of my more perceptive members affirmed.

In spite of its outrageous title, *Wrecking to Build*, it probably was not too bad judging by the kind remarks and compliments of the people after the service. Now I am not so sure, for I have learned that congregations are eager to say nice things to their minister, however uncomplimentary their remarks are in private.

So we were duly launched on our new adventure in one of the inner city churches of the great steel city, just across the Allegheny River. Its suspension bridges pleasantly reminded me of the famous Chain Bridge over the Danube in Budapest, the lovely city of my birth. Once, the area had boasted of palatial mansions of the city's millionaires. Much later, in movies set in this location, I saw some of these.

These historic mansions had been transformed into private schools, headquarters of insurance and business firms, and office buildings. The modest middle-class homes had become cheap rooming houses, and down near the riverfront, we had some cheap taverns, houses of prostitution, flop-houses, plus considerable juvenile delinquency. Sometimes our women had their purses snatched away as they left the church in the evening after prayer meeting, choir rehearsal, or an occasional Sunday evening service. It was still deteriorating.

Our missionary, a strikingly pretty, slender, blond girl who had the courage of a genuine Christian missionary and dared to visit in all of the unsavory nooks of this quarter, told me one day of a visit to one of the cheap rooming houses. There, a mother complained about a frightening experience the previous night. They were awakened by the shrieking of their baby, and when they rushed to the cradle they saw a big rat jump out and scuttle away.

On a parish call to one of our families, I found them living in an apartment badly needing redecorating, and repairs to the bathroom and sink. In answer to my indignant inquiry, they informed me that one of the nearby churches owned the house — willed to them by a devout member who wished to provide for the future of her beloved church. It was another depressing illustration of the interaction of church and society in my beloved America. It provided me with a good example of the impact of culture upon the life of the church in our American society, which I used fifteen years later with telling effect in my class "Church and Society" at Boston University.

This was a sadly over-churched area. A generation or two before, there had been enough wealthy and middle-class residents to build and support about seven large and prosperous churches. The splendid edifices and their furnishings still gave evidence of the wealth of better days. Now, the ever-shrinking congregations, their constant and sometimes desperate struggle to make ends meet, the low resources of new members mentally and physically as well as financially, and the growing pessimism on the part of ministers and church officials created a bleak spiritual and emotional climate that undermined enthusiasm and evangelical zeal. Only the cheapest kind of revivalism flourished — concentrated in a couple of run-down church buildings that had been sold by their discouraged congregations. The churches carried on an unwilling and sometimes unconscious competition with each other, which only added to our unhappiness and spiritual depression.

However, we recognized but little of this during our quick visits while they were considering our call. It was a delightful reprieve from the hopeless situation of our Hungarian missions that caused a breakdown in my health. Dear Doctor Mary, an osteopath and a member of my new church, recognized my condition. One day she said to me, "Since the Depression, I am not capable of giving my church my previous financial support. Permit me to give you, my pastor, all the treatments you need to restore and maintain your health, as my special contribution to the church."

We accepted her gracious offer and within a year my health was almost normal again. And how I needed her help! Her treatments were a welcome change from the innumerable pills another kind physician, a medical man, had been feeding me. When she passed on a few years later, I found another osteopath whose treatments restored the use of my right arm, crippled by arthritis and the pressures of my new field.

My new church was one of the oldest in the city. They had celebrated their centennial only a year or two before. Almost from the beginning, it was served by highly educated ministers of liberal sympathies. It was very influential in denominational and community affairs. The daughter of the minister who had served two generations before told me, in a burst of confidence, that one of the deacons had slapped her father's face after a Sunday morning service.

"Why? How could that be?" I inquired incredulously.

"Oh, he had preached the first chapter of Genesis and declared that the world was not created in six days." However, the church stood by its pastor and he carried on.

His successor continued this tradition and became an important figure in the life of the city as well as the life of the Baptists. His three daughters were still prominent in the church and became our staunch supporters and friends.

The man who followed him recognized the inevitable downward trend of the community and the church. He declared that he would not stay while it transformed into a garage or gasoline station, and left.

My immediate predecessor and dear friend, who recommended me and gave me opportunities to preach for him a couple of years before his resignation, was a young man. He was very gifted in dramatics, passionately on the side of the underprivileged, very modern in his theological views, and a good pastor. Perhaps he was ultra-dramatic in his preaching. When under the compulsion of an idea, he tended to ignore people as if he did not see them, as in fact, he did not. Ann and I were very fond of him because he and his wife thought well of us and became our friends while we were still only missionaries of tiny foreign language groups. He particularly endeared himself to me at a pastor's summer conference by his close attention to my devotional talks and his prayer: "I believe, Lord. Help Thou my unbelief."

It is to the credit of the church that they dared to call us to their pulpit. Not infrequently, as my Ann drove the women of our church to some of their meetings, they would make snide remarks about "those foreigners." With her charming smile, she reminded them that she too was a foreigner.

"No, not you, Mrs. Kautz, you are one of us."

And I can't forget one Sunday when a fine violinist, one of our members, was leaving the church with a bouquet of flowers my Ann had given her in appreciation of her music. As we shook hands, she remarked flippantly, "Don't I look as if I came from a Hunkie wedding?"

I smiled and responded, "Ah, indeed you do." She did not remember that she was talking to a "Hunkie." We were fully accepted by all except perhaps for some underprivileged folk, whom we had unconsciously robbed of their feelings of pride and superiority against foreigners. How often, later on, we experienced the same kind of reaction to the Negro in the South by poor Whites!

Despite our foreign background and a slight accent, which they said they found charming, they accepted us more wholeheartedly than had our own compatriots in the Hungarian churches. Fortunately, I was a good speaker, and so was my Ann, whose personality, charm, social ease, and merry spirit, coupled with a deep spirituality and earnestness, endeared her to all.

We felt honored by their call and the apparent opportunities in a grand old historic church and a large membership — certainly as measured by our previous experience. They reported a membership of five hundred twenty-five, over seven times the total membership of my three mission churches! I needed an entire year to discover that one hundred twenty-five of these were not even on the roll, and next year had to report about one hundred fewer members even though we had over thirty accessions.

The choir, of good size, was a similar disappointment. Their leader, a Welshman with a big voice, was in much demand as a singer at community and Masonic meetings. His voice must have deteriorated and, I am afraid, he lived in the past. Not infrequently I had to pray earnestly for renewed inspiration after the choir had harrowed my feelings with their singing before the sermon. But this was a new, big church, and so I endured their performances more charitably. Not until our chorister's death two or three years later were we able to build a lovely women's choir whose singing always filled my heart with gratitude and inspiration.

They offered me a low salary, twenty-five hundred a year, no parsonage, no auto expense, and no premium toward the denomination's pension fund. All these had to be met by ourselves. However, even so, this was $700 more than we had received on our mission field, and my provident Ann — bless her! — felt certain that we could make ends meet. We were so happy about the new and, to us, splendid opportunity that had come so unexpectedly that it appeared divine leading. We lost no time with protracted discussions concerning finances.

At the end of the year, they offered to raise my salary. They had, by their own confession, never paid such a low one to their previous pastors and seemed genuinely concerned about it. Although I had given up my mission work, we had not lost our missionary passion. I inquired about their contribution to missions that year. It was rather low in my judgment.

"If you raise your giving to missions by one third," I told them, "you can forget about giving me a raise." They did so. At the end of that year, however, they did not repeat their offer and had forgotten just how their contribution to missions had been increased. Nevertheless, I still had the satisfaction of knowing that their giving to missions was not reduced again during the seven years of my pastorate. We had not been so happy since our first pastorate in the little rural church while still studying at Colgate. We worked very hard and richly deserved our vacations in Wildwood, New Jersey.

In our fourth year, one of our trustees told me, "Mr. Kautz, I doubt if there is a single person in the church who doesn't like you." I was delighted until I remembered the warning of Jesus, my Master: "Alas for you when everyone speaks well of you...."

Yes, that first year was a honeymoon, and we went on our summer vacation to the shore determined to return full of energy, determination, and plans for the coming years. We had found accommodations at Reverend Fisher's farm in Rio Grande, New Jersey, in a garage transformed by three high partitions into three small rooms. We carried water from a pump outside. It had a woodburning stove inside for cooking, an ice box, oil lamps, cement floor, cold shower, and very simple furniture. All of us loved the ocean, only four miles away, where we would spend most of our time. Our rent was extremely low, so we did not mind the primitive accommodations at all.

My Ann even baked bread, which she shared with our genial host, whose heart was as large as his vast abdomen. He would sit by and chat as he watched her knead the dough. It reminded him of his mother, he told us. And when he discovered how fond of raspberries Ann was, he supplied us with all we could eat from his farm. We became fast friends and supported him by our presence at all his services, and occasionally I preached for him. For seven years we went back to enjoy our wonderful host and the ocean.

About the second week of that first summer, a pimple developed on the back of my neck, which did not respond to the usual treatment. Preaching in a friend's church at Vineland I dared not turn my neck at all. To prevent giving a wrong impression, I explained that while I did not belong to a "stiff-necked generation," I was somewhat incapacitated by an unwelcome guest sitting on my neck. After dinner, a physician, a member of the church, examined my sore and suggested that it have surgical attention. Was it absolutely necessary? I did not want to spoil my family's vacation by entering a hospital about forty miles away. He assured me that the ointment that he prescribed ought to draw the pus.

We returned to our garage-cottage in high spirits. Unfortunately, my boil did not drain very well, and after a few days, we visited a local physician who assured us that if we bathed the boil several times a day with a hot boric acid solution it would heal. One evening, as Ann was performing this chore as my nurse, I fainted away. The pain was unbearable. We hastened to call on our physician again who gave me some large greenish-blue pills and light-heartedly assured my worried wife that she was in no danger of losing her husband.

Doped by the pills, I dozed fitfully that night until dawn. I could not stay in bed any longer. Quietly throwing on some clothes and wrapping my head in a heavy towel to protect myself from the infamous Jersey mosquitoes, I went out and walked until eight o'clock.

When my wonderful family awakened, they were immediately ready to take me home. Quickly, we had our breakfast, packed our car and started for Pittsburgh, nearly three hundred miles away. Knowing that we had a long exhausting drive through the mountains, my brave little wife drove steadily even through a bad thunderstorm in the mountains where cars were parked on both sides of the road waiting for the storm to pass, stopping only for gasoline and oil and to check our tires.

Toward evening, I insisted that she stop for supper. I threatened to jump out of the car if she did not. She recognized my desperation and stopped long enough for a quick meal, which she and the children needed badly. I myself was too sick and dopey to eat at all. Around ten o'clock that night, we stopped in front of our own physician's office in Pittsburgh. He examined me and slowly, gradually, suggested my immediate entrance to Mercy Hospital. I assured him that I was ready for immediate surgery and "did not care if he cut my head off," so excruciating was my pain. He took me to the hospital at once, while Ann and the girls went home.

Mercifully, the anesthetics took immediate effect and I knew nothing until hours later. Dr. Gold informed my Ann as soon as the operation was over, and assured her that, barring complications, I should soon be on the road to full recovery. He praised her for not permitting me to drive, for the poison had already begun to seep into the bloodstream and would have spread quickly with the movement of my arms and shoulders.

For the next two weeks, I wished I had died. The continuous pain; the exhaustion; the necessary but humiliating attention to my physical needs; sometimes by shy embarrassed student nurses and an unsympathetic, indifferent older nurse; the daily dressings; and the snipping-away of unwanted tissue made the experience something of a nightmare. I recall vividly one day lying in a semiconscious state, feeling as if I were a wreck bobbing up and down on the waves, and unable to pray. Finally, a weak, vagrant thought crossed my mind: "God, you have to do it all now."

Until then, I would have considered it inconceivable that a time could come when I would not be able to pray! This was a new existential insight into religious psychology, and with it came a new, vivid, and deep sympathy. No, it was empathy now, with those who are ill and suffer. I determined thereafter that I would forgive the sick, everything. How I wish that every clergyman, physician, and nurse would have such an experience sometime early in their lives. How the processes of healing might be sped up in a climate generated by such people. I did have a nurse I called "my good nurse." Physically unattractive, but oh so kind and thoughtful that I can never forget her. After my release, I wrote an eloquent, warm letter to the superintendent commending her, and sent her a nice check the next Christmas.

I also had a curious delirium, that impressed me deeply and provided a sermon topic. I was back on the seashore, surrounded by a vast multitude singing as if their throats would burst: "We are born and we die. We are born and we die." It sounded like the theme of a symphony I had never heard. I kept saying to myself, "I must not forget it," while humming it as that vast choir sang. Then I heard a woman's voice cry, "Let him live! Let him live." And the throng replied: "We are born and we die. We are born and we die." This lasted for a time, then I slowly came to, humming the theme. With full consciousness, unfortunately, it faded away. To my everlasting regret.

My family happened to be in one day when my surgeon came in with a nurse to dress the wound. My fearless elder daughter Eloise asked permission to look at my wound. The surgeon tried to dissuade her, but she insisted. "All right," he finally said, "look." She did, and fell to the floor in a dead faint. No wonder. It was a wound as large as a fist, my wife later told me. The doctor simply shoved her under the bed with his foot, and completed the dressing. She did not make a second request.

The stench from my wound must have been overpowering. I recall wondering why two of my friends from church sat at such a distance, across the room from me. They did not come again, although I spent thirty days in the hospital. Slowly, as my condition improved, I too became aware of the foul smell.

As I regained my strength, my will to live reasserted itself fully, and I became quite eager and impatient to return home. My surgeon explained that it was possible to hasten the process of healing by pulling the skin closer together and leave an opening about the size of a silver dollar that would fill with growing tissue. They would have to do this under anesthesia, which would make the operation painless.

But now that I was no longer in constant and excruciating pain, I did not relish a second operation, even if it was only a sewing job. On the preceding night I prepared myself before I fell asleep by reciting the words of Jesus in John 14, "Peace I leave with you..." and planned to do the same inaudibly the next day before I went under. So it happened. And just before I lost consciousness, I managed to say, "Well, Lord, here we go. You and I on a new adventure together." My surgeon told me that I went under beautifully and quietly.

But, the next day, and a few days after that, I had severe pains in my shoulders and arms as protesting nerves sent their indignant messages over being pulled taut with the shrunken skin on my neck. Finally, after thirty-one days in the hospital, I went home. It was like heaven, although I missed the constant attention and service I had become accustomed to at the hospital.

A few days later, our elder daughter left for college, leaving home for the first time. I had planned to go along, but my exhaustion prevented me. I watched them leave the house and drive away. Then I went back and wept bitterly.

I was kept out of the pulpit for another month while I recovered my strength. Our church treated us marvelously. They invited a former assistant pastor to fill the pulpit and to meet all the duties and obligations of a full-time minister. They paid his salary as well as my own so that we had no financial worries. They surrounded us with their love, attention, and prayers, and so enabled us to meet our trial with faith and gratitude.

I hardly need to state that we plunged into the work of the church with new enthusiasm and dedication after that. They rallied around us beautifully and we had another very successful year, not only in accessions and finances, but in a new unity and cooperation that brought happiness as well as success.

The next summer when we returned to our cottage, I felt a dread welling up from my subconscious that seemed to increase with every mile. In spite of this, I insisted on returning in order to conquer it somehow. I tried not to betray this, but I am afraid my family sensed it in my increasing gloom. A few days after our arrival, I was walking alone on the beach, and suddenly the buried memories of pain and anxiety burst to the surface in heartrending sobs. When it was over, I was healed, and I could enjoy our vacation once more.

22 - A Happy Interlude

We had not imagined that we could find so much beauty in Pittsburgh. Its notoriety because of the smoke-filled atmosphere had prepared us for cinder, dirt, billows of smog, and sooty handkerchiefs. And in truth, there was plenty of this. Nowhere else did we have to clean the wallpaper in our rooms or come in from calling with big splotches of soot on and inside our coats and shirt collars. Most houses looked a dirty brownish grey.

But on one of the few clear evenings, we happened to be on Mount Washington. Looking down upon the confluence of the Allegheny and Youghiogheny Rivers as they form the Ohio, our wondering eyes gazed on an unforgettable scene. Blinking and winking street lights in the "golden triangle" and on the surrounding hillsides, millions it seemed, reflected in the rivers below the dark, purple sky with its countless silent worlds on high. The busy, dirty, noisy steel city below made it seem like a dream — another world. In the distance, there was a red glow in the sky pulsating with the strange billows of white-hot steel in the mills and the newly dumped red slag.

Later, we saw the trains of slag, fresh from the mill with their strange, jar-like containers on freight cars, dumping their contents one by one, each leaving a glowing, cascading, red stream down the hillside. And the mounds of slag piles from the coal mines! They contained a lot of unsaleable coal that somehow caught on fire and burned with a million flames, small and big, blue, yellow, red, and white. It made a visiting preacher exclaim: "Brother this looks like hell!" Perhaps, but it had a unique beauty, an eerie, demonic beauty.

We lived on the edge of a hill overlooking Riverview Park, with its trees, bushes, winding drives, and walks, and miles beyond was the silver ribbon of the Ohio River. In the winter, the miracle of snow transformed the scene into a veritable fairyland, especially at night when the lights in the park came on and every bush and tree sparkled with an unearthly loveliness, and the distant, silent autos threw their beams of light to search the shadows for their secrets. Our back porch and kitchen window looked upon this marvelous panorama, and we never had our fill of it. Some of my best sermons, fairest visions, and dreams were born here. In one of my sermons, composed out under a summer sky on a hilltop in the park, I was carried away by the memory of that soothing and inspiring environment. I cried out with rapture, "Once again Mother Nature took me to her bosom." But the next day, Sunday, in my sermon I exclaimed: "Once again mother bosom took me to its nature!" My congregation came to with a start and my young people looked at each other with delighted grins.

At least once a year, around Easter time, we visited the flower show at the Phipps Conservatory. Artists must have planned and planted the flowers, trees, and bushes in riotous spots of color. Whether a tropical scene or a humble rustic cottage in the woods, always it was an enthralling experience. I remembered that this and the free treasures of the palatial Carnegie museum and library, a stone's throw away, were the gift of wealth to the community. I almost forgave the unjust economic order that compelled millions to live in ugly ghettos, giving to the wealthy and powerful the means for these charities.

And how often we feasted on the treasures of the museum! They were a constant recreation and inspiration. At least once a year they had an art show where we viewed the paintings, drawings, and sculptures of a new and rising generation. Often we shuddered in horror at their fantasies and sometimes enjoyed their unusual and new presentations. Always, we found plenty of material for our family discussions.

There was a very wealthy lady in our membership who learned about my musical gifts, mostly underdeveloped, and through a mutual friend occasionally sent me a ticket to the concerts of the Pittsburgh

Symphony Orchestra. It was there I heard for the first time the Fifth Symphony of Beethoven, to me the greatest of them all. With its opening trumpet call of destiny, "tra-ra-ra-ra, tra-ra-ra-ra!" The unearthly beauty of sound filled my being to overflowing, and before it was over I broke into sobs. The people around me gazed at me in wonder.

Olin Downes was a frequent commentator, a great blessing to this illiterate music lover. His interpretations opened up worlds of meaning for which I am eternally indebted to him.

The orchestra was revived in our time, and at first was guided by the batons of guest conductors, excellent in my eyes but not to the eyes of knowledgeable sponsors who wanted a superlative leader who would transform it into one of the great orchestras of America. They found this man in a stocky, stern, peppery Hungarian, Fritz Reiner, a cruel conductor who drove the musicians to distraction, but in the end, left behind an outstanding symphony orchestra.

Just about that time, Texaco sponsored a series of live opera broadcasts from the Metropolitan Opera House in New York City every Saturday afternoon. We settled ourselves comfortably in our front room, turned on the radio, and bathed our spirits in the glorious singing and beautiful music, forgetting all the unpleasant and worrisome problems of life, utterly relaxed at the end, and ready to put the final touches on my next sermon and on Sunday school lessons.

And with my office at the church, with its beautiful stained glass window and spacious desk! There was beauty all around me which always means so much to my ever-thirsty esthetic sense.

My Ann and I threw ourselves into the work. The midweek service took on new life and increasing attendance. On Sundays, Ann taught the women's class with her characteristic enthusiasm, and to growing attendance. I did my best in preaching with good, if not uniform, success. The temptation to put too much into a sermon was always a handicap to me, and organizing the material was painful slavery. Also, the desire for vivid and concrete presentation away from the abstractions and speculations of theology and philosophy, for the sake of the less-educated listeners like young people and children, made additional demands on my inventiveness, originality, and imagination. Fortunately, I have the gift of gab and had years of self-training and discipline in our mission churches in simple, vivid, colorful, and practical preaching in order to reach the comparatively uneducated immigrant members of my mission churches.

The Bundle of Life was one of my particularly intriguing ideas, which I had to create on short notice, in which I tried to challenge all of us who were tied together by life's struggles, hopes, fears, joys, and sorrows.

"It surely was a bundle," my little wife reproved me.

However, one of my most intelligent and best-educated members sought to comfort me with the kindly-meant (but hardly complimentary) observation, "But it contained some good nuggets of thought."

On the way home from one of our Sunday services, my perceptive elder daughter at sixteen years old, observed, "You presented beautiful ideals to us this morning daddy, but you did not tell us how we may achieve them."

Shocked, I pondered her remark and concluded that there was considerable truth in it. From that time I made a special effort to harness my imagination better to make my sermons more practical. I discovered, however, that some and perhaps many of my listeners, preferred to hear and admire beautiful ideals rather than be bothered with the tough challenge of applying to them in our everyday world. Yet, some people in every congregation welcome challenging sermons. As my colleague in one of our downtown churches said with deep sincerity, "Give us one of your good disturbing sermons."

I was committed to preaching the full Gospel. It was applicable to individuals and families, government and private enterprise, business and management, finance and international problems, war and peace, etc. So I preached. It was not as difficult for me to preach on or refer to such topics as it was for my poor little wife. "I can tell on the back of the necks in front of me how they are taking your sermons," she said.

I had a new insight into the problems of a conscientious and loving wife of a minister. I had to admit that it was much easier to have the self-expression of preaching as well as the supporting notion that one was speaking God's special word to our generation.

Nevertheless, at the beginning of my fifth year, one of my faithful trustees assured me, "You know, Mr. Kautz, there is not a single person in the church who does not like you." It was a wholly unsought and unexpected statement, unrelated to our conversation, therefore all the more significant and tremendously reassuring. Almost immediately, however, I remembered my Master's words: "Woe when all men speak well of you." My anxiety to please Him returned.

I always remember with gratitude Mr. Rope, a Y.M.C.A. secretary, whose Christian dedication, liberal and hospitable mind, sympathy and loyalty, added much to my inner security, and inspired the best preparation. In addition, two very intelligent, self-educated young ladies, office secretaries, and rapt listeners added to my assurance and freedom in preaching. At the close of my pastorate they were kind enough to say, with evident sincerity, "Under your preaching, we had a university course." I felt, and still do, that such praise was too flattering.

In any case, my wife and daughter, my loving but merciless critics, kept my feet on the ground. My young people were fine listeners, too. Some of them were very able. One of them, a high school student remarked after worship, "You know, you don't preach an easy Gospel." The tone of voice revealed both approval and guilt. Even my simpler, less-privileged members showed no difficulty in getting the point of the sermons, like the one who thanked me with troubled eyes and trembling lips. Then there were those who responded only or mainly to one note: evangelism, economic injustice; comfort, etc.

My growing awareness of their needs, of which not the least was a well-rounded development in Christian character and personality, demanded an ever more thorough preparation immersed in prayer. I was determined not to give the Holy Spirit reason to whisper to me as He did to a German preacher of the Middle Ages: "Edwin. Edwin, you have been lazy!"

For some years I had been aware of the weakness of pastoral prayers. Too many ministers of that day depended wholly on the inspiration of the worship hour and prayed extemporaneously, resulting in a repetition of words, phrases, clauses, and ideas, with much emotion and little thought. As I thought of my more intelligent and better-schooled members, I felt the necessity for better preparation, and for my pulpit prayers, to finally write them out.

Once, at a large meeting, a brother minister led a long prayer. Repeatedly, I found my mind wandering and I had to lasso and drag it back to the prayer. This shocked and humiliated me. Then came the warning: If you, a dedicated pastor with an able and disciplined mind and good education, can be guilty of this, what about the members of your congregation during pastoral prayer? Is there any use or any sense to a prayer that not many follow, or follow only intermittently?

Slowly, I worked out a new approach, making the pastoral prayer considerably shorter and the invocation and post-sermon prayers somewhat longer. In the invocation, I included adoration and thanksgiving. The pastoral prayer was confined to communion, intercession, and petition. The prayer after the sermon consisted of repentance, a plea for pardon, dedication, and consecration. In addition, I was careful to formulate the prayers in such vivid, concrete, unexpected and yet simple language that the congregation would be carried along to pray with the pastor, and so transform it from a solo-performance into truly congregational prayer. To my knowledge, only one family, a somewhat limited one, complained. Prayers should not be read, they insisted, but spoken "as the Spirit gave them utterance." They could not understand how the Spirit could inspire a minister carefully composing his Sunday prayers.

This determined me to seek the reaction of a pair of intelligent, well-educated, experienced members of the congregation, whose father had served as a pastor in our church. Some years previously, he was a very able, eloquent preacher and community leader. In response to my earnest and insistent pleas for their honest evaluation, they assured me that my prayers were an improvement. One of them replied, "You know Mr. Kautz, I always thought that when my father led in prayer, it was the opportunity to say my own personal prayers. It never occurred to me to follow my father and make his prayer my own. But recently I find that impossible. You carry me along in spite of myself."

"Is that good?" I asked,

"Oh yes."

From that time on I had no misgivings, only increased caution lest my prayers sound as if read or too formal. No longer did I feel somewhat ridiculous when I announced, "Let us unite our hearts in prayer."

Ours was a widely scattered membership with the core living within two miles of the church. Some of my most faithful attendants at worship came a distance of sixteen miles. Our parish calls piled up a total of a little over one thousand miles a month. Some of our shut-in members insisted on a pastoral visit several times a month. Some every week. This, with hospital calls, visits with prospective members, consultations with unhappy or troubled folk, increasing denominational and community responsibilities, oversight of all our church organizations with participation in their meetings and preparation for these as well as the services and the Men's class made an increasingly heavy load of responsibility.

While the results were surprisingly good, they began to taper off after the first four years, and our Sunday school, the steady feeder of new members in every church, had fewer and fewer children. Something had to be done, but what? The most immediate and least expensive possibility was to change our weekly bulletin. If we reduced the space for the order of service and made a place for an insert on the front page, space for inspirational paragraphs would be doubled. A commercial printer had an unusual variation of typeface available and offered to do the job for a surprisingly small sum for a church. This was very successful.

It added to my satisfaction to receive the praise of my fellow pastors, and better still, note some of my ideas in their bulletins. Every week fewer and fewer bulletins were left in the pews, and the interest of the congregation grew. They began to distribute these to their neighbors and friends. Our shut-ins, absentees, and inactive members found a new interest in our church and its activities. But this was not enough.

I discovered that the church had an income of $600 per year from a small endowment fund. This was added to the fund each year. It seemed to me that if this were used as the base for the salary of a missionary, the returns would be both more immediate and more meaningful. I suggested this possibility to our trustees. But the most influential member, who always had his way, turned it down cold and flat. There was no discussion. It seemed better not to antagonize him. Accordingly, I presented the need to the secretary of the city mission society, offering him, or a member of his board, a place in supervising our shared enterprise. There was no dialogue. He simply refused. Next, I tried to interest my most prominent layman, a person of some wealth but not a millionaire. We worked out an estimate, using the investment income, plus an annual gift from him, and a smaller sum to be included in our yearly budget, or the salary of a missionary.

I was happy to be able to kindle enthusiasm. I began to talk about new possibilities for the church. Everybody was concerned about the situation. About fifteen years earlier, their pastor had prophesied that the church would be displaced by a gasoline station, and resigned. The needs of the community, my vision for meeting some of these, the promised revival of the Sunday school, and the financial possibility to undergird it soon had everybody talking, most of them favorably. Opposition slowly melted away, and I was empowered to find a missionary who might undertake the task.

My search finally ended at the Baptist Institute, where they had a graduate who had not been placed. One of the teachers wrote to me about her with unusual enthusiasm, sent a small photograph, and backed up the letter with a personal visit. Miss Martz herself came for an interview. She was a shy, lovely girl, big blue eyes, golden hair, fairly tall and slender, and with dimples that framed a charming smile. Immediately I felt that she was the right person for us, with her deep dedication, eagerness to work — certainly an easy person to work with and not an ambitious sergeant who would try to push the commandant around.

We looked over the church and its facilities, saw the underprivileged area, frankly talked over the problems we faced and the small salary we were able to pay, and arranged to meet the deacons who had to recommend her. She met them and spoke to them the following Sunday, answered their questions, and won them with her modesty, frankness, and dedication. Her physical loveliness and charm were matched by her spiritual appeal. She received a unanimous call and soon disarmed what was left of the opposition, including the cold, hard boss of the trustees and our grumpy sexton.

Her influence was soon felt. To see her walking up and down those rows of cheap rooming houses, making friends with the wives and children of war workers, many of whom had come from the South. Bringing new hope and cheer to the lonely, friendless, discouraged folk of our big steel city was an inspiration in itself. She had known poverty and loneliness and was able to speak their language. Sometimes, however, she was terribly depressed and suffered from nightmares as the sights and sounds of our area haunted her dreams.

She met a family from the deep south. While the husband earned more money than he had ever dreamed of making back in their little home town, he was now becoming a drunkard, leaving his large family only five or ten dollars a week to subsist on. She inadvertently, one day, stumbled into a street of prostitutes. She listened horror stricken to a mother who was awakened at night by the shrieks of her baby, and rushing to his crib, found a rat jumping over the side and scampering away. It had been gnawing at the little one's ear! It was not too unusual to have the purses snatched out of the hands of our women as they walked the streets after choir practice. Surely our lovely Miss Martz had guardian angels with her to escape molestation.

My wife adopted her as our daughter, aided her in every way, fed her with bountiful and tasty meals, and put her down to rest when she looked very tired. More than once she had a good nap on our front room couch. It was a joy, and she was so appreciative. They attended meetings, went shopping together, and gave moral support to each other.

She began to train new teachers, introduce worship centers in the Sunday school, participate in the youth meetings, tell the junior sermon at Sunday worship, and sing in the choir. To sum it up, she gave all she had.

By the end of the first year, we had about sixty new children coming to our Sunday school.

Finally, the denomination took notice of her, and after two years, drafted her as one of six outstanding missionaries and set her to work in the new Winning the Children to Christ Campaign. Not the least important part of her success in this was meeting a winsome and prosperous bachelor in New York State who won her in marriage.

Our social and Sunday school rooms had not been renovated in many years and their shabbiness finally demanded action. The old genteel tradition decreed wall-to-wall carpeting. Thinking of the neighborhood and the new programs, I advised good oilcloth. But the ladies, thinking of their lovely houses and willing to raise the money, insisted on carpeting. And they won. It was far more beautiful than my plan would have made it. But, the saving might have enabled us to keep Miss Martz at least another year. Later developments in the community, and work with its young and uncontrollable elements, caused greater concern about the carpeting than for their salvation.

Our youth group of twenty-five high school boys and girls, about equal in number, was a continuous source of joy to us, despite the inevitable difficulties and problems that arise in such a group. Their adult leaders, Misses Bertha and Mary Lees, very personable and able, provided wise and dedicated guidance. They were always present at the meetings, well prepared, and ready for emergencies. Our young people admired and loved them.

About one third of them lived eight to sixteen miles away and had relatives in our membership, or they themselves belonged to our church. They were schoolmates and traveled together. The rest lived at a distance of one to five miles from the church. Most of them were at our services of worship on Sunday. Their most successful series of meetings centered around courtship and marriage. We advertised these and invited young adults and any others who might be interested. This resulted in a four- to five-fold increase in attendance and generated great enthusiasm. I gave a brief lecture introducing the particular theme of the evening, followed by questions and discussion. Our Youth were accustomed to the free and untrammeled expression of their ideas, and we usually had a grand time and difficulty closing the meeting on time.

One of our best members was Neil Gallagher, a Roman Catholic. He was a fine, thoughtful boy who never missed a meeting and took his turn at Bible reading, prayer, and presenting a topic for discussion. He learned to "pray from the heart" instead of the book and was as good a Christian as any of our own youths. The others so admired and loved him that they elected him president. One of our deaconesses who had two boys in the organization came to me with a violently eloquent protest and demanded that I do something about it. To elect a Catholic boy president of a Baptist group was a scandal. She would not put up with it. In vain did I point out that Neil was as good a Christian as our own young people, notwithstanding our doctrinal and other differences, and that as Baptists our youth had the privilege and freedom to elect their officers. Four responsible adults were always present at the meetings to watch, guide, and save them from serious errors. She had considerable influence and was adamant, and could create quite a disturbance if she wished. I was helpless and could only pray and ride out the storm. Fortunately, her good sense and Christian conscience prevailed.

Bessie Hoff was a member of our church as well as of the youth group. A pretty and headstrong but lovable girl. She and Neil fell in love and wanted to marry. Her mother came to me, distraught at the prospect. I must do something about it! Bessie assured her mother that she would not become a Roman Catholic nor would she take instruction and sign her children away.

Neil was equally determined to remain a Catholic. The strongest reason was his oath to his mother on her deathbed that he would not forsake the church and damn his immortal soul. He no longer believed that only Catholics would be saved, but either because of a lingering superstition or a noble sense of honor, he could not break the oath to his mother.

Bessie insisted on marriage in the church, before the altar, but in view of her staunch resistance to what his church demanded, Neil's priest refused, although he might unite them in the rectory. Poor Neil! He went on a regular pilgrimage interviewing every priest within reach, but in vain. Finally, the "radio priest" of Pittsburgh, Father Cox, took pity on them and consented to unite them.

The young couple now wondered about going through with it. They did not want to hurt me. But after frankly discussing with them the problems they would face in their marriage, I assured them that their happiness and success was my paramount concern. I promised to be present at the ceremony and privately pray for them. For some reason, the kind rector did not appear, but sent an assistant to perform the ritual.

After their marriage, the young couple continued to attend their own churches but came to our youth meetings together. On a visit to their humble little home, I found that they read the Bible and prayed together every day. I keep wondering how they adjusted to the coming of children, if they had any.

23 - Can't Escape Trouble

We had no men's organization in our church. The previous pastor had organized one, but it had faded out. The president was never reconciled to this. When a new family of eight joined the church — a family that included three men eager for a men's club — the organization was revived. Gus, the head of this big family, was a go-getter — enthusiastic, hard-working, and open-minded. We invited interesting speakers, always followed by free discussion, a social period, and complimentary refreshments. Within a few months, we had large groups of men present and delegations of men came from other Baptist churches to see how we did it. A new optimism began to pervade the church.

One day, I received an urgent call from Gus to visit him in jail. He explained that he was accused of accepting bribes in his capacity as a building inspector. Tearfully, he explained that it was all due to a malicious action by some enemies, and he pleaded with me to come to his trial as a character witness. I promised to, of course, and took along the chairman of our board of deacons. At the trial, it became clear that he was guilty, and after a lecture by the judge on public morality, not daring to look at us, he left the courtroom sobbing.

My good deacon and I were crushed. So were the men in our club. They had no heart to continue. The new optimism changed to renewed pessimism about the future of our church. And some of the older, more privileged members of the church were more firmly fixed in their prejudices against the "riff-raff" moving into the community surrounding the church. Gus's family was too hurt and ashamed to continue coming to our church. Our visits, sympathies, friendliness, and prayers were in vain.

Then came a coal strike in the mining towns around Pittsburgh. Not one newspaper, as I remember it, had anything kind to say about the miners or their union. They carried cartoons of John Lewis, their chief — a big hat on a big head pulled low over fierce eyes staring under bushy black eyebrows. He looked more like a tough gangster than a responsible labor leader. But the miners worshipped him as discovered in my previous parish, and for good reasons. He had forced the mining barons to pay their workers a living wage and to reduce accidents and hazards in the coal mines. I recall no support from the clergy. At an interdenominational open-air service in a public park nearby, I wove into my sermon on the Kingdom of God a strong statement in their favor. To my pleasant surprise, the congregation responded favorably and there was no unpleasant reaction — quite a change from the reaction of the steel barons only a few years before.

About this time, the President of the U.S. Steelworkers union, Mr. Murray, a devout Roman Catholic, developed a deep concern over the chasm separating labor and religion. We called upon a dedicated young leader in the union, John G. Ramsay, to build a bridge over the chasm. Mr. Ramsay, who viewed with sensitive, open eyes what the Great Depression was doing to the working man, was the son of a steel mill superintendent. He threw himself into relief work, but soon came to see that this was not enough. He organized a rather unusual steel union local in which the meetings began with prayer. Liquor, cursing, and swearing were forbidden, and hatred of management was discouraged.

In the Presbyterian church, where he and his family were members, they were no longer welcome. Instead of smiles and greetings, they were met with frowns and cold stares. Often their former friends lust looked over them and the pastor through them. His father sternly ordered him out of the home and forbade his return unless he gave up "this labor foolishness." Fortunately, his admiring wife stood by him, as did his Christian conscience and the Lord of that conscience, Jesus Christ. But the sweet, irenic spirit of this dedicated man won out in the end, and, ultimately, he was reinstated in the respect and admiration of the community, even in the love of some. This was the man whom Mr. Murray, the steelworkers president, chose to be liaison officer to the Protestant churches.

One day, Reverend Louis Holzer, pastor of a prominent Baptist Church and president of the Protestant Ministers' Meeting of Pittsburgh, called me on the telephone. What did I think about inviting Mr. Ramsay to address the next meeting? He expressed his misgivings, knowing that many in the clergy had strong anti-union convictions, and wondered if the results would be good enough to justify the risk of calling such a meeting. I strongly urged him to go ahead and promised to undergird the effort with my prayers. He did.

Again, the non-violent, gracious, sweet spirit of this tall, handsome man with a hint of the South in his soft voice, his patient listening to our probing and not always friendly questions, his honest and sincere replies, won respectful and earnest attention. Almost two hundred of us gave hearty applause at the end and nearly all filed into the dining room as guests of the Steelworkers' Union to continue our conference on labor unions. The ice was broken. Ministers of the religion of the Nazareth Carpenter began to look with less prejudice upon the organized workingmen of our day and upon their aspirations. It felt like a miracle — it *was* a miracle.

During these years, Willard Uphaus, a Methodist minister, surprised me in my office with the request that I head up the first Religion and Labor Conference in America. It was to be held in Pittsburgh, with a large sponsoring committee of prominent leaders of religion, labor, and other outstanding citizens. But why me? Why did he not find one of the more prominent ministers of the city to lead the movement? Apparently, they had hesitations similar to that of the outstanding clergymen of Homestead a few years previously. They could not afford to be closely associated with organized labor. How could I refuse? I consented with gratitude for the opportunity, but also with some trepidation.

Again, it was our good fortune that Willard Uphaus was a gentle spirit filled with a great love for his fellows, especially workingmen who had been so shabbily treated, and for the church that was suffering deep wounds because of its neglect of the working man. His never-fading smile, soft voice, patience, sincerity, non-violent spirit, and ability to organize and inspire made a deep and favorable impression upon all who knew him.

The First Religion and Labor conference was a great success. Outstanding clergymen — Roman Catholic, Protestant, and Jewish — gave eloquent and thoughtful addresses extolling honest labor and condemning rapacious management. Prominent labor leaders challenged the churches to support their just and noble aspirations and to remember the great prophets of the Old Testament and the Founder of Christianity, who was a working man. In the discussion period, there was a frank interchange of appreciation and criticism. It was a large meeting. Since then, the Religion and Labor Conference has grown into a significant movement.

In Pittsburgh, I also had firsthand experience with the functioning and influence of city politicians. A young couple with their child began to attend our church. The husband was of older American stock with Scottish background. The wife was the daughter of Russian immigrants. They were poor. He was unemployed. With their little girl, they came to church and Sunday school regularly and listened with rapt attention. I called on them in their home, a dark damp apartment of three rooms in a basement. For a little while each day the sun paid them a visit at one of the windows. I was deeply concerned about them and tried to supplement the city's charity by judicious yet generous amounts from the church's communion fund. They never hinted even distantly about receiving such help and were always very grateful. This both pleased and hurt me. Gratitude is one of the loveliest flowers of the human heart. On the other hand, it was our obligation to encourage and help those in need. I am happy to note that one of our dedicated deaconesses invited them repeatedly to her home for Sunday dinner, and a few others followed her example.

The time came when Mr. McDonald expressed the decision to follow Christ and join our church. But he became ill. My visit revealed that he was a very sick man, and the doctor we called insisted that we take him to a hospital. Allegheny General was only about six blocks away. I telephoned the superintendent at once, explained the situation, and requested that they admit him without delay. He informed me that they were crowded and it might take a few days. A week passed. I called again, but only heard more excuses and assurances. Another week passed. I called the hospital and explained how serious the situation was, their unhealthy house and the threat of illness to his family, and asked for an immediate and favorable decision, but in vain. Every few days I called my sick friend's home, prayed with them, informed them of my efforts and about the hospital's reactions.

Almost a month had passed. On my next pastoral visit I did not find him home. I was frightened, but his wife assured me with great relief that he was in the hospital at last. How did that happen? The political boss of their ward had heard about their plight, called, and the next day the hospital ambulance carried her husband to the hospital. This experience hammered home the unpleasant impression that a ward politician had more influence with the medical authorities than a religious leader. If only our story could have a happy Hollywood ending. Alas, it was not to be. My friend grew steadily worse and finally left this evil world.

The wife called me to officiate at his funeral. The church provided one of the very few floral pieces. But there was a line of about ten autos and a special one for the minister. He had a very nice if inexpensive coffin and quite a few mourners. Most of them I gratefully remember from our church. I wondered who was paying for the funeral. On the way to the cemetery, I learned from my young driver that it was an act of charity on the part of the city, solicited by the ward boss. He was a very kind and thoughtful man, he assured me, who at Thanksgiving, Christmas, and Easter, always provided generously loaded baskets of food containing everything needed for a holiday dinner, and looked after the poor in various ways throughout the year. No wonder they voted his party at every election and kept the ward safely democratic. I do not doubt that Republican bosses in underprivileged areas frequently did likewise.

Keenly aware that this leads to corruption in government, I nevertheless could not blame the poor who were often immigrants or refugees from the poverty of the South, especially when I recalled the corruption on every level of government — municipal, state, and federal, and the corruption by the robber barons of finance and industry. Well at least I could preach on it and I did. But how inadequate that is, although it often proves a therapy to pastoral confusion and guilt.

One of my deacons, a simple, unschooled but dedicated person, was suddenly taken ill in the night. We called several physicians, but they would not come unless assured of their fees. He died. This happened once more when one of our women called me in despair, with an identical result. I was shocked beyond words. I began to wonder about the ethics of the medical profession. How fortunate was I to have a medical doctor and an osteopath among my members! They could not turn their own pastor down. I like to believe that they would not have done so to others either.

Nor could I get over the prejudices of medical men against osteopathy. They were so imprisoned by their theories that they were unable to see its benefits to those like me who were not made well by their pills. And I keep wondering if the same attitude accounts for the rise and success of Christian Science and similar schools of healing. Nor am I blind to the same weakness in religion and in the social sciences.

I suffered for several years because of our church choir with its disharmonies, and the powerful-voiced choir director, who changed from the tenor to the bass, soprano or alto as he felt them weaken or go off-pitch. The situation was eased by his sudden death. His successor was one of our own members, a very knowledgeable man musically and a member of one of the outstanding industrial choirs in the Pittsburgh area, but uncertain in his leading, which produced some startling effects. My musical ear suffered tortures, but my character and soul developed. I grew in patience, forgiveness, and understanding and worked harder than ever on my sermon preparation and prayer to make up for my choir's inability to musically mediate the inspiration of the Holy Spirit. Under the pressures of worship, awaiting the choir's selection and enduring their poor performance, I developed considerable self-control and did not betray my desperation to the congregation, the choir, or its director. I comforted and encouraged him when he was discouraged by the performances. He did his best, as well as our volunteer singers, and I had no right to demand, or expect, what they were unable to give.

After a couple of years, he resigned. During those few years, the conviction ripened in my mind that we might be able to have a smaller but superior women's choir. After some cautious inquiries and conferences, we discovered a woman who had proved herself a capable chorister in a neighboring settlement house and was willing to build a choir for us. This was a hobby for her, and the salary she requested was within our means with only a little strain on the budget, which we hoped to overcome with good music. Miss Meire was a jewel. In a few weeks, my recurring uneasiness during choir numbers disappeared and I was able to lead in prayer without the necessity of soothing the harrowed feeling of the congregation as well as my own. They sang like angels, and their participation was a means of spiritual grace and aesthetic delight. On special occasions, gifted members of her other choirs gladly joined with ours and added to the beauty of our services.

Our lovely daughters were a great blessing to us. They were active in both Sunday school and in the youth group. They sang in the choir, were very friendly to all ages, and were loved by all. Our elder daughter had astonishing persistence like her mother. In her junior years she received many a spanking for her temperamental and inadequate piano practice. Later in the college where she taught under professors who ignored or cut her, she was very lonely. In one of her letters she wrote:

"Dear mother; thank you so much for your lickings when I was lazy at piano practice. What a relief in my periods of loneliness to play and play until it has dissolved and I am fit to go on again."

At every opportunity, my Ann had made inquiries about colleges. She was eager to see our daughters in schools where scholarly standards were high, the cost was within our means, and had a spiritual atmosphere. Since Ann's parents were the first Baptists in her native town in Czechoslovakia, both of us had served as Baptist home missionaries and now served a Baptist church, it was unthinkable that our daughters would not attend a Baptist college. Alas, our inquiries in which we explained our needs and backgrounds brought no favorable replies, and in some instances, no replies at all. Apparently, it made no difference that Eloise, the older one, was second in her large graduating class of 300, highly recommended by her principal, active in school affairs, and a potential leader. She was an independent and self-reliant person who did not hesitate to take issue with her social science teacher — a retired colonel, almost reactionary in his political and economic views who persecuted her by his references to our "Little Miss Pink."

When Eloise left for college, her shy, fearful, nervous younger sister, Elaine, developed into a self-reliant, brave little person. At her high school commencement, she delivered a splendid address on Simon Bolivar with perfect poise as the salutatorian.

One summer we were fortunate to be entertained by a prominent Baptist lady of wealth in a rest home for missionaries that she maintained. Here, a young woman who went to Burma as a college teacher from our first little church in central New York, was the hostess. She had suggested our names to her employer. While we were there, enthralled by the beauty of New Hampshire, surrounded by people with similar ideals and aspirations, feasting upon the best food and conversation, and our children in a nearby camp, we had one of the most relaxing and enjoyable vacations of our lives.

There was a Baptist Junior College for girls in town with a lovely campus, fine buildings, and good standards of scholarship. We wondered if we could send our girls there for a portion of their college experience. At lunch one day, several of the town's ladies were our guests. Of course, they knew about the college, and were its active supporters. When my Ann made a cautious inquiry about entering our daughters, their reaction, in manner rather than words told us, "Who do you think you are? This is a swanky school. It is for children of socially prominent and wealthy families."

But life, or as we prefer to think, Divine Providence, rendered poetic justice. Years later, when our Eloise was earning her master's degree in education at Syracuse University, on the recommendation of the head of the English Department, she was called to teach at the same school, Colby Junior College. Dr. Sawyer, the president, thought well enough of her to invite her father for a series of lectures on international affairs. One of her youthful ambitions was realized when I was introduced as Miss Kautz's father! In one of our conversations, Dr. Sawyer said, "I cannot thank you enough for your daughter. You have no idea what she means to our school." We swelled with unchristian pride and Christian gratitude.

Yet we had some conception of her service there, for one day she wrote:

You know, daddy, how I fought against coming here to teach a bunch of rich kids. I wanted to serve the poor as you and mummy had done all your lives. But I am beginning to realize how poor some of these rich kids are. Imagine a father not coming to his daughter's graduation because he happens to play in a golf tournament, and sending a hundred dollar check instead! What kind of people are these?

In another letter:

The other day the president called me to his office and presented the case of a student who had been expelled from several dormitories. "Won't you take her into your small cottage, and see if you and your girls can help her? This is her last chance. If she fails to measure up to our expectations, she's out."

"But we have such a happy, cooperative climate. We don't want it poisoned. And we are a little democracy. I could not force this girl upon them."

"Well, try and see what you can do. I hate to admit failure."

So the young professor presented the case to a special session of her girls. They spent an evening far into the night discussing all aspects of this challenge. They decided to give the delinquent a final opportunity to make good.

The girl moved into the cottage. At the close of the first day, there was a knock on Eloise's door.

"Come in."

In came the new girl. She apologized and said, "You don't know what you and the girls have done for me. This has been the happiest day of my life!"

Our younger daughter, Elaine, was more gifted musically. She had a very sweet voice and sang like a bird. On our trips, still memorable because we sang in harmony, mother and Eloise carried the tune, Elaine added her alto and original harmony, sometimes ascending above the melody in a glorious soprano, and daddy added a tenor or bass. The only rift in our song-fest occurred when Mummy or Eloise wandered off-pitch or sang, according to Elaine, "like a Blue Jay." How we wish such experiences to other families. Elaine was gifted with an artist's eye and an artist's hand. She helped eagerly in selecting materials for dresses and in sewing them. However, she had little patience or persistence with things she did not care for.

Both of them were our proud supporters, loving observers, attentive listeners, and not always gentle critics. As both became college students, their critical faculties were sharpened and we had to watch our diction, grammar, and style very carefully. On the way home from church, daddy's sermon or mother's teaching in the women's class were carefully discussed, sometimes with the critical assurance and superiority of adolescents. However, their admiration and love were always a healing balm. And how could even adults learn humility, or continue to develop it, without occasional and repeated humiliation?

Once, Eloise was on a brief vacation from college, and as usual, expected to come to church with us. Her mother suggested that she attend the youth class, but she insisted on going to mother's class.

"What would you do in a class with middle-aged women?"

"I'd listen, try to learn and participate in the discussion."

After a lengthy debate, her mother proposed a condition. "All right, come, but only if you promise to give a frank criticism of my teaching."

"Well, mother, you leave sentences unfinished, you have dangling participles, you confuse tenses and persons, but I'd rather hear you teach than anybody else."

This was incisive, and true. My Ann never had much patience with grammar in any language. Her thoughts often outran her speech and she often forgot to complete a sentence, but she had vitality, charm, enthusiasm, and a down-to-earth approach that made her a fascinating speaker.

24 - For Lack of Vision

Unfortunately, our shy, rather fearful, uncertain, and withdrawn "little girl" Elaine was constantly overshadowed by her quick, aggressive, vocal, and energetic big sister Eloise. Only when Eloise had left for college did Elaine blossom out at home, in church, and in school. We did all we could to protect and help Elaine, but we have to confess a lack of success in this respect. We made the mistake of entering her in the same college that her big sister attended, and before the year was up, she insisted on going to another school. We recognized the need and consented, but not without misgivings because she was transferring to a state college from a religious school. But it worked out quite well. She graduated cum laude and became a campus personality, which her big sister never achieved, and she was a good student. At last, she was a person in her own right — Elaine Kautz — not just Eloise's little sister.

Both of them were injured spiritually by the teaching at the religious school where the approach to Bible study was extremely conservative. There the Bible professor emphasized memory, literal acceptance of the book, and the professor's views. They discouraged questions and independent thinking on the part of the students. The unfavorable reaction on the part of our sincerely religious daughters to the Bible persists to this day.

They were in college together when Eloise received an invitation to the Junior Prom. The girls in her house were all agog, for she was the only one so honored in their house. This was the outstanding social event of the college, and the cost to the gentleman was considerable. It was a flattering invitation, but Eloise was *not* eager to accept it. To her housemates, however, this was a prestigious affair and not to be missed. Finally, she accepted. Then she telephoned Elaine.

Elaine said, "But Eloise, did you forget that daddy has a Candlelight Communion Service on the same evening?"

"I guess I did. But never mind. I'll call the gentleman and decline with many thanks."

The girls were astounded. She couldn't — she mustn't do that! But she did exactly that, and was at the communion service instead. It hurt us all the more that with such a spirit, they had to study the Bible under such an uninspiring, word-chewing literalist. Even so, they did gain a rather complete though superficial knowledge of its content by sheer memorization.

When Eloise was in her last year in high school, she had decided to become a medical missionary. This both pleased and troubled us. Her decision was in line with our own outlook and life work. She had a strong motivation for service, practical and direct as she had seen it in the lives of her parents. But as they watched her development they suspected that she had dramatic and literary rather than scientific gifts. One day, I took her on a walk and confronted her.

"Have you decided what you want to be?"

"What a question! You know I want to be a medical missionary."

"Of course, but we wonder if your aptitudes fit you for some other calling."

"Now daddy, I know my own mind." She could be very determined. "And I am committed to missions and medicine."

"Splendid! But do you remember how the physicians you consulted discouraged you from going into medicine? How positively they asserted that it was no field for women?"

A cloud came over her features and I was almost sorry I spoke at all. The sparkle of enthusiasm faded. And I was not at all sure how much I believed in the doctors' objections. I knew something about male objections and prejudices in almost every field when women sought admittance. And through the ensuing years, I spoke in scathing terms about the privileged and prejudiced males whose fragile egos sought to escape competition with the despised female. But my concern about her basic aptitudes overrode other considerations.

I had learned that Stevens Institute of Hoboken, NJ, had developed a series of basic aptitude tests that had helped thousands to make the right choice regarding their occupation. So I suggested to my big girl the possibility of taking these tests. She was adamant. She knew what she wanted to be and we were not in a position to waste twenty-five to forty dollars. Indeed we were not. Not with my salary of $2,500 per year, but wasn't it more important to save the time and tuition fees that might be spent in vain before she discovered her mistake? My little firecracker went off again and I ceased. Nonetheless, I was determined to go ahead. There were too many warning signs indicating that she might be shunted onto a wrong track and in the wrong direction.

That summer, interrupting our seashore vacation in Wildwood, New Jersey with the pretext of visiting our relatives in New York, we drove through Hoboken, stopped at Stevens and explained. Our firecracker went off again. When the sputtering died down, I explained that we would lose the fee already paid, and we were entitled to the peace of mind the tests may bring to us. Moreover, the tests may reveal that she was right, her emotions might be undergirded by the findings and we would no longer be able to object to her decision.

Acknowledging the force of our arguments, but still grumbling, she went in. It was a long weary wait before she came out. Disgusted, she described the tests and shared the findings. She was a born teacher they told her. That was the last thing she wanted to do! Was she fit for anything else? Why, yes. She would make a good lawyer.

"Well, we could have saved our money," declared my Ann, who had no confidence in the newfangled notions and discoveries that always intrigued me. "I needed no tests to see that the way you argued with me from your earliest childhood." Since the tests also revealed definite indications of literary gifts, Eloise must also try to write.

Ann was partly right, however. Elaine was not benefited by those tests at all. Apparently, only strong, well-defined traits could be measured. Though our independent, headstrong daughter registered as a pre-med student, at the close of the first semester she came humbly, of her own accord, to another of our conferences.

"I wonder what I should do. I don't like my pre-med courses. I got a 'B' in chemistry but I don't understand it. I just memorized."

"Well, perhaps the testers were right. Why don't you change your major to education?"

"But I want to help people directly."

"Well, Jesus did both. Now, which has proved of greater or longer lasting benefit? Teaching or healing?" After pondering this for a while she admitted that His teaching has been the supreme blessing. Then we discussed the probability that all vocations are important. She changed her major and immediately experienced a sense of accomplishment and self-realization.

Around that time, we saw a street sweeper working away in front of our church. "Do you realize," I asked my daughters, "that that man's work is as important as mine?" Shock and unbelief registered in their faces. They thought of their father in his preacher suit and his dramatic position at Sunday worship, people listening carefully to his sermon, and thanking him for helping them. How could the work of this uneducated man, in his soiled clothing pushing a broom, compare with their daddy and his activities? So I continued.

"What would happen if no one swept the streets?"

"It would get pretty dirty."

"How dirty?"

"It would accumulate to quite a depth."

"What then?" They were thinking quite hard now. "How about health?"

"We'd be in danger of epidemics and many more people would die, adults and children and babies."

"And to whom would I preach then?"

The point was well made and it kept them from becoming the

insufferable snobs so many educated and privileged people are, even in our beloved and democratic America.

In her senior year, Dr. Purdy, head of the English Department, recommended that she enroll as a graduate student in English at a University, and apply for a scholarship. Also, it was her year for practice teaching in a good high school nearby. Soon after she began to teach, she wrote rapturous letters about her experiences.

"Now I know that I am basically a teacher. This is what I was born for." And in the same vein, she simply pushed the unwelcome idea of further schooling out of her mind.

Kind Dr. Purdy's letters went unanswered. Finally, she appeared in her class one day as Eloise was preparing to leave the room, and whipping out an application blank made the ungrateful brat fill out and sign it. Then Dr. Purdy herself mailed it and her favorite English major received the scholarship and went on to Syracuse for her Master's, where they awarded Eloise two fellowships

Perhaps my most successful job in my Pittsburgh pastorate was the winning of forty North Side churches for a campaign of social evangelism. We had more cooperating churches than the famous and popular Billy Sunday, the converted baseball player, years before. This in itself was a great achievement. We were very fortunate in securing my good friend Charles Wells. As a lecturer on current problems in the light of the Gospel, he drew cartoons as he talked to illustrate his themes, and was eloquent, dedicated, and humorous. A reporter and world traveler, he was in a class all by himself! We had set up a large interdenominational sponsoring committee of prominent lay citizens composed of members in our churches, and the clergy.

Their names appeared on every letterhead printed for the meetings. I composed vivid, pointed paragraphs for the Sunday bulletins of the churches, and worked unceasingly in the background to suggest, check, encourage, and do what others could not, would not, or forgot to do.

I won the interest and cooperation of the superintendent of the big

Carnegie library in our area. He was an agnostic but in full sympathy with our goal of enlisting the cooperation of the Christian churches in creating a social consciousness and conscience. Through his influence, the large assembly hall with over one thousand seats was rented to us for the cost of the heat, light, and janitorial service. We rented space for large advertising cards of our own in every trolley car passing near the library.

The choirs of the larger churches were drafted, each for one service. They rendered beautiful, inspiring selections. Our women's choir, augmented by some excellent voices of our chorister's other choirs, made its unique contribution. Every church contributed its quota of trained ushers who did their important tasks unobtrusively and well. Prominent laymen presided at the meetings, and the clergy led in reading the Scriptures and at prayers.

The first meeting started well. The hall was crowded. Suddenly, all the lights went out. We sat in darkness, nervous and helpless, until someone started a Gospel song. Our nervousness dissolved in a warm feeling of Christian fellowship and enthusiasm, and when the lights came on both the speaker and the crowd were keyed to noble expectations. After the benediction, hundreds remained in the hall for the question period — a regular feature of these meetings and in some respects the most exciting and informative. It was an auspicious beginning — another precursor of success.

Mr. Wells had, as I recall it, an extraordinary and fascinating background. He was the son of Quaker parents in California. To their great distress, he lost his faith in college. However, he remained fast friends with his wise father. Wells became a news reporter and traveled all over the world. He was in Hitler's Germany, heard the mad genius speak, and observed his hypnotic power over his divided and misguided people. He was in Stalin's Russia, too, saw the persecution of religion, and dug to its roots in the ignorance of its clergy, the Russian Orthodox Church's blind, selfish enjoyment of the hierarchy of its privileges, wealth, and power under the Czars, and their lack of concern for the plight of the poverty-stricken masses.

Owing to the restrictions of the regime, he had not had his mail forwarded to Russia, and on his return to Berlin he had a boxful of accumulated mail awaiting him. Starting with the earliest postmark, he read his mail from his parents. As he read the last letter, it informed him of the sudden death of his father. The shock of losing his dearest friend drove him out into the night, and he walked the streets of Berlin until the early hours of the morning. Then from somewhere, somehow, there came the conviction that his father was not dead, but alive.

This, in turn, led to the discovery of his faith in Christ. Then came the question: What shall he do with his life? Because of all he had seen in his travels, he was led to give himself to the unique task of interpreting events at home and abroad, and the big questions and problems of our age in the light of the Gospel. He continued his travels to keep abreast of new developments, and established listening posts in various parts of the world to keep informed. The challenge of a group of Christian businessmen led him to establish a non-profit publication, *Between the Lines*, which I, along with many others, came to look upon as the most informing and least prejudiced source of controversial news and events.

The meetings elicited great interest as revealed by the attendance and the question period. The aim was not the gathering of new members, but the creation of a vivid awareness on the part of ministers, lay leaders, and church members in general of the relevance of the Gospel and its challenge to our age. It made the preaching of the Gospel in our churches much easier and encouraged the faint in heart among us to speak the truth with greater boldness.

I was greatly heartened by the success of our cooperative enterprise, and it led me to speak to my fellow pastors of endeavors of a much closer cooperation and unity. Our union services on Sunday nights during Advent and Lent, at which the pastors preached in turn, indicated a real interest in cooperation. To all of us pastors, it was evident that the continued deterioration of our area would make not only our word but the very existence of our churches increasingly precarious. Something more had to be done. But what? I collected information about six or seven of our churches in the downtown area of the Lower North Side, and then my imagination began to soar.

I envisioned one federated or united church with two to three thousand members, specialized ministries, large resources in endowment funds, and building values amounting close to one million dollars; a men's group of five hundred and women's organizations of over one thousand members; outstanding adult, youth, and children's choirs, Sunday school and youth groups in proportion. All of this permeated by new hope and optimism in facing the need and the challenge of the community.

The ministers of these churches met frequently to discuss such a possibility. All were agreed on the need, yet again and again vague apprehensions, born of narrow church loyalties, love of their beautiful though largely empty buildings, not to speak of the possible loss of our own jobs kept haunting us. But the vision beckoned insistently enough to lead us to call a meeting of our official bodies to discuss the matter. About sixty laymen appeared, along with their pastors, and discussed the possibilities for over two hours. We adjourned with the decision that we'd report to larger groups in our churches and meet again for further discussion and to formulate recommendations. Alas, the meeting was never called. Our narrow church loyalties, the opposition of denominational secretaries, fear of the new and unknown, and the discomfort that may be involved in the necessary adjustments cooled off the enthusiasm leaving only vague regrets that such a splendid vision would not be realized.

Once again, I saw and predicted the doom hovering over us as I had in my last mission field and at the school among the Hungarians, and previously in Vernon, New York. Sick at heart, I tried to do my daily work, but now without a vision. Since then, half of those churches have gone out of existence. One or two rather ignominiously.

No less discouraging was it to deal with the executive secretary of the local association of Baptist churches. I invited him to negotiate an agreement with our church to use our building as their headquarters, paying reasonable rent and enabling the church to keep going until the final closing of the work appeared advisable. On our part, we would agree to deed to the Baptist Association the property, furnishings, and endowment fund. This meant an offer at a dollar value of $75,000 to $150,000. He never responded. Not even to discuss it. Perhaps he expected all this to fall into his lap in a very few years anyhow.

But a few years later, a gifted but aggressive and unprincipled man wormed his way into this pastorate, led the church out of the association and Convention and into heavy indebtedness, without fulfilling his rosy promises, and left the church to struggle along as best it could. Exploited and bereft of its capable but discouraged lay leadership, it continued as a thin shadow of its former self lost for good to the Association. Denominational leaders who heard about my offer were astounded at the blind attitude of the secretary. One of them had warned me beforehand that I should not expect any help from him.

My brother pastors in the three other Baptist churches of the area were almost as much to blame. I had suggested to them the formation of a close federation of our churches to plan together and to concentrate our resources where most needed. After a few meetings they withdrew, and this experiment, too, was nipped in the bud. Shortly after, another Baptist church closed its doors.

We made a few halting steps toward cooperation with a Negro church, only a few blocks away, but we found it a one-way street. They did not respond.

In the midst of such discouraging experiences, it helped somewhat to be elected moderator of the association. They were having a difficult time. Enthusiasm was at a low level with general dissatisfaction and poor cooperation. It appeared wise to follow the practice of presidents of the American Baptist Convention and visit all the churches of the association with an inspirational message and an opportunity for them to discuss the general situation. Perhaps a group of prominent pastors would be even better. The secretary's icy reception of the idea made this impossible, and so we stayed in the same old rut.

Both of our girls were in college now, and my Ann grew lonely. Efficient in homemaking, her household duties quickly done, she found time dragging very slowly. The day she sent our younger daughter off to college she went to one of the big department stores and applied for a job. Within a few days, she was one of their sales ladies. When she brought her first check home she gave it to me with a shining face and eyes aglow with success and love.

"For years you have given me your paychecks. Now it is my privilege to bring you mine." For her sake, I was glad but she saw how my face fell and she asked, "You're not happy about it, are you?"

I replied somewhat ashamed, "I guess I am still of the old school. My sensitive masculine ego is hurt, humiliated, I guess. I know what your job means to you and I don't have the heart to ask you to give it up. I'll get over it." I did, but not for quite a while. I experienced how difficult it is to make the heart feel what the mind approves as logical.

How good it was to get away for our summer vacation at the shore in New Jersey. The warm sun, the music of the breakers, freedom from the pressing cares, and unending pastoral duties of the church. Our renewed family togetherness gave us the complete relaxation we needed. At nearby Cape May, there were nightly concerts of classical- and semi-classical music by a good little orchestra that soothed our troubled souls and inspired hopeful thoughts. They played in a little frame auditorium, built over the breakers, which gave an unusual accompaniment to the music above.

One evening came the thought: "All this loveliness we enjoy tonight arose out of the ancient primeval ocean, life by some inner compulsion reaching out and up in ever-changing forms to increasing complexity and newer, greater possibilities, until mankind appeared and began his cultural development. From animal grunts and noises came song and speech, the making of musical instruments, the invention of musical notation, and the composing of melody and harmony."

And now many millions of years later — here I sat lost in contemplation and wonder at the vastness of perspective and the wonder of it all. I no longer heard the orchestra, although I knew that the violins were still there with the scraping of horsehair on catgut, guided by strange symbols; circles, semicircles, dots, and tiny flags on paper, producing divine music born in the mind of a deaf musician who never heard it with his physical ears!

The symphony set in motion airwaves that entered my ears, struck upon the tiny eardrums that transmitted these as nerve impulses to my brain, and changed to an ecstasy of feeling. Why, why this continuing miracle! Surely, surely, this fantastic, impossible experience could not be the result of the chance play of blind forces, the unceasing dance of molecules, atoms, electrons, neutrons, and all the rest! To be an atheist or agnostic makes more staggering demands on credulity and belief than faith in a Creative Intelligence guiding such developments. It yielded a sermon that I preached with great joy and satisfaction. The title: *Music over the Breakers*.

We went back to our daily tasks, problems, and disappointments with new strength and courage. We needed all of it. A mad genius was amuck in Europe. The bad peace of Versailles and Trianon exploded. The world was on fire.

25 - The World On Fire

A mad genius was amuck in Europe. The bad peace at Versailles and Trianon, the impossible task of holding a nation in subordination forever, the aid that was too little and too late to the weak democracy of Germany, the postwar fears and resentments, and the impassioned and reckless promises and threats of a paperhanger on the way to dictatorship made a witch's brew in the cauldron of aid. Nervous, tired, and frightened Europe threatened to run over and flood the continent with another conflagration — truly worldwide this time. The historical forces, set in motion at the "peace" conference, kept pressing against their confining bonds and it was too late to start other forces to counteract and redirect their incalculable energies. We shall not tell the history. Others have done it better.

The excitement in America, too, was increasing month-by-month, week-by-week, day-by-day. The Monday luncheons of the ministers, occasions of pleasant conversation, became more and more serious — troubled dialogues of men who were concerned with offering an adequate message for those anxious days. As the lightning flashed, and the thunder and roar of the storm clouds broke over Europe, our conversations became excited, concerned, and penetrating. Over and over again we discussed various attitudes a Christian might take towards the wholesale murder of God's children by each other. Our executive secretary took an intense and peculiar satisfaction in telling us about his sergeant in World War I and his vicious bayonet drill. The rest of us were rather disgusted, but most felt that they could not ignore the threat of Nazism. A very few of us Christian pacifists could not reconcile our convictions about loving our enemies, who were also our brothers under God our Father with indiscriminately slaughtering them, their women, their children, and their elderly, as modern warfare demanded. Some of us questioned the propaganda of the Allies that depicted the Germans as beasts and spread the atrocity stories of concentration camps. We still remembered the vicious propaganda of World War I over the signature of Viscount Bryce, a highly ethical leader, later revealed by Philip Gibbs in *Now It Can Be Told* and *More That Can Be Told* as pure fabrications. In the end, the strongest feelings of each man determined his course of action. However, only a very few of my colleagues sank to the pagan attitudes of those days. The pressures kept building up in the church, too.

Sympathy grew for our English cousins in their terrible ordeal. There was the growing threat from Germany, as nation after nation was conquered by their blitzkriegs, and suspicion that the shocking stories of brutality, torture, and wholesale anti-semitic persecution and extermination might have been be true (and to the more impressionable *were* true). Packages for Britain, no more silk stockings from Japan, and continuous discussion about the war in Europe kept feeding the well-founded indignations and the consequent war fever of our people. The *America First* movement that was designed to keep us out of the war weakened and died. Lend-Lease of food, goods, war material, and ships edged us closer to the brink of a horrible abyss.

All this was vividly and painfully illustrated by the outstanding lay leader of our church. He was a very dear personal friend of our family and my staunch supporter. He was a splendid Christian — upright in all his dealings, possessed of strong ethical conscience — and was a generous supporter of the church and of various good causes. He attended church regularly and listened to my sermons with an open mind and heart, voicing now and then thoughtful and tactful criticism. I loved him and his family dearly. It was the most satisfying and happiest relationship we ever had with a parishioner. When my car wore out, he helped us with a very generous check to buy another, though he was displeased by all the chrome just coming into fashion. We were often entertained in his palatial home out in the suburbs. He was of English extraction and his family had played an important part in the life of an influential Baptist church in England. One day, with justifiable pride, he told me that the municipal council, with important problems before it, often took the position: "Let us find out what church X thinks about it."

He undoubtedly had relatives in England. Naturally, he was deeply concerned about the course of events, just as our citizens of German, Polish, Czech, French, and Scandinavian origin were.

My heart went out to him in his increasing agony. His wife told me that he walked the floor at night, frequently until the early hours of morning. He was also worried about his only son, whose death would be the end of their line. Against all this, my arguments concerning brotherhood, love, and non-violence were of no avail. Nor did it help to point out that the British Empire was not built by the voluntary invitation of their subject peoples, but mostly by bloody imperialist wars. England had been made rich by those conquests. I did not want our boys to go and die for an empire — not even for the British Empire on which the sun never set. And if the Germans wanted to build an empire of their own, they were doing only what the English, French, Dutch, Belgians, Spanish, and Portuguese for centuries had done before them.

He was honest enough to admit the force of this, and when his wife of German origin rose to support him in his fierce denunciation of the Germans, he reminded her that my pacifist position was the only one justified by the teachings of Jesus.

He tried to educate me about the Germans. One day, he threw a book to me — almost at me — that was published in 1914. It was one of the many propaganda histories of those frightful years. I recognized it at once for what it was. But to him, it was Gospel truth, probably because it justified his position. In spite of the increasing tension between us, however, our invitations to Sunday dinners continued, and we tried to find inoffensive topics of conversation, mostly in vain. Finally, one day, to my horror, he burst out with "Germany must be conquered, all the men castrated, and that nation forever kept down to prevent them from starting wars!" I gazed at him in sore amazement. My sensitive, gentle, Christian friend was now a casualty of war.

My sermons were of no help. I felt conscience-bound to preach on themes relating to the threat of war and on brotherhood. My wife accuses me, even now, of overdoing it. No matter what my sermon theme or Bible text was, I somehow brought in brotherhood, if not the word, its application or illustration. She was quite unhappy about it, as were others in our membership. But nobody stayed away or reduced their contribution to the church, the usual and most accepted ways to show unhappiness with and disapproval of a pastor. How could I stop preaching nonviolence and love and brotherhood when the nation and the world were sinking into the bloodbath of the ultimate infamy and sum of evil, war?

After one of my sermons in which I had vividly and concretely applied the Gospel to the problems of our society, there was a deadly stillness and a sparking tension in our car as we drove home. Finally, I spoke. "I'm afraid you did not feel very comfortable during the sermon this morning. Scarcely anybody thanked me."

"Why must you preach like that all the time?" cried out my wife, my dearest, kindest, severest critic.

"Yes, daddy," the children continued in support of their mother.

"I know I ought to be more careful. What if I had upset too many people and the church asked me to leave? How could we give our daughters a college education?"

"Daddy, don't talk like that!" my eldest daughter reproved me. "You just go on and preach what you must, what your conscience tells you. I'll be ashamed of you, all of us will be if you do otherwise! We'll make our way somehow."

For the rest of that day and all that week, there was singing in my heart. Surely, I had not lived in vain when my own child holds me to my ideals.

In those days, full of threat, insecurity, and darkness, I longed for every bit of hope and cheer, and a sign of the presence of the loving and omnipotent Intelligence. Jesus had taught us to call our Father. I was in the big public library in Oakland one Saturday afternoon in agonizing preparation for my Sunday sermon. A rainstorm came up. Buckets of water pounded on the windows. Spears of lightning flashed constantly. Thunder roared incessantly. It was one of those days when it was easy to imagine the imminent end of the world. When the storm came to an end, I went out and started for home, deeply depressed. As I walked along, I suddenly became aware of a puddle. I stopped. There, in a mud-puddle before me, was the concentrated glory of the sunset with its colors of brilliant gold, red, light green, purple, and blue. I gazed at it in wonder, then my beauty-loving eyes filled with tears of gratitude. "How could I ever doubt Thee, Oh Father, who fillest the earth with Thy beauty?" I prayed and went home strangely comforted and at peace.

Suddenly, the international situation exploded into our faces at Pearl Harbor, unexpectedly to us but perhaps not to our government. In just a few hours, the Japanese forces destroyed the surrounding forts, the port, and our naval and air fleets stationed there. The nation reeled under the shock of this disaster. We were wholly unprepared for this. Why? It is still argued vehemently. Our West Coast was open to the enemy. All that week I attended my duties in a daze, praying for light and for the courage to do what was right. So, what *was* right? Oh, it was clear enough to me, an American citizen, that what was right was to defend my country. Of course. But my Christian conscience and imagination saw very clearly that participation in the mass murder of my brothers was wrong. What guidance, what inspiration, what word of comfort could I bring to my people, to our youth, to their parents, and to those few influential community leaders who were members of our church? Saturday night came around, and still no light. When my Ann was asleep, I went into another room and, after agonizing prayer and inner turmoil, I wrote out as carefully as I was able the statement I would read to the church the next day:

A STATEMENT TO THE CONGREGATION
December 14, 1941

Our nation is at war. I believe in democracy, which among other things, means the rule of the majority, and I accept my nation's decision in Congress and shall abide by it.

I live in a democracy for which I am profoundly grateful. I will not try to obstruct the will of the majority. I will do all I can to make my country strong and an agent of God's will according to the vision granted to me and in ways compatible with that vision.

Our government has granted freedom of conscience to the conscientious objector. In doing so it acknowledged a loyalty higher than loyalty to the state, namely, loyalty to the Kingdom of God. I am grateful that my country has taken this position. Otherwise it would have been like the totalitarian states.

I love my country, but my primary allegiance belongs to God. I believe that this is truly Christian, and also that it is truly American, for democracy and freedom cannot exist without a freedom of conscience. The danger to this nation comes not from people who have too much conscience, but from those who have too little. My conscience does not allow active participation in war.

I plead for unity in the church of Jesus Christ, in love. I will not call into question the devotion of another follower of Jesus Christ because he disagrees with me on this war. I ask for the same consideration from others.

In the First World War, I was entitled to exemption because I was a student for the Christian ministry. I preferred to waive exemption for three reasons:

1. I did not wish to be considered a coward.

2. *I wanted to prove my loyalty to America.*

3. *As a Christian pacifist I wished to register my protest against war.*

I stated this before the draft board, and was assigned to the Medical Corps, spent six months at the Base Hospital in Camp Upton, and received an Honorable Discharge.

I feel that I owe you this frank statement even as I have stated my position in my preaching all along. I trust that this will save our beloved church, and its pastor, from idle or ignorant gossip, and provide a defense against malicious misrepresentations.

"Here I stand. God help me, I can do no other."

(signed)
Edwin L. Kautz

The congregation accepted my statement graciously. Perhaps they admired their pastor's courage, and probably their Christian consciences did not permit them to take a strong, contrary stand. I promised to look after the welfare of all our youth as well as their loved ones, and all others who may be called into the armed services of the nation. I also offered to resign if they so desired. They did not ask for it nor did they suggest it. With a heavily burdened heart, I started my service through the terrible war years with a new appreciation of my people, whose continued support gave me an added sense of security and spiritual poise. A month later, I received a letter from the Council on Christian Social Progress of the Northern Baptist Convention, from which I quote the first paragraph:

The ultimate aim of every war is the establishing of peace. Our nation is now engaged in a second world-wide conflict. It is clear that the peace which we gained at the close of the last war was built upon a decidedly insecure foundation.

We must do better this time. Christians will fail in their stewardship if they do not give serious and prayerful thought to the kind of social order that will follow when hostilities have come to an end.

Greatly encouraged, I immediately established a course on the causes of war and conditions of a just and durable peace. My wife was to teach a Sunday school class of younger women, and I of men. As a beginning, I used an outline that I had presented to an interdenominational summer assembly that I had sent to Dr. Poteat, president of Colgate Rochester Divinity School, who was kind enough to call it the best statement he had seen on the subject.

In reply to a letter by Professor William C. Mather, chairman of the Council on Christian Social Progress, I wrote as follows:

Lessening the cruelties of warfare, keeping men's consciences awake with respect to humane treatment of enemies has always been considered one of the important tasks of the Christian Church.

Cynics have even accused Christianity of taking this easier way to satisfy its conscience in preference to the sterner demand of creating a world order where wars become unnecessary.

Influential voices in our nation are voicing the demand for retaliatory and indiscriminate bombing of civilians in the enemy countries. Surely, the Christian bodies of our nation ought to say something about that. Are we to make war on defenseless women and children? Shall we practice that for which we condemned the totalitarian powers? We are concerned to keep the fair name of the United States unsullied by unnecessary cruelty. We are anxious to wage the war, if wage it we must, in such manner as shall give the common people of all the world a new confidence in America and make possible a peace with less bitterness.

Has it not been stated repeatedly on good authority, that indiscriminate bombing of civilians has no military value? Surely, we can dispense with it then from a purely utilitarian point of view.

I suggest that we petition our government in the name of our common humanity and in the name of the Christ who taught us to love our enemies, to refrain from such practice.

Kindly convey this suggestion to the proper committee. You will be interested to learn that our Board of Deacons has approved the suggestion of your council to form study classes on a "Just and Durable Peace." I myself shall teach our class of thirty younger men, and my wife will teach another class of the same size of younger married women. In all, this will cover an outline of about sixty pages, and we expect to give six Sundays to it.

Identical letters were sent to the Minister's Council and the Christian Council of Allegheny County.

At the annual meeting of the Northern Baptist Convention, there was a long, excited debate on a recommendation to the churches of the Convention concerning their attitude toward the war. The movement to line up our churches for war in support of our government was led by Dr. Poling of the Baptist Temple in Philadelphia. Against such action, Dr. L. B. Mosely, pastor of the First Baptist Church of Pittsburgh, led the debate.

At the psychological moment, when the tide had turned in favor of a firm Christian declaration opposing church support for the war, Dr. Poling dramatically produced and read a letter from President Roosevelt expressing the strong hope and wish for our support of the government in such an emergency. However, the President's wish and request was denied by a formal vote. This was a new and unique step by a large Christian body marking a new attitude toward war and government. It was eroded somewhat only by the cruelties, deceptions, and atrocities of the Nazi regime, and the fear of world domination by the "supermen," who were proving themselves so subhuman. But strong Christian aversion to wars remained.

All these, and other developments, strengthened my hand and convinced the church that I was not a lone fanatic tilting at windmills. I now set myself to bring what comfort and strength I could to our youth and their anxious parents. No pastoral prayer was offered without remembering them. In my prayers, I struggled against the repetition of identical phrases, words, and ideas so that these petitions would not become meaningless tautology unable to unite and move the worshippers to earnest petition. We held farewell services for them without the usual maudlin elements, affixed their stars to our service flag, and dedicated the same in a ritual without pagan ideas. We kept them in constant remembrance with paragraphs in our Sunday Bulletin and with extracts from their letters, while sending our Bulletins to the ends of the earth. We gave them a warm, joyous welcome whenever they visited at home.

At the same time, I endeavored to keep all of us from the all-too-human but degrading trait of hate for God's children who were engaged in the same senseless heathen slaughter on the other side. A new attitude was beginning to permeate our population — that war was a "dirty job" that had to be done, but not for glory or high adventure. Certainly, our boys did not go to war with the enthusiasm and the singing of those who participated in World War I. All this, and the new climate so generated, made my war against hate more meaningful and successful than it could otherwise have been. And no one to my knowledge impugned my motives for the misfortune of having been born in Hungary (with one very painful exception to be told later).

INTERCESSION FOR OUR BOYS IN THE ARMED FORCES

Oh Thou, who makest the wrath of man to praise Thee, we commend these, our boys, to Thy loving care as they go through the fires of war. Sustain them by Thy love, grant them a vivid sense of Thy presence, make them centers of radiant faith in our Heavenly Father who cares for all men.

May theirs be the courage of Christ to live up to their noblest convictions, may their lives be clean in order to be strong, and a source of inspiration to their comrades. Save them from hatred, cruelty, and the curse of drink and illicit pleasures. Keep them tender at heart and wholesome and good soldiers of the great white Captain who loved them and laid down His life for them.

Out of their awful experiences may there rise an inexorable hatred for war and an unshakeable determination to build a world brotherhood.

May suffering cleanse and enlarge their vision, until they too shall see what Jesus dreaded, and until their hearts too shall burn with the same divine compassion for all mankind. We humbly beseech Thee make us worthy of their confidence and sacrifice.

We ask it all in the name of Him who died on a shameful Roman cross in order that we may be sure of Thy eternal love for us. Amen

Our first casualty came all too soon. David Council was not a member of our church, but a faithful attendant at services. A winsome high-minded boy of a fine family, beloved by all of us. He was in the Air Force, and in an accident dashed to his death at Alamagordo, New Mexico. We gave him a beautiful funeral without the usual tear-jerking reminders that God was on our side, or that this was His will and we have to be reconciled to it. We covered his star with gold, and pledged ourselves not to forget him. It was difficult in this war to use the accustomed prayers of previous wars even for those who were not conscientious objectors. The indiscriminate bombing and wholesale strafing on both sides, the drafting of populations, made the use of words like "heroes," "martyrs," "self-sacrifice," etc., turn to dust and leave a bitter taste in the mouths of thoughtful people.

Soon our youth encountered the tough and ugly realities of war, like the chaplain in the merchant marine one of my boys told about, who got drunk and resorted to prostitutes on shore leave, and then tried to conduct divine worship and exhort the boys to clean living. Another, the brightest of our youth who served in Patton's army in Germany, wrote to me telling of the wanton destruction of a beautiful piano in a home where they were quartered, and how his comrades laughed at him when he protested. And there were other stories, far worse, that they could have told. Since my own grandfather told me of the atrocities by the soldiers of Francis Joseph in the Italian campaign, and his share in them, I was not surprised.

I had enough imagination and empathy to understand and feel the reactions of soldiers in the heat of battle and the tortures of conscience to seek escape and forgetfulness by any means — unless their softer feelings were numbed by discipline, indoctrination, and "blooding." Our boys were not good killers until this had been done to them. Who was I to pass judgment on them? Only deep sorrow and profound dejection were possible to me that men, created in the image of God for whom Christ died and for whom, millions of them, Jesus was the model personality, could sink so low, indeed below the level of animals.

Years later, after a sermon at the University Baptist Church in Austin, Texas, a Jewish youth requested an interview with me. We met at the regal social building of the University of Texas, where he was a student. He had flown in a bomber in Asia. They went on daily bombing flights over Japan. The boys in his plane were good "Christians," read their Bibles, and prayed before going on their "missions." After they had unloaded their bombs, they swooped low over the fields where old men, women, and children were working, and strafed them, leaving them dead and wounded in their wake.

I expostulated with them "Why do you do this to these harmless people? Suppose Japanese fliers flew over *our* fields at home and did this to our old men, women, and children! How would you feel?"

They laughed at me and shouted, "They're only Japs! Monkeys!"

"Please tell me, explain to me if you can, how these religious boys could be so heartless."

I was too honest to put him off with sociological reasons about the warlike culture in which they had lived that had conditioned them, and to the propaganda of that culture in war that made it easy for them to kill and to joke over their enemy's grotesque motions as they were shot. For in all our Christian churches there was the eternal reminder of the Savior who taught his followers to love their enemies and who, in the agonies of the cross, prayed "Father forgive them."

Here was a Jewish youth, inclined toward agnosticism, whose conscience was more sensitive, and whose heart was more tender than that of the "Christian" boys. No, I had to drop my head in sorrow and shame and confess our sin. At the same time, I could not help thinking that perhaps their gruesome, macabre humor served to save them from madness.

In line with my pledge, I introduced a study of war and peace, beginning with the Bible and on through "Christian" history. We looked at the gory stories in the Old Testament, justified by the doctrine of a vengeful, national god, partial to his people, helping them to conquer and enslave the Canaanites and fighting with the armies of Israel against the heathen. We followed with the visions of the great prophets who dreamed of a world of peace, at a time when violence, cruelty, and bloodshed were accepted everywhere. And the story of the anonymous author of the Book of Jonah who reproves the patriotic expectation and satisfaction of seeing his nation's most powerful enemy, Nineveh, destroyed.

If Jonah had no heart for the children and the dumb animals in that great city, his God did, and when God did not destroy the city, Jonah petulantly cried, "It is better for me to die" than to see his God concerned about their enemies! What a revolutionary tract, even for our time many centuries later! No wonder that preachers found it easier to argue about the size of the fish's throat and the details of Jonah's submarine journey. Not until our atomic bombs were dropped on Hiroshima and Nagasaki did most of us hear the Voice: "Get together or you will all perish!"

How well do I remember the day when we learned about Hiroshima. For days I lived in a daze. My nation, the United States, had done this frightful deed. The most idealistic nation in all the world, I sincerely believed, and the most Christian. In the wink of an eye we killed one hundred thousand people and maimed many more thousands for life in an ocean of fire — helpless women, old people, and little children as well as men and soldiers. My imagination pictured that scene of horror in terrifying detail. We had "out-Hitlered" the mad paperhanger. Could an airplane crew perpetrate that and not go mad?

The soul-searing doubt insinuated itself into the minds of thoughtful believers: What kind of God can permit this? Can it be a God of love? Is there a God at all? Once again, as so often throughout man's existence, we were tempted to unload our iniquity, depravity, and guilt on God. We could not entertain the thought that precisely in a world like this can heroism, moral character, a love like that of Jesus and true ethical greatness develop. Nor could we accept the implications of our faith that made room for creatures with a certain freedom of choice on God's good earth, which could effectively and tragically neutralize the expression of divine love. We wanted to believe in an unlimited Almighty God and in human freedom. This contradiction was tearing us apart.

My course on war and peace in the men's class and with our youth was not very successful. It was too disturbing and the war that enveloped us was trouble enough.

An agent of the War Department called on me one day to inquire about the loyalty of the chairman of our board of trustees who had found employment in a war plant. An odd person that agent was, either under the influence of liquor or drugs. I still wonder how he landed such an important job.

An F.B.I. investigator also appeared at my home one evening on a similar errand. He was a clean-cut, intelligent, college-bred gentleman. Everything the War Department agent was not. After I had answered his questions about my church member, I requested the right to question him in turn. He readily consented.

"Well, I suppose not even Mrs. Roosevelt can escape our F.B.I. investigation?"

"No, she could not."

"I suppose Norman Thomas would have to run the gauntlet?"

"Yes."

"But why? Don't the communists hate socialists? Was not Mr. Thomas one of their most determined enemies? Then what sense is there in mistrusting such a man's loyalty to our government?"

He did not answer that. Perhaps he wasn't able to. I have wondered ever since.

Then came the president's order to send all Japanese, including citizens of the United States, native-born and naturalized, into hastily erected concentration camps, to which our government gave the more euphonious name "relocation camps." Such a name did not have the horrifying connotations of the other. But the prisoners therein confined received scant comfort from the name. Probably, for the first time, thousands of our own citizens were confined in such camps without due process of law. And without justification — only rumors, accusations, and slanders of greedy White neighbors coveting their choice farms, neat houses, and other property.

Working unconscionably long hours and supported by family solidarity and cooperation, they had become dangerous competitors of the individualistic, Caucasian Americans who now saw an opportunity to grab, for a pittance, the property of these solid, hard-working "Yellow bastards." And the unprincipled politicians and demagogues of California used the incipient but groundless panic of the Whites to make such expropriation of the properties of these Japanese immigrants and their American-born offspring an easy matter.

In vain did police chiefs, even in far-off Hawaii, report the Japanese citizens' behavior faultless, and the assurance that, if necessity arose, they could arrest them overnight. The president ordered that they be shipped to the "relocation camps," ostensibly for their own protection, within a few days. The camps were in desert places, dusty and hot in the summer, and freezing cold in the winter. Their hastily constructed barracks provided none of the amenities of their homes. No wonder that some became embittered and returned to Japan after the war. Yet most of them remained loyal to the nation that, in spite of its proclaimed ideals, had humiliated them so unjustly. And the most decorated group in our armed forces was a *Nisei* (second generation Japanese) battalion that fought for us in Italy and in the Pacific area.

And it is a sobering fact that the Negro stevedores, on the transport that would carry them to fight on our side against Japan, attacked the Japanese Americans on their way to the internment camps.

After the war, teaching a course in sociology in a Baptist College in Texas, I assigned the study of various racial and immigrant groups to my class. Subdivisions of five students were to report on each group: background, traditions, achievements in history and in the United States, etc. They themselves chose the groups. No group and no individual was even willing to consider a report on Japanese Americans, so powerful was the impact of race prejudice and of our wartime propaganda, though several groups were willing to report on the American Negroes. Finally, I myself undertook this assignment, in vain I fear. They did not even want to listen to such a report. I was worried for a long time.

Our treatment of Japanese Americans, particularly citizens, had hurt me deeply. How could my country, my beloved America, act so unfairly and so wickedly toward them? Were those of German, Italian, Austrian, or Hungarian descent, whose colors and features enabled them to get lost in the crowd, less perilous? Were not the Japanese actually *less* dangerous because of their very differences of race, so easily recognized? Was not this simply a new combination of racial and economic prejudice, or another example of racial discrimination so prevalent among White Americans?

But let us return to my pastorate in Pittsburgh during the war. My beloved but sadly confused and troubled lawyer friend began to stay away from our services. I visited him in his office and expressed my concern, both as his pastor, and his friend. I expressed my deep appreciation for his support and friendship and asked him not to let me down. His reply was an accusation that my friendship was a cover for exploiting him. I could not believe my ears, for my friendships were never based on selfish calculations and manipulations. I am well aware of my follies and sins — may the Eternal Goodness forgive me — but disloyalty to a cause or a person was never one of them.

I left in a dream. A horrible nightmare. True, he had often entertained us in his palatial home and surprised us with presents, even gave us $200 to help us buy the new car, badly needed in my work, but none of it was expected, still less planned for, but a beautiful plus of our friendship for which we were unspeakably grateful.

What could I do to prove to him how wrong and without foundation his accusation was? I simply had to return his cash gift. Another friend counseled against this, pointing out that when he gave his gift he did not feel that way, and I should hurt him to return it. But would I not injure him more by allowing him to continue in his unfounded suspicion?

Accordingly, I gave the money to several good causes and sent him a statement of these and the reason for my actions. He did not deign to reply.

A few months later, Miss Muriel Lester, a social reformer twice nominated for the Nobel Peace Prize, was in Pittsburgh to speak on Christian pacifism. She was Secretary of the *International Fellowship of Reconciliation*, and was making her last tour of America before her retirement.

She had renounced wealth to found the famous Kingsley Hall, a settlement house in the slums of London. She was host to Gandhi on one of his trips to London and went to India to follow him.

Her sparkling personality and the authority with which she spoke from the depths of the Spirit had made her one of the best known and loved lecturers of our day. She was one of twelve women selected by Professor Thomas Kepler for his definitive anthology of saints of the devotional life from the first century through the twentieth.

She made a profound impression on me, and I felt led to confide the story of my broken friendship and ask her advice on restoring it. In return, she sadly confided that because of her pacifist convictions she had a similar experience with a very dear friend, and it proved impossible to reestablish the broken friendship. I would simply have to carry the wound in love, until my friend was ready for it, or to the end of my life.

Years later I learned that my friend confided his suspicion that I was a Hitler agent to one of the Baptist secretaries. The breach was never healed. I carried the aching wound for many years.

26 - Painful Transition

As the war spread in extent and intensity, so did the tensions at home. Fortunately, increasing victories at the front and good earnings at home balanced somewhat the grief of those whose loved ones paid for our successes in the field with crippled bodies and minds, torture, and death. We pastors had to bring comfort, courage, and sanity to our people in a world gone mad. Hatred of the enemy increased as the "superior race" began to bombard London from the continent with a terrible new weapon, and as the "little yellow men" proved their superiority in ever enlarging conquests in the Pacific.

It became easier to preach against war in general as its destruction of life and property and the slow erosion of our democratic freedoms increased, but also more difficult to take a stand against this particular holocaust since it appeared to be the only way to stop our enemies, the genocide of the Jews, and to build a new world in which peace and freedom would be safe. The hope of a new international organization cast a ray of light into the dark night of war's insanity. Prayers had to be kept Christian, but was this possible when victory over the mounting evil and our enemies, who were the visible embodiment of evil, appeared possible only in their continued slaughter, who were also our brothers for whom Christ died? In this terrible dilemma, each of us did what was demanded and permitted in our hopes and fears, devotion to the Father of all men, but also in increasingly chauvinistic patriotism, the profits and losses of organized violence, and the needs and wants of our people.

Somehow my congregation, on the whole, accepted my continued preaching and teaching of Christian pacifism, some of them, perhaps many, with increasing discomfort, subconsciously wished for a moratorium on a love that includes our nation's enemies. To satisfy this longing was impossible for me. Yet my people trusted me and endured my pleas to withstand hate and cultivate love.

Perhaps it was in part because our young people serving in the armed forces of the nation were looked after conscientiously by the less pacifistic, less outspoken, or more militaristic pastors. And the stories our youth brought home about our boys were not as complimentary as our war propaganda pictured them. All of us, who knew something about it, were terribly concerned at the frightening sag in the morals of our boys and girls amidst the pressures of boredom, killing, and the temptations to escape from these pressures by illicit pleasures.

Then, the Atomic Bomb! Was it necessary? So it was argued. But later we learned that Japan was already making overtures for peace, that her armed forces were widely scattered and her cities in ruins. In fifty years, perhaps, we shall know the truth. I heard Dr. Urey, one of those who had worked on the bomb, tell us on two separate occasions that our government promised the atomic scientists the bomb would not be dropped on a city but on an unpopulated area. According to him, our government broke its pledge to these scientists. This he stated at two public meetings in Pittsburgh at the Soldiers' and Sailors' Memorial Hall and the First Baptist Church.

It was fortunate that I was able to take a brief vacation at the seashore in New Jersey. The blackout was depressing, but the stars came out in unaccustomed splendor. Their light speeding over the frightful vastnesses of space somehow imparted hope to my despairing soul. As the breakers came in, they changed into innumerable diamonds as if a gigantic hand had scattered them over the sand. It was a sight not seen before, when men's brazen lights blotted them out.

Now and then I visited the Tabernacle where famous preachers held forth. One evening, sauntering along the street, there came across the radio a strong masculine voice. Who was it? We had tuned in on the ceremonies of Japan's surrender. General MacArthur was speaking on war and peace. He kept insisting that the solution to the problem of war was not military, but theological. I listened in amazement. A general turned preacher was challenging us to think about war — his specialty — in Christian dimensions. No wonder he won the admiration and affection of some of our enemies. The occupation became a unique and successful experiment in guiding democracy to a conquered nation. How fortunate we were!

Soon after, we had the privilege of the leadership of another great soldier, General Marshall, who was also secretary of state. His plan of reconstruction was made available to our allies and enemies, as well as our vast resources to rebuild their shattered economies. I can never forget the moving statement of a German to our traveling group in Germany: "Do you think we can ever forget how you came to us, with your energies after the war, and helped us to our feet?"

How tragic that Russia, so rigidly bound by her Communist ideology, was unable to accept our generous offer extended to her, also. How different are the consequences and our relationships today?

Somebody ought to document the many stories of soldiers and non-combatants reaching across enemy boundaries to express their penitence over the slaughter, and their compassion for the enemy. Reverend Roger Williams of Greensburg, Pennsylvania tells about a member of his church who killed a German soldier on the battlefield. As he examined the pitiful possessions of the dead man, he found a letter and the address of his mother. He almost forgot about it, but back at home he was overcome by guilt and forced to write a letter to the mother asking her forgiveness. In due time, her reply came.

Among other things, she wrote, "Thank you for writing to me and sending me my son's possessions. While my grief is great, I do not blame you, for you were obeying orders, as was my son. Come and be my son in place of my own."

Beautiful, ah yes, very. But not enough. The slaughter and blind obedience to orders must be prevented. The victorious allies made a tardy and unhappy beginning in the trials of the war criminals at

Nuremberg until the court refused to accept the contention of the defense that the accused were only obeying orders.

Back at home, I became a member of an interfaith committee on preparing the families of our veterans for their return home. It proved to be quite helpful in providing guidelines to ministers and lay leaders in understanding and counseling with the soldiers and their relatives.

After more than seven years in that inner-city church, four of which, until the outbreak of the war, were very happy indeed, I felt justified in putting out feelers for a new opening. To my increasing uneasiness, only one or two inquiries came. One day, one of my friends, a fellow pastor, called me on the telephone and told me about the concern of all my friends about something I ought to know, but they were afraid to hurt me. After assuring him that I should welcome whatever it was (what are friends for if not to share in love what I ought to know?) he informed me that whenever the pulpit committee of a good church inquired about me the executive secretary steered them in other directions. He told them that while Kautz was a good pastor, he spoke with an accent — to which my church had never objected — and he is a *C.O.* (conscientious objector to war). This finished me with every pulpit committee.

Needless to state, I was shocked. It was clear that because I took Jesus seriously neither my superior denominational officer nor the pulpit committees considered me fit to lead a church. Apparently, my usefulness as a Christian minister was at an end. After a painful but thorough discussion with my faithful Ann, it was decided that I would go back to school, earn a graduate degree in sociology, and try to break into college teaching.

Fortunately, about the same time Dr. Franklin, Dean of the School of Education at the University of Pittsburgh, called and asked if I would teach an extension course in religious drama.

They had just lost the professor responsible for most of their courses in religious education. The professor knew about my work in Bible drama and recommended me highly for teaching it at the University.

This was one of the joyous tasks I had voluntarily assumed because of my love of drama. People had come from a number of churches and their reports had created a reputation for the church and myself, of which I was unaware. At our plays, people did not laugh or talk in the wrong places, but were deeply moved as evidenced by the almost breathless silence and the sounds of silent weeping. And now this labor of love and joy opened up a new avenue of self-expression when I had the greatest need for it.

I accepted, of course, and found a class of about twenty ministers, missionaries, and other lay church workers. They were so appreciative that, within a month, the Dean called me into his office and asked if I could teach another subject during the next semester. What a pleasant surprise. Our conversation revealed that we each had taught courses that might be tied into one. He had given his course at the University of Pittsburgh, *The Religious Outlook in America*, and I had given to churches and ministers my lecture *War and the Christian*. He asked for a syllabus on a course that we would call *The Present War and the Religious and Moral Outlook in America*. When I submitted my syllabus he admitted: "This outline and bibliography are much better than mine was." It was also successful.

The genuine appreciation and friendliness of Dean Franklin inspired me to ask his counsel. I told him in brief outline the story of my life beginning with our coming to America. At the close, he said, "Mr. Kautz, if you were a Methodist and I had known all this, I would have done everything in my power to place you in one of our colleges. You have so much to give."

Then he called into consultation Dr. Elmer, Head of the Department of Sociology, and together they worked out a combined course in sociology and religious education leading to a Master of Arts degree that would provide me with a broad appeal to college deans. I learned a great deal (even though a few of my professors were very dull and boring). And I shall forever be indebted to Dr. Franklin and Dr. Elmer, for the inspiration of their friendship and the opportunity they provided for continuing my checkered career.

Finances were a big problem. Our daughters were still in college and my salary was barely enough to provide for our necessities. However, as an instructor in the School of Education, I received the munificent sum of $200 per semester. My dear friend, who had made me aware of my problem in the ministry, prevailed upon a fine young minister in a large and wealthy church of another denomination to have me called as his assistant. My salary as director of religious education and youth amounted to $200 per month. My wife found employment in a religious bookstore, and so we were able to continue without insuperable difficulties to keep our girls in college and to finance my own education.

So we said goodbye to Sandusky Street Church, and at 54 years of age, I was back to school for my master's degree, hoping that in another year I may embark on my new career — college teaching. My work at the church and my studies fitted together very nicely and mutually reinforced each other.

It was a very fruitful and happy year. The worship periods in Sunday school became interesting, even exciting. Soon all looked forward to each Sunday with eager expectations.

The young people had discontinued their meetings Sunday nights after several years of struggle, and I was expected to resurrect them. A large committee spent several months in careful preparation on an adequate plan to revive the youth meetings. We were very ambitious, looking for attendance of one hundred to one hundred fifty, whereas the previous best was around twenty.

Several times various members of the planning committee including the pastor, frightened by the ambitious plan I kept pressing for, were ready to fold up. Somehow we kept going and the result was the greatest series of programs for youth ever put on by this big church. Alas, they found it too much work and did not continue the following year. I was no longer there.

This was a church of over one thousand members. They never had to worry about finances and owned a beautiful building — one of the loveliest and most impressive in the entire city. It was an inner-city church on a street of department stores. Its members came to the services from considerable distances. They owned valuable real estate around the church from which they derived an income of around $50,000 a year. There was no organized effort to gain new members. In fact, they expected prospective members to be attracted by its prestige. All this provided no incentive to build their membership. There were some truly dedicated members, but their number decreased year by year.

They had a colossal pride that slowly eroded their devotion to Christ and their dedication to missionary outreach. The pastors they attracted were less and less dedicated, and the last I knew of them, they had only a shell of a church. What a pity! For a while, as I discovered much later, some of the members thought of inviting me to be their pastor. But the most influential board member soon quashed that by saying, "We want no Hunkie in our pulpit."

Finally my course was completed, and at an impressive commencement received my Master of Arts degree, having earned an "A" in all my subjects.

Now I was ready for a new beginning. I had the feeling that I might be invited to join the department of sociology. My thesis advisor, Dr. Phelps, appeared pleased with my thesis, *The Hungarian Baptist Movement in America*, a socio-historical study. I wrote it as a participant observer, having served as president, editor, member of important communities, and consultant to the American Baptist Home Mission Society, etc. It was not as dry as a library thesis. Dr. Phelps assured me that he had read every page. A real compliment!

Soon after, he called me into his office. Thorough disgust registered on his face. I asked him what was wrong. He told me how Dr. Elmer and he had hoped to have me teach with them at the University. "You have so much to give, but they won't employ you!" I thanked him for his concern and my heart sank.

Some days later, Dr. Elmer signaled to me when he spied me as I went past a long line of students at his desk. He offered me a chair. I hesitated to take his time, but he insisted. He wanted to explain why they could not invite me to join the staff, as they desired.

"Did you know, Kautz, that for twenty years sociology was the stepdaughter of colleges and universities?"

"No," was my astonished reply. "But why?"

"Because to the average member of the boards of trustees, sociology was synonymous with socialism."

I could hardly believe my ears. How could they have been so stupid? But he assured me that it was the truth.

"And now," he continued, "they are scared out of their wits by the bomb, and they want us to build strong sociology departments. We lost a whole generation of teachers, and now they want young faculties who will continue the work when we pass off the scene. I am very, very sorry, and I hope you can find an opening elsewhere worthy of your gifts and efforts."

I thanked him and left, wrapped in deep gloom. Another dead end. We sent out scores of applications, mostly to church-related colleges, hoping that they would appreciate my religious background. Most of them did not reply, and not a single Baptist college. A dean from Texas was kind enough to express his regret at not being able to employ me, stating that I must be a very interesting teacher. Even this drop of encouragement helped my sagging spirits. My appeals to leaders of my denomination were of no avail.

I had completed my work at the church and we were without an income except for the small salary the bookstore paid my Ann. Fortunately, our children were on their own. I was fifty-five and about to start a new career. Would any school want me at that age and with only an M.A., not a Ph.D.?

To complicate matters still more, a Slovak Baptist Church near our home in Duquesne was suddenly left without a pastor, and hearing about my wife of Slovak parents, came to our home and invited me to become their pastor. I could preach in English. They felt sure of our success in spite of my Hungarian past. My lovely wife charmed them and they insisted on returning to receive a favorable answer.

That same evening, I received a long distance telephone call from the president of the oldest women's college of the Southwest, in the heart of Texas, a Baptist institution. He wanted me to become Head of their Department of Sociology and associate professor. He told me that the University of Pittsburgh recommended me, and informed him that I was a Hungarian Baptist. Southern Baptists supported the movement in Hungary, and some very able Hungarian students had received Doctor of Theology at the Southern Baptist Theological Seminary. Hungarian Baptists were well known as a dedicated, conservative group. Therefore, he was eager to have me, especially in such a controversial area as sociology.

But I was not at all eager to accept the invitation. It was too far from our children and friends, and the anti-Negro prejudices and discriminations of the area repelled me. I was afraid I would not fit in at all. The schedule of fifteen class sessions per week in five different courses, including two non-sociological, one in economics, and another in the government of Texas looked impossible. The salary was contemptible. He said he would write and call me again. When I informed him that I simply could not come for the salary offered, he said he was not able to offer more but he would consult with his trustees once more and call me again.

He did, and offered the munificent sum of $2000 and an apartment for nine months, and I would have to find something else for the remaining three months. As to race prejudice, he informed me that they had Mexican girls from Texas, and Chinese and Japanese from Hawaii. This, he thought, implied that racism was not such a difficult issue.

In a college blue book, I looked up the information on the school. I found it to be a rather large school of a thousand students, fully accredited, and of appealing description. I was not in a good bargaining position, so I accepted and left within the week.

27 - Texas and the Fascinating Frontier

So, this was Texas! I had viewed its endless plains for hours, dry and hot. In the air-conditioned Pullman coach, this did not inconvenience me until I stood outside on the station platform. Since no one met me there, I found my way to the bus station with my heavy bags, and boarded a rickety bus to the little college town — a county seat with an impressive courthouse. I learned later that because the old families had kept the railroad out of their town, the new railroad town grew like Topsy while the college town remained a sleepy little place.

Dusty and tired, I presented myself at the president's office. He received me cordially, and with his lady, took me to dinner at a good restaurant. On the way, he mentioned the wonderful smell of nature. I found it rather unpleasant — not at all like that of the hills and valleys of Pennsylvania because of an odd smell of decay in it. Since then, I noticed this smell several times as I traveled through the south. Once, another traveler asked me, with deep longing, if I had ever smelled the bayous on the lower Mississippi. Yes, I had. To me, they stank. To him, they were fragrant. Is it all in our minds?

After dinner, they drove me to my room in a house owned by the college just off the campus, where they rented rooms to anyone, adding thereby to the income of the school. My room was hot and had no fan, so I had to leave my door unlocked and partly open during the night. In my aching loneliness, I pictured my loved ones back with me in our cool and comfortable home, and prayed earnestly for them. Then, slowly, to the music of myriads of insects, I fell into a troubled sleep.

I lost no time in making preparations for my classes. While not knowing who would teach sociology, the college had not ordered textbooks. I had to do this immediately. Until they arrived, I had to depend on lecturing. Fortunately, I had some of my college notes, and the library had a few good books on sociology, so I managed, studying day and night, mostly in my bathtub while immersed in cold water. I soon discovered that the scholastic standard of the school was about equal to that of a good high school in Pennsylvania. This enabled me to keep comfortably ahead of my students. They were lovely, eager young women, but quite a number from rural backgrounds simply could not understand what I was driving at for quite a few weeks. Not until my third year was I able to hold my students to college standards, and then only those who had previous classes in sociology.

Still, it was a demanding schedule, fifteen hours a week in the summer heat of that semi-tropical country. Not at all like the America I had known. Neither was their quaint, soft drawl, so different from the harsh accents of Yankee-land. The president of the school attempted to pressure me into teaching eighteen hours a week, including at least one class on Saturday. I simply refused. Then, I would seriously consider teaching during their summer session? I would. But later, when I learned that in one hundred-plus heat they would pay me one month's salary for six weeks, I withstood all his blandishments and pressures and steadfastly refused.

There were plenty of children in the house where I lived, including somebody with a coronet who practiced it "religiously" day after day. I had to go to the college library to study and miss my comfortable, cool bathtub. Finally, at the risk of making enemies of my fellow tenants, I presented my complaint to the administration. They understood and decreased the noise. Happily, I lost no friends.

The food was delicious. I never ate such good food at an institution. The fact that I was a guest of the college at meals until my wife arrived made it taste even better. But our students were not satisfied — a typical reaction to even the best institutional meals. My necessary exercise to keep fit consisted of a couple of walks a day to the post office downtown and back. Everybody else rode. Not long after, I heard remarks about the crazy damn Yankee who walked in the heat.

I also visited the open-air market where the region's farmers sold their produce. The crude blank features, lackluster eyes, and ill-nourished bodies of those rural slum dwellers depressed me so much that I gave up those visits. Some of them actually looked sub-human and reminded me of some people living in city slums. But they are different and I have not been able to analyze that difference.

Soon after my arrival, the president took me on a tour of vacant faculty housing facilities. They were terrible little shack-like houses with decrepit furniture. I told him that not even during my poverty-stricken college days did I ask my wife to live in such quarters, and I would not do so now. One of them was fair and might be considered, but it was occupied. Finally, he showed me one that I thought could be made attractive. He tried to talk me out of it. The school was receiving a nice rental for it. Well, I simply would not consider any other. Finally, he consented but insisted that he would have to charge me rental for the furniture.

The upholstery on the sitting room chairs was dirty and torn and needed to be covered and refinished. The dining room furniture was very nice, and that of one bedroom adequate, but that of the second bedroom was quite decrepit. The second bedroom was left as it was, for we brought our own bedroom furniture. The rental for furniture was fixed at $10 per month, and we had to pay for the electricity, gas, and water.

I rented the furniture, hoping to keep this a secret from my wife, and succeeded for the first three months. Once she was happily settled in our lovely new home, she might not be too disturbed, for her good taste and hard work had always made our living quarters beautiful. But she was shocked and never forgave the administration this picayune saving at our expense in addition to our very low salary of $2,000 for nine months plus the apartment of four rooms.

Finally, after subletting our furnished apartment in Pittsburgh, my wife arrived. To keep her company, our daughter took a week's vacation from her teaching and accompanied her.

They drove through Tennessee through the black of night over narrow roads, through thick forests, and where only dim lights here and there barely indicated human habitation. It was rather scary for them. They drove through a cloudburst, then found primitive accommodations for the night. They admired the crepe myrtle, the live oak, and other strange trees, and were scared out of their wits when they stopped to gaze at an enormous black bull.

When they reached our new home, the engine gave up the ghost. It would not start. We had to call a mechanic to examine and repair it. The three of us slept in the double bed in my single room and were guests of the college at meals. What a shocking contrast to our beautiful apartment in Pittsburgh. But, thank God, we were together again. After two months of painful separation, none of that mattered.

For a week Elaine was the guest of the girls, a different one each night. In that short week, she heard more college gossip than I did in three years — most of it harmless. Toward the end, she made the observation, "Do you realize, daddy, that these girls are about five years ahead of us northern girls in social maturity?"

No, I did not. I had been too busy to notice it. But now I opened my eyes and discovered how right she was. Social graces, the ability to deal with men, dressing well, and their easy conversation became very evident. They were indeed attractive and winsome.

One of them invited my daughter to a special restaurant in a neighboring town. There, she introduced her to Mexican food, which she found quite tasty. But her mother and I have never learned to appreciate it. On the way back, as people crowded into the bus, the driver kept announcing and demanding, "All Negroes in the back. All Negroes move to the back."

"Who does he think he is to talk like that to colored people?" my reckless daughter demanded. "Shhhhh" her scared companion, a girl of Texas, warned. She knew that "the eyes of Texas were upon them." But my brave, indignant daughter continued to sputter away in a lowered voice until they left the bus. I assured her that her attitude and action was right, even if the students and faculty disapproved.

Since mine was a new voice in the town, I received quite a few invitations to speak. The local luncheon club, the junior chamber of commerce, three parent-teacher groups and others were eager to hear what the new "Damn Yankee" professor had to say. My first address to the local luncheon club was *Ideals and Actualities of Communism*, comparing these with our democratic ideals and practice. They were rather surprised at my daring exposition, but took it in their stride and even voted their appreciation. The president of the local bank wrote me a note of appreciation and invited me to visit him for a chat.

After that, other invitations came. I spoke on family life, my specialty, and warned against narrow prejudiced conditioning of our children, and the need for laying broad and deep foundations for our American democracy in the family and in our schools. I emphasized the curse of racism and the necessity for rethinking their general attitudes in this entire area, under the pressures of our time in the light of our Christian ideals, our democratic professions of democracy, and the findings of anthropology.

After one of these lectures to a local parent-teacher association, a super-patriotic Texan businessman said he wanted to beat up the "Damn Yankee." I learned later that only the determined stand of a local newspaperwoman, our Associated Press reporter, saved me. Most of the time the reaction was not so violent, but pleasant and appreciative. How fortunate that I was well-informed, an unusually able and attractive speaker with a good voice, and a Baptist minister as well as a college professor. Intellectuals were still under suspicion in many parts of that great state and not infrequently won support by pandering to the prejudices of the populace. Especially of the poor Whites.

My barber, Jeff Murray, was a great comfort. He was a self-educated man, a thoughtful and unembittered Negro. I refused to bow to the general, prejudiced practice of calling him by his first name. Instead, no matter how his other customers stared, I called him "Mister Murray." I had more intelligent conversations with him than with many of my colleagues on the faculty. One day, when we were alone in his shop, he told me about a number of unpleasant experiences. The most recent one had occurred only a couple of days previously. One of the inevitable discussions started on the "Negro problem," and the men who filled the shop discussed it, as usual, with more heat than light. One of them, a poor White, asserted in a loud voice, "Negroes ain't got no souls!" Nobody took issue with him.

Mr. Murray had seven children, all college-bred, who had migrated to the North where life was easier. But this ignorant White felt greatly superior. My visits with my good Mister Murray were inspiring experiences and I looked forward to them. When he became ill I called on him in the hospital and prayed with him, also on his wife at home to bring her such comfort as I was able, and followed it up by calling on them in their home. This started a kind of whispering campaign against the "damn Yankee nigger lover."

Texas was fascinating. I was entranced by the songs of the mockingbird, which Thomas Jefferson had called the sweetest singer on our continent. Roses bloomed, even around Christmas. We picked ripe figs off the bushes and pomegranates as well. We were delighted by the vivid colors and beauty of various cacti, and peeled and ate the fruit of one. When fodder was scarce, the farmers would burn the thorns off cactus leaves with blowtorches and fed the thick luscious leaves to the animals.

One day, after several weeks, I became aware of a strange feeling, as if something were pressing me down. Gradually I realized that the trees were rather short and their foliage much closer to the ground than that of our majestic elms and oaks in the north. When I stated that some of them were three- to four-stories-tall, they insinuated that this was a tall Yankee tale. Such trees were beyond their experience. I was informed later that this shortness was due to inadequate water.

Bugs were plentiful and grew to a generous size. We had flying cockroaches about two inches long. When anyone walked across the campus toward evening they constantly waved their hands. At first, I wondered if this was a new form of exercise until I, too, learned to wave mine to keep the mobs of mosquitoes at bay. One morning, as I walked to class, I heard a loud crackling underfoot. I was amazed to discover that the sidewalk was covered with snails.

At another time, as I went for my evening walk, bugs covered the street lights, and they popped underfoot, and also popped like rapid-fire shots under the wheels of cars. I rushed back and took my Ann out for a ride to see this plague. The white enamel walls of the bus terminal had turned black with their bodies. It was awesome. It reminded us of the plague of locusts in the Bible. The next day they were swept up and carted away.

But such things were accepted as a matter of course by our girls and the natives in general. Going to lunch one day in the college dining room, we found a whole colony of ants on our table. The house mother sitting at the table calmly swept them to the floor with her hand. How dear old Dr. Schweitzer would have approved!

One day, as we drove along a country road, we suddenly noticed an enormous snake stretched from one side to the other. It had appeared so unexpectedly that we were unable to stop the car and ran over the poor animal with quite a jolt. When we looked back it was nowhere to be seen. We were told it was a harmless breed, but it surely frightened us. However, there were some poisonous kinds, too. One of our instructors found and killed three rattlesnakes in his yard where his children were accustomed to playing.

And it was hot, oh so hot! From April through November, my poor Ann's clothes were always damp around the waist. In a talk with the librarian at Baylor University in Waco, I speculated how it must affect the speech and movements of Texans. She commended me on my insight and complained of Northerners who failed to see that what looks like laziness is simply a necessary adaptation to a hot climate.

For years up north we'd had a garden. It provided me with exercise, a joy in growing things, fresh vegetables or, at least, a flower plot. The grounds around our new home were quite barren and we were determined to pretty it up. I started with some cannas to cover up the posts on which the house rested. In spite of my regular and generous watering, they soon dried up. Then my neighbor and colleague planted a vegetable garden. That, too, was a failure. The college gardener tried his hand at it and was successful in the first year only. He claimed that chemicals in the water were responsible. So, gradually, we all gave it up.

During our Christmas vacation, we drove up to our apartment in Pittsburgh, Pennsylvania. We discovered that our envious neighbor had stirred up trouble with our new landlord and our tenant. She resented our subletting the apartment. Consequently, we decided to sell all our furniture for a pittance and gave up our old home where we had been so happy.

On our return to Texas that first Christmas, we had a pleasant surprise: blossoming rose bushes and other flowering shrubs. We discovered soon enough, however, that winter could be very unpleasant. The cold blasts from Canada had no mountain ranges to cross, and arrived in Texas in great blasts of frigid wind. We saw the thermometer dip over sixty degrees in twelve hours to twelve below zero one winter. That was "very unusual," the natives assured us. With our house on stilts, the doors and windows very high and not very airtight, and tiny gas heaters, one in each of the five rooms with high ceilings, it was difficult indeed to keep warm. We often spent hours in the social hall or the library where central heating made the climate bearable. When the temperature went down to twelve below zero, the water pipes froze and we had drinking water delivered to us by truck for several days. Classes were suspended and school life slowed down almost to the point of hibernation. When snow fell, our girls were dismissed for the day to build snowmen, engage in snowball battles, and frolic in any way their imaginations suggested. We saw a native get stuck at a turn and tie a piece of twine to one of his back wheels to give him traction. After considerable hesitation and discussion between us about whether we should try to help without insulting the driver's masculine pride, my Ann went out, started the car and pulled him out of the snowdrift.

On a visit to our Baptist pastor, we discovered that they had closed off most of the parsonage and lived in a couple of rooms through the winter, and we learned that this was a common practice. Open fireplaces were still found in many homes, not as decoration, but as a necessity. We soft city dwellers from the north, however, had to keep close to the fire and keep turning around as one side of our body roasted and the other froze.

Our social life in the college lacked the richness of what we had enjoyed in the Pittsburgh area, where we had scores of friends of all classes, special connections with ministers, university professors, and community leaders. In the little college town, we knew no one. While the small population in town and college should have facilitated the making of acquaintances, the general cultural climate was rather dry. It certainly did not help that we had come from the North and spoke with a slightly foreign accent. Slowly, we made contacts with members of the faculty and with my students, but did not succeed in breaking the invisible wall that separated town and gown. Only once in our three years stay were we invited to a home of townspeople, and it was to give a lecture to a small group.

With my students, we succeeded so well that on Saturdays we had ten to twenty of them dropping in for chat and refreshments. My lovely Ann, a charming hostess, had made a fine home that delighted them, especially those whose background was in crude frontier villages with their poor houses, poor furniture, and a general lack of beauty. For my lectures in class, I prepared my lessons carefully and presented the material vividly and concretely using illustrations from my own experiences that, coming out of a different milieu, were new to them —

even exotic. They were always interested, but especially so when I had to challenge some of the general presuppositions and prejudices of their great state and special subculture. In their evaluations of my courses, they often made these observations. Many of them praised my courage and my willingness to listen to them, as well as my ability to stand my ground.

Once, our Dean of Women asked me point blank, "Professor Kautz, what do you teach our girls? In every room I visit they are discussing your courses." I hardly knew how to answer. It would have taken too long to reply adequately. I don't know if I invited her to audit my classes, but I should have.

She liked us, however, and we became good friends. One evening, around nine or ten o'clock, she was in our house sampling our delicious, juicy Hungarian fried chicken. There was a knock at the front door, and there stood two of my students, who had run across the street from the campus to have a brief visit with us. I invited them in and whispered that the Dean was visiting with us. They were frightened out of their wits, for they were in their pajamas, ready for bed, and had just slipped into their coats for an informal call. All of this was against the rules. How could they face the Dean? Feeling secure in our friendship with the Dean, I insisted that they come in and, since she was not on duty, she would overlook their one misbehavior. So it happened that the Dean was very cordial and understanding, but they hurried back to their dormitory as quickly as courtesy permitted. There were no echoes of this innocent adventure on the campus, at least none that reached our ears. Good Dean!

My Ann often invited faculty members for informal tea or coffee and they were glad to escape their restricted quarters and visit in our lovely home. They remarked upon the warm, friendly atmosphere, and were eager to visit.

We invited the president and his wife for dinner. They were surprised and delighted to notice how we had transformed the apartment into the most attractive home on the campus. They lived in a fine house and reciprocated by returning our invitation. Once or twice a year they had a big formal evening in their home for faculty, the town's elite, and the military command from Camp Hood with their wives. Nearly all the men were in tuxedos, the officers in parade uniform, and the ladies in beautiful gowns. It was a gala occasion with splendid refreshments, though with dull, boring conversation until the guests left.

Some of us on the faculty stayed to help clear away things and then relax in the pretty parlor while the president and older faculty members reminisced. Perhaps it was on one of these occasions that the president's wife complained about the difficulty of finding adequate servants.

"Well, my dear," responded the president, "this is a democracy after all, and you can't blame even simple, unschooled people for their unwillingness to do what is considered servile tasks." I respected and loved him for that.

We had a Founders' Day banquet each year, a beautiful occasion, with lovely table decorations and a wonderful meal. Our girls looked like princesses. For faculty, ladies, and guests, it was a black-tie affair with a very enjoyable program. The two cultural societies on the campus entertained once or twice a year with well-prepared programs and tasty refreshments. But the best part of the evening was the informal conversation at the end when we got closer to both students and faculty. It was considered an honor to be invited. Three, or four times, the school invited musicians and other performers to entertain the college and the town.

Gradually, we developed more intimate contacts out of which some true friendships grew. A significant one was Reverend Hagar, pastor of the nearest Moravian Brethren church in a rather large town nearby, and his family. It was the president who called his attention to us, realizing how much we needed congenial social contacts — suspecting that these may not be found easily by "damn Yankees." Perhaps it was because of our common immigrant background. They were Czech and bilingual. All of them used Czech in their churches, spoke it in their homes, read

Czech newspapers, and were proud of their heritage. They were just entering into a period of adjustment I had experienced in the Hungarian Baptist churches up North, always painful, sometimes critical, and always involving the very future of such churches. The older members and ministers insisted on continued use of their native tongue, while their youth felt more at home with English, which they understood better, and, as Americans, considered *their* native tongue. They had lived in Czech villages for three generations or more, and in their comparative isolation, did not have to endure the pressures of Americanization present in the urban areas of the North.

When my newfound friend shared his anxieties with me concerning this problem, I told him about my struggles in similar situations up North. He was greatly relieved to find someone with whom he could frankly discuss problems that often gave him sleepless nights. He was their outstanding leader, and felt the heavy burden of leading his people across this wilderness of conflicts, problems, uncertainties, and lack of understanding. I was only too happy to bring to him empathy, understanding, a little wisdom, and much Christian love, and so ease somewhat his almost unbearable burden. He often asked me to preach for him, and when he finally collapsed and died, mine was the privilege of officiating at his burial.

His family and many of his friends became our dear friends. They were thinking of extending a call to me to become their pastor, which was a real honor since I was a Hungarian, and their countrymen had strong prejudices against mine. The fact that my wife was of Slovak descent would have made their adjustment easier. However, we were happy and fulfilled in our college environment and did not wish to change again.

Visiting in the villages around Temple, I found interesting contrasts in culture. The Czech and German villages had attractive houses and churches, with well-kept gardens and clean streets. Their homes had handsome (even if not always expensive) furniture, rugs, carpets, and lace curtains like homes I had known in the North. Not so in the Anglo villages with descendants of immigrants from the United States, where all these were lacking. We were entertained in a home where there were no curtains, no rugs, torn window shades, and furnishings so battered that we began to think we ought not to accept a fee for preaching from a church whose members were so poor. In the course of our conversation, however, I learned that my host's income was at least twice my own. We puzzled over this for a long time.

One Sunday, I preached in another rural church. After the service, a young man rushed up to me all out of breath.

"Are you professor Kautz? Are you, are you?" he panted.

"Why yes, I am."

"Did you live in Massachusetts?"

"No, but my daughter married a Bostonian, and we visit her every summer."

"Well, when you get to Massachusetts the next time, kiss the ground for me!"

"Why? What's the matter with you?"

"During the war, I was stationed here at Camp Hood. I fell in love with one of these lovely girls and married her. After the war, she prevailed upon me to move to her town and live in her house. I did." Then, sinking his voice to a whisper, he continued, "But, you know, we had a better barn for our cows than the house we live in now." Then he disappeared into the crowd.

On my Ann's next trip up North, to welcome one of our grandchildren into the world, Ann engaged two Texan gentlemen in conversation at dinner and tactfully referred to what looked like poverty to our uninitiated northern eyes. In reality, it was only a lack of concern about the furnishing of their homes. They patiently informed her that since the climate was so warm, they spent more of their time in the open rather than in the house, and the furnishings were not very important. Cattle and oil were the most valuable possessions. They spent their time and energy on those.

On another occasion, after church service, we were entertained at dinner at the home of a public school teacher educated at our college. After the meal, she showed us her garden. The flowers were lovely. Evidently, a great deal of care had been lavished upon them. The vegetable garden was equally well kept. I was a few steps behind the ladies as we walked between the rows. Suddenly, to our astonishment, she stopped, lifted her skirt a bit, spread her legs, and urinated.

Our experiences repeatedly hammered in the fact that this was indeed frontier country.

In this culturally poverty-stricken area, the radio broadcasts of the Metropolitan Opera Company were a godsend. We ought to buy nothing but Texaco gasoline for the rest of our lives in gratitude for sponsoring these broadcasts. They transformed our dreary Saturday afternoons into feasts of beauty and joy. If only the present sponsors of television would do likewise! Even the great traditional center of culture in Boston gives so many bleak and boring hours of noise, mindless entertainment, and primitive orgies of sex and violence, in so far as it is permitted. Thank God for an educational channel that respects our intelligence, for the Boston Symphony Orchestra for its inspiring music, and for the recently organized civic opera company with its excellent offerings that enchant our ears and eyes with beauty.

One of our happiest and most meaningful experiences was a surprising invitation to a barbecue on July fourth with another professorial couple from a neighboring college. We had set out to visit a new section of that amazing state. At a gasoline station, we inquired about a good place to eat. We were in luck, the attendant informed us, because that very day the local veterans' organization was giving a barbecue to all in that town.

We explained that we were from two other towns and hardly eligible. He insisted, however, that we go, for we would be welcome guests. And so it was. We received a royal welcome, were placed at the head of the line, and formally introduced to all. Apparently, they felt honored to have two professors and their wives as guests.

In two enormous trenches large slabs of beef were roasting. Old-fashioned, round, new wash tubs were filled with potato salad, vegetables, and bread. After a delicious meal, we left with many thanks.

Another of my delightful experiences was the sociological trip with my class. We visited the state prison in Huntsville. How the poor convicts gazed at my lovely students with admiration and respect. All wanted to sit in the electric chair and did so. They asked innumerable questions of the warden, who was delighted with them.

Perhaps their biggest surprise was the visit to a Negro orphanage. The grounds were lovely, well landscaped, and centered in a beautiful rose garden. The superintendent came out to greet us and present each one of us with a red rose and a smile. The offices, living quarters, and classrooms were spotless. The uniforms of the nurses were clean and attractive, and the children were well dressed and happy. It made a profound impression on my students. It was shockingly different from what they had heard about Negroes. Some lifted the bed covers to see if the "amazing" cleanliness was more than surface. It was. I am certain from experience that many White homes were not as clean as this Negro orphanage. We left deeply impressed, hugging the children and carrying our roses. It was the only place where we'd received a gift.

A visit to the headquarters of Alcoholics Anonymous was another surprise to them. "Why, they don't look like alcoholics at all," they whispered to each other. They were a happy, intelligent-looking crowd, and, as we learned from their testimonies, from every class of society. Several of them described their miserable lives before they were released from the curse of drink, faced up to their various problems, and acknowledged their helplessness. My religious students listened entranced as they heard how these people lived soberly a day at a time, depending on a (the?) Higher Power to give them the strength. To admit their helplessness, their illness as alcoholics was very, very difficult indeed.

It was a glowing report they gave in chapel a few days later. All stressed their visit to the Negro orphanage, expressing their warm admiration for everything they found. The meeting at Alcoholics Anonymous made a profound impression — so much so that they could compare it only to a high-level prayer meeting. In view of their deep religious interest, this was high praise indeed.

28 - The Cancer of Racism

Two charming young people from Shanghai provided us with the color and flavor of the Far East. One of them, Cho San, a girl of twenty, was the daughter of a wealthy manufacturer of chemical fertilizers. She was lovely, magnetic, temperamental, and stubborn, but also full of winsome traits. We practically adopted her, and she came and went as a daughter, and was a welcome guest at our meals when the tasteless, strange American foods repelled her. We encouraged her to raid our icebox to find choice morsels that tempted her. But we were never able to teach her to like milk. In her culture, it was considered a food unfit for human beings — not even when Dr. Huang, our Chinese surgeon friend, explained its nutritional qualities. Although at first, he too was nauseated by milk. He had learned to drink it and tried to encourage her to do so.

Cho San was surprised when we occasionally ate in the kitchen, for in Chinese homes, even of the upper classes, that was the dirtiest section of the house, and people, especially guests, did not enter it. She compared it to our spotlessly clean kitchen and marveled at the contrast. Often while my Ann was taking a nap on our front-room couch, she would sit on the floor resting her back against it, and study her homework. Once, as we talked about life in China, she broke into sobs, but would not tell us why. Later, she explained that the Chinese frowned upon emotionalism. When her mother said farewell to her at the dock in Shanghai, they just gazed at each other without kisses nor embraces. "But we felt all that you feel," she assured us.

Cho San told us that one evening a week was reserved for the family. After an unusually fine meal, they told each other their experiences during the week. The father told about his business, his successes, and problems, giving his views on the government and the challenges and shortcomings of the Chiang Kai Shek regime and of communism. The mother discussed her problems with the household help and with the children. An older daughter, who was concertmaster in the Shanghai Symphony Orchestra, played one or two new selections that they were preparing for a concert, and so on, and down the line until all of them, two boys and three girls, had reported their experiences and observations in school and the city. The parents were hoping to send all of them out of the country before the Communists took over, and succeeded in this with all but the eldest daughter, who became a dedicated Communist. All four have made a success of their lives in America.

Cho San apparently felt thoroughly at home with us, even though her jealous student friends from the East tried to alienate her. They assured her that we did not really care for her but were only interested in her as we might of something exotic, like a tree, flower, or bird. She often went with my Ann to her office in the church where she worked as a secretary and Director of Religious Education. There, she studied her lessons.

Once, she came to us with an agonizing headache. My Ann suggested that she take a couple of aspirin pills and lie down in one of our rooms, which she would not do. But finally, we prevailed on her, assuring her that in our home we would not permit anybody to disturb her. Then we went to our separate rooms for our customary siesta. Suddenly we heard the front door softly open and close. We jumped up, but she had already crossed the street and was running across the campus to her dormitory. To say that we were surprised would be a mild statement indeed. She never volunteered an explanation and we never asked. Dr. Huang later told us that it was not considered proper for a girl to sleep away from home. Why? He was not sure but perhaps it pointed to a former age when it was not safe.

Our unmarried daughter Elaine came down to visit us one summer. She fell in love with an attractive Texan working on his Ph.D. at the University of Texas. They became engaged and we began to plan for the wedding. It occurred to us how nice it would be to ask our "adopted" daughter to be the bridesmaid, but she excused herself and gave as the reason her lack of an appropriate dress. She had some lovely Chinese dresses and we assured her that one of them would be very acceptable, or we could find an American dress or rent one that would be suitable. She sullenly refused while giving no reason, nor could our friend the doctor explain her behavior.

It was she who told us about the young Chinese intern at a famous clinic in the neighboring town of Temple. He had fled from St. Luke's, an Episcopal missionary hospital in Shanghai, because of his dislike of Communists. The change was a difficult one. From chief intern and surgeon, he'd found himself demoted to a mere assistant, and limited to sheer observation with no opportunity to practice surgery. He was depressed by his inability to polish up on his techniques, to learn American techniques, and continue his professional development. He feared that he would fall behind even in his Chinese training and become a less competent surgeon than he had been in Shanghai.

He missed his many Chinese friends, and the relaxation and beauty of Chinese opera, of which he would intone for us some very strange sing-song tunes. He ate American food without relish and learned to drink milk with disgust. In fact, our "daughter" told us, he was at the point of giving up his dream of surgery in America. Then, after repeated requests that she bring him to our home, she failed to do so, again without explanation or excuse. My wife drove over for him, found him as he was leaving the clinic, introduced herself and invited him to go with her. He must have been very homesick, for he gladly accepted her invitation and came with her.

They found me ill in bed. Were we embarrassed! His first impression must have been "How clever, they have free medical advice and treatment." I apologized profusely. Something in our mutual need reconciled us to the situation, and the evening became the beginning of a wonderful friendship. We looked forward to his visit every Saturday and kept him for dinner. Our Hungarian food must have been more flavorful and appealing, for he ate generous portions of it. After a while he offered to prepare some Chinese food for us, bringing such ingredients as he could discover in our markets. Periodically, our "daughter" joined him in this, and later another Chinese girl joined and we had quite a dinner party every Saturday night. They even invited two Chinese boys from another college. But how different was this food from that served in Chinese restaurants! After a few weeks, we ate it with greater relish than our American cooking.

One day, I was unable to find our doctor at the hospital and inquired for him at the intern's living quarters, but in vain. As I was leaving, one of them asked, "What shall we tell him, who called?"

"Oh," I replied with a suppressed smile, "just tell him, his dad." Their eyes popped but they did not dare to question me. They must have engaged in considerable speculation about the mixed marriage of which my "son" was the issue, and about his mother, who, judging by her son, must be a beautiful woman.

Dr. Huang was a handsome young man, and the nurses at the hospital tried to entice him to their parties. But for Saturdays, his invariable reply was, "Sorry, my pa and ma are expecting me."

We wondered how, being a couple nearing sixty, we could attract him with their sedate ways rather than the young student nurses and interns. We discovered that he had a very high standard of sexual morals and was repelled by the free and easy ways of our youth. A devout Episcopalian, he seldom missed worship. He appealed to a number of the girls in our college, and some of these southern belles were lovely indeed. But our "son" remained courteously at a distance.

Once we engaged him in a rather intimate conversation about marriage. He admitted that he found our girls very charming, but he dared not take any of them back with him, where, according to their age-old tradition she would become his mother's "slave." No American girl could be expected to be happy in such a marriage. Later, I discovered that he also would have to face prejudice and discrimination because of his racial intermarriage.

One evening our "daughter" was showing us her photo album. In it we came across a picture of a tall and very handsome youth. In reply to our questions, she revealed that he went to school with her. They had been very fond of each other, but she broke off the affair. Why? Didn't she love him? Yes, she did, but her parents objected to him. Why were they opposed? Because he is an Eurasian, an offspring of White and Asian parents? Was that so bad? It was a disgrace. I filed this away in my memory as an interesting and live example of Chinese race prejudice. Later it helped us to explain our White anti-Negro prejudice. Years later I learned that the Chinese considered themselves superior to all the other people of the earth. How galling it must have been to endure, for centuries, exploitation and conquest by the uncouth, hairy, White barbarians of the West! Perhaps we are paying for it, even now.

One day she came to our house livid with anger. We wondered why. She simply could not endure the racist remarks of our White students. Who do they think they are? Gods? She sputtered away.

"That's very mean and reprehensible indeed," my little lady agreed, "and you know us well enough by now to realize how strongly we ourselves condemn race discrimination and prejudice. But tell me what the Chinese call us Whites in China?"

She looked surprised and was silent.

"Didn't they call us foreign devils? Aren't the Chinese prejudiced also? Would your parents permit you to marry a White man?" She hung her head in eloquent silence.

Somewhere in our sacred Scriptures, there is a proverb: "Cast your bread upon the waters and after many days you will find it." It had puzzled me for years until I discovered that it had a figurative meaning.

Our younger daughter had come down to Texas for an operation to have us near her. When they discovered at the famous clinic, where our "son" Dr. Huang was an intern, that she had to go twice under the knife, we were very uneasy. Dr. Huang assured us that he himself would escort her to the operating room, remain during the operation, and see her safely into her own bed. How fortunate! During surgery, the table began to tilt but our faithful friend was there and saved her from sliding to the floor. On the way to the operating room, the attendant almost upset the cart. He saved her again. What rich returns our simple hospitality to a foreigner yielded, of which this was only a sample. Perhaps it all came about because we ourselves had also been homesick strangers in America.

In my teaching, the most interesting, exciting, and controversial area was that of race. As soon as we reached that chapter in our introductory sociology, everybody wondered what I would teach. I overheard a remark of one of my students as she left the classroom, "Do you think he's a Yankee?"

Little Jo was probably one of my brightest and most fascinating students. She confessed to plowing through Marx's *Das Kapital* by herself. She was always wide awake in class with eyes glued on the instructor. She was very proud of her ancestry, claiming descent from an English dynasty, the Stuarts. She was equally proud of the way they took care of "their Negroes" on their plantation. She often visited the families with her mother providing them with medicines, advice, and financial aid. She told all this so unselfconsciously. I shall always regret that I was not able to visit them and see for myself.

She challenged me one day with the statement:

"We have only one political party in our community. I bet you can't guess which."

"Oh," I replied, "that's easy, the Democratic Party of course."

"No, it is not."

"You tell me."

"It's the White Supremacy Party!"

"Do your Negroes vote for that party?"

"Of course. All of them."

Apparently, it never occurred to her that anything was wrong with that situation.

She waylaid me at every opportunity to quiz me on any new thing. She seemed to go along with the findings of anthropology on race without any difficulty. One day, however, she broke into my presentation in a shrill antagonistic voice:

"I don't believe a word you say."

For a moment I was bewildered. Recovering, I responded, "Well Jo, you know how I emphasized at the beginning of this course that no one has to believe anything the text or I say, or the information they find in their collateral reading. But I expect them to know the information given, and to give an adequate statement on why they don't accept it. Would you mind telling me why this sudden and hostile reaction?"

"If I believed what you are teaching us I would have to believe that my grandfather fought in vain for the Confederacy."

She never came to class again. Loyalty to her grandfather had built an impenetrable wall in her mind against the truth, not only of science, but against the teaching of the Declaration of Independence, the Constitution, and the teachings of Jesus, who she claimed to follow.

I found it useful to reinforce the teaching of science by appeals to these ideals, which my students admired but hardly understood. Their sentiments were on my side, but they were aghast at the implications. Yet many of them stated in their evaluations of the course: "I appreciate your courage to state your convictions as you do."

They were astounded to discover that there was another side to the Mexican War, and none of them had ever heard that Abraham Lincoln had called it a war of empire. And of course, Robert E. Lee was admired far more. Nor had they ever heard about the condemnation of slavery by Washington and Jefferson, both Southerners, or by other founding fathers.

In another of our discussions on race, the little niece of the Bible professor protested timidly one day.

"But professor, what about the Bible?"

"Well, what about it? Does it not teach that all of us are the offspring of one pair of common ancestors, Adam and Eve? That God is the father of us all and we are brothers? That Christ died for all of us?"

"Oh, I don't mean that."

I knew what she meant, for by that time I had heard the strange, belabored twists of religious doctrine by which they justified racial prejudice and discrimination. So I asked her to bring her Bible to the next class session and read the troublesome Scripture passage. She did. It dealt with the unhappy experience of Noah who did not know the power of wine and was found naked in a drunken stupor by his son, Ham, who was laid under a curse with his descendants because he had found his father's state amusing.

"And who were the descendants of Ham?" I asked.

"The Negroes, of course."

"Is that what your Bible says?"

"Yes."

"Read it please."

She looked at the passage and was silent. I insisted, "Please read what the Scripture actually says."

Almost inaudibly she said, "The Canaanites."

"Were they Negroes?"

"No."

"Then what are you talking about?"

Our students did not have the nerve to speak up against their professors, but there was a wonderful opportunity to bait their professor of the Bible, who received his Doctor of Theology degree from the outstanding seminary of the Southern Baptist Convention. They gave him a very uncomfortable hour at the next session of his class. He never forgave me for this. And he never saw the terrible implications of his teaching about the character of God and the superstition of a curse.

The same student made a trip to Chicago one summer and could hardly wait to tell about it in class.

"The Negroes up north were not dirty, ignorant, shiftless, lazy, and thieving like their own Southern Negroes."

"Why not?"

"They are a different breed."

To suggest that perhaps the real reason was that they had opportunities to develop such as never existed in the South was totally unacceptable to her. I was amazed to discover that one of my colleagues from the North had the same impression and attitude. She insisted that I visit the "deep" South to understand why Southerners felt as they did toward Negroes.

The same Bible professor's son, who had studied race problems with me, dropped into my office one day for help. That same day, in a literature class, the lady professor dragged into her lecture an indictment of Negro soldiers in World War II, especially for their cowardice. The young man recalled my reference to this by a Southern study group, but found it was exactly the opposite. It was in my files and I gave it to him. At the next session of her class, he read some of their significant findings. She demanded the source. He carried it up to the desk. When she discovered that those were the findings of a competent Southern group, she was speechless and never referred to it again.

The news of these happenings spread like wildfire. They tended to lower the esteem of the students for some instructors, demanded greater care in teaching and more careful study on their part, and they centered their resentments on this "damn Yankee" who was always making trouble. Some of them stopped talking to me and turned away when they met me on the campus. It was very unpleasant for me, too, but I was helpless. Somebody had to tell the truth about race, and my classes were the logical place to do so.

My task was not made easier by my passion for correlation. I felt for years that teachers, even at colleges and universities, gave no help to their students to tie in their courses with the others. As a result, the graduates too often graduated with compartmentalized minds, often hermetically sealed off from each other. Consequently, I had to touch on, reinterpret, and add information in economics, history, government, and religion to enrich their understanding of life. But this again exposed me to sniping from my colleagues in other areas. No matter. It had to be done.

One day, I reminded my students of the parable of the Good Samaritan. Bringing it up to date, I inquired, "What would happen to me if I stood on the steps of the Courthouse in this town and told a story in which the rogues were White pillars of society and the admirable character a Negro?"

They looked shocked and replied unanimously, "You'd better run."

Sometime later, I asked the pastor of the local Baptist church in a prayer meeting whether Jesus would apply this parable to the persecuted Negro of our day and make him the hero of the story, and the solid and substantial White citizens the bad guys. There was a moment of shocked silence as the congregation stared at me. I felt exceedingly uncomfortable. Then the pastor firmly declared that Jesus would. I was grateful for his courage. I was not alone, after all. Later, he declared to some important people in town that he considered Professor Kautz the best Christian on the campus. That was rather extreme, but it helped me, I am sure, to last for three years on the faculty.

From time to time it seemed evident that the assumed inferiority of the "nigra[2]" was rooted in a psychological need to feel superior, especially for the poor Whites, who thus had a group whom they could despise. Occasionally, we had a few veterans in our college who later transferred to another school. One of them came up to me after class and told me how shocked he was at the previous session of the class when I told about the inhuman treatment slaves received in "the good old days," which their parents and teachers had not dealt with honestly.

"I went home mad," he confessed, "and told my father about it. But my father assured me that you had told us the truth. My grandfather had two "bucks" he'd used to breed like animals, and then took me through

---

[2] Offensive ethnic slur for an African American.

the shacks where they lived. I felt you ought to know this."

I thanked him and took courage. On the whole, my students trusted me even when they could not quite believe me. They were willing and even eager to listen to my presentations and admired my "damn Yankee" courage. Only when they returned after vacations did they look unhappy and suspicious after they had been warned by parents, relatives, and neighbors not to believe me. Still, day after day, often until late at night, they discussed my course. I fear this did not make me any more popular with my colleagues.

I was especially impressed by the thorough acceptance of this racism on the part of my girls with German names, golden hair, blue eyes, and fair skin. I suspect that their ancestors were liberals who had fled from an oppressive regime after the unsuccessful revolution of 1848 that had swept the continent. The surrounding racist culture in Texas had reversed their liberal tradition and they became as prejudiced as their Anglo friends.

We had a most offensive experience in a large Methodist church in another town. It was a Mother's Day service, and for some inscrutable reason, the pastor kept emphasizing the supremacy of the male and that the woman was only a vessel. My wife and daughter almost walked out. Then he ranted about the sin of miscegenation. He had a Negro mammy, therefore he appreciated Negroes, he insisted, but he simply had to draw the line at intermarriage and any social mingling which would lead to that. Nowhere did we hear that it was the White who was guilty of breaking through the wall of separation, not the Negro, that it was the White who had been guilty of exploiting the Negro sexually because of the power of the White owner. Miscegenation was started on the plantations by the White master, but nobody spoke of this. We spent some time analyzing the Negro problem and slowly, painfully arrived at the conclusion that it was a White problem. It was the White master who undermined the Negro's self-esteem by making his wife a concubine and so making healthy Negro family life impossible. The White master even made the religion of Jesus, the religion of brotherhood, a psychological prison for the Negro so as to keep him in subjection more easily. Even so, there were many slave insurrections conveniently hushed up in our textbooks. They do not fit the picture of the happy Negro so carefully painted in our southern tradition.

Never before had I known so many girls with boy's names. I was told that fathers were so determined on having sons that they named them long before birth. When the child proved to be a girl, she was given the expected boy's name but with a feminine ending like Jo, Johnnie, etc. It was probably rooted in frontier psychology and the need for men.

My course, *Marriage and the Family*, was very successful. All of my students were eager to marry, and welcomed all the light I might shed on success in family life. The only problem was the attitude of the president, who requested me to omit all references to the sexual side of marriage. But how could I avoid that and give only some idealistic references that would skirt around the realities and avoid the problems of adjustment in this area? Would I not mislead my students and deserve their contempt by a cowardly silence? Did I not owe them a wholesome, realistic, and constructive education, and also with idealism? Was this less important than finances, divorce, etc.? The president and I could not agree. I continued as before.

I had not studied either the history or government of Texas. Now, the government of Texas was one of the required courses, and I was requested to teach it. So I had to immerse myself in both and keep well ahead of my students. They were thoroughly patriotic Texans, utterly convinced of the righteousness of their ancestors in their revolution against Mexico, and utterly unaware of Abe Lincoln's statement that the Mexican–American War was a war of imperialism, even as were most northerners. I called their attention to the book by a Mexican author that presented another and quite unwelcome picture.

I sent them to watch the elections at the courthouse. They reported with surprise and indignation that the voters filled out their ballots at long tables in view of everybody so that there was no secret ballot in Texas, or at least in Belton. What should they do to have this practice corrected? They decided to write a letter of protest to the governor and the legislature. I am not aware that they received a reply.

In my course, *Social Aspects of Industry*, they had more receptive attitudes, probably because they had heard about the rapacity of high finance. They shared this with other agrarian states and resented the urban finance and industry that exploited those living off the land. They used the terms capitalism, socialism, and communism without any clarity of meaning. Later, my students in the North had similar difficulties. We drew up some careful definitions and comparisons, and they themselves policed and corrected false statements and generalizations in class. However, it was difficult for them to face up to the shortcomings of capitalism: bloody strikes, depressions, its corruption of national and state legislatures, company towns, conspiracies in price fixing, quality, etc. In fact, they were progressively uneasy as I endeavored to make them face up to these. I well remember the remark of a veteran, the owner of a little restaurant who stopped at my desk as the class was filing out:

"You know, Mr. Kautz, we really believe you but we hope to make our pile before things change." It was a good summary of their attitude and that of millions of our citizens both North and South, East and West.

We had always been faithful worshippers and dedicated church workers. However, in Texas, we found church services increasingly boring, and, in time, we attended purely out of a sense of duty. The emphasis was on revivalism, and at the close of each service, there was an impassioned plea to give ourselves to Christ and to join the church. Often a lengthy exhortation was added with vehement gestures more fitting at a football game or rally than at worship. Very few sermons were aimed at building Christian character, and none at correcting the evils and inequities of our social and economic system. The preaching tended to be very emotional, repetitive, and concerned purely with personal salvation. I did not hesitate to discuss this with my students and challenge them to broader, deeper Christianity. They kindly listened to my exposition, wondering perhaps whether I was discussing religion or sociology.

Once a year, we had a revival on campus with very emotional singing and preaching. Many of the students went forward in tears when the altar call was given to rededicate their lives to Christ, and to individual students to ask their forgiveness for some wrong done to them. It all seemed thoroughly genuine and very moving. However, I never saw any of the faculty respond.

Also, it was very impressive to see almost the entire student body respond to the invitation of the local pastor at the first church service of the school year, and line up around the walls to express their desire to unite with the church. This was repeated every year, and the students became active, involved members of the local church instead of mere names in a distant one.

At breakfast every day, we shared in devotions on the radio. One morning, I suddenly became aware of something different.

"This does not sound like a Southern preacher," I observed. At the close, the announcer informed us that the speaker was from Austin. "I really got something this morning," I said to my wife, "let us look him up and get acquainted." Some days later, when I called at his office, introduced myself, and told him how I happened to come, he gripped my hand in both of his and exclaimed, "God love you!"

It was the beginning of a meaningful and inspiring friendship. His brethren of the cloth were suspicious of him throughout the state, as well as in the capital. Perhaps the fact that he had a degree from Yale had something to do with it. Moreover, his church was the first Baptist church in the state that welcomed and integrated Negroes. Because of his superior tact, wisdom, and patience, plus Christian love, his church appreciated his leadership and was loyal to him. Whenever he had to be absent from his pulpit he called on me to preach. And how I could preach to that congregation of about twelve hundred, most of them educated men and women with a large number of faculty members and students of the University of Texas! Never before or since did I have such an opportunity. I did not hesitate to apply the Gospel to the problems of the nation and the world.

He surprised me one day by asking that I preach for them during community revival week.

"But I am not a revivalist and I am not good at that kind of preaching."

"I want you precisely for that reason. My fellow preachers and my denomination will not forgive me if I have no services this week."

"What shall I preach about?"

"The will of God for the individual and the world, as you have done on Sundays."

"How far may I go?"

"The sky is the limit."

I thought to myself, "You do not know what this means," and accepted.

My president was kind enough to release me those five evenings when I assured him that it would not affect my classwork unfavorably. I was sure it would not.

My general theme was the Kingdom and the Rule of God, and on successive evenings I dealt with specific areas. These included social and economic justice, war, race, and international relations. Every night we had a very good congregation frighteningly attentive. I preached my heart out making strong appeals to the minds of my listeners as well. But the crown of it all was the pastor's reaction. One evening after the sermon, he stood up with tear-filled eyes and said to his people: "You heard real preaching tonight, truly prophetic preaching. Let us never forget it." All the way home on that sixty-mile trip my heart sang in gratitude and humility.

He was a brave man. He was also very wise, and had an uncanny feeling about changes in the climate of his church. His youth leader was inclined to be impatient with him and wanted him to go faster, but he would not be pressured. A younger and less-patient pastor came to one of the biggest churches in town. My friend was worried that he would not last and tried to restrain him. It was such a comfort and joy to have another preacher on his side, for at times he was very, very lonely. But the new pastor had a vital, outgoing, and very attractive personality. He was a popular preacher with a strong, healthy, emotional emphasis, and the moving eloquence characteristic of the best Southern preachers. These atoned for his apparent recklessness, and he stayed on for quite a few years. Since then, both of them have achieved national prominence.

My friend's confidence and admiration were reflected by the members of his church. Some of them entertained us in their homes on weekends when I preached in their church. One of them introduced us to a very new, very Texan expression of hospitality, when he served us with coffee in bed — a lovely way to awaken guests. Another, the chairman of our college board of trustees, with his lovely wife, entertained us repeatedly and became our friends. We were conscious of a warm welcome on the part of the staff and the members of the church.

Prejudice was not limited to "nigras[3]." Quite general, though less powerful, was the Texan prejudice against Mexicans. In my (advanced) course in ethnic and race relations I gave them a selected list of some of these and asked the students to choose one and report on it to the class: German, Italian, Jewish, Negro, and Mexican Americans, and others, were chosen without difficulty, but not a single one would accept the report on Japanese Americans. War propaganda was partly to blame, but in the subsoil of the unconscious there was the rock of racism. Otherwise, why weren't German, Italian, and Hungarian Americans also confined in concentration camps under the euphonious name of relocation camps? Surely, Japanese Americans were more easily recognized than the others, and therefore less dangerous. Police chiefs of Hawaii and California found no evidence of disloyalty and had assured the President that they

---

[3] Offensive ethnic slur for African Americans.

could pick up suspects on short notice. What mysterious and hidden forces made the utterly un-American, unconstitutional, and illegal herding of thousands of our own citizens into those camps?

Since everyone positively refused to report on Japanese Americans, I myself spent a whole hour on them. All through my report, I was conscious of a distinct hostility in the averted eyes, bored expressions, lack of questions, and unwilling writing in their notebooks. Over and over again I had to emphasize that they did not have to believe what I was telling them, but they would certainly be quizzed on the material on the next test. So I hoped against hope that some gnawing uneasiness about their attitude would impel them to read and think about the matter.

Nor did it help to point out the fact that a Nisei battalion was the most decorated unit in Italy and later went to the Far East to fight against Japan. To them, and to my students, they were only "Japs" and "monkeys!" The son of my colleague, the Bible professor, was a member of the class, and prejudiced like the rest.

Slowly we became aware of a new, cool draft in our relationships with the people of the church in Austin. It took quite a while to discover that this emanated from the college. Things were quickly coming to a head. Underground rumbles had penetrated the church office and I noticed a new frostiness on the part of the office secretary. At the same time, I began to have restless nights. I would be awakened by an indefinite, formless fear. Finally, several of my junior and senior students came to our home and informed us of a plot to force me out of the school. They mentioned the Bible professor as the chief conspirator. They were very indignant and excited and wanted to stage a strike of protest. I begged them not to. I explained that, as a Christian and a Baptist, I could not injure the school's reputation. And if some of the faculty members and administrators acted in such mean, underhanded, and pagan fashion, I still had to act as a Christian. Very unwillingly and painfully they accepted my reasoning and promised to be quiet.

Within two or three days I was called on the telephone by the chiropractor of the town, a mature man, who periodically took courses at the college. His voice shook as he urged me to come to his office at once, for he had something to tell me that had disturbed him greatly. When I arrived, he burst into a denunciation of the Bible professor who had just left.

"Imagine," he stormed, "that hypocrite had the nerve to come here with a petition he had drawn up to have the board of trustees refuse your appointment for the coming year. I told him that I registered for your classes because I had heard disturbing rumors about your teaching and I was determined to find out the truth. I found you to be the best Christian on campus, and I certainly would not sign such a scandalous accusation, which declared that you were undermining the morals of our youth. So, he stormed out and slammed the door. You must fight this!"

I explained my position and asked him to follow my example and make no trouble. Certainly, the administration had not indicated that they were considering such a course of action, and even if they were, they may decide in my favor. Certainly, I would expect them to do so, for I had done no wrong. He promised to forbear.

Not long after, the president called me into his office and asked me about my plans for the following year. I assured him that my full intention was to return and continue teaching. He hinted at the dissatisfaction of some teachers who taught Summer and Saturday courses. I reaffirmed my opposition to courses on Saturdays, resulting in an eighteen-hour week with the variety of courses that had been assigned to me, and I was not eager at all to teach during the summer session in the intense heat at the low salary of one month for six weeks. Nevertheless, I was willing to try it the following year. So we agreed, and I left his office feeling that my appointment was safe.

Yet, a feeling of uneasiness and insecurity persisted, and I decided to call on a new friend in Austin, who happened to be an influential member of the Board of Trustees at the college. He was most sympathetic. Over refreshments, encouraged me to hold out, and emphasized how much the Baptists of the South needed college professors like myself. Greatly heartened, we embarked on a trip to the West, and then to Boston in the East.

29 - Lightning Strikes

We had just bought a new Ford. We had unexpectedly come across a young friend of ours who had attended the same church and college as I did in New York City. He was now an automobile salesman in Texas selling Fords. New cars were still very scarce after the war, but we needed one for our trip, since ours already had 98,000 miles on it. However, one had to find an inside track in order to get one. Our Northern friend was the answer of providence to our problem. Soon we were on our way.

On the road, we discovered in a vivid experience what a flash flood was. It was in Odessa, Texas, where torrential rain suddenly filled the road with water up to the doors of the cars. We barely had time to escape to a small elevation into a gasoline station. Here, we sat for hours watching the thick accumulated traffic move slowly through the flood like a line of boats. Trunks and the insides of cars were flooded. It was a fascinating and sad sight. Twilight was falling fast by the time we found refuge with the family of one of my students.

The trip across New Mexico was uneventful and hot — exciting and fearsome in some sections of the road. It was a hair-raising drive, over narrow mountain roads without guardrails, one side skirting a precipice, the other touching the mountains, periodically running under an overhanging rock, and hot, so hot, and we were quite drenched with sweat, and exhausted when we stopped for the night.

Until the sun sank beyond the horizon of the desert, we were miserable. The pail of ice carried in front of us in the car to cool us was no great help. At last, darkness covered the desert. It proved to be an uneventful though eerie night, without a moon. Only the sparkling stars punctured the black velvet sky.

The trip through Arizona was so hot that we had to take refuge in an air-conditioned cabin. We stayed in it most of the day, slept, and rested until my Ann's fierce headache subsided.

Around six o'clock the palms outside our cabin began to wave vigorously. My restless Ann was eager to continue. I begged her to be patient, but patience is not one of her strong traits. She pointed to the palms — how they waved in the strong wind. It had to be cooler, much, much cooler. We packed and stepped out into the breeze, only it felt like a hot blast from an oven. We felt it foolish to unload again and stay for the night, and equally foolish to drive on in the merciless heat. Somehow, by a silly logic we decided that to drive on would be wiser.

We made a brief stop at Blythe, an American oasis, for a general check-up, then on through the vast silence of the desert, lit up here and there by the shafts of light of passing cars.

As always, we took turns driving and napping, and after a good stretch, an almost uncomfortable coolness surprised us. My Ann needed covers as she curled up on the back seat for her nap.

As the gray light of early dawn stole across the land, I barely discerned a long double line of palms coming out of the dark. They marched past us on both sides of the road. With their tall smooth trunks, a small umbrella of fronds at the top, they looked strange and foreign — un-American. I had the uncanny impression that we were entering Egypt. Suddenly, Ann awakened and in a startled voice demanded:

"Where are we?"

"In Egypt, love." I told her.

"You are dreaming," she protested wearily and rubbed her eyes. "But where are we?"

"Looks like Egypt to me."

She popped up and stared. "Yes, but these are American houses," she exclaimed. "So we are still in our good old U.S.A.," she sighed, greatly relieved. "I guess it's only California. You and your corny jokes!"

Soon we were in the City of Angels, where we spent a few days visiting with old friends who had come years before and found it a good city to raise their children. We had a peculiar lack of interest in seeing another metropolitan area, even famous Disneyland, and just hurried through Hollywood. On all of our trips, we found people far more interesting.

Here a very dear friend joined us, eager to show us interesting sights we might miss on the way home. Then, on toward San Francisco. The ocean drive on the brow of a mountain chain with its sheer cliffs dropping to the sea was a very unique and fascinating experience. To our left stretched the deep, deep blue of the Pacific Ocean until in the vast distance it met the lighter blue of the sky, spread out above like an equally vast dome, on which cloud ships were sailing to mysterious ports. On our right, more mountains. It was Ann who noticed their unusual and peculiar formations, like primeval giants sprawling in every conceivable position, quite overwhelming, like mythical creatures of an age long past.

We found San Francisco with its many hills, its great bay and the famous bridge arching over it like the fantastic creation of superior beings, its Chinese quarter giving an intriguing Asian atmosphere — a unique city. Some day we must go back and explore it.

Then down into the valleys. Taller and taller trees towered into the sky. They became wider and wider, green giants such as I had not dreamed of. "Where are we?" I cried. Our sly friend informed us that we had entered the redwoods. We stopped our car in a clearing and began to walk. We paused before a giant redwood in amazement that grew as we read the inscription under it. It had stood there when my ancestors came off the steppes of Asia and crossed the Carpathians to found a new home along the Danube and Theiss rivers, about 900 A.D. It was already a giant when the Savior trod the dusty roads of Palestine. It was a mighty tree when Moses led his people out of captivity into the promised land, and coeval with ancient Egypt. It overwhelmed me. We whispered to each other in the ghostly silence with not a single trill of a bird or the noise of an animal. Then we noticed that some ancient forest fire had burned out large concave spaces in the middle of many of them. Yet they lived on, a vivid testimony to the power of life. We walked through the trunk of that giant tree pictured on postcards cut open into a tunnel with a car driving through it. That was interesting and gave a vivid idea of the enormous thickness of the tree, but we felt it was a desecration of that wonderful living thing. By all odds, this was the most impressive and awe-inspiring sight on our trip.

"You have a letter waiting for you. It looks very important. Apparently, it is from the college in Texas where you are teaching." This was the greeting of our hostess, the wife of Dr. Distefano, my beloved friend of prep school and college days. We had reached Omaha, Nebraska where we expected to renew our old friendship.

To Ann and me it was like a black storm cloud, for it was an unexpected and unnecessary message from the Chairman of the Board of Trustees. What could it mean? We read it quickly and with a sinking spirit. It informed us that they were not renewing my appointment for the coming year. They emphasized that they had nothing against me, I was an excellent teacher, etc. etc., only they just were not in a position to engage me for the coming year. It was a bewildering letter from a badly confused board, desperately trying to forestall any unfavorable action by me. It would be untrue to state that I was not tempted to make trouble for them, but my Christian conditioning gained the upper hand. That they themselves did not feel right about it was clear by the pledge they gave to continue my salary for three months if I did not find another position in time.

Evidently, the Bible professor had done his underground campaign very well. Later, a mutual friend informed me that the chairman of the board was sick about it and slept poorly for days. He knew me well, for we had repeatedly been guests in his lovely home in Austin. It was organizational loyalty and the pressure of the president and the board that compelled him to go along.

In the middle of summer, when nearly all teaching positions in colleges had been filled, I was without a job with little hope of finding another for the coming year. What shall we do?

It is needless to point out that our happy vacation was finished. Quickly we bought or borrowed a college blue book. Or was it a World Almanac? We formulated a plan to visit every college along the highway within fifty miles each side of the road all the way to Boston where our daughter lived. Our visit with our dear friend and his family was cut short, and two days later we were on our way.

It was a weary, discouraging journey. The miles stretched endlessly before us with never an encouraging word, although every college official was courteous and very sympathetic. Some days later, we arrived at Wilson College located in Chambersburg, Pennsylvania at around nine o'clock in the morning. At once, I called up the president, introduced myself, and asked for an appointment after he'd had his breakfast. He came down to meet us immediately — an extraordinary gesture of courtesy. When I told him my story, he exclaimed: "Why didn't I know about you three months ago? We needed someone just like you to teach our courses on marriage and the family."

As I recall those very discouraging experiences, I am greatly comforted by my wife's addition to my story as I tell it to our family and friends: "You should have seen him. Proud, erect, shoulders back, he went from one discouraging interview to the other."

But as the summer wore on and we continued to send out innumerable letters and received no encouragement, even the loving, comforting welcome and offer of a home by our loved ones could not keep my spirit from sagging. To have something useful and worthwhile to do, I began to write this autobiography. So, out into a nearby park, I walked every day. Praying, reading the Bible, and recalling our past victories against adverse circumstances beginning in distant Hungary, I slowly regained the courage to press on.

The joyous hospitality of our son-in-law, Proctor Houghton, who did special shopping every Saturday at the Market in Boston to provide us with the best, his ready, hearty laugh, his invitation for us to move in with them until we knew what to do — all this and much, much more was like medicine with miraculous power.

Their eager curiosity concerning my childhood gave me additional motivation for writing my autobiography and helped to take my mind off the bleak present. After all, I was fifty-seven years old and without a Ph.D. I had a checkered career, and rejections of my applications for teaching at little, backwater colleges. My daughter kept encouraging and begging me to try for an appointment on the faculty of Boston University. How could I expect a wonderful urban university with twenty-six thousand students to be interested at all in me? Finally, her insistent pleas and confidence in her daddy prevailed. During the previous summer, I had dared to present myself to Professor Albert Morris, head of the Department of Anthropology and Sociology. I gave him an outline of my life, beginning with our migration to America and closing with our conference and this dialogue.

"What is your age?" he asked. My heart sank.

"We might as well terminate the interview," I replied, "I am fifty-seven. That fact finishes my prospects everywhere."

"Not with me. We need someone to teach marriage, and if I had my way, I would not have anybody under forty years of age teach that course." I gave an inaudible sigh of relief.

"Do you have a Ph.D.?"

"No, sir. And that is another reason why even small colleges cannot consider my application. Apparently, it seems to be very important for the status of the school, and as an assurance to prospective students and their parents, that the education offered will be first-rate. But, you see, I am not interested in research. I can do it well, as you may discover in reading my M.A. thesis. But I am a born teacher, as are my wife and daughters. My students never doze in class or find it boring, and I myself live at my fullest when I teach."

"Keep in touch with me and send me your personal data. We ought to have someone to assist in teaching Family, Marriage, and Introduction to Anthropology and Sociology."

This had provided a gleam of hope on my dark horizon. My daughter, wife, and son-in-law continued their kind but insistent encouragement, and at last, I made my way to Professor Morris' office for the second time. But he was away, teaching in British Columbia. My heart fell. It would be too late to employ me when he returned. And so we began to make preparations for our return to Texas, to arrange for moving with our possessions to Boston and to continue our search for a position in New England.

By the grace of God, I was able to send a courteous reply to the college in Texas refusing their offer to pay my salary for another three months. I was human enough not to offer any relief to their consciences for their outrageous conduct by accepting their offer. But I expected them to pay our moving expenses, which they did with alacrity, though my wife prophesied their refusal.

We delayed our departure as long as possible in order to confer with Professor Morris. At last, we could wait no longer. I wrote a letter instead, stating my readiness to come at once and giving my daughter's address should they decide to call me. Giving her the addresses of a number of possible stops, where we may be reached, we set out on our final trip to Texas.

On our arrival, our neighbor informed us that Boston had been calling us for three days. We telephoned our daughter at once and learned that Professor Morris was eager to introduce me to President Marsh as soon as possible. The University would pay our expenses. However, he very carefully and emphatically explained that this was not an appointment. Ann and I agreed that we would be able to pack our belongings in three days and set out on our return, and I would be ready to teach the following week.

And so it happened. On our return, we were greeted most heartily by the President, the Dean of the College of Liberal Arts, Professor Morris and members of the Department of Sociology. I was immediately appointed. Professor Morris, realizing the unusual strain we had undergone and the need for time to adjust to the new situation, limited my teaching load to six hours per week. I lost my fancy title, Head of the Department of Sociology, and my status as Associate Professor. I'd become Assistant Professor — a healthy status at a wonderful university.

Remembering the warning of Dr. Phelps at the University of Pittsburgh that I discover as soon as possible the tender areas in new situations and teach accordingly, I asked Professor Morris to inform me. He assured me that I was quite free to teach whatever I considered necessary, using only reasonable tact. A few years later, I discovered that there were some modifications to this freedom. I was eager to introduce a course in the Sociology of War. My department head approved, but when he presented it to the Dean of the University, he objected to it on the grounds that "nobody will take it except a bunch of pinks." Yet, how different the climate was from that of the school in Texas, as evidenced by the action of the Committee on New Courses that approved my course by a great majority even against the judgment of our College Dean, who felt compelled to go along with the Dean of the University.

We had regular departmental meetings at which the faculty members spoke their minds frankly, and this was true of the college faculty meetings. Professor Morris was a true democrat and eager to know the thinking of the department on all matters, including the appointment of new professors.

What a relief after the rather autocratic regime in my former situation!

The workload was heavy, but not to be compared with that of the former college where the president tried his level best to make me accept eighteen hours of teaching a week, including two non-sociological courses.

It was with genuine joy and enthusiasm that, after a rest of about six weeks, I started my regular teaching. Many of my students were very able and conscientious, especially my Jewish students. Most were well prepared for college, and I was able to hold them to a high standard.

Again, how different from the little college in Texas.

However, the standards varied considerably in the various colleges and schools of the University. That of the College of Liberal Arts was probably the highest. We had difficulty sometimes in adjusting to the standards of some of the other schools. It was a terrible shock to be compelled to fail half of a class in an important examination. Even more so to have their dean ask for special consideration and a passing grade for a student whose father was a B.U. graduate, a very active alumnus, and a generous contributor. Fortunately, this happened only once to me.

It did not take long to discover some important big holes in the high school education of my students. For example, almost none knew anything more about Patrick Henry than "Give me liberty or give me death." Not one of them was aware that he did not want a United States of America because his supreme loyalty was pledged to his own state of Virginia — a nation with its own armed forces, flag, government, money, etc. He could not envisage any flag flying above that of Virginia, not even that of the United States. How much easier it would be to win our people to a real commitment to the United Nations and to lessen their resistance to world government if this were generally known and adequately interpreted!

Nobody knew that Abraham Lincoln called the Mexican War a war of imperialism. Very few remembered anything about Dollar Diplomacy, or how Teddy Roosevelt boasted about the acquisition of the Panama Canal Zone, when he said, "I took it." Or the ruthless pacification of the Philippines, and about the impact of other such items of ignorance on our relations with the Latin-American nations south of the Rio Grande. No one knew that of all the treaties we made with the Indians, only one was kept, or why the Indians lived in peace with the Quakers of Pennsylvania when the frontier everywhere else was ablaze, or when and why the "savages" became savage. Apparently, nobody remembered the Irish riots in New York City during the Civil War, if they ever learned about them, which were far worse than those in our Negro ghettos today.

Nor did any of them realize how cruel and bloody our own revolution had been while they were greatly indignant of revolutions elsewhere in our own time. Nor had anybody called to their attention how much worse it might have been had a parliament, the royal court and the center of power been in the colonies, and not thousands of miles away in England.

Once, I asked a young instructor in history if sociology had made any difference in the teaching of history.

"No," he replied without hesitation, "Why should it?"

"What do you teach?"

"Facts, nothing but facts."

"But," I ventured to say, "What about the meaning of those facts?"

With tremendous assurance, he replied, "That's up to them to find out for themselves."

I was sorely troubled, for I knew from experience and observation how difficult it is to find meanings for some facts, and how badly interpretation is needed at times. Sociology was a vastly important subject because it enabled me to touch on so many aspects of our American society and culture.

Teaching introductory sociology in one of our affiliated colleges gave me an opportunity to point out evils in our nation's life that we had overcome, and some still waiting to be corrected. Propaganda history had done its work well. In the third session, as I was about to open the class, they started to sing at the top of their voices, "God Bless America." I was startled at first but joined them immediately. Then I reminded them that no matter how often and earnestly we wish and pray for divine blessing, it cannot come unless we develop a great passion for truth, because the God we worship is the God of Truth and also the God of Love, who is intent on making the spirit of brotherhood prevail in our social relationships.

While still in Hungary, where Roman Catholicism was the established religion, I was told about a very splendid and significant annual service on the Field of Blood near Budapest. It was a service of the Consecration of Weapons. In *The Sociology of War*, I pointed out the terrible degradation of the religion of Jesus, the religion of Love and Brotherhood, in blessing and sanctifying the horrible means of mass murder of our brothers, and expressed the hope that this was no longer a practice. However, one of my students, a faithful Catholic and a veteran of the war in Korea, raised his hand and told the class that in that war, he himself was involved in that ritual. My students were aghast. They had never heard of it.

In the same course, we considered possible solutions to the problem of war, including Gandhi's doctrine of non-violence. I confessed that I myself was a Christian pacifist and gave an exposition of the meaning and strength of this position.

In the next session, I presented the weakness of this doctrine. At the close of the class, one of my students preparing for the Christian ministry reproved me. How could I speak out of both sides of my mouth, so eloquently presenting the pacifist position and then arguing against it? I pointed out that as a teacher it was my duty to do both, though I was still a Christian pacifist. He left the room sadly, shaking his head.

One of my surprises was at a summer session when I became acquainted with an "Uncle Tom" from the South, a pastor about forty-five years old, who had been sadly corrupted by his conditioning. He wiped my desk and chair clean at every session. I was embarrassed by what looked like servile behavior. After the final examination, which he failed, he begged me in tears to give him a passing grade so that he may get his degree and continue to teach. I am afraid that my reply was not very kind. But looking at this servile victim of a corrupt system, I did give him a passing grade. I have wondered ever since if my action was just. I like to believe that I erred on the side of love.

Did not I, who considers loyalty oaths unfair and useless, sign a statement that amounted to such an oath before I was employed by the University?

I was surprised one day when one of my students, a Christian minister, told me how startled he was to find a professor of sociology who had any sympathy at all for religion. I assured him, on the basis of my own experience, that this was possible, fair, and decent, but that even professors of sociology may be prejudiced in certain areas. I remembered and told the story of my professor of sociology at the University of Pittsburgh, one of the outstanding sociologists of our land, who had a severe reaction against the religion of his own family. This became a strong prejudice against all religion that started to soften only toward the end of his illustrious career. This social scientist, trained in objectivity, was for many years a victim to his prejudice in the field of religion. How often we who pride ourselves in our objectivity, plant the seeds of prejudice in the minds of our students and are hardly aware of what we are doing to them.

This experience was underscored by another, when a professor of our own department said at a public debate that he could not discuss religion because he did not know what it was, since there were so many kinds. Here was a social fact, religion, staring him in the face, but because of its rich and varied content, which my learned colleague could not reduce to a simple definition, he would not and could not discuss it.

These were matched by an older student who protested my "dragging" religion into discussions in my class *The Family*. He was a professed atheist and could not see how a social scientist had the right to present religion as a possible help to family living.

I pointed out that it could be a blessing or a curse depending on its nature and quality. I myself had been an atheist for a few years and now was a Christian. I knew that not all Christians are good people, and not all atheists are bad. To prove my objectivity and fairness I gave him the professor's chair to expound his atheism to the class at the next session. They reacted with boredom. Curiously, he did not appreciate the opportunity.

It proved to be rather difficult to go contrary to the conditioning students had received from the mass communications of our society.

Take, for example, the ideas about sex and love. To practically all of them, love equaled sex and love was sex. In any case, they approved of the equation. In conjugal love sex is basic. But sex apart from respect, kindness, tenderness, the desire to help the one we claim to love and to be the finest person, can hardly be called love. They agreed. Several of my female students in variant forms made the statement: "I wish men would look at me and treat me as a person, not just a body!"

I spent two or three periods discussing what love really is, and its implications for the individual and for society. Yet on the final examination, the ideas of the mass media too often prevailed.

In connection with this, I recall the remark of a college counselor in North Carolina. With a snort of disgust, he said, "Your students up north are well up on sex techniques, only they don't know what love is." He had a point.

The author of a textbook on marriage asked me to read his manuscript. Sex was its predominant theme, not character or personality or adequate knowledge of the various factors that make for success in marriage, and it included a rather complete list of sexual perversions that he evidently considered necessary for a successful marriage. Fortunately, the book was ultimately refused by the publisher.

I was often disturbed at the general failure of proponents of sex education to present ideals as well as biology, and character as well as pleasure even after they had begun to talk or write about family life education.

In economics, I had a different problem. One had to watch what one might say about the Sacred Cow of Capitalism. To them, it meant that the instructor was leaning toward communism, which of course had nothing to commend it. When I presented the ideals of communism they would scarcely pay attention. When I completed my exposition I asked if these reminded them of anything. Two or three courageous souls thought that it sounded like the ideals of the Gospel. An indignant outcry drowned them out. How could atheistic communism resemble Christianity? We went over them again comparing each to Christian teachings. Yes, there were real and striking similarities. We finally concluded that we were dealing here with a religion without God. Did we not see in these a basic reason why they appealed to people in a world of ruthless competition and the exploitation of the poor and weak by the rich and the powerful?

Then we dealt with the actualities of communism. Here there was no difficulty. Our mass communication had constantly emphasized the cruelties of the regime, its oppression, bloodshed, violations of democratic and human rights, the liquidation of the wealthier peasants, etc., etc. Free medical treatment and hospitalization were considered wrong because these were communist reforms. But these were sorely missed by the Hungarian refugees who fled to America after the unsuccessful revolt against the Russians. They were staggered by the costs. This one illustration must suffice. Grudgingly, as we dealt with social improvements, my students admitted that there seemed to be a few good things in communism.

They struggled painfully to define and differentiate capitalism, socialism, fascism, communism, and democracy. It was difficult to leave behind the easy, confused thinking of their conditioning. However, we made some progress, though slowly — especially the brighter students who enjoyed playing ping pong with words from the jargon of sociology, economics, politics, and psychology. I got the class into the habit of demanding an explanation of such terms or the use of simpler terms. Here too we made some progress.

My classes enjoyed my vivid and concrete presentations. Sometimes, however, my enthusiasm and excitement carried me away, and before I realized it I was shouting. Most of my students welcomed my exciting presentation, but after one of my classes, a troubled young lady came to my desk and warned me that the next time I started to shout she would leave the class. I promised to control my excitement better and succeeded fairly well, for she did not leave the class. It cramped my style, however, for I had to subdue my enthusiasm. Later, when I read her paper on the development of personality in the family I received an insight into her problem. She came from a loud, argumentative, scrapping family, in which she had been quite unhappy.

My assignments sometimes created arguments between the students and their parents. However, the latter to my knowledge never complained. Once in a while, they brought appreciations and compliments. One day, a young man told me about the visit of a friend in their home, a prominent professor at Harvard. The student was engaged in writing a paper on the formation of personality in the family. It was based on five chapters and discussions in class, and the students had to apply the material to their own development. It was not an easy task, and they grumbled generously about it. The professor asked about the assignment, and when my student explained, his comment was, "Well, at last they are beginning to do it right."

One of the very real surprises occurred in *Church and Society* which, along with *Sociology of War* had not been taught previously. In place of the final examination, my students had to write an essay on an approved topic related to the course supported by adequate research. A girl of Orthodox Jewish background chose *The Impact of Christian Missions in Africa*. Would this be acceptable to her parents? She replied that they would not have to know about it. Anyhow, this intrigued her and she would do it. In due time, she presented her findings to the class. It sounded like a missionary's presentation. I listened in amazement as she defended her findings in answer to the interruptions and objections of another Jewish student who had attended the Jewish seminary in New York City. Finally running out of patience with him, she asked, "Have you ever read a book on Christian Missions?" He admitted that he had not. "Then I advise you to read up on it and then I'll talk to you," was the astonishing reply.

My Jewish students, with the background of forcible conversions in the Middle Ages, persecutions by Christians in modern times, and the anti-Semitism rampant all over Europe, were unable to look fairly upon the missionary movement or evangelism. Nor were missionaries perfect. Some of their doctrines and methods had been crude. My students felt that missionaries won their converts by all kinds of tangible, material benefits. It must be confessed that too often in the beginning there were a considerable number of "rice Christians" among the converts — those who joined a church not because of profound spiritual convictions, but because of material benefits.

My students failed to realize that the Gospel by its very nature required sharing what we had with those in need, that we would deny it if we only preached and did not express the love of God with deeds of helpfulness: Feed the hungry, clothe the naked, heal the sick, and take a stand against the evils that impoverish and corrupt men. True religion as Jesus declared in His unforgettable statement, "The Sabbath was made for man, not man for the Sabbath," consisted of serving man. Alas, there had been also more emphasis on fear than on love.

How different was the view of my Hindu Swami friend. He was greatly admired in the universities around Boston and frequently lectured on Hinduism. After we had known each other for some time and had learned to love and trust each other, we had a very frank discussion about the relative merits of Hinduism and Christianity. He was offended at the missionary invasion of India. I had to admit that sometimes it looked like invasion and imperialism. But at its best, it was simply a sharing of the best of what we had in the Christian religion — the teachings of Jesus and their implications.

Then I pointed out that in both cultures both religions had their shortcomings. Christianity had approved of witchcraft, slavery, the divine right of kings, absolutism, exploitation of the common people by the aristocracy and the barons of finance and industry, to mention a few evils that for centuries were not condemned by the church. Gradually, however, as the Christian conscience slowly developed, these were weakened and disappeared. On the contrary, the evils in Hindu Society hung on. Impatiently, he brushed aside my statement by saying that he was talking about religion, but I about Sociology. Unhappily, I observed, that perhaps that was the basic trouble with the religion of India. Nevertheless, our friendship continued until his death.

My Christian students were quite unfamiliar with the persecutions of the Jews by the Christians and showed a positive aversion to hearing about it in its tragic and horrible details. I made *Stranger than Fiction* (Lewis Browne, 1925) required reading for them.

It was in such and similar experiences that the real value and joy of teaching lay. I fully agreed with Professor Barnes who stated repeatedly, "If I were able, I would gladly pay for the privilege of teaching." What a happy experience it is to see the dawning of a new idea or truth on a student's face, even when that experience reveals the pain of disillusionment with what he had known, or believed he had known. But what pain to the conscientious and concerned teacher to feel helpless with fearful, stubborn, or tradition-bound students.

But now that I am retired, I am back in the ministry, my first love. But I still teach as I always did, "Even at the breakfast table," my Ann facetiously remarks. And my charming, gracious Ann is my full partner, for with my reduced energy she has to assist me in all my ministerial duties, pastoral visitation, presiding at worship, etc. It is amazing how superior she is to me in energy, vitality, and common sense. We take only interim pastorates now, ranging from two to ten months, with generous vacations in between. Some of our most delightful experiences and greatest successes have come to us in these pastorates. Perhaps it is because, as my Ann so often remarks, "We stay long enough to be loved, but not long enough to have our clay feet discovered."

For the past fifteen years we have lived with the Houghton's, our daughter's family, an extremely happy life, sharing their joys and trials. With our four grandchildren, it has been a very, very happy experience. We are grateful to them beyond words for their generosity, fellowship, and love.

And now we think often about the last and greatest adventure before us. We are not too eager to stay on, for we are beginning to discern the signs of the last great weakness. We are immensely grateful for all of the experiences of the past and for all of those whose lives have touched ours. All of them have helped us to grow in wisdom, faith, and maturity, even and especially those who have caused pain. We gladly and fully forgive all who have hurt us, because we too are "sinners saved by grace." And, as Christmas approaches again, we pray with Tiny Tim, "God bless us, every one."

Thanksgiving, 1966 Edwin L. Kautz

Appendices

Árpád (895 - 907), first ruler of the united Hungary
(detail of Árpád Feszty's 1894 cyclorama *Arrival of the Hungarians*)

Appendix A - Hungarian History

Editor's note: In the original manuscript, the author recalled mining his pride in Hungarian heroes in order to find strength in a fight with New York street thugs. It has been placed in this appendix to prevent it from interrupting the storytelling flow.

[I imagined myself] among the wild horsemen whom Arpad led into Pannonia at the head of seven tribes united into one people. Their chiefs had mingled their blood in a sacred ceremony thereby symbolizing their new unity. They not only conquered the rich plain along the Danube but became the scourge of Europe as their intrepid horsemen made deep invasions into the settled lands of the west. After a while, however, as the armed men of these lands and their leaders discovered the strategy of the wild horsemen, just off the steppes of Asia, they convinced them by a series of defeats of the necessity for staying within the borders of the Carpathian Mountains.

Their new leader, Stephen, recognized the need for a firmer unity and control in order to be accepted by the new nations in the west. He asked for missionaries of the faith common to those peoples, and the Pope sent in missionaries whose passion for the conversion of these heathen matched the fire of their warlike hosts. The leader's zeal was equal to the objective he had set. Whole villages were driven into the water and baptized. In recognition and appreciation of his labors, the Pope sent him a crown and a title unique in Christendom: "Apostolic King of Hungary." For at least two hundred years longer the heathen religion of Hadur (Lord of Battle) with its sacrifice of a white stallion continued secretly in sacred groves. But the back of paganism was broken. The new nation guided by the strong hand of Saint Stephen, first King of Hungary, set its face toward the west.

It was fortunate indeed for Christendom because this virile people, powerful in its military virtues, became the bulwark of Europe. Again and again the pagan hordes of the East swept like a flood to its borders, sometimes spilling over it until it seemed that the nation was dead; but resurrection always followed. After the invasion of the Tatars, the King, on inspecting his devastated kingdom, found vast stretches denuded of their population and only the charred ruins of hundreds of villages. He had to invite settlers from the west to restore the nation.

Then came the Turkish invasions, two centuries of almost continuous fighting, until at last only one fort, Eger, remained in Hungarian hands. At the crucial hour when the infidels made their final assault, the women rushed to the walls, throwing boiling oil and water, rocks and fire upon the invader, wrenching sword, spear, and mace from the hands of their wounded and fallen men and beat back the Janissaries, the flower of the Sultan's troops.

There was Kinizsi who rushed into battle with a sword in each hand, and when the sanguinary battle was over he led his men with wild abandon in a victory dance carrying a dead Turk in each hand and a third one in his teeth. And there was the glory of Szigetvar, a mud fortress in which Zrinyi Miklos held up the army of the Sultan for two precious weeks, which saved Vienna. With his pitiful little force of a few hundred men, he defied the greatest force the Turks ever had, 150,000 men. Again and again, the Sultan flung his vast army against the tiny fort in vain. Again and again, the enemy concentrated their fire upon the crumbling walls, so tradition tells us.

Finally, Zrinyl assembled what was left of his brave defenders, addressed them in fiery words, placed one hundred gold pieces in each pocket of his best uniform saying, "Let not the man who finds my body go unrewarded." He commanded the gates thrown open and a cannon fired into the infidels massed before it, and leading his men in a surprise sortie, died fighting. The Sultan propped up on his throne saw nothing, for he had died sometime previously, in a fit of rage over his inability to capture that mud fort.

But Hunyadi Janos, Commander-in-chief of the King's armed forces was the greatest figure of this tragic period. Leading his southern army to the border, he met the Turkish at Belgrade. Greatly outnumbered, as usual, but fired by the thought that they were defending Christian civilization as well as their own land, they threw themselves upon the hated infidel, inflicting terrible losses on them and forcing them to retreat. It was a very costly but momentous victory. When the Pope heard about it he celebrated a solemn 'Te Deum' of thanksgiving and decreed that the bells of Christendom be rung every noon 'unto eternity' in commemoration of this battle which saved Christendom. But it cost John Hunyadi's life.

It was logical that when the nation had to choose a new King, the nobles elected Hunyadi's son, Matyas, who is celebrated ever since in the history of Hungary as Matthias the Just. He also was a great military leader, keeping the borders clear of all invaders. He was a great Statesman, a scholar, and an eminent patron of the arts. His court was one of the important centers of Renaissance culture, where artists, musicians, architects, and scholars were welcomed and encouraged by the King's genius to produce great works, which shed luster on his court.

He was beloved by the common people. One day after a banquet, so the story goes, he rose from the table and cried, "Follow me my lords," and led them into the vineyard where peasants were at work. Taking a hoe from the hand of an astonished serf he commanded, "Follow my example," and briskly set to hoeing the vines. The well-filled, corpulent, and somewhat befuddled gentlemen of the court looked at their monarch in amazement. Then each one took a hoe from the nearest peasant and engaged in this hard labor.

Soon they were sweating, grunting, and cursing under their breath, but they had to keep at the job as long as the King did. The peasants looked on in awe and amazement. Finally King Mathias returned his hoe to its owner and sternly addressed his court; "I wanted you to know from experience how hard is the lot of the peasant who supports us, so that you may never despise him!" The peasants cheered their King until the whole countryside was filled with the echoes.

From time to time, he would travel through the land incognito to see for himself the conditions prevailing in his kingdom. He came to a village where the head was also a judge who exploited not only the villagers but wayfarers who passed through his village, compelling them to work for him without pay, sometimes for days. This he did to the stranger who had just arrived in the village, forcing him to pile up loses in his courtyard. An hour or two later the glittering royal escort galloped into the village and greeted their King. When the evil judge learned the truth he threw himself on his knees before the King to beg for his life.

Appendix B - Life In A Sect

Editor's note: Likely originally written as a separate essay, this was in the original manuscript after the chapter "Churches on Trial." It was agreed amongst the preparers of this book that a better placement would be as an appendix so it would not interrupt the flow of the author's life story.

Educated Hungarians considered themselves Europeans and boasted, with some justification, that their nation had saved Europe and Christian civilization repeatedly. Budapest was a cultural center with its university, the opera, great library, art gallery, and the National Museum. Yet the upper level of culture was rather thin and the masses had little more than an elementary education. Nor was there much opportunity in this poor and largely agrarian society with its millions of landless peasants who were proud and stubborn in their ancient ways; a heavy undigested mass in the nation. Yet it was undoubtedly these very qualities which enabled them to outlast the invaders who swept like tidal waves over this unhappy land through the centuries. It was a tragic situation that forced so many of its intellectuals, artists, and musicians to seek opportunities in other lands. The masses lived cramped, thwarted, frustrated lives burdened by taxation, militarism, a state church, a reactionary aristocracy, and a lack of educational opportunities.

Then the hungry maw of the American industrial machine reached across the oceans for cheap labor. By flamboyant advertising and the reckless promises of not too conscientious agents, the occasional success story of immigrants and the miracles of modern transportation, they gathered these restless masses and took them to the "promised land."

Some were artisans, some peasants, a few professional men, a few fleeing from the clutches of the law. Some seeking new opportunities, some concerned only about money enough to secure financial independence for themselves in the Old Country. Some, perhaps many, came to escape military service, many to establish a better future for their families, and some were driven by a restlessness which they were not able to explain. They were mostly men, but a few girls came to earn a dowry and sought employment in domestic service or in cigar, shirtwaist, and other factories.

In America, they found a strange new civilization. Language, folkways, foods, the tempo of living, were all new and at times very strange. Freedom from taxation, or so it seemed, never a sight of a soldier, free libraries, high wages by European standards, freedom to come and go if one had the money and knew where to go, free land if one wanted it and knew about it, vast cities where people crowded together in small dark rooms with few places where children might play, garbage and filth in the streets, often thrown out of windows, the prejudice and contempt of "Americans," Tammany Halls, panics, booms, terrible train wrecks, the great spaces, millionaires, skyscrapers, fires — everything in gigantic proportions and many other strange things — all demanding adaptation as quickly as possible.

Of necessity, they flocked together for security and fellowship, as near the Eastern seaboard as possible, unless indeed they were directly transported from Ellis Island in special trains or coaches to mining or steel towns. Their funds and knowledge were limited and their friends were few. Stores, churches, lodges, benevolent aid societies, theaters, saloons, banks, newspapers, real estate, and insurance agencies arose to meet their peculiar and pressing needs. In the big cities and in steel and coal centers, compact little Hungarian quarters formed with a life all their own. There, one heard the language of the Old Country, smelled its cooking, worshipped according to the dear old ritual, danced the *csardas, Körmagyar*, polka, and the waltzes of Strauss to the accustomed fiddling of gypsies, and read the unbelievable items about America and the familiar news from Budapest; from Parliament, and from the town or the village of one's birth, and the gossip and news of the Hungarian colony in American-Hungarian journalese in the papers of one's own mother tongue.

Away from the tradition and exactions of established churches, a large proportion broke away from organized religion. Bars in the basements of churches did not increase the respect of the laity for church or clergy, even when they accepted them for reasons both of pleasure and of financing the church.

In the Old Country, church tax took care of the maintenance of buildings and the salaries of the clergy. Consequently, they had not learned to support religion by voluntary contributions. Not only did the Roman Catholic Church own vast areas of the best land and receive full financial support as a state church, but some of the older, well-established Protestant churches as well were aided by the state.

Life in this smaller and more comfortable world, this bit of Hungary transplanted into America's soil, was more familiar and more secure, and more meaningful. Slowly, as whole families found their way to America the children were enrolled in Hungarian language schools on Saturdays, attended Hungarian churches on Sundays, and, for recreation, went to Hungarian plays, dances, and outings.

At first, very few intended to stay in America. But then they learned about the advantages the New Country offered to their children, many of whom failed to fit into the feudal caste and military system in Hungary. While they were still strangers in the United States, and would probably be considered "Hunkies" for the rest of their lives, they realized that after breathing the free air of the New Country, they would stifle in the old.

In fact, most of them became marginal people and remained so for the rest of their lives, not at home in the new culture and cramped by the old, not accepted fully by Americans and looked upon with suspicion by the regime in Hungary, for they were tainted with the ideas of American democracy and human dignity. Their very considerable savings were sent back to the Old Country to support relatives, to buy land, to provide a living in their old age. These were welcome, but they themselves were not. It was far less expensive to live in the Old Country; American dollars lasted longer, and there were no pensions or social security as yet in the United States.

Within this smaller world of Hungarian immigrants, there was another, very, very small world, composed of the Hungarian Baptists.

In one place at least the mission was started by one who was converted in an English-speaking church. So far as the writer is aware, the other missions were started by immigrants who had a conversion experience in the Old Country. Some had become rather worldly, and, heeding the siren call of rich America, came, like others, to make money. A few had heard about the mighty Baptist movement in America and about freedom from persecution in this blessed land and came to the "Promised Land" to find this new freedom.

It must be emphasized that in Hungary for decades the state and established churches — Catholic (all branches of it), Lutheran, Greek Orthodox, and Reformed — had persecuted the despised little sect, the Baptists. These were apatriotic, Bible-loving, clean-living group of people to whom the church was literally the family of God, and who insisted on restoring the Apostolic purity of life and ritual of the primitive Christian church. The fear of "worldly" clergy for their prestige and livelihood, was another reason for persecution. The democratic brotherhood of the Baptists, and its implied threat to the feudal privileges of the prelates and aristocracy, and the insistence of this "sect" that clergymen be examples to their flocks — which the rather worldly-minded and clergy resented — only increased the fears and hostility of the clergy.

As an example of this democracy consider this story from Budapest. A high official in the government monopoly of tobacco, with the title of Royal Counselor, was converted, and on his way to the office met a servant girl. Lifting his tall silk hat he greeted the girl as "my sister" and, transferring his cane, carried her market basket to her door, while people looked on in astonishment.

Baptists set up their little fellowships everywhere. First, they met in homes, then in stores, then, as persecution relaxed and as their personal lives won the acclaim of serious-minded folk, in houses of prayer, until finally, the government declared their faith accepted and extended to them its protection. Yet, in remote places, bishops, superintendents, and pastors of the other faiths and minor government officials still continued to persecute them.

They were not revolutionaries except in an ecclesiastical sense and in personal ethics. They insisted on a rather Puritan code; a renunciation of all worldly amusements, the single standard of sex morals, regular church attendance, uprightness in all things, and willingness to suffer for the faith.

As an indirect result of their work, some consecrated laymen and ministers of the Reformed Church established the Awakening Reformed Movement which emphasized the Baptist teachings of personal probity and of a fervent religious life, and probably renewed the entire Protestant life of Hungary. It even influenced the Roman Catholic Church. Years ago, an unhappy Roman Catholic priest told the writer, how in his seminary days, he and some of his fellow seminarians were in the habit of dropping in on a small Baptist congregation in Budapest, meeting for prayers in a cellar, where they heard simple, unlearned people pray more eloquently than a bishop, and that without a prayer book.

On their arrival in America, the few Baptists found no powerful hierarchs or clergy to persecute them, as in the Old Country. However, most of them were not able to quench the inner fires of the Spirit. They soon discovered that ostracism, stonings, and beatings were their lot whenever they dared to proclaim their faith to their neighbors, distribute their tracts, or preach their beliefs in the open air.

Often, they did not realize until years later that they had a right to protection by the police; and sometimes the police too failed them in strongly Roman Catholic neighborhoods, as in Chicago, even as late as 1925.

But when they were aware of their right to such protection, they often refused to avail themselves of it. They were afraid of weakening the effect of their witness by their unwillingness to accept persecution, and by accepting the protection of the state, which both to them and even to some of their persecutors had been an agency of oppression in the Old Country.

They protested against intemperance, drunken revelry, the unfaithfulness of men and women separated from their families, and in the midst of the tensions of life in an alien culture, against the corruptions of the clergy — many of whom drank freely and were not too careful about marital loyalties or about unsocial compensations for celibacy.

They insisted that the purity, fervor, and organization of the primitive Christian church be considered the standard for all Christian churches today. The reading of novels, newspapers, and all but edifying literature was discouraged. They became even more puritanical than the believers in the Old Country, for example: to the prohibition against smoking, they added another against drinking, which they took over from the intense anti-alcohol campaign of American Protestant churches.

In those early days, a young man was sitting down to his Sunday supper. His younger brother, aged twelve, came in from an American Baptist Sunday School where they had had a stirring temperance lesson. As the older brother, about twenty years old, was about to pour out a glass of beer, the younger gripped his arm and with intense feeling pleaded: "Please don't touch that stuff anymore!" The older boy pondered the request, then under the influence of a sense of obligation as the eldest in the family, he corked up the bottle and never drank again.

Let no one imagine that for the believers this life was bleak or unsatisfying. They had been converted because they had been dissatisfied or unhappy or conscience-stricken; or because life had seemed harsh and cruel and meaningless; or because they had had a revulsion against the licentiousness that was prevalent; or because they had some innate desires for clean and meaningful living; or because they had felt insecure and unsatisfied with superficial friendships.

Within the new spiritual fellowship, they were children of God, who had come home, the "twice-born," the family of God, bound together by a spiritual kinship that originated in the heart of the Eternal. This was more meaningful and precious than the ties of physical kinship, for within the latter one often missed the clean, uplifting, deeply meaningful comradeship of the Christian Gospel. They lived in a new world. The old world was doomed, its face was set against God — the highest, the best, the eternal reality — and therefore condemned and marked for destruction.

Since their emotional life was constricted into a religious channel their religious life became all the deeper, swifter, mightier, a fiery flood. Ecstatic dreams and visions were not infrequent. The writer has often read how such movements led to sexual excesses and immorality, but his own knowledge and experiences impel him to testify that such phenomena in this movement were comparatively infrequent, and the inevitable discipline by the fellowship — usually excommunication — was swift and merciless; the offender had brought dishonor and shame upon the "Household of God."

There was equality and freedom within the fellowship not found in the established churches, Catholic or Protestant. The leaders — laymen at first and ordained clergymen later — were conscientious shepherds of the flock, calling frequently — at least once a week in the early years — giving counsel to their members in all sorts of problems, without fees, and receiving very modest salaries. They were not too well educated and lived close to their people. Speaking their language, living irreproachable lives, and constantly exposed to the scrutiny of the small fellowships, they were loved and trusted.

There was, of course, a certain percentage of misfits. Much of this was due to the rapid expansion of the work and to the consequent necessity of accepting individuals who perhaps were fitted to do a fair job in the early situations but were not equal to the demands of the more complex situations later.

All of the members had the same rights, all the affairs of the church were discussed and voted on by the membership. Women had the right to voice their feelings in both religious services and business meetings and voted on all questions as did the men. Prestige was the result of superior piety, wisdom, and service.

All this was a far cry from the autocratic and "worldly" churches all about them. There were no dues or entrance fees to worship as in the other churches. The members contributed voluntarily according to their zeal and ability. Some of them were tithers. This enabled them to point to achievements altogether disproportionate to their numbers as compared with other groups. They won the admiration, envy, affection, hatred, or whatever reaction the members of the Hungarian community were conditioned to; but they could not be ignored.

Their family life was so wholesome that this too attracted and challenged others. Their freedom from prevailing vices led to home ownership and prosperity. Such visible tokens of the benefits of the good life could hardly be ignored.

From the beginning, every fellowship had a youth hour at which the members and friends could find self-expression; both old and young. In these meetings they spoke of their experiences through the past week, gave testimonies, confessed their sins — mostly in general terms — recited religious poetry, monologues, dialogues, gave religious plays, prayed, sang solos or duets, or gave instrumental solos or ensembles, read from religious papers some particularly good short article, gave brief expositions of scripture, exhorted, etc., etc.

Later almost every church had a band; some of these became quite famous in Hungarian circles. Splendid choirs were developed. All these were innovations that later were eagerly copied by the older, established churches.

Within the first ten years, Sunday Schools were established

everywhere. The happy, informal, fervent atmosphere attracted many children, young people, and adults until in sheer self-defense the older churches had to follow suit. Sisterhoods, brotherhoods, and vacation Bible schools were developed to meet special needs and to keep the members busy and happy within the fellowship.

All sorts of opportunities were grasped for social gatherings. At first, when the churches were small, they gathered in homes for simple refreshments, conversation, gossip, and singing. One of the features was the use of drawing for Bible references, which were marked on tiny cards and contained anything from promises to reproof. Sometimes these applied rather pointedly to the circumstances of the persons drawing them and made a profound impression.

Later they gathered in the same manner in their church buildings for anniversaries, name-days, birthdays, weddings, and conferences. The meals were free "love feasts." In fact, they were called *szeretet vendégseg* (hospitality of love).

They had no patriotic pride or prejudice. They looked upon patriotism, more or less consciously, as a worldly attachment and emotion. They were citizens of heaven and of the New Order about to descend from heaven. Sometimes, as in Homestead, Pennsylvania, around 1908, this fellowship of believers was composed of various nationalities: German, Hungarian, Slovak, Croatian, and Serb. Sometimes all of these languages were used in conducting services. Later, language difficulties and the patriotic fervor and prejudices engendered by World War I, made separation inevitable.

This little world, so briefly and inadequately described, was not without its weaknesses and faults. The customary faults of democracy, such as too much talk, slow action, and demagoguery, found their way into it, as well as the petty gossip, snooping, and the spiritual pride of small exclusive religious fellowships. One of its chief weaknesses was its success in thoroughly isolating its members from the Hungarian-American community.

In later years, they sought to open the doors into the larger Hungarian and American community by artificial means. Increasingly, they took part in various movements, joining various "worldly" lodges and organizations, both to penetrate into the larger world with their testimony and because of uneasiness in the narrow, restricted outlook and activities of the fellowship. The youth has been particularly restive in this situation. This is particularly true of the second and third generation brought up in the faith without the bitter lessons of the "old" life, with its tensions, struggles, and the victories and the sweet security of the "new" life after conversion.

Anichka (Anna, Ann) Lukacs (Lucas) at age fifteen
with her parents in Stara Tura, Slovakia (1909)

Appendix C - Anna Lukacs Kautz Biography

Editor's note: This essay was apparently written by the author's first daughter Eloise, to be read at the 1988 funeral of his widow Anna. It's included here because it fills in some details of Anna's life not covered in the main manuscript.

Anna Lukacs Kautz was born on March 24, 1894 in Stara Tura, Slovakia. She was the eighth child in the Lukacs family. Only three lived beyond infancy. The other children of John and Katherine died of diphtheria.

Little Ann was refused entry into the private Slovak Lutheran schools because she had not been christened, for her parents had become Baptists, a despised Christian sect.

As a kindergartner, she entered the public schools — the domain of hated Hungary, the occupying power. She was the only Lukacs child to learn the hated Hungarian language.

Her parents, evangelical Baptists, made their home a house church. All Baptist visitors and missionaries found lodging and care with them. Nationalities were irrelevant. All people were God's children. Indeed, although her father was a dedicated evangelical Baptist according to Ann, he continued his search for truth, even exploring Darwin's teachings through the book he kept on top of the chifforobe.

As a child, Ann was ostracized because of her family's convictions. She used to tell of stone-throwing by village children. When hit and hurt, she'd run into her father's sheltering arms crying, "Is this what it means to suffer for Jesus?"

"Yes , little Ann," He'd reassure her. "Remember Jesus loves you."

At the age of fifteen, tiny and ill with grief over the death of her beloved, crippled sister, Ann came to this country. An illegal immigrant, she pretended to belong to a friendly family which was accepted into America. Her oldest sister at Ellis Island met her, but within three days, told her to find a Baptist Church to help her. Her sister had her own life to live. Ann was confused and frightened, but with the help of the Slovak Baptist minister's wife, she found a job taking care of a dying Irish lady. For a whole year Ann was so homesick that she thought of suicide.

Then came an extraordinary opportunity. She was invited to do housework and live in the home of a Baptist executive and his wife who were officers on the Home Mission Board of Baptists in N.Y.C.

What a disappointment! Unlike the help at her parent's home, she was not considered an equal. Not only did she have to use the servants' entrance to the house, but her mistress checked all the food that was eaten, actually counting each evening the slices of bread. The humiliation was not only painful, but confusing. What about the fellowship of Baptist Christians? It shook her faith and beliefs to their foundations. When she left this family, they wept and beseeched her to stay, asking how she could leave a "Christian" family when she herself professed to be a "believer?"

Her next position was doing housework and living in the home of a prosperous German Swiss family. Evidently, she captivated them, for they offered to adopt her. She would be their only child! Grandma Burkhardt even made Ann beautiful hats and gowns in the latest fashions.

Her dreams, however, had been well planted. She wanted to be a missionary, and that meant education. In addition, she was now teaching Sunday school in a small Hungarian Baptist Church, where the membership glowed with the warm, welcoming, enfolding love of God. There she had met a serious, dedicated young man, Edwin Kautz, who was preparing for a ministry to Hungarian Baptists.

Sadly, her "foster" parents, the Burkhardts, let her go. Strongly disapproving of an education for a girl, also, they thought that this "child" was involved with an impractical idealist who probably had tuberculosis. They offered no support other than a welcome if she should some day return.

Determined, adventurous, sparkling Ann went to the Baptist Missionary Training School in Chicago. Her beloved fiance went to Colgate University in Hamilton, N.Y. Ann graduated with excellent grades. While in school, she taught herself to play the piano well enough for Sunday school. In addition to scholarship funds, she had earned her way and paid for some of her expenses with her meager savings.

Five years of engagement ended in a great wedding celebration. Baptist dignitaries honoured these two outstanding young students with their attendance.

Ann joined Edwin for his last years at Colgate where they also served as minister and wife in the rural community of Vernon, N.Y. How they enjoyed the wholesome community and warm love of their parishioners!

Times were hard for them. They dug dandelion greens for vegetables and gathered fallen apples for applesauce. Their first child, Eloise Katherine was born. Their life in Hamilton and Vernon was a treasured beginning to their service together, for they always functioned as equals in their mutual careers. This was symbolized by the action of her husband, who took Ann's maiden name, Lukacs, for his middle name. It did not seem "right" to Edwin for the woman to always take the man's name as her name. He insisted, "Are we not man and woman equal in the eyes of God?"

At last they had a fulltime pastorate in West Pullman, Illinois in the Hungarian Baptist Church. There Ann taught Sunday School where she was the piano player and Religious Education Director. She supported Edwin's work and nurtured their family. There, their second child Elaine Ann was born. Then Edwin received a call to head the Hungarian Department of the Baptist Theological Seminary in East Orange, N.J. Eight idyllic years followed, filled with struggle and challenges as they trained young people for the ministry. Their students came from Hungary as well as from the homes of Hungarians in the United States.

Lonely summers for Ann, while her husband visited Hungarian

churches stretching from Chicago to NYC, became opportunities to teach her own children as well as the children in the East Orange Baptist church. Their home was a haven for all of Edwin's students as well as for visiting Baptists. Each Sunday during the school season, Ann provided an evening meal for about twenty students. Edwin led discussions and singing, while Ann led the devotions and played her beloved piano. Their home was filled with music and joy. With her efforts and her husband's excellent teaching, the Hungarian Department grew until its students were half of the total number of students in the school.

Then came the depression! Their dreams of making the Hungarian Department part of Crozer Seminary in Upland, Pennsylvania collapsed. The Seminary was closed.

Off they went to Pittsburgh to serve in three tiny churches so scattered that one hundred miles of driving was necessary each Sunday, and Ann did most of the driving! Yet Ann always hovered over her daughters. She had refused to live in the parsonage three blocks from the steel mills. It was also in the "red light" district of Homestead, and she thought it too much of a sacrifice to raise two high-school daughters there. She also decided that Eloise and Elaine should have to attend only one church regularly or they would become "turned off" by driving one hundred miles on Sunday to three different churches. Building on her missionary training, Ann became Religious Education Director in the Mckeesport church as well as chauffeur and homemaker for her family. By this time both Ann and Edwin felt that most Hungarian Baptists should now become active in the American Baptist movement. There was no longer a need for Hungarian language churches. Their task was finished and they would have to find new work for the Lord. They accepted a call to a large English-speaking church, the Sandusky Street Baptist church in Pittsburgh. At this time in their ministry, two unrelated events occurred which challenged Ann's life. Their two daughters went to college, and World War II broke out.

Thirty years earlier, Ann and her husband had come to the conclusion that it was against God's will for human beings to kill each other. They had become pacifists and would not mute their call to love, even though it was a time when war called to hate. They spoke out for Jews when the U.S. turned away a ship loaded with Jewish refugees from Germany. Ann and Edwin insisted that love needed action to supplant the violence of war. Christian brotherhood should have no boundaries. In their own lives they had risen above hatred. By their marriage, they had demonstrated that love could surmount national enmities. In times of war, such convictions, especially when spoken publicly and dramatically, were unacceptable. A happy ministry became a painful service.

When their daughters graduated from college, Edwin and Ann decided that he should return to his great love — college teaching. Encouraged by Ann, at fifty years of age Edwin entered the University of Pittsburgh for his MA in Sociology. During this time, their older daughter was married.

Upon graduation, he found a position at a Baptist school in Belton, Texas: Mary Hardin Baylor College. Ann found a position as a church secretary. Their younger daughter, Elaine, was married at the college.

Again, forthright action and teaching about equality for all of God's children brought criticism. The college President demanded that no U.S. history about Black and White relationships and no discussions about current problems between Blacks and Whites were to occur in Edwin's sociology classes. In fact, they were reprimanded for entertaining their Black barber, a friend of theirs, in their home. Blacks were to be kept in their place, and they were presumed inferior to Whites.

During the third summer vacation while on the way East, a letter reached them, saying their services at the college would no longer be needed. Despair gripped them! They were now in their mid fifties. It seemed that no one would employ a man that age who had only an MA degree! However, Eloise's husband Proctor, recognising his father's-in-law's excellence in teaching, scheduled appointments with colleges in the Boston area. Each one confirmed their fears. Too old!

Need a Doctor's degree! After many weeks, they desolately returned to Texas to claim their belongings. They planned to return to Massachusetts and live with their older daughter, her husband, and their two preschool children in a tiny bedroom with a double-bunk bed.

Before they reached Texas, a call came from Boston University. Edwin was hired by the Sociology Department at the College of Liberal Arts to have the ten happiest years in his professional life. Ann became a lively organiser for the Boston University Women's Council, as well as undertaking major responsibilities at the First Baptist Church in Newton.

Ten years of interim pastorate work ensued after retirement from Boston University. Among these pastorates were several years at the prestigious First Baptist Church in Brookline. Again, Ann's vitality and missionary training came to the fore. These years were the "dessert" of their lives.

But Edwin, in his late seventies, fell one summer evening. Then followed seven years of deterioration while his dying brain brought unceasing agony to them both. He sensed the control slipping away and the advent of undesirable personality changes. Ann insisted on giving full time care for her beloved husband of fifty years, only to discover his inadequacies and his exhausting demands. An empty-headed, shambling shell, Edwin fell again and died of a fractured skull. Ann was then alone for the first time in fifty-five years. Could she rebuild a life of productivity and joy?

With her adventurous spirit, she ventured forth again — this time to Newton City Hall as a receptionist, eventually winning an award for ten years of volunteer service. She helped establish a Senior Citizen's outlet in City Hall for selling items made by seniors throughout the city. Her church work continued. Her radiant smile cheered those around her. Later, shingles, Parkinson's, and arthritis began to overwhelm her, but her zest for life and her liberating, growing faith in God's love and care enabled her to stimulate young people to "get their education." As they showered her with their love, she gave them courage to live their own lives joyously and productively, always sharing with them the love of God for all His children of all backgrounds and beliefs.

Little has been said of her intense love for her family, her teaching at home, and her insistence on good nutrition. Little has been said of her mischievous tomboy antics — chasing her grandchildren up trees or squirting them with water. Little has been said of her hard work at home, her clean house, her shopping shrewdness, her canning abilities, or her money management. All these ordinary tasks in our culture were unstintingly performed with excellence by little Anichka Lukacs, Anna L. Kautz, 1894-1988, ninety-four years, nearly a century of life and love for Jesus.

She lived a vital life, zestfully refusing to conform to this world, but seeking to transform it into the kingdom of an intelligent, loving God.

refused. It did not seem fair; they had not been sent for us. "You stick (stuck) up?" she rasped. It was not possible to convince her by courteous explanations. She had practised this for years with glad acceptance.

She injected herself into our work with the youth and the women in the other mission, had her picture taken with them, and was able to interpret these to the mission Board as new angles, new advances in her work. It was totally unnecessary, unsought and largely unappreciated. It only convinced us more firmly against taking on her work too at the parent-church.

Finally, a few years before her death she began to drop hints here and there concerning an inheritance she was leaving for her friends; her relatives had passed on. She would even show a few precious objects, such as a ring and a watch and give the impression that one or another would receive it on her death, asking them to hold it in confidence. In consequence she had more attention and service than ever before. When she died she had an expensive funeral, a bronze casket, enclosed in large wood coffin lowered into a grave carefully lined with thick cement. It was the largest funeral in the community that year, for she had distributed her charities to many and many more had heard about her and the grapevine had informed them of the wealth to be distributed after her death. It was a splendid occasion, one she would have enjoyed, as she doubtless did in planning it.

First carefully then feverishly the expectant "heirs" began to look for a will and her possessions. There was no will and only a few pitiful posessions of little value. They began to suspect each other and wound up accusing each other of filching

Page of original 1966 manuscript, from Chapter 19 - The Great Depression

Appendix D - Editor's Notes and Acknowledgements

by Scott Marshall

The author of this book was my grandfather (my mother's father). It was dated at 1966, presumably when the first draft was finished. He was 75 at the time. I was told that it was unsuccessfully submitted to publishers. More recently I'd heard that the book was at least to some degree encouraged by and dictated to the author's oldest daughter, Eloise (my aunt). A photocopy of his complete 521 page manuscript was submitted to each of his seven grandchildren. This book was produced from one of those copies, which was scanned to a pdf file and subsequently transcribed by computer into editable text using the OCR process (Optical Character Recognition). The author's brother's grandson, Robert Allen Kautz, edited the computer file to correct the computer's errors and to add the author's handwritten revisions. This book was edited from that file. Some additional research was needed to ensure historical accuracy (the author mentioned the unreliability of memory in his Preface). The goal of final editing was to end up with a book with consistent syntax that was enjoyable for the average reader and preserved most of the style and voice of the author.

Since English was the author's second language, some editing was required to make the text clear and flow well for modern American readers.

Among the editing required was the verification of foreign names and their spellings. For example, the steamship the author crossed the Atlantic Ocean on he called "The Bluecher" in his original manuscript. We found that the actual ship was named the SS Blücher (after German

Field Marshal Prince Gebhard Leberecht von Blücher, who had helped defeat Napoleon at the Battle of Leipzig in 1813). Several ships carried von Blücher's name. The one in which the author steamed to America was a Barbarossa-class ocean liner built in 1901 (two years before his voyage). It was scrapped in 1929.

Additionally, the author switched many times between telling his story in the first-person and the third-person, sometimes in the same chapter, and sometimes in the same paragraph (first-, second-, and third-person refers, respectively, to "I", "you", and "he" or "she"). For example, the author referred to himself as "little Eddie" in many of his boyhood stories, but in others called himself "I". Later, regarding his first teaching job, he called himself "the young professor" but sometimes in the same chapter reverted back to "I." It's not entirely clear why he'd done this. Perhaps it was because of long breaks, and he'd forgotten the perspective he'd been using. Or, perhaps, it may have come from a need to put some emotional distance between himself and his story in certain places, so as not to relive too vividly some of his heartache. In some sections, he appeared to use third-person perspective out of shyness about being thought boastful.

While it was important to preserve the author's voice, it was decided that the final book needed to be consistently in the first-person perspective without the reader having to wonder at times if the author was talking about himself or about someone else. We changed nearly all of the third-person syntax to first-person in singular, plural, and possessive forms when the author was referring to himself. This greatly improved the narrative flow and clarity and helped the reader connect emotionally to the author's thoughts, feelings, and experiences. For example, "They burned their fingers severely" became "We burned our fingers severely."

Still, some of the author's at times quirky syntax, no doubt from English being his second language, was left as is to preserve some of its color, tone, nuance, and personality. There was concern that editing might distort the author's voice, but it was decided, for this volume, that story would take precedence over the style. If voice, color, and style interfered with the reader's appreciation, then the narrative flow would have priority.

Finally, I'd like to acknowledge the help of my friend Valerie, a retired copy editor, Linda Marshall for more help with editing, and Stephen Csik, a friend who'd grown up in a local Hungarian community who helped me with firsthand knowledge of the Hungarian language and culture. I also give my thanks to the local writer's group, led by author Nancy Demme, for their interest and support, and for contributing their thoughts to this endeavor.

www.ingramcontent.com/pod-product-compliance
Lightning Source LLC
Chambersburg PA
CBHW021823090426
42811CB00032B/2000/J